THE POLITICS OF IRISH EDUCATION

1920–65

THE POLITICS OF IRISH EDUCATION

1920–65

Sean Farren

The Queen's University of Belfast
Institute of Irish Studies 1995

Published 1995
The Institute of Irish Studies
The Queen's University of Belfast

Grateful acknowledgement for financial assistance is made to the Cultural Traditions programme of the Community Relations Council which aims to encourage acceptance and understanding of cultural diversity.

British Library Cataloguing-in-Publication Data. A catalogue record for this book is available from the British Library.

ISBN: 0 85389 595 3

Printed by W & G Baird Ltd, Antrim
Cover and design by Rodney Miller Associates

To Joseph and Mary Farren

Table of Contents

Acknowledgements

In the writing of this book particular thanks and appreciation are due to many people. In the first instance I would like to acknowledge those whose professional skills facilitated the accessing of documents and data relevant to the study. For permission to consult and publish original source material and for their practical assistance I wish to express my deep appreciation to the directors, librarians and staff of the following: the libraries of the University of Ulster, University College, Dublin, Trinity College, Dublin, the Public Records Office of Northern Ireland, the State Paper Office (now the National Archives) in Dublin, the National Library of Ireland, the Central City Library, Belfast, the Linenhall Library, Belfast, the diocesan archive of Down and Connor and the archdiocesan archive of Armagh.

I am also indebted to other scholars who have ploughed some of the same furrows and whose work has been an inspiration. In this respect, I would like to acknowledge in particular the scholarship of Professor Donald Akenson, Professor John Coolahan, Professor Donal Mulcahy and Dr Séamus Ó Buachalla. Their pioneering work has revealed the complexity and diversity of issues that need to be addressed in the recent history of education in Ireland.

Thanks are due to Joan Maguire and in a special way to Dr Brian Walker of the Institute of Irish Studies at Queen's University, Belfast for his persistent encouragement. Also to Joan Erskine and Kate Newmann for their meticulous guidance and advice in bringing the text through its final stages. To Dr Roger Austin a special word of thanks is owed for comments and advice at an early and critical stage in the research. To my students over the years whose interest in many of the issues addressed in this book was an important spur to my research special thanks are also due.

In a very personal sense thanks and appreciation are owed to my parents and to my wife Patricia, whose support was undiminished in all of the endeavours associated with this work. To my children I wish to say thanks for their forebearance and their interest while Ciara's assistance was particularly important at a very crucial time.

SEAN FARREN
August 1995

Abbreviations

A.S.T.I. – Association of Secondary Teachers of Ireland

I.A.A.M. – Incorporated Association of Assistant Mistresses

I.N.T.O. – Irish National Teachers' Organisation

I.R.A. – Irish Republican Army

N.I.H.C. – Northern Ireland House of Commons

N.I.L.P. – Northern Ireland Labour Party

U.T.U. – Ulster Teachers' Union

Introduction

Published accounts of education in post-partition Ireland have almost all concentrated exclusively either on developments in the south, or on those which occurred in the north. Until now, only Donald Akenson's two separate studies, *Education and enmity* (1973) and *A mirror to Kathleen's face* (1975), have afforded students of the period the opportunity of drawing parallels between developments in both parts of post-partition Ireland in an area of considerable public interest and which, at the establishment of both states, shared the same administrative and curricular structures. This study is an attempt to explore these developments in one volume in order to more sharply make the comparisons and contrasts which their divergent histories from 1922 invite.

The 90 years preceding partition had witnessed the gradual development of the national school system under the auspices of which schools had been built throughout the whole of Ireland. As a result, elementary education became accessible even in very remote parts of the country with pupils following broadly the same curriculum whether at school in Antrim or in Cork. Second level, or intermediate education as it was officially called, though considerably more restricted in terms of access, had also been developed with pupils again following similar syllabuses the length and breadth of the country. Both states inherited, therefore, quite an extensive network of schools at both levels which whatever about the inadequacies of the systems within which they had operated had provided levels of education that bore favourable comparison with what was being attained elsewhere in Europe at the time.

Education was not, however, a service which developed apart from the more general issues of the day. Politics and religion had long affected that development and would continue to do so as this study constantly reveals. At one level, church and state had experienced a long relationship in matters educational in Ireland, mutually supportive in an exclusive sense in the case of the state and the established church, i.e. the Church of Ireland until the early nineteenth century. Then the other major churches, most notably the Catholic Church, began pressing for their role in education to be recognised and supported as well. Hence the creation of the national system and of a new set of church–state relationships in education. At the more popular level where politics also interwove with religion and in the context of those developments from which emerged the political forces of Irish unionism and of Irish nationalism, education became one of the battlegrounds on which confrontations between both were fought. Immediately prior to partition such confrontation was acutely evident in the manner in which the Catholic and

Protestant churches together with their political allies clashed with each other over the proposals to reform education in 1919, mirroring the wider constitutional conflict raging at the same time. Following partition these same forces continued to confront each other, openly in the north and more covertly in the south.

The interplay between education and the wider political context is highlighted for each phase of the period discussed in this study in order to identify the source and some of the principal determinants of these confrontations. What is revealed may well appear to invite harsh judgements on many of those responsible for education in both parts of Ireland over the period studied. If such judgements can be made, then so be it. More important, however, at this point in our history is to evaluate the educational policies and the developments which flowed from them in order to more deeply understand ourselves and those influences which have made us what we are. Conditions and circumstances will never be the same again for education as in the years from 1920–65. Different times and different circumstances prevail today, but some of what we are was shaped by the education received during these years and that is what makes its study pertinent.

As the finishing touches are put to this work, the first twelve months of the ceasefires declared by the paramilitary forces from both sides of the community in Northern Ireland are drawing to a close. So, as we attempt to lay the basis for more positive relationships within the north and between north and south in Ireland, it is not untimely to begin posing questions as to what we could expect from our educationists, policy makers, managers and teachers, over the next several decades that could cement the fragile peace of 1995.

SEAN FARREN
Portstewart
August 1995

1

Seeds of Diversity:
Education in Ireland in 1920

The Irish systems of education

Despite the political storm that had begun to rage throughout the country, the school year of 1919–20 provides a useful basis from which to take stock of the condition of first- and second-level education in Ireland on the eve of the country's partition. That year was the penultimate one during which education at both levels was administered on an all-Ireland basis. It was also the school year which was to witness the last major but vain effort to restructure both systems before responsibility for them was turned over to the new authorities, north and south. Also, during that year significant steps were to be taken to lay the foundations for the reforms to be introduced once those authorities did assume that responsibility. For these reasons the school year 1919–20 is an appropriate vantage point from which to review the forces and developments which had shaped what was to be the educational inheritance of Ireland's two political entities as well as being one from which to anticipate how that inheritance might be further shaped within these new contexts.

In 1919–20, first- and second-level education was being provided by a combination of public and private initiatives which had resulted from a set of uneasy compromises mainly involving the major churches and the country's British controlled administration over the course of the nineteenth century. At first, or primary level, the various churches, through their network of parishes, were the main providers of what were termed 'national' schools and on the eve of the country's political partition this network of national schools was a very extensive one indeed; approximately 9,000 such schools were in operation in 1919–20. National schools were essentially local institutions, built on land acquired by their local managers, supported, financially and otherwise, by their local communities and subsidised by the Board of Commissioners of National Education in Dublin.

Second-level, or 'intermediate' schools were provided on a much more restricted basis. Fewer than 500 such schools were in operation in 1919–20. For the Roman Catholic community, secondary education was available mainly in colleges and schools conducted by diocesan clergy and congregations of nuns, priests and brothers. A small number of schools catering for Catholic pupils were also conducted by lay people.[1] For the Protestant com-

1

munity a range of philanthropic and church-affiliated bodies conducted secondary schools. Financial assistance of a limited kind for intermediate education was available from the Board of Commissioners of Intermediate Education, also located in Dublin.

The boards of commissioners

National and intermediate schools operated within quite separate and distinct legal and administrative frameworks under their respective boards of commissioners. The Board of Commissioners of National Education was the older of the two, having been in existence since 1831[2] while the Intermediate Board only dated from 1878.[3] The establishment of both boards had followed long periods of debate and controversy as to how public assistance for schools should be provided. Much of the debate had been caused by the problems successive governments had had with proposals for assisting Catholic schools. Direct funding for such schools had for long proved unacceptable to the British government with the result that boards of commissioners which would act as intermediaries between the state and school authorities were established in order to circumvent the problem. In the case of the national schools, managers were invited to apply to the Board of Commissioners of National Education for recognition which, if granted, entitled them to receive a percentage of capital costs to establish and maintain a school. In addition, the board paid teachers' salaries, published and provided textbooks, operated a system of inspection and generally attempted to play quite an interventionist role in the promotion of elementary education.[4]

Second-level schools received funding on the basis of the results obtained by each school's pupils at the annual examinations conducted by the Board of Commissioners of Intermediate Education.[5] This board was much less interventionist than its sister board in the sphere of elementary education, but this is not to say that it was non-influential in the development of second-level education during the period of its existence. As an examining body, the Intermediate Board set syllabuses and, by this means, determined to a considerable extent curricula in intermediate schools. Otherwise, however, intermediate schools were essentially free from direct scrutiny by their board since no inspectorate existed at this level until the last decade or so of the board's existence.[6]

Membership of the boards

Both the National and Intermediate Boards were composed of laypersons, an exception being their chief executive officers, termed their Resident or Assistant Commissioners. The actual number of members on each board had been altered over the years since each had been established. In 1920 the National Board consisted of 20 members, while the Intermediate Board comprised 11.[7] The Lord Lieutenant of Ireland appointed the commissioners and it was to him they addressed their annual reports. Each board appointed its own full-time staff under its respective resident or assistant commissioners. One resident commissioner directed the affairs of the National Board, while two assistant commissioners directed those of the Intermediate Board. The lay members of each board met regularly to review the operation of their respective administrations and to consider matters of policy.

A glance at their credentials reveals that most commissioners were drawn from the upper ranks of the churches, the judiciary and the universities. In 1919–20 they comprised five bishops and an ex-Moderator of the Presbyterian General Assembly, seven lawyers including the Lord Chief Justice of Ireland, the Provost of Trinity College and several other academics and members of the Irish 'nobility'. If the social status of the commissioners was 'high', it probably took second place to their religious affiliations since the denominational mix on the boards was no accident. Indeed from the establishment of each board care had been taken to ensure that both main-tained an 'acceptable' balance as between Roman Catholics and Protestants.[8] In the case of the National Board, the balance which existed in 1919–20 dated from 1860 when, as one response to strong Catholic criticism of the national school system at the time, the government had increased the number of com-missioners from 14 to 20 and allocated half to Catholics.[9] A similar balance was reflected in the composition of the Intermediate Board.

Aims of national education

The central aims of the national system of education were laid down in 1831 by E.G. Stanley, the Chief Secretary of Ireland in his famous letter to the Duke of Leinster, then Lord Lieutenant of Ireland, outlining proposals for the sys-tem. According to Stanley 'one of the main objects must be to unite in one system children of different creeds'.[10] As later expressed by the Board of Commissioners for National Education, this aim read as the provision of 'combined literary and separate religious education'.[11] High-sounding and unifying in their intent as such sentiments may have appeared, behind them lay a history of division and rivalry between the Christian churches in Ireland and the consequent problems for successive governments which, before 1831, had attempted to devise schemes by which basic education could receive a degree of public funding. Schemes to provide such funding in the earlier decades of the nineteenth century had not proved wholly suc-cessful. Pressure from the Roman Catholic Church, in particular, for direct government funding for its schools, had faced successive governments with an embarrassing dilemma since Protestant opposition, political as well as church, to direct funds being made available to Catholic schools was very strong, not just in Ireland, but in Britain as well.

Constitutionally, the United Kingdom of Great Britain and Ireland was a 'Protestant' state and still, in the early nineteenth century, suspicious and at

3

times openly hostile to Roman Catholicism. In political terms the Papacy was regarded as a foreign power whose interests were frequently viewed as inimical to Britain's. Allegiance to the Pope was, therefore, seen not simply as a religious matter, but as a political one as well. Hence the charge of treason which some still levelled at British subjects who happened to be Catholic.[12] It followed that the provision of public funding for schools which might preach treason could, in itself, be also seen as treasonous.[13] Second, at a religious level, since Roman Catholicism was heretical in the eyes of Protestants, what justification could there be for a Protestant state to support schools in which heresy would be propagated ? Indeed, within the established church, i.e. the Church of Ireland, the view still prevailed that it was its exclusive responsibility to inform the Catholic Irish of the error of their ways and to convert them to the 'truth'.[14]

Roman Catholics, however, formed the major denominational community in Ireland and their church's demand for public money to support Catholic education was difficult to ignore. Prior to 1831 attempts to provide some public funding for Catholic schools had involved rather indirect means, but growing Catholic opposition to the Society for Promoting the Education of the Poor of Ireland,[15] the channel through which such support for elementary education had been directed, had led to a major inquiry being commissioned in 1824.[16] Following this inquiry and several more years considering the matter, the government's proposals for a national school system eventually appeared as outlined in Stanley's letter.

Denominationalism – a key characteristic

These proposals were intended to meet a number of competing and conflicting demands. Schools associated with the new system would be designated as 'National Schools'; they would be open to children of all denominations and none; separate, denominationally based religious instruction would be safeguarded while all children would receive their 'secular' education in common. Hence the phrase 'combined literary and separate religious education' which came to summarise the aims of the national school system. Laudable as these aims and conditions might have appeared at one level, in effect their only real virtue was that they allowed the government to provide a subsidy for popular education in Ireland.

Denominationalism was to prove too hardy a plant to smother under any scheme for 'united' education. Given the social and religious realities of Irish life, the aim of providing 'combined literary and separate religious education' ran completely counter to the wishes of the major churches. The result was that, faced with a set of interests with considerably greater moral and ultimately greater political influence in Ireland, the government was forced to compromise and to modify some of the unifying features intended for the national system towards a recognition of those interests. The outcome was a system that became more and more explicitly denominational over the course of the following decades.

So, while the original framework of the national system remained intact until the country was partitioned, within it a whole series of compromises aimed at addressing and allaying denominational fears had been made. Nonetheless, the fact that the framework remained intact was, in itself, a remarkable achievement given a situation in which the main agencies upon which the system depended, i.e. the Irish churches, were almost permanently suspicious of, if not openly hostile to each other and where political allegiances served only to reinforce such attitudes.

Protestant attitudes

The two main Protestant churches in Ireland, the Church of Ireland and the Presbyterian Church had been very opposed to the national system at its inception. A large majority in the former decided to have nothing to do with the new system and, to rival it, established the Church Education Society in order to provide support for Church of Ireland schools and so avoid their being subject to what were regarded as the objectionable regulations of the Board of National Commissioners on religious instruction.[17] This society operated with some considerable success until post-famine times. However, by the time the church was disestablished in 1870, the Church Education Society was in rapid decline[18] and its capacity to provide support diminished as more and more schools under Church of Ireland management affiliated to the national system.[19]

Within the Presbyterian Church, especially in northern counties, strenuous opposition to the new system was also expressed. There were several grounds to this opposition, one of the main ones being the right of access to national schools which, according to the regulations of the National Board, had to be granted to the clergy serving the denominations of all children enrolled in each school. Many Presbyterians feared that granting such access to national schools under their auspices to the clergy of other churches would imply recognition of the latter. Given the strong antipathy of many Presbyterians to Roman Catholic clergy in particular, opposition to the national school system became widespread within that community.[20]

Following unsuccessful efforts to establish a rival system under Presbyterian auspices,[21] efforts focused on changing the regulations of the national system so that school managers might be allowed a greater degree of control over their own schools in order to determine for themselves who could be granted access, as well as other matters pertaining to religious instruction. After a rather short campaign in the late 1830s, the pressure mounted by the Presbyterians was successful[22] with the result that schools under Presbyterian auspices then quite readily joined the national system. Greater control was conceded to local managers by accepting that schools not vested in the board could be recognised as national schools. As many commentators have pointed out,[23] this concession to the Presbyterians marked the first major compromise by the Board of National Commissioners towards denominational interests. It was a compromise from which the other churches were not slow to learn.

By the early twentieth century the main Protestant churches were so well integrated into the national system that they had few, if any complaints about it on grounds of principle. Many of their spokespersons had, in fact, become, at a rhetorical level at least, quite favourably disposed towards religiously mixed schools and critical of the Catholic Church for its firm opposition to denominationally integrated education.[24] This is not to say that the Protestant churches were indifferent to religious instruction as part of education. Whenever the prospect of any significant change in the system was raised their insistence that religious instruction be provided and that ministers of the various churches, or their representatives, have access to schools was stated in unequivocal terms, as a commentator in the *Church of Ireland Gazette* was to point out during the great debate over reform in 1919:

We claim for our children the best education the State can provide; and we also claim for them the right to be taught their religion by those who believe in it.[25]

These demands apart, the Protestant churches appeared willing to encourage interdenominational mixing at pupil level, at least. However, the strong opposition to such a prospect on the part of the Catholic Church rendered the general emergence of denominational mixing in schools impossible in the Irish context.

Catholic attitudes

Despite opposition by some, a majority of the Catholic bishops had accepted the national system with some considerable enthusiasm when it was first announced. Bishops in many dioceses encouraged their clergy to apply to the Board of Commissioners in order that the schools they managed could become associated with it and receive the financial help which it was making available,[26] with the result that a large number of schools under Catholic management became 'national' schools within a short period of time after 1831.

However, from 1850 onwards a marked change in official church attitude took place. While this change did not result in the Catholic Church actually withdrawing its schools from the national system, apart from a small number under the auspices of religious congregations,[27] relationships with the National Board became fraught with many difficulties. The signal for this change was contained in pronouncements at a major synod of the church held that year in Thurles, County Tipperary. There it was decreed that only schools under Catholic auspices could be regarded as satisfactory for the education of young Catholics.[28] In other words, what the bishops were saying was that the ideal for them was a system entirely under Catholic control, not merely a system regulated to a considerable extent from the outside and which was intended to cater for children of any or no religious denomination. In effect the bishops' claim amounted to a demand that denominationalism be the basis for a national system of education, a demand that was, in theory at least, in direct conflict with the aims expressed by the National Board. This claim was to be reiterated with increasing frequency following the Synod of Thurles. The years 1859–62, in particular, witnessed a concerted effort to persuade the government to this viewpoint. Pressure was mounted, beginning with a statement by the bishops in favour of a denominational system, together with a 'Memorial' to the government to the same effect.[29]

Responding to Archbishop Paul Cullen of Dublin, who was a prime mover in organising the church's campaign, the government stated that it would adhere 'to the principles in which the National System had been erected . . . [because] . . . if those demands were conceded . . . the National System would be overthrown, and a system of sectarian education substituted for it, calculated to revive social divisions in Ireland – and to stimulate feeling which it is the object of every just and liberal government to allay'.[30] Despite this rebuff, Cullen persisted and used the occasion of the Powis Commission of Enquiry into Education in Ireland, 1867–9, to press the church's demands saying in evidence that:

. . . a denominational system should be established so that in their respective schools Catholics and Protestants may give to children the fullest instruction in their own doctrines.[31]

While no major concession was gained by the church on its central demand for an explicitly denominational school system, some success was achieved in the sense that membership of the Board of Commissioners was increased to twenty with half of the places going to Roman Catholics.[32] Furthermore, the display of religious symbols was, as a result of a recommendation of the Powis Commission, no longer subjected to earlier constraints.[33]

The campaign against 'mixed' schools was pursued by the Catholic Church through constant pressure on its own members to ensure that Catholic children only attended schools under approved Catholic management[34] because, despite the fact that most national schools were conducted under the auspices of one religious denomination or another, many schools enrolled pupils from different denominational backgrounds. Added to the basic objective of the church to ensure a Catholic education for all Catholic children was a widespread fear of proselytism and schools under Protestant auspices were seen as prime instruments in attempts to induce young Catholics away from their religion. Parents were frequently reminded of the evils of 'mixed' education and of their responsibility to ensure that their children received their education in a Catholic school. Only such an education, stressed the bishops, would protect their children against the 'dangers' facing them. In a pastoral letter on St Patrick's Day, 1861, Cullen warned parents that:

... never was your zeal more necessary when a licentious press every day assails the holy Catholic Church, maligns the Apostolic See and spreads the vilest calumnies against our holy religion. Unless your children be well educated is it not to be appre-hended that their faith may be shaken by the assaults of enemies whose arts they have not been prepared to encounter ...[35]

The campaign against 'mixed schools' was particularly directed at the model schools, 28 of which had been established by the National Board by the early 1860s. Set up as one element within the board's plans for teacher training, the model schools were the only national schools directly under the board's own management. One of their aims was to exemplify the benefits of (denomi-nationally) 'united education'. Yet, despite guarantees provided for religious instruction and despite the fact that some of the model schools had obtained the support of local clergy, they were denounced as unsafe for Catholic chil-dren and Catholic managers were prohibited from employing teachers who had taught in them.[36]

To judge from enrolments in national schools after the 1860s the church's campaign against 'mixed' education met with considerable success. The National Board's own statistics indicate that 1867 was the year for which the highest percentage of schools with some degree of interdenominational mix-ing was recorded. In that year, 57.4 per cent of the national schools through-out the country were reported as having some denominational mixing in their pupil intake, a figure which had dropped to 25 per cent in the last school year when such statistics were reported, 1912–13. The decline coincided too obviously with the intensification of Roman Catholic opposition to interde-nominational schooling for it to be accidental.

Catholic apprehension

The case for a truly denominational system was strengthened by the Catholic Church's wider concerns at this time, concerns that were to trouble the church well into the twentieth century. To Archbishop Cullen, as to many leading figures in the Catholic Church of this period, the times were not aus-picious for Catholics. State power and its concomitant secularism, for which the 'licentious press' was seen to be the natural voice, were judged to be on the increase and both threatened the faith and the institutions of the church. Church opposition to state involvement in education was a key element in its opposition to the growth of state involvement in many spheres of life as the nineteenth century progressed. In continental Europe at this period the posi-tion and authority of the Catholic Church were being seriously affected by the growth of state power, not least in countries like France and Italy, tradi-tionally Catholic countries, but by then coming increasingly under politically secular influences. In such countries state attempts to control education resulted in bitter and prolonged conflicts with the church.[37]

Nationalists further aggrieved

In addition to their general political grievances, further grounds for nationalist suspicion towards the new regime's educational policies arose from the latter's antagonism towards their Gaelic heritage. While some unionists had participated in and others had supported the revival of Irish and of Gaelic culture generally, their support had ebbed away and had become quite muted as the language movement became more political and more stridently nationalist.[36] Nationalism, the Gaelic revival and Catholicism were, by 1920, almost inextricably linked in the unionist mind with the result that many unionists accused the Catholic Church of fostering an extreme nationalism in its schools. William Corkey, a leading Ulster Presbyterian, a convenor of his church's Education Committee and later a leading opponent of Londonderry's educational reforms, in a pamphlet entitled *The Church of Rome and Irish unrest: how hatred of Britain is taught in Irish schools,* expressed views widely held in sections of the Protestant–unionist community. Corkey strongly attacked the teaching of Irish history and the general manner in which Gaelic culture was being fostered in Catholic schools in the period from 1900.[37] At the opening of the Northern Ireland parliament the unionist M.P. Henry Mulholland re-echoed these views when he attacked national schools because they 'tended towards disloyalty rather than towards loyalty'.[38] According to Mulholland,'the primary and ultimate object of education is the production of loyal and patriotic citizens'.[39] When matters relating to the teaching of Irish were raised in parliament similar antagonisms surfaced amongst unionist members, one of whom argued that, '. . . there is no need for an Organizer of Irish language instruction. What do we want with the Irish language here ? There is no need for it at all'.[40]

Londonderry himself did not display a great deal of sensitivity towards nationalist feelings about such matters when controversy developed over changes in regulations for the conduct of the Intermediate Board's examinations in 1922. The regulations for these examinations, which that year were still set and administered from the board's offices in Dublin, were changed to permit candidates to answer questions in Irish in subjects other than Irish itself.[41] Reaction to this change was quite hostile within the Ministry of Education in Belfast, and Londonderry stated that '. . . I will not for one moment allow the use of the so-called Irish language in the Intermediate Examinations for Northern Ireland'.[42] He then announced that, because of this and other changes, the examinations would be cancelled for Northern Ireland.[43]

Such attacks on Irish were interpreted by nationalists as further evidence of unionist hostility to their community as a whole and so only served to reinforce their opposition to the new state and to justify their non-participation in any attempts to develop its structures and institutions. In this conviction they were sustained and supported not simply from within their own community in the north but also by the policy and actions of leading nationalists in the south. From the south a policy of non-co-operation with the new northern authorities, co-ordinated and directed principally by Michael Collins, was being intensified from early 1922 just as final arrangements for the transfer of the administration for the north from the south were being made.

Although he had signed the Anglo-Irish Treaty and had argued tenaciously for it in Dáil Éireann, Collins would appear to have been profoundly unhappy about its provisions for Northern Ireland. He undoubtedly expected that the boundary commission proposed in the treaty to review the territory of the north in the light of the wishes of local people would result in major changes being proposed, changes which would render the new state non-viable and so hasten political unity.[44] Nonetheless, it also appears that Collins wanted to underline what he regarded as the north's non-viability and inherent instability through a campaign of both active and passive resistance within the nationalist community.[45] The increased I.R.A. activity of the spring of 1922 was the mainstay of the first, while an economic boycott and various other forms of non-co-operation with the Belfast government became the basis for the second.[46]

Education's most dramatic contribution to this campaign was to be evidenced in the refusal by teachers in over 200 Catholic managed schools to accept the authority of the new Ministry of Education in Belfast.[47] These teachers endeavoured to retain links with the educational authorities in Dublin, who, under Collins' instructions, continued paying their salaries.[48] Publicly, the Catholic Church attempted to maintain a degree of neutrality on the issue saying that non-recognition was a stand taken by the teachers themselves.[49] However, as Mary Harris points out, there was considerable consultation between representatives of the new government in Dublin and Catholic school authorities in the north aimed at encouraging non-recognition of the northern regime from the autumn of 1921.[50] Launched in the spring of 1922, the boycott campaign, at its height, involved some 700 teachers from 270 schools, approximately one third of Catholic national school teachers. Once the south became embroiled in civil war, from June 1922 onwards, the campaign lost much of its momentum and Collins' death in August hastened its end. In September the southern authorities decided that no further salary payments would be made.[51]

In common with the whole campaign of nationalist resistance to the northern regime, the education boycott had no positive outcome. It only intensified existing inter-communal antipathies and rendered more difficult the achievement of a *modus vivendi* between nationalists and unionists. It also had the further effect of reducing the possibility of co-operation at an educational level between the two Irish administrations in such areas as teacher training where the possibility of maintaining an all-Ireland framework had existed.[52] In addition, the ending of the boycott marked the virtual end to active official support from the south for nationalist opposition to the new regime in the north. Preoccupied with their own critical concerns the southern government of 1922 and its successors were to provide little more than verbal support for the nationalist community until the 'troubles' of the 1970s. Thenceforward, the nationalist community was on 'its own' and had to begin the painful process of adjusting to a situation to which it was psychologically firmly opposed. It was to prove a difficult process and one in which education was to play a very significant part.

Effects of the Catholic – nationalist stand

A number of commentators, notable amongst them D.H. Akenson,[53] have been harsh in their judgement of the Catholic Church for its non-participation in the Lynn Committee and of the general nationalist stand taken at this time. Akenson may well have been correct to describe this non-participation as 'the single most important determinant of the educational history of Northern Ireland from 1920 to the present day'.[54] However, Akenson's failure to take full account of the wider political context, not least the fact that the British government had, only several weeks before the establishment of the Lynn Committee, opened negotiations with Sinn Féin on an agenda which must have placed at least a question mark over Northern Ireland's future, indicates that he did not fully appreciate the constraints operating on the church and on the whole nationalist community at this critical time. Church participation would have given Northern Ireland a legitimacy which nationalist politicians throughout the island were withholding and which constitutional nationalists in Northern Ireland itself did not even tentatively confer until some years later. Furthermore, despite Londonderry's liberal-sounding remarks and his appeals for co-operation from all interests, unionist attitudes, at government level, did not always reflect any real appreciation of, much less sympathy for nationalist values, or of that community's problems. Had Londonderry waited until negotiations between Sinn Féin and the British government had been completed before establishing his committee, when northern nationalists would have had their position clarified, and had the direction of educational reform been less obvious, it might just have been possible for nationalist leaders to have adopted a less negative approach to educational reform and perhaps to other matters as well.

The Lynn Committee deliberates

Despite the absence of co-operation from the Catholic–nationalist community and against the background of considerable civil unrest, the Lynn Committee quickly set about its business. The membership of the 32 person committee was, inevitably, predominantly Protestant in religion and unionist in politics. Several leading Protestant churchmen were among the members, including the Primate of All Ireland, Archbishop Charles D'Arcy of Armagh, Bishop John Grierson of Down, Rev. J. Bingham, a leading Presbyterian, Rev. Dr W. Strahan, a former Moderator of the Presbyterian

Church, and Rev. W.H. Smyth of the Methodist Church. All five of the unionist politicians on the committee had declared themselves in favour of local authority control of education and some, like Lynn, were particularly hostile to the Roman Catholic Church's claims on education.

The committee submitted an interim report in June 1922, following which Londonderry set about drafting an education bill. This bill was presented to parliament in the spring of 1923 and was on the statute book in October of the same year.[55] In its interim report the committee expressed deep regret at the absence of Roman Catholic representatives and at the failure of any Roman Catholics who had been invited to do so to give evidence to it:

It is greatly to be regretted that . . . Roman Catholic interests have not been directly represented. We have been anxious to give the fullest possible consideration to the views of all denominations and we greatly regret that our invitations to Roman Catholic institutions and organisations to give evidence have also been refused.[56]

The committee went on to state that it had, in spite of this absence, endeavoured to take account of the Catholic Church's known views on education:

We have throughout been careful to keep in mind and to make allowance for the particular points of view of the Roman Catholic Church, so far as known to us, and it has been our desire to refrain as far as we could from recommending any course which might be thought contrary to their wishes.[57]

The extent to which these views were acted upon in the committee's recommendations can be judged in the discussion which follows in this and in subsequent chapters.

Structural recommendations

As had been anticipated the interim report recommended the creation of local education committees to act as education authorities. These, it was hoped, would become the main providers of the education service. Existing school managers would be invited to transfer the control and management of their schools to these committees. Schools so transferred would thenceforward become the responsibility of the local committee and would be fully financed by it. Also, in time and according to developing needs, these committees would be responsible for providing new schools. The Lynn Committee was clearly of the opinion that such a development would be the best possible way of ensuring a high standard within the educational service and that every effort would be made to build a unified system on it : 'We think that if possible all schools should be under the local committee and that inducements should be offered to bring this about'.[58] In other words, the committee hoped that all schools would be transferred, a hope that it is difficult to believe was realistic in the context of known attitudes in Northern Ireland.

One matter that required particular attention in any proposal to establish public control of schools in Ireland was what, if any, would be the future role of the churches in education. Since most schools had been established under some form of church auspices they were part of the fabric of local church life. School buildings were available for various church functions and teachers, being usually of the same denomination as the sponsoring church, were expected, or at least encouraged, to play an active role in parish activities. It was not surprising, therefore, given its composition that the Lynn Committee was quite sensitive to the relationship between the churches and their schools and to how that relationship might continue in the future. Indeed, in evidence to the committee, representatives of the Protestant churches had emphasised the need for a positive and close relationship to be maintained.[59]

The Lynn Committee was anxious to ensure that wherever church schools would be transferred, account would be taken of this relationship in the deeds of transfer. It recommended, for example, that existing uses of school buildings outside of school hours be allowed to continue and it clearly hoped that the churches would be amongst the interests represented on local education committees.[60] Above all, the Lynn Committee displayed its sensitivity to the churches' role in education in its recommendations on religious instruction. Here it was strongly of the opinion that the new system should adhere to the original aim of the system of national education, i.e. the provision of combined literary and moral education with separate religious instruction. The committee warned that 'strict care should be taken that the existing rules and regulations of the Commissioners of National Education with reference to religious education . . . should be continued'.[61] This led the committee to recommend that religious instruction be provided on a regular basis during the hours of compulsory schooling, provided such instruction met with the approval of the parents and that the right of access to schools by the churches be retained.

By displaying such sensitivity the committee was taking heed of what the various Protestant churches had stated in evidence to it and also of what several spokespersons for those churches had been saying in public comment about the principles upon which they expected the restructured educational services to be based. For example, Bishop Grierson of Down, a member of the Lynn Committee, made it clear how he expected religion to be treated in the new system:

The essential point is that religion should be taught in our schools. We one and all would insist upon that. A merely secular education does a cruel wrong to a child. It is fundamentally unscientific; for it leaves a part and that the most tender and most important part, of the child's personality uninstructed . . . public opinion generally of our province demands an education that will in its schools teach the young mind the fact of God and the facts of the revelation of his love.[62]

The view that religion should be placed at the centre of a public system of education was not, however, a unanimous view within the Lynn Committee. Adam Duffin entered a note of dissent in which he argued for an essentially secular system of public education because he was concerned that religious instruction within the hours of compulsory education would be anomalous in what would, in effect, be state schools. If, he argued, religious instruction was going to be provided in such schools then there were no grounds for treating other schools, i.e. voluntary schools, any differently on the question of funding simply because they wished to protect their form of religious education. Duffin concluded that schools fully funded by the state:

> ... must be devoted to secular education only, so far as the State provided machinery is concerned, but where it is required on behalf of any considerable number of children I do not see why there should be any difficulty in affording opportunity and facilities for giving religious education under the auspices of the Churches, without interfering with the primary work for which each school is supplied.[63]

In other words, Duffin argued for the decision the government was eventually to make in the 1923 act, i.e. that religious education could only be provided outside the compulsory curriculum. His was not the majority view of the Lynn Committee nor, as was to be made abundantly clear in the reaction to the act, was it the majority view within the Protestant community in Northern Ireland. Church involvement in education was generally accepted and the expectation that religious education should be part of general education was scarcely questioned. The only significant support for Duffin's views came from sections of the teaching profession itself. The views of the president of the U.T.U., Isaac McLaughlin, on this issue have already been quoted. Although representative of an element of teacher opinion, it would not be correct to claim that McLaughlin's views were widely held throughout the community, or indeed throughout his own profession. The concept of an explicitly secular system of education remained very much a minority preference.

Curriculum reform

In addition to its recommendations on the control and management of schools the Lynn Committee proposed changes in the curriculum for elementary schools, most of which would prove to be non-controversial. Essentially these changes amounted to a readjustment in the number of subjects taught in the different classes of elementary schools. The one change which did give rise to some controversy, though of a rather muted kind, was that relating to the place of the Irish language. The committee recommended that Irish, hitherto available as an optional subject from standard three, be available in the future only from standard five. The reason given was that this was more in keeping with current practice on the introduction of other second languages like French. This recommendation, which was accepted by the ministry, was greeted with hostility within the nationalist community where it was perceived as further evidence of the new regime's antipathy towards its cultural values.

While the recommendation on the place of Irish might have been justified on the grounds of educational thinking of the period, a number of other recommendations give weight to the view that political concerns were indeed exercising the minds of members of the Lynn Committee, for which educational arguments were only a convenient cloak. Although it was not explic-itly stated, these concerns seem to have arisen because of the political values which Catholic schools were perceived to be fostering, values which many unionists believed should not be subsidised in any way by their (Protestant–unionist) state. The committee argued that all schools should be obliged to inculcate appropriate civic values, at the core of which lay loyalty to the northern state and to the British Empire. For example, one recommen-dation regarding the choice of history textbooks seemed to have been based on William Corkey's allegations about the approach to history in Catholic schools when it stated that:

... the power of the Ministry to regulate and to supervise the books used in schools should be very strictly exercised in the matter of historical text-books and readers. No book bearing upon the subject of history should without previous official sanction be permitted to be used in any school under the Ministry.[64]

It is unlikely that the members of the committee had Protestant schools in mind since no question had ever been raised about the kind of history taught in them, at least not by Protestants and unionists. Strong suspicion that the teaching of history in Catholic schools was subversive was not just part of unionist rhetoric. A comment by the then assistant secretary in the Ministry of Education, Lewis McQuibban, reveals that it was a view endorsed at offi-cial level as well. In a memorandum to his minister in October 1922 about the recommendation that history and Irish be mutually exclusive options in elementary schools McQuibban wrote:

I agree with this recommendation in as much as the kind of history that would be taught in schools where it is desired to foster the study of Irish would be likely to have a bias of a very undesirable kind.[65]

Further evidence that particular political concerns exercised the minds of members of the Lynn Committee is to be seen in the recommendations made regarding the teaching of 'civics'. Loyalty to the constitution of Northern Ireland and to the British Empire was explicitly stated as an important edu-cational objective in the recommendation that:

All state-aided schools should aim at cultivating a spirit of respect for law, obedience to constituted authority, and no aid should be given to any school in which principles are inculcated subversive of the authority of the state ... No books should be used in state-aided schools to which reasonable objection might be entertained on political grounds. All teachers should as a condition of their recognition be required to give an undertaking to carry out faithfully the regulations of the Ministry. Further, as recom-mended elsewhere in this chapter, the duties and responsibilities of citizenship should be included in the instruction given to pupils in the schools. The special importance of this aspect of educational work should be emphasised in the training college. In addition, we consider it desirable that the Ministry should encourage in all state-aided schools the flying of the Union Jack on suitable occasions.[66]

As far as the Lynn Committee was concerned its members were obviously of the opinion that all schools should transmit the values of British citizenship despite the fact that it must have been obvious that for most Catholic schools such a task would be unacceptable, not to say impossible. The committee's claim to have borne in mind the needs of Catholic schools was rather narrowly interpreted, being confined exclusively to questions of management and religious instruction. No account was taken of the general cultural values and practices of the Catholic–nationalist community. This failure further served to bear out some of Cardinal Logue's fears that the committee would be inimical to Catholic interests.

Nonetheless, the members believed that the overall aims which they were drawing up for education in Northern Ireland were being determined within a progressive framework. In particular, the members saw their recommendations as being closely in line with educational developments in the rest of the United Kingdom and, as Londonderry himself pointed out ' . . . the goal of the education Ministry in Northern Ireland is to give the boys and girls of Ulster the advantages possessed by children in other parts of the United Kingdom'.[67] In this sense education policy was in keeping with the general motivation behind much government planning in Northern Ireland, of maintaining parity with the rest of the United Kingdom.

First controversy

As the northern government proceeded to assume its responsibilities for education there was one immediate issue with which it was faced, the resolution of which was to mark the size of the gulf opening up between approaches to education north and south. The issue was how to provide facilities for teacher education. St Mary's College in Belfast, in line with the non-co-operative attitude of the Catholic–nationalist community at the time, made no attempt to establish any formal links with the Ministry of Education following the latter's establishment in 1921. This attitude did not have any significant practical effect since graduates from the college in the period of non-co-operation, 1921–23, were not hindered in any way from taking up teaching posts in Catholic schools. The problem facing the ministry concerned the supply of Protestant teachers, male and female, and the supply of Catholic male teachers, all of whom had, up until then, to seek teacher training places outside Northern Ireland.

Protestant teachers and Catholic male teachers usually received their training in one of the southern colleges. Catholic students could choose between St Patrick's College, Dublin and the De La Salle College in Waterford. Protestant students of the Presbyterian denomination usually chose to attend the Board of National Education's Marlborough Street College, while those of the Church of Ireland had their own college in Kildare Place, Dublin. Once the authorities in the south began to assume full responsibility for government in January 1922 they set about introducing a number of important changes in elementary education which carried profound implications for teacher training. These changes were to result in Irish and Gaelic culture generally receiving a greater emphasis within the curriculum of the training colleges, a development not likely to find a warm welcome within the northern ministry. Secondly, the new Department of Education in Dublin decided that to maintain the existing number of teacher training places in the new state could result in a serious over-supply of teachers or in the state subsidising the training of teachers who would only be required for schools in Northern Ireland. As a result a question mark was immediately raised over the future of the college in Marlborough Street because most of its students, being from the north, would return there and so its closure would have least impact within the south. Obviously the authorities in the Irish Free State had not anticipated the possibility of any co-operation with their northern counterparts on this matter despite the fact that the latter had been hoping that the existing arrangments for teacher training might continue in some form, as a ministry memorandum of the time clearly suggests:

. . . [The Ministry] were willing to enter into joint arrangements for carrying on the existing training system, but such proposals have so far been entirely ignored by the Provisional Government and the action of the latter in modifying the existing college timetable without reference to the Ministry is plain evidence of their obstructive tendencies. The whole policy of the Provisional Government is being directed towards giving what the Ministry in Northern Ireland regard as undue preference to the Irish language in all schools and colleges under their jurisdiction, and their action in this respect is being pushed as far as circumstances permit, directly or indirectly in Northern Ireland.[68]

There is a touch of irony in a note on the memorandum which commented upon the effect which co-operation in the field of teacher education might have played in north–south relations generally:

If there is any field of administration, more than any other, where joint and harmonious action between North and South might be expected to produce good results in the direction of bringing the Irish people together it is in the educational field . . .[69]

With the prospect of co-operation with the south no longer feasible, the Ministry of Education had to determine how the future supply of teachers for schools in Northern Ireland could be assured. An internal ministry committee to address the question recommended the establishment of a non-denominational college in Belfast to be known as Stranmillis College. Meantime, the ministry made arrangements with the Church of Ireland Training College in Dublin for the latter to continue training teachers in accordance with regulations of which it, the ministry, approved.[70]

The Church of Ireland Training College authorities hoped that these arrangements would continue indefinitely, thus guaranteeing student numbers for a college which otherwise would be cut off from one of its major sources of recruitment, the northern counties. Unfortunately for the college, this was not the ministry's intention and once a decision was reached to establish a college in Belfast, there was no interest in maintaining a link with a southern college, however Protestant or however willing that college might be to maintain those links.[71] The termination of the arrangement was the cause of considerable disappointment within the Church of Ireland.

Dr Henry Kingsmill Moore, principal of Kildare Place, expressing his regret, wrote of the desire he had of keeping up the 'continuity' and of promoting 'the feelings of goodwill and fellowship of which our country stands so sadly in need'.[72]

Had attempts at a similar arrangement with the Roman Catholic male colleges been successful, north–south co-operation in teacher education might well have endured beyond this period. However, since not one of the Catholic colleges was prepared to provide a course of teacher training acceptable to the ministry in Belfast alternative arrangements had to be sought for Catholic male students.[73] A number of Catholic students did enrol for the course at Stranmillis but when church authorities made clear that they would not be employed in Catholic schools and when it became clear that facilities would not be provided at St Mary's for male students, negotiations were opened with the ministry to find an acceptable solution. A separate college for Catholic male students was rejected as impractical given the small numbers that would be involved. Proposals for a hostel under Catholic Church control where students would reside while attending Stranmillis College also came to nought.[74] Eventually arrangements acceptable to both the Catholic Church and to the ministry were agreed in 1925 whereby male students would be trained at St Mary's College, Strawberry Hill, London with their fees and maintenance paid for by the northern ministry. While satisfactory to the church, this compromise was achieved at the price of co-operation between north and south in the first instance and, secondly, of more local co-operation between the Catholic Church itself and the management of Stranmillis College which could have had profound effects for the training of northern teachers from the very beginning of the new system's existence.

Reform in the Irish Free State

The south inherited all the elements of the public administration of education which had developed under British rule in Ireland. Included in this legacy were the educational administrations established to service the Boards of National and Intermediate Education. Both boards were soon abolished by the new authorities (the National Board in 1922 and the Intermediate Board in 1923) and their administrations placed under one executive, before eventually being merged into a single Department of Education in 1924.[75] This restructuring of the administration was virtually the only major structural reform in education introduced by the new regime in its early years. There was no attempt whatsoever to effect the kind of structural changes which had been contained in the ill-fated MacPherson Bill and which were about to be enthusiastically embraced by the new administration in the north. Instead, the educational reforms introduced focused almost exclusively on transforming the schools into key agents of the revival of Irish and Gaelic culture generally.

Since the establishment of Dáil Éireann in 1919 two important initiatives had been taken, aimed at promoting curriculum reform. The outcomes of these were to receive the approval of many of those destined to take charge of the administration of education in the Irish Free State. The first was the convening of the National Programme Conference by the I.N.T.O. in 1921 to plan for the future of primary education. The second was the decision by Dáil Éireann, also in 1921, to establish a commission to undertake a parallel exercise for the secondary sector.

The I.N.T.O.'s initiative arose out of an anxiety about the pace at which curriculum change to promote Irish might take place, and was aimed at ensuring that a greater emphasis on Irish would respect the position of teachers, many of whom had little or no knowledge of the language. A degree of concern had begun to spread throughout the profession in 1919–20 when it was reported that pressure was being mounted on individual teachers in some parts of the country to adopt the programme for Irish published by the Gaelic League. Grounds for the I.N.T.O.'s concern increased as the Gaelic League became quite strident in its demands and there was particular concern over the fact that some schools were being unofficially visited by members of the league and of Sinn Féin to check on the extent to which the call for a more 'Gaelic' curriculum was being heeded. According to T.J. O'Connell, general secretary of the I.N.T.O. at the time:

In that year, 1920, patriotic fervour had reached its highest pitch. Chief among the national ideals, next to an independent Ireland, was the revival of the Irish language. In pursuance of this ideal, the Gaelic League, without prior consultation with the I.N.T.O. or the school managers, had published an educational programme for immediate adoption by the schools . . . It must be assumed that those who framed and were responsible for this programme would have understood that immediate compliance with its demands was a virtual impossibility in the majority of schools . . . Word began to reach I.N.T.O. Head Office of visits to schools by local enthusiasts who demanded that irrespective of conditions or difficulties the League programme should be put into immediate operation . . . It was fortunate, therefore, that steps had been taken to convene a national representative conference, at the same time as this attempt to impose the Gaelic League programme was under way.[76]

Therefore, partly in response to the league's demands for a more 'Gaelic' curriculum, but also to ensure that whatever changes would be made would have the co-operation and support of the teachers who would have to implement the changes, the I.N.T.O. at its 1920 annual congress adopted a motion calling upon its central executive and the Board of National Education to take an initiative to ensure that the teaching of Irish would be carefully controlled. The motion was as follows:

. . . while not more than fifty per cent of the children of school-going age attend school it is futile to expect that the Irish language can be revived through the schools . . . [and so we] ask the National Board in conjunction with our Executive [i.e. of the I.N.T.O.] to frame a practical programme so that at least one hour per day be devoted to instruction in Irish within school hours. That proper facilities be provided for instruction in Irish by extern teachers in schools where such is necessary.[77]

Acting on this motion a decision was taken by the congress to 'frame a programme, or series of programmes in accordance with Irish ideals and conditions'.[78] From this decision developed the National Programme Conference convened by the I.N.T.O. The wisdom of the I.N.T.O. in taking this initiative was further underlined by resolutions endorsed by the Gaelic League at its annual conference that same year which envisaged quite radical and rapid moves to Gaelicise primary education. Following up on its educational policy adopted two years earlier these resolutions demanded that:

. . . no teacher, trained or otherwise, shall be regarded as qualified to teach in an Irish National School unless fully qualified to give instruction in the full programme . . . existing teachers over fifty years of age to get three years to qualify. . . those in control in every secondary in Ireland should be required to teach Irish, Irish literature and Irish history to every student attending school; . . . that in English speaking districts the teaching of Irish should be such that all subjects should be taught through Irish in all secondary schools in five years . . .[79]

The problems which these demands would have caused had they been implemented in full were clear to the I.N.T.O. The demands reflected the zeal of those who were convinced that restoring Irish as the first language of the citizens of an independent Irish state was essential to that independence. To them it was not an impossible task and opposition was not to be brooked, though in adopting such an absolutist approach the absence of any concession to, or consideration for other traditions in Ireland was clearly evident – only one tradition was being regarded as central to the cultural basis of the school curriculum in the new Ireland.

National Programme Conference

The National Programme Conference was intended to include all major interests connected with primary education in Ireland at that time and while all were invited not all chose to attend. The conference was, however, attended by representatives of a number of important national bodies, the I.N.T.O. itself, the Gaelic Athletic Association, the Gaelic League, General Council of County Councils, National Executive of the Irish Labour Party, Aireacht na Gaeilge (Ministry of Irish), Dáil Éireann and the Association of Secondary Teachers of Ireland. Acting as special adviser to the conference was Professor Timothy Corcoran whose views on the restoration of Irish as well as on the role of the Catholic Church in education were well known and have already been noted. Notable among the organisations absent from the conference were all those which were most representative of Protestant teachers and unionist opinion generally. Although not formally convened as such, it was in the event, a conference which could be described as almost exclusively representative of nationalist opinion.

The conference commenced deliberations in January 1921 and adopted the following terms of reference to guide its work:

(1) The adoption of a minimum National Programme.

(2) Additional Subjects, and the circumstances under which such additional subjects should be made compulsory.

(3) The consideration of the best means of applying items (1) and (2), including the question of National and Local Administration, Training Facilities, Teaching Staffs, School Premises, Attendance, Provision of Text Books, etc.[80]

Such comprehensive terms of reference suggest that the conference intended to take the opportunity to consider not just the programme of instruction, but also structural matters, teacher training and school attendance legislation as well. However, it is interesting to note, that while all other items from its terms of reference are mentioned in the final report, nothing is said or recommended on the matter of 'Local Administration'. Perhaps memories of the 1919–20 controversy were too fresh for anything to be said and it can only be inferred, therefore, that it was decided to make no recommendation for change, since to do so might have risked confrontation with the Catholic Church and so endanger every other aspect of the report. The report of the conference was submitted to Dáil Éireann where the Minister of Education gave his approval to the programme and indicated that it would be brought into operation in national schools.

The educational aims expressed in the report reflected the sense of nationalism prevalent throughout the country at the time and the desire to inculcate future generations with a deep sense of their Irish identity and in particular of their Gaelic heritage. Language, history, music and song would all reflect this desire very explicity in terms of their actual content. As the aims for history stated, its study should:

. . . develop the best traits of the national character and . . . inculcate national pride and self-respect. This will not be attained by the examining of dates and details but rather by showing that the Irish race has fulfilled a great mission in the advancement of civilisation and that, on the whole, the Irish nation has amply justified its existence.[81]

Understandable as the desire to inculcate a sense of Irishness was, this desire was also motivated by a degree of Anglophobia evident, for example, in the guidelines produced for the English programme which recommended that the selection of authors to be read in the higher classes should:

In order to bring pupils as far as possible into touch with European thought and culture . . . be mainly directed to the works of European authors, ancient and modern, drawn from the many good translations which abound. English authors, as such, should have just the limited place due to English literature among all the European literatures.[82]

Educationally sound as these sentiments might appear at one level, they were expressed as part of an attempt (which probably owed much to Professor Corcoran's advice to the conference) to minimise Anglo-Saxon cultural influences in Ireland and to maximise those of continental Europe.[83] Corcoran's attitudes towards what he described as the 'Anglicisation' of Irish minds led him to argue that Ireland's links with continental Europe were a more natural element in the nation's culture than were British links. Pointing to such Irish clerical scholars as Philip Lombard and Luke Wadding who had been forced into exile in continental Europe, Corcoran claimed 'To that tradition, and to that direct mental intercourse with Europe and especially with the Latin peoples of Europe, we must avail ourselves of our new freedom in order to return'.[84] As E. Brian Titley points out, Corcoran 'only grudgingly conceded a place to English language and literature in the educational scheme of things. But, curiously in view of its emerging role and influence at the time, no such privilege was to be accorded Anglo-Irish literature . . . '[85] Titley goes on to quote Corcoran's attitude towards the latter and his case for its exclusion from the curriculum:

Of great, dignified, national prose writing, Anglo-Irish literature has none to show . . . Poor and trivial as it often is in form and content, it would certainly, if so used and thought upon, prove a formidable obstacle to the restoration of Irish to full literary use and study.[86]

Indeed school syllabuses in the south over the following three decades were, as a result, to contain only limited reference to Anglo-Irish writers.

As well as dealing with the new 'national' requirements the conference took the opportunity of addressing a number of the criticisms which had been expressed by educationists regarding the *New revised programme* of 1901. In particular the 'overloading' of the curriculum which had frequently been complained about was tackled by proposing a new, reduced 'minimum' programme together with recommendations for additional subjects as indicated in the conference's terms of reference. That apart, no other major changes were recommended.

Intermediate education

Intermediate education in the south was also coming under similar pressures to those which were affecting primary education in 1921. In that year the Gaelic League's annual conference drew up a list of demands to be presented to the Board of Intermediate Education, all concerned with promoting the Gaelicisation of the curriculum. Foremost amongst these demands were the following:

(a) That in examinations the questions in every subject should be set in Irish as well as in English.

(b) That candidates should be allowed to answer in either language.

(c) That in the 'groups' [subjects were grouped in various sets, e.g. classics, modern languages, which included Irish, commerce etc.] Irish should be substituted for English as a common subject.

(d) That in the papers in history and geography the paper should be so constructed that full marks may be obtained by questions bearing directly or indirectly on Ireland.

(e) That English read in Irish schools should be as far as possible emptied of specifically English thought and culture.[87]

There were two obvious strands to these demands. On the one hand, as the first two demands indicate, a concern that the Irish language receive equal treatment with English. On the other hand, as the rest of the demands indicate, there was an attack on the dominance which English 'thought and culture' were perceived to have achieved in Irish education. Subjects like history and geography usually only considered Ireland within the wider context of the British Empire, while English required the study of established British, rather than Irish authors, perspectives and approaches which would obviously be unacceptable to those of a nationalist outlook. The demand that English be replaced by Irish as a common subject underlined in a dramatic way the Gaelic League's aim of reviving Irish as the daily language of the Irish people. As such, Irish was entitled to enjoy a pre-eminence within education which required that it replace English as a 'common' subject which all students would be required to study.

Within Dáil Éireann steps were being taken at this time to prepare for changes at secondary level through the establishment of a Commission on Intermediate Education charged with making recommendations on curriculum reform. This commission, which operated through separate subject committees, commenced its deliberations in September 1921 with a brief that stressed the new national context within which education would soon be operating and the need for '. . . a programme of secondary education which would meet the national requirements while allotting to the national Language its due place therein'.[88] According to Proinsias Ó Fathaigh T.D., who officially initiated the proceedings of the commission on behalf of the Dáil, the revival 'of the ancient life of Ireland as a Gaelic State, Gaelic in language and Christian in its ideals'[89] were the over-riding objectives contained within that brief. With Professor Corcoran as their adviser, six sub-committees prepared recommendations for reform of different areas of the secondary curriculum.

Much of the groundwork for the commission's recommendations had been laid in the deliberations of the Molony Committee (1918–19), especially as far as the structure of the curriculum was concerned. In line with the latter's recommendations, the commission proposed the reduction in the public examinations to two, one at fifteen plus, the second at eighteen plus. Significantly, in a move to free areas of the curriculum from the constraints of the past, it also proposed that considerable freedom of choice be allowed to schools in the selection of texts for the humanities subjects. As far as promoting Irish and Irish culture was concerned the commission's general recommendations were very similar to those of the Gaelic League. This was particularly so as regards the right to answer questions in either English or Irish, and in the fact that questions on Ireland in history and geography were to enable candidates answering such questions to obtain full marks. In the curriculum in general, Irish was recommended to have the same status as English but not replace it as the Gaelic League had demanded.[90]

With both the National Programme Conference and the Intermediate Commission at work in the months leading up to the establishment of the Irish Free State in December–January, 1921–2, and to the creation of the country's first educational administration under nationalist control, considerable preparation was obviously under way towards implementing the kind of educational programmes which the new authorities believed would be appropriate for that new situation. Commenting on the anticipated direction of these reforms and in particular on the influence of the Gaelic League on them, the *Times Educational Supplement's* Irish correspondent wrote in August 1921:

It would be simple blindness to dismiss the Gaelic movement and its activities as futile zealotry or a mere mask for a political conspiracy. Those who do so seldom show themselves equally zealous for their own educational ideals and in any case are shutting their eyes to the probable course of events. Hitherto the movement has not only received little backing among Unionists and Protestants but has been accorded most lukewarm support by the leaders of Nationalist politics. But among those who are certain to be the first rulers of Southern Ireland will be found many like their chief [de Valera] wholehearted in the determination to make Ireland Gaelic speaking. At present the income of the Gaelic League is stated at about £6,000 to £7,000 and there is no large fund of capital. If so much can be done with so little what can be accomplished by men in command of the nation's capital.[91]

Indeed, for many who were to guide the educational fortunes of the new state this determination was underpinned by a sense of triumph that the time had at last come when a long-oppressed culture would flower again. As one writer in the Gaelic League's journal wrote:

Tá Caisleán Bhaile Átha Cliath i seilbh Ghaeil faoi dheiridh ... Ní bheidh an 'Bórd Naisiúnta' ann feasta leis an teanga a bhascadh agus a bhearnadh.[92] [Dublin Castle is at last in the possession of the Irish ... The National Board will no longer exist to beat and smash the language].

In both parts of the island 1921 closed and 1922 opened with considerable expectation that educational reform of the kind long sought by the dominant interests in each but blocked or at least seriously inhibited under the old regime, was imminent. Just beneath that expectation, however, lay fears, suspicions and apprehensions as to what such reforms would actually entail.

3

Storms of Controversy:
Education in the North 1921–23

1923 Education Act

THE 1923 Education Act was a major piece of legislation, repealing as it did, in whole or in part, 17 earlier pieces of legislation and introducing significant structural change affecting the ownership, management and financing of schools in Northern Ireland. The most important structural change introduced by the act was contained in its provisions for the establishment of local education committees to control, manage and provide schools within their respective areas. This change, based as it was on the general principle that local democratic involvement in the provision of education was highly desirable, had been central to the reforms recommended by the Lynn Committee and, as noted previously, long advocated in government circles prior to partition and strongly supported by many unionist politicians and members of the Protestant churches.

According to the act, local committees were to be composed of representatives of the local authorities in the areas they served, as well as of other persons deemed to have an interest in education.[1] The legislation also provided for the establishment of school committees to be responsible for such matters as the care and maintenance of school buildings, as well as acting in an advisory capacity on a range of other issues – not, however, the appointment of teaching staff.[2]

Existing schools were to be invited to transfer control and management to local committees which would then assume full responsibility for their maintenance and development.[3] In order to safeguard the interests of trustees whose schools would be transferred certain guarantees could be negotiated in the terms of transfer[4] and, in addition, the act recommended that local education committees consider the desirability of providing representation on school committees for the 'trustees or persons' by whom schools were being transferred.[5] Under the terms of the act, trustees who did not wish to transfer their schools could retain 'voluntary' status.[6] However, voluntary schools would only be considered for capital grant aid if management committees were established on which the relevant local education committee would be represented by a ratio of four trustee representatives to two local authority representatives (hence the term 'four-and-two' which entered general currency from this time for schools with this management structure).[7]

Voluntary school managements not willing to accept this structure would only receive minimal forms of financial support, e.g. for lighting, cleaning and heating as well as teachers' salaries. No grants would be available to such schools for capital development except on a very discretionary basis.

The case for these provisions and their clear financial implications was, first, to make transfer an attractive proposition by making the alternatives relatively unattractive. Second, and more directly related to the basic principles of the act, it was argued that a greater degree of public accountability was essential in a system which would make increased public resources available to schools. Third, it was not considered appropriate in a modern system of education that schools should continue to be managed solely by persons who were, in effect, part-time managers. It was also hoped that school committees would provide an appropriate mechanism for counteracting the negative effects which many had identified as being associated with the managerial system, providing a direct voice for parents and other local interests.

These provisions clearly marked a significant break with the structures which had been in place since 1831. Not only was the control and management of schools to be affected, but most significantly for those agencies interested in providing schools, also the basis upon which public finance would be made available to schools. The National Board had been empowered to allocate grants of up to two-thirds of capital expenditure and since such grants had been available without any condition for public representation in the management of national schools, the new provisions were to be seen, especially by the Catholic Church, as a change by which its schools would be seriously disadvantaged if their traditional system of management was retained.

On the question of religious education the act contained provisions of a kind not recommended by the Lynn Committee and which were, moreover, open to the interpretation that religion was to be relegated to a less than central position in schools which would be operated by the new local committees. The Lynn Committee had recommended the retention of the definition of the aims of education used by the National Commissioners, i.e. 'combined secular and separate religious education' which would have meant that religious education would have been an essential part of education in all public authority schools. Instead of adopting this principle, the act indicated that schools were to provide 'an education both literary and moral, based upon instruction in the reading and writing of the English language and in arithmetic'.[8] Religious instruction as such was to be treated not only as separate in the National Commissioners' sense, but no longer part of the required curriculum, as the act made clear when it obliged education authorities to merely:

... afford opportunities for catechetical instruction according to the tenets of the religious denomination of the parents of the children attending any public elementary school, being provided or transferred school, and other religious instruction to which

60

those parents do not object . . . and those clergymen or other persons (including teachers at the school) to whom those parents do not object shall have access to the children in the school for the purpose of giving them religious instruction.[9]

In other words, religious instruction was no longer to be an essential part of education except where it might impinge through 'moral education' and only in so far as education authorities were obliged to provide facilities for religious instruction was its importance formally recognised. Teachers, moreover, while not precluded from providing religious instruction, were no longer to be obliged to do so. Furthermore, in dealing with the appointment of teachers, the act stipulated that henceforth all appointments to public elementary schools would be made by the relevant education authority, and not by the committee of the school concerned. The act also prohibited any account being taken of the religious beliefs of applicants for a teaching post in provided or transferred schools.[10]

Other features of the legislation included new regulations regarding the employment of children, a scheme for the provision of school meals, proposals for a school health service and an improved scholarship scheme for pupils wishing to proceed to secondary school.[11] In contrast to the provisions on grant aid, religious instruction and the appointment of teachers, these other provisions were to prove non-controversial.

Conflict on two fronts

The controversial provisions of the 1923 act were to bring the new administration in Northern Ireland into conflict with both local communities. The Catholic-nationalist community saw itself adversely affected because of the new conditions for grant aid. These conditions were interpreted as effectively depriving its schools of public funding unless the church would agree to a degree of public representation in their management and such a condition the Catholic Church was, of course, not prepared to accept. Conflict with the Protestant–unionist community was to arise for a number of reasons, firstly because of the new conditions governing religious instruction and the appointment of teachers. Later, the question of church representation on school and local education committees was to be added to these sources of grievance.

Of the two conflicts in which it was to be immersed, that with the Protestant–unionist community was potentially the more serious for the government. Bringing, as it did, the government into conflict with sections of its own supporters, it threatened to undermine or least seriously impair its capacity to govern and, thereby, to pose a question mark over the very existence of Northern Ireland itself. Conflict with the Protestant churches on the scale which was about to be witnessed could hardly have been anticipated. Over the preceding decade these churches seemed to have fully supported the campaign for increased democracy in education in Ireland and it must have been expected in government circles that once guarantees would be given that religious instruction could be provided in publicly controlled schools, acceptance of the new arrangements would be virtually automatic. The contrast between the position adopted by the Protestant and Catholic churches over the MacPherson Bill must have served to strengthen this anticipation. Indeed no less a person than Church of Ireland Archbishop D'Arcy had, in September 1921, clearly signalled his firm approval of the general principles upon which the Education Act would be based when, speaking to his diocesan synod, he expressed his support for popular involvement in education, for a local educational rate and for a school system which could bring children of different denominations together.[12] Yet , despite such views and despite the general stand of the Protestant churches over the previous decade, conflict of a very bitter-kind was to develop between them and the government. It was a conflict which would demonstrate the strength of traditional Protestant beliefs in Northern Ireland and the capacity of the Protestant churches to act just as vigorously as the Catholic Church had a few years previously when it had judged it necessary to do so in order to protect its own interests.

The government's case

Before examining Protestant and unionist reaction to the legislation in detail, it will be helpful to consider carefully the government's and, in particular, the Minister of Education's arguments for the act. In his speech introducing his bill to the Northern Ireland Senate, Londonderry outlined the principles upon which he claimed its main proposals were based.[13] The first principle and one to which he was to frequently appeal over the next two years, was that of democratic control of education. Arguing that a centralised system of controlling education was entirely out of date, Londonderry claimed that the 'Bill is making the long step from the centralised system to a system of democratic control',[14] that it was in keeping with the spirit of the times and with the need to provide local people with a say in the development of education. The second principle enunciated by Londonderry concerned the thorny issue of religious instruction. The minister believed that Northern Ireland was and wished to remain a Christian society and that the government should support this desire. However, this did not mean that the state should assume direct responsibility for imparting Christian beliefs and he argued that the state's role should be a neutral one in this area. Nonetheless, he was careful to say that : 'The state is non-sectarian, but not secular in the sense that it takes no interest in the moral upbringing of the children. The state, as does the individual, looks to the churches to give the lead in Christian idealism . . .'[15]

The key issue was the extent to which the state should become involved with the churches in helping the latter to meet their responsibilities and how central a role the churches should be afforded. Londonderry does not seem to have properly gauged the strength of church feeling on this matter and he, rather naively, seems to have thought that their co-operation could be obtained on his terms. Nonetheless, he was mindful enough of past divisions to appeal to the churches not to allow themselves to '. . . become a stumbling block in the way of an ideal system owing to a determination to segregate their flocks and create from birth a division when union is so essential to the well-being of this province'.[16]

The minister's concept of co-operation with the churches within a system of education, publicly financed and democratically controlled, was, however, one in which the churches could no longer play the same role or exercise the same influence as previously. He acknowledged as much when he paid tribute to them for their work in education in Ireland in the past, implying that their role would no longer be as central in the future.[17] He was also at pains to argue that denominational instruction could not be formally provided within the kind of system envisaged in his bill and that while he would agree to facilities for such instruction, outside the hours of compulsory schooling, being provided, beyond that he claimed 'the state cannot go'.[18] To justify his stand Londonderry was able to point to the fact that the same principles had been enshrined in the 1902 Education (England and Wales) Act which had established local education authorities in both countries and which had removed the churches, especially the Church of England, from the central role which they had previously played in the provision and conduct of schools. More significantly in terms of the wider political issues which came to be associated with the act, Londonderry and his officials also believed that they were precluded from going any further in terms of facilitating religious instruction by section 5 of the Government of Ireland Act[19] and, at this early stage of Northern Ireland's existence, the government was very anxious not to enact any legislation which might be found to be contrary to its own constitution. To do so would, it was feared, invite the British government to reopen the whole constitutional issue and because of the great sensitivities surrounding education, there was a particular anxiety to avoid such dangers in this area. Such fears did not, however, appear to concern those from the unionist community who came together to oppose the act and to do so with such determination as to eventually pressure the government into violating that constitution.

Moral but not religious instruction

To avoid accusations that his approach to religious instruction suggested indifference to the general moral education of the young, Londonderry laid considerable stress on the care which had been taken to ensure that such education would be part of the compulsory curriculum. In his Senate speech of 4 June 1923, he stated that '. . . we are determined that moral instruction shall be associated with secular education'[20] and he went on to stress that the kind of moral education he had in mind would be based on Christian principles. Later, in an article published in 1924, he again spelt out his arguments on this point, writing that :

The Churches are, I believe, ready to admit public management of the schools as soon as they are convinced that religious instruction will be assured as it is under their own management. We have endeavoured to meet these views by providing that ethical instruction be given during the hours of compulsory attendance and that a daily period shall be fixed in accordance with the regulation to be laid before Parliament during which clergymen and other persons to whom the parents consent shall have access to the children in all provided and transferred schools for the purpose of giving them catechetical instruction in which the teachers may take part. It is difficult to see how we could have greater assurance of religious instruction . . .[21]

Difficult as it may have been for Londonderry to have seen how it might have been done, the churches did indeed expect him to provide that greater assurance and until it was provided they were to remain at loggerheads with the government.

Despite the optimistic note which Londonderry struck in public, he could not have been totally unprepared for some of the hostile reaction which surrounded the act when it was passed. At cabinet level several meetings devoted considerable time to the question of religious instruction, the minutes of which reveal intense debate on the matter. Following publication of the bill, Londonderry reported to his colleagues that the (Protestant) churches were pressing him 'to allow denominational teaching within the hours of compulsory attendance'.[22] With the support of several ministers, he successfully argued against any concession in this direction.

Among those supporting him were several who favoured a completely secular education in public elementary schools with one parliamentary secretary referring, without very much evidence, to what he described as 'a wide feeling against clerical control'.[23] Londonderry himself was also inclined to view clerical opposition as not being representative 'of the opinion in the province' and that 'it was largely manufactured by certain interested ecclesiastics'.[24] Interestingly, however, the Prime Minister who, in 1925, was to negotiate the first settlement with the Protestant churches over his Education Minister's head and who was probably more sensitive to the depth of feeling that was being aroused on the matter of religious instruction, thought that it might be wise to adopt a scheme to allow such instruction in accordance with the churches' demand.[25] However, his suggestions found no favour amongst cabinet colleagues at this time.

As for the Protestant churches themselves, they were not easily dissuaded by the minister's attempts to reassure them that all would be well under the new arrangements. They had each made their positions on religious instruction clear in their evidence to the Lynn Committee and had expected that the legislation would have taken full account of their demands. The Board of Education of the Presbyterian Church had, for example, argued to the committee 'the futility of all education if divorced from right moral principles'[26] and had recommended that a curriculum of joint secular and separate religious instruction be adopted, both to be required elements within the curriculum. The Church of Ireland and the Methodist submissions followed similar lines.[27] Throughout the early months of 1923 several attempts were made to persuade the minister to change his mind in order to make religious instruction part of the compulsory curriculum. Noting the evolution of the controversy the *Times Educational Supplement* reported 'daily fights in the Northern press over the Education Bill' and commented that there was a 'strong feeling in favour of the Lynn Committee's recommendations' on religious instruction.[28]

Fearing for the success of his proposals, Londonderry moved swiftly to try to defuse the controversy and, by some clever use of language, made it appear that he had conceded on the question of religious instruction. Speaking in the House of Commons in April, and, perhaps quite consciously, reiterating the kind of language used in the Presbyterian submission to the Lynn Committee, he stated it had never been his intention to exclude from the compulsory curriculum 'the lessons of Christian teaching and those moral principles to which we all subscribe'.[29] So, he proposed to 'include in the Bill such provisions as will ensure that instruction of this description will be imparted to the children . . . [emphasising that] . . . unless we lay down . . . our adherence to Christian principles and the belief we hold in the necessity for associating Christian ethics with secular teaching, we shall not be discharging the duty we owe to the rising generation'.[30] As a result, clause 7 of the bill was amended to include the word 'moral' alongside 'literary' to indicate that both were part of the aims of education.[31]

The minister's words announcing this amendment were warmly welcomed by several M.P.s who believed that the fears raised over religious instruction had now been satisfactorily allayed. Robert Anderson M.P. said that '. . . the House as a whole has been delighted by and the community will receive with the greatest relief, the statement by the Minister of Education that there is no intention and never was any intention of putting religion out of the school'.[32] Fears were further allayed when a later amendment made it clear that teachers would be permitted, though still not obliged to provide religious instruction.[33]

While the minister did appear to have addressed some fears by his decisions to amend the bill, he seems to have maintained a degree of deliberate vagueness around the definition of 'moral education'. Robert McKeown M.P., the minister's parliamentary secretary and the person who moved the amendment to clause 26, described it 'as a thing that might run through the daily work of the school. It does not refer to religious instruction . . .'[34] As Akenson points out, Londonderry was under no illusion himself as to the distinction between moral and religious instruction. His quotation from the minister's letter to the Church of Ireland Bishop of Down, Connor and Dromore on the question of religious instruction makes the distinction clear:

. . . and now let me come to that other type of instruction which I shall call for the sake of clearness, not religious but moral instruction . . . Such teaching must by necessity be absolutely undenominational;. . . It thus cannot include reading from pages of the Bible itself . . .[35]

Despite such a clear distinction, Londonderry's willingness to introduce an amendment had the effect of defusing the controversy over religious instruction for the time being and allowed attention to focus instead on the proposals for the appointment of teachers.

Teacher appointments

The fact that the proposals concerning the appointment of teachers also became a matter of immediate controversy must have caused even more surprise to the minister and his officials. It was true that some concern over the appointment of teachers in public elementary schools had been conveyed to the Lynn Committee. At that stage, though, the concern was primarily that a church should retain some presence in schools it transferred, and did not relate specifically to fears about religious instruction or the appointment of teachers. The Church of Ireland's submission, for example, had recommended that Church of Ireland teachers should be appointed to any schools which that church would transfer.[36] However, the significance of this issue only emerged when it became clear that religious instruction would no longer be part of the required curriculum and, consequently and more importantly perhaps, that teachers could not be obliged to provide it. If teachers would only be appointed to teach the secular aspects of the curriculum, their religious beliefs could be disregarded, a fact underlined by the prohibition in clause 66 on taking such beliefs into account when appointing them. The door was, therefore, theoretically being opened to the appointment of teachers with any religious beliefs, or none, to teach in public elementary schools. Since such schools would be attended mainly, if not exclusively by Protestant pupils the issue became of immediate importance to the Protestant churches. The managers of Catholic and of other schools which would not be transferred were to remain free to make their own appointments. Furthermore, since the bill proposed that the regional committees and not school committees would be the appointing authorities, the question of who would control these authorities also became pertinent to the issue. In predominantly nationalist areas the committees would be likely to contain a majority of nationalists who would not be seen by unionists as likely to act in unionist interests. Hence, the spectre of teachers from all kinds of backgrounds generally described as inimical to Protestant interests, was invoked to protest against what was alleged to be an attempt to deprive the Protestant community of a say in who would be permitted to teach its children. One unionist M.P. accused the Minister of Education of attempting to put , 'Socialists and Roman Catholics into your schools . . . putting in men who burned the Bible . . .'[37] and according to the same M.P., William Coote, a conspiracy would be devised as, he alleged, had already taken effect in the United States of America where:

. . . fifty three per cent of the teachers in federal schools in the United States are Roman Catholics today although their own hierarchy will not allow their little children to be brought into these schools. The same is going to happen here . . . if that clause is continued . . . I venture to say that before fifty years the North of Ireland will be Roman Catholic for you will have financially rooted them in the soil, you will have Catholics and Socialists. Heaven help Ulster and its generations with such teaching of the little children.[38]

Exaggerated as this expression of fear about a Roman Catholic 'take-over' of 'Protestant' schools was, the basis to it must have appeared real enough to some, especially those like Coote who was from a border constituency with a large nationalist community. Opposition to this provision was not confined solely to those of a conspiratorial outlook, as the more measured words of a Canon Browne of the Church of Ireland illustrate:

Church of Ireland managers had agreed that giving the regional committees the appointment of teachers was one of the chief obstacles to the transferring of schools to the education authorities: the leaders of the Presbyterian and Methodist Churches are in full agreement with the Church of Ireland on this point.[39]

Dr Hugh Morrison, M.P. for Queen's University, who was to become a strong opponent of the 1923 act, also identified the procedures for the appointment of teachers as likely to be very contentious. Speaking about the problems which could arise in predominantly nationalist areas over the appointment of teachers to 'Protestant' schools, he argued that the Catholic Church did not want such an invidious situation and that it was one which the 'Protestant churches will not submit to . . . [because] . . . you cannot allow Catholics to control the appointment of Protestant teachers while they themselves are not affected by the regional committees in other districts'.[40]

Nevertheless, despite these apprehensions there were some voices within the Protestant churches arguing that the minister's proposals should be given a chance, as Dr Grierson did saying that :

. . . the old order is changing and now clerical managership has to go and it is right that it should go. The new measure would in the end have happy results and he did not believe that the old relations between the teachers and the clergy would be greatly disturbed.[41]

The teachers through their unions also welcomed the proposals on appointments, seeing in them an opportunity, at last, of being freed from many of the commitments which clerical management had imposed on them. Many teachers had long harboured resentments at being almost obliged, as part of their conditions of appointment, to assist in church related activities.[42] To them, the new proposals were stating that only professional considerations should count in all future appointments to transferred and provided schools. Speaking in support of these proposals J. Smyth of the Ulster National Teachers' Union claimed that:

. . . denominationalism has cursed our country with a multitude of small struggling schools, often housed in mere hovels, lacking in most facilities for efficient teaching . . . The teachers in these schools owed their appointment not to their scholastic attainments nor to their efficiency as school keepers but to the favour of interested parties or to their willingness to perform duties altogether outside the province of a secular teacher.[43]

As for the government, it was hoping that 'common sense' would prevail since it was convinced, as Robert Anderson stated, that it was hardly conceivable that :

. . . regional committees would for a moment think of appointing somebody out of harmony with the views of the people as whole . . . In the appointment of teachers for those schools regional committees ought to be trusted to do what is right by teachers, by the children and by education as a whole.[44]

Anderson was probably correct in his assessment of what was most likely to happen since it was most unlikely that unionist-dominated regional committees would appoint teachers other than would be acceptable to their local communities, while the few nationalist controlled committees would be more than likely to respect the wishes of local Protestant communities given that Catholic schools would not be subject to any interference at all in the matter of teacher appointments. Unfortunately his view was not shared by most of the leading spokespersons for the Protestant churches. Instead, pressure against the proposal mounted and demands that the relevant section of the bill be amended were made, otherwise it was threatened that many schools would not be transferred.[45] A joint statement by three leading clergymen of the main Protestant denominations on the matter of teacher appointments in September 1923, just before the legislation was enacted, called for appointments to be made by school committees and for the religious denomination of applicants to be a relevant factor.[46] The three argued that their concerns were motivated by their fear of what might happen in regional committees controlled by Roman Catholic majorities. Such situations, they argued, required a measure of legislative reassurance by which the education of Protestant children could be safeguarded against any attempt to impose Roman Catholic teachers on them.

To the government, however, opponents of the proposals were missing the point. Since the bill indicated that transferred schools would no longer be denominational schools in any formal sense and would, as *public* schools, be open to all sections of the community, control and management had to be fully in the hands of public representatives. The churches, the government argued, would continue to have their interests recognised in various ways since it was expected that church representatives would be nominated to regional and school committees and that facilities would be made available for religious instruction in transferred and provided schools. Confident that its case was a strong one, the government refused to bow to pressure and believed that time would reveal how groundless the fears expressed really were. As the *Belfast Telegraph* editorial writer put it at the time:

The pulpit has even been used on occasions to create unfounded fears by the circulation of statements which were unwarranted. The public realised that the keystone of the New Act is popular control and they instinctively resent the implied imputation that while they can be entrusted with far graver responsibilities in all that makes up national and local government they cannot be entrusted with control over the appointment or dismissal of those who are to teach their children: exercising that control through the medium of popularly elected bodies that must from time to time account for their stewardship at the bar of public opinion.[47]

This was precisely how the government saw the issue and as Hugh Pollock, Minister of Finance, was to put it later in the year the demands of the Protestant churches were essentially demands for maintaining 'denomi-nationalism' in education.[48] So, with little parliamentary opposition mobilised against the bill, it was finally passed with a substantial majority in both houses and was entered on the statute book in October.[49]

Opposition mounts

The passage of the bill into law did not, however mark an end to controversy. What the first year of debate demonstrated was the firm intention of the Protestant churches to campaign to ensure that their interpretation of the educational needs of Protestant children and their views as to the circum-stances in which these needs should be met would prevail. However irra-tional and unreal the government might have considered the churches' fears about the effects of educational change, to many Protestants they were nonetheless real, deeply rooted fears and would not be easily allayed by rational reassurances. If the first round went to the government and to Lord Londonderry in particular, it was to be the only round they would win and their victory was to prove a short-lived one.

In parliament, Londonderry's colleagues heaped praise on him in very fulsome terms when the bill was passed with Senator Joseph Cunningham claiming that :

. . . the people of Northern Ireland are very fortunate in having secured one who has taken such a considerable interest in this question of education. The noble Marquess will be forever remembered particularly by the working classes who may be bene-fited by this measure.[50]

The teachers' unions also warmly welcomed the act, as did editorials in that most dependable of newspapers, from the government's viewpoint, the *Belfast Telegraph*.[51]

However, with little delay the Protestant churches soon rallied support for their attack on the act. From October 1923 until March 1925 when the first amendments to the act were passed, it was virtually an all-out onslaught on the government by the churches and their allies throughout Northern Ireland. The failure of the government to meet the demands of the Protestant churches for substantial amendments before the bill was passed led to a much more intense and more public campaign of opposition to the new act than had been witnessed prior to its passing. Almost all shades of Protestantism and unionism outside of parliament to begin with, and then gradually inside it as well, began clamouring for change. Signalling the beginning of this onslaught, one churchman, speaking at the Church of Ireland synod in the Clogher diocese a mere two weeks after the act was passed, said that: 'They must never rest until an amending Act was brought in or the Church of Ireland, Presbyterians and Methodists would turn against the government'.[52]

Even the Church of Ireland Primate, Archbishop D'Arcy, who had asked in December 1923 for the new act 'to be given a chance'[53] was in January 1924 arguing that:

Protestant managers and Protestant parents will desire to be quite sure that Protestant teachers are appointed to Protestant schools . . . Our Ulster people are a religious people. It is quite impossible that they desire a system of education more thoroughly secularized than that of any other part of the United Kingdom.[54]

Later at a meeting of representatives of the Protestant churches in March 1924, D'Arcy presided when a resolution was passed calling for amendments to the act, especially on the matter of teacher appointments:

We reiterate our conviction that the only satisfactory solution of the question is an amending Act. At the same time we are willing to enter further conference to see whether it is possible to meet the situation for the present by means of regulations, especially with reference to the appointment of teachers in transferred and provided schools.[55]

While the immediate emphasis was on the appointment of teachers, once the controversy was reopened it was not confined to this matter and the exclusion of religious instruction from the compulsory curriculum re-emerged as the second central issue. The campaign was led by some of the most notable of the Protestant clergy, among them William Corkey, then convenor of the Presbyterian Church's Education Committee who, when moving the adoption of the report on primary education at the General Assembly of his church in June 1924, linked both issues, arguing that:

The old system had been made up of combined secular and separate religious instruction, but under the new Act religious instruction was taken away altogether as a fundamental part. Again the Education Act took away any safeguard they had as to the appointment of teachers, while it made the giving of religious instruction optional on the part of teachers. If there was no regulation for religious instruction in the Act religious instruction remained optional. They did not want sectarian teaching; but they wanted the teaching of religion to their children on the broad basis of their Protestant faith.[56]

Corkey's remarks indicated quite clearly that the changed status envisaged for transferred schools should in no way affect their 'religious' characteristics. In schools attended by Protestant children religious instruction should be provided according to Protestant beliefs, school teachers should be obliged to provide it and such school teachers had, therefore, to be Protestant themselves. That is what the Presbyterian General Assembly formally demanded when a resolution reflecting very closely the views expressed by Corkey was adopted:

Whereas the National Board of Education had for its fundamental principle the imparting of 'combined secular and separate religious instruction' thus giving recognition of the fact that all real education must be founded on a religious basis, and whereas the Commissioners of National Education assumed (as for example in the management of Model Schools) that such instruction would be imparted by teachers in full sympathy with the religious convictions of the parents of the children the General Assembly deeply deplores the passing into law of an Education Act which departs from these principles and thus deprives the people of Ulster of two cherished and long established rights.[57]

The Presbyterian Church was now fully committed to campaigning for change and throughout the rest of 1924 considerable effort was devoted to mobilising local presbyteries in support of its demands and to combining with the other Protestant churches to ensure success. The churches relied on three weapons in their campaign. The first was their refusal to sanction the transfer of any school until the terms of transfer were such as satisfied their demands. As one clergyman quite bluntly stated: 'if they were going to have merely secular education the church should not transfer the schools'.[58] The second weapon was to focus attention on the attack which, they alleged, the act was making on the place of religious instruction in education. They did so by claiming that the act was essentially an example of secularising legislation which, by placing religious instruction outside the hours of compulsory schooling, was an attack on education itself. Also, by placing the appointment of teachers in the hands of regional committees the churches argued that the act made it possible for teachers not acceptable to the Protestant community to be appointed to teach Protestant children. In even simpler terms the act was represented as taking the Bible out of schools and, as Coote had stated, allowing for the appointment of 'Socialists and Roman Catholics' to Protestant schools. A large leaflet which was prepared for wide distribution, but not used because the government agreed to amend the act in March 1925, bluntly made these points by asking if people were aware:

1. That the Education Authority is forbidden to provide Religious Instruction (Clause 26) ?
2. That the Committee appointing teachers is expressly forbidden to pay any regard to the religious views of any applicant (Clause 66)?
3. That, therefore, the door is thrown open for a Bolshevist or an Atheist or a Roman Catholic to become a teacher in a Protestant school?
4. That the object of the National Education Board,viz. Combined secular and separate religious instruction for all denominations (though recommended by the Lynn Committee) has been set aside for a system which is secularist in its terms and tendencies ?[59]

To meet these concerns the churches asked that the act be amended to allow simple Bible instruction to continue as previously and that some means be found of ensuring that schools attended by Protestant children would have Protestant teachers.[60]

The third weapon was a campaign of public meetings which the churches were well placed to organise and which was to have the effect of causing considerable unease in political circles, particularly because of the government's concern about Northern Ireland's constitutional position. It was a particularly unhelpful time for the government to be faced with such a degree of unrest amongst its own supporters. The Boundary Commission envisaged by the Anglo-Irish Treaty in 1921 had only recently begun to function and was engaged in taking evidence as to where the actual border between north and south should be. Nationalists harboured hopes that the commission would make such recommendations as might question the whole partition settlement. Any widescale dissension within the unionist community would, the government further feared, be exploited by those who would wish that settlement undone. So it was clearly very much in the latter's interest to maintain the highest possible degree of solidarity in unionist ranks.

Government resistance

Within the Ministry of Education the advice to Londonderry was that he should stand firm. His permanent secretary, Lewis McQuibban, was convinced that the Protestant churchmen were demanding something which in principle could not be conceded and was caustic in his criticism of what he regarded as their lack of leadership:

... clerical managers want to force an obligation of teaching religious instruction of a particular kind ... the churches want public expenditure and that they should retain denominational privilege . . . are they not lacking in the qualities of leadership so essential for men in positions of such enormous responsibility . . . Are they not out of touch with the spirit of the times.[61]

While Londonderry was not quite so forthright in his comments, nonetheless throughout 1924 and up until virtually the moment when concessions were made, he and the government argued the case against changing the act. In the minister's view his clerical opponents had simply misunderstood the intentions of the act as far as religious instruction and the appointment of teachers were concerned. Speaking in Belfast in January 1924 he claimed that:

... with the provisions made under the Act and above all by the concession of the right of entry which the clergy of Ulster unlike the clergy of England have secured, I maintain that Religious Instruction is safe in Ulster so long as the people of Ulster remain religious people and so long as the churches maintain their influence over her people . . . I ask the opponents of the Act a very simple straight-forward question: Do they mean to imply that by giving the control of the local services of education including the appointment of teachers to education authorities composed of persons directly representative of local bodies elected by a 'deeply-religious people' the Ministry of Education is risking the cause of religious instruction?[62]

The question was not quite so straightforward as Londonderry suggested. In these remarks Londonderry was really asking whether, if the churches valued a role in education for themselves, they could ever allow this role to be removed, however slightly, from their own very direct control over key aspects of education. The answer in the case of Northern Ireland was a resounding 'no', notwithstanding the fact that the public authorities were themselves sympathetic to the beliefs, values and attitudes of those most likely to transfer schools.

It has to be understood, however, that the Protestant churches in Northern Ireland were not, as churches, acting out of character in opposing the terms of the act. What they displayed was the same apprehension that any other church would have displayed at the idea of no longer being able to determine and guarantee beyond the immediate future the manner in which religious instruction would be imparted. Londonderry's attempt, therefore, as he said in the same speech, 'to urge on the people of Ulster to have confidence in themselves' by taking greater control through democratic institutions for education was not going to be met with any sympathy from the churches as far as religious instruction was concerned.

Two quite different approaches to education were in conflict and the differences between them were further revealed by Londonderry when, in March 1925, almost on the eve of the government conceding amendments to the Protestant churches, he further argued that :

> . . . it would be a violation of every principle of religious liberty that such instruction [i.e. religious instruction] be given in compulsory hours. In the second place the Government are not prepared to place any legal obligation upon teachers to give religious instruction . . . in the third place Government are not prepared to enable the new education authorities to provide Religious Instruction . . .[63]

Contained in those words was the view that a public system of education could only be secular and that any formally religious dimension to education could only be accommodated within the non-compulsory part of the curriculum. In support of this stand, he again invoked the Government of Ireland Act saying that the government was not 'prepared to initiate legislation which they are advised would be at variance with the provision of that Act'.[64]

In public, at least, Londonderry appeared to have the full support of his Prime Minister who argued, like Anderson, on the more pragmatic grounds that he found it '. . . inconceivable that a committee constituted on those lines [i.e. elected by the people] would select as a teacher anyone they felt was unsuitable from any point of view'.[65] In other words, Craig was saying that committees composed of representatives who, in terms of religious affiliation, would be Protestant would be most likely to only select teachers suitable in every respect (and that to include giving religious instruction) to teach Protestant pupils. However likely this situation would be, the churches remained unconvinced and the government had to face the reality that, not only were the churches effectively mobilising support for their case outside parliament, but that they were gaining support inside as well.

Members who had previously accepted the government's assurances on religious instruction and on the appointment of teachers began to argue the Protestant churches' case. Robert Crawford M.P., one such member, was by the spring of 1924 seconding the amendment moved by Dr Morrison, who had been one of the most persistent critics of the act, to have sanction withheld from those sections dealing with religious instruction. In support of his stand he made it clear how much he had accepted the churches' demand for compulsory religious instruction:

It is our duty as members of the Government of Northern Ireland to make arrangements that every child be taught the everlasting word of God. I believe that this house and this Government should have made sufficient regulations and in that respect I consequently second this motion.[66]

But as yet the government was in no danger and the amendment failed by 24 votes to 4.

Unease with the act was not, however, confined to backbenchers. Craig himself, as several cabinet minutes reveal, felt from the start that some compromise would be necessary. As early as March 1923, when the draft bill was being discussed, Craig had argued that religious instruction might be allowed during compulsory hours on certain days of the week. Later, in September of the same year, he argued, in cabinet, that teachers in transferred schools should always be of the same denomination as the body by whom the schools were transferred.[67] Obviously Craig felt that both matters were likely to be controversial and it was probably no surprise to many that it was he who, in the end, directly negotiated with church representatives and agreed to have amendments introduced.

It was not for some time that the political necessity for amendments became clear. After all the act continued to retain considerable support outside of parliament. In particular the teachers' unions were becoming very anxious lest the advances which they regarded the act as having achieved for their members be lost in the face of church and growing political opposition. Like Londonderry they believed that in reality the act posed no threat to religious instruction since most teachers were likely to co-operate in providing it. Speaking at the annual congress of the U.T.U. in 1924 its general secretary made this point, saying that:

We believe that the facilities for the giving of Biblical and catechetical instruction in the Act of 1923 are as great as those provided under the Charter of 1832; and if the clergy and the persons duly appointed by them take advantage of all the facilities provided for religious instruction in the Act there will be no danger of the future citizens of Northern Ireland growing up in godlessness or in ignorance of the Holy Scriptures. As the official representative of the U.T.U. I wish publicly to state that the teachers will do their duty in this respect as zealously in the future as they have done in the past. Compulsion would defeat the object we all have in view, i.e. the moral and spiritual welfare of the future generations.[68]

This point was strongly reiterated as the climax of the first phase of the controversy was being approached in early 1925 when the same union's executive passed a resolution stating that 'while teachers are quite willing to continue the giving of religious instruction as heretofore they would most decidedly object to compulsion being applied'.[69]

Fundamental priorities

As the campaign for amendments began to coincide in early 1925 with concern about wider constitutional issues affecting the outcome of the Boundary Commission's deliberations those orchestrating that campaign found themselves in a position of some political strength. The prospect that the commission might recommend changes to the border between north and south was of considerable concern to Craig's government[70] and he was determined to present a united unionist front against any territorial change which could be regarded as to Northern Ireland's disadvantage. Any hint of disunity, such as that threatened by the dispute over education, was, to say the least, unwelcome. With churchmen, like Dean R.G. King of Derry, claiming that the 'Ulster government has declared for entirely non-religious education',[71] the possibility of a church led, or at least a church inspired attempt to undermine support for the government within the unionist community, was not a completely fanciful one.

That threat was evidently growing as support for the churches came from an increasing number of Craig's own backbenchers, from the Orange Order and from more and more leading voices within the churches themselves. The scale of this support could no longer be ignored and so Craig decided, whatever Londonderry might think, that steps be taken to allay the Protestant churches' concern over the 1923 act. A hastily arranged meeting took place between Craig and representatives of these churches on 6 March, the day after the latter had held a large meeting in Belfast in order to increase pressure for change.[72] At that meeting Craig agreed that he would consult with his colleagues and that a government decision would follow quite quickly. The decision came the following day and consisted of a commitment to introduce an amending bill which would remove the prohibitions in clause 26 on the provision of religious instruction and the further prohibition in clause 66 on taking an applicant's religious affiliation into account when making teaching appointments. The combined efforts of the Protestant churches and of the Orange Order proved too formidable as the Rev. William Corkey clearly revealed in his account of these events:

The terms of settlement were accepted by the secretaries of the United Churches Committee and the representatives of the Loyal Orange Order on the clear understanding that when the prohibitory clauses had been deleted the Act would be administered in sympathy with the views of the overwhelming body of the Protestant people in Northern Ireland. In other words, that no objection would now be taken by the Ministry, or by the Borough and Regional Committees to the insertion in the deeds of transfer of Protestant schools of the two vital conditions:-(1) that Bible Instruction would be given each day by the teaching staff of the school and (2) that in the case of a vacancy in the teaching staff the teacher appointed by the Education Authority would be from a list of three nominated by the local education committee of the school.[73]

The amending legislation was introduced in the form of a very short bill and quickly passed through all its stages by 13 March. Craig was, therefore, able to face the general elections held the next month, his party united and the threat of major divisions in the unionist community removed. His reward was another overwhelming victory for the Unionist Party.[74]

An unconstitutional measure

Behind the scenes, however, there lurked dangers for the future which, if they had become public in the spring of 1925, could have had very serious consequences for the government and for the constitution of Northern Ireland. The dangers lay in the very negative view taken of the amendments by the Governor of Northern Ireland, the Duke of Abercorn, who was obliged to scrutinise the constitutionality of all legislation. Abercorn wrote to Craig on the day the act was passed indicating that it was only to avoid embarrassing the government that 'reserving' the bill had not been advised :

Moved . . . by the desire of not causing to your Government the embarrassment which reservation in the exceptional circumstances of this case might have created the Secretary of State has decided not to advise reservation of the Bill. At the same time I learn and am asked to let my Ministers know, that His Majesty's Government, in case it should be found expedient, after the Bill has become law, to determine the validity of the Act or any of its provisions, hold themselves at liberty to advise His Majesty in accordance with Section 5 of the Government of Ireland Act to refer the question here-after to the Judicial Committee of the Privy Council.[75]

Despite his concern that the legislation might have been constitutionally invalid Abercorn obviously allowed the wider political context to influence his judgement and this was quite an extraordinary decision, given his role as guardian of that constitution. In mitigation he did sound a warning to the government, the importance of which only becomes apparent when viewed in the context of the government's next amending act in 1930 and, more sig-nificantly, in the context of the controversy which was to surround an even later piece of educational legislation in 1947.

Had the nationalist opposition been more aware of what was happening and, even more importantly, better organised to probe the issues involved, it may well have been possible to have mounted an effective constitutional challenge to the 1925 amendments. As it was, only the nationalist press high-lighted Londonderry's stand on the constitutionality of the original act and his commitment given at the very time when Craig was preparing to nego-tiate with the Protestant churches. In an editorial on 10 March the *Irish News* quoted the minister's comments to journalists a few days previously:

There are certain constitutional limitations imposed on the Government of Northern Ireland by Section 5 of the Government of Ireland Act, 1920; and the Government are not prepared to initiate legislation which they are advised would be at variance with the provision of the Act. They cannot pay for the teaching of religion.[76]

No wider heed was paid to these comments and within a week, those limi-tations had been breached and, privately, the governor had clearly acknowl-edged that to have been the case.

Religious instruction or Bible teaching

Confident that the churches had now won their case on the matter of re-ligious instruction and teacher appointment, managers who wanted to transfer their schools attempted to have suitable terms on both matters included in deeds of transfer. That confidence was not to last very long because when the formulation below was suggested by the United Committee of the Protestant Churches and the County Grand Loyal Orange Lodge of Belfast, it was rejected by the Ministry of Education[77] and a further period of controversy with these churches and their allies ensued. The general formulation proposed for terms of transfer was as follows:

1. That Religious Instruction shall be given by the teaching staff as heretofore on a programme to be approved of by the persons transferring the schools.
2. That in the event of a teacher being transferred who on religious grounds is objectionable to the persons or Body transferring the school (or the persons transferring and the local School Committee) it shall be competent for the persons or Body transferring the school, on giving due and reasonable notice to the Education Authority to terminate the lease of notice.[78]

What, in effect, was being sought by this request was to use the amending act as an occasion for obtaining more positive commitments regarding the appointment of teachers and the provision of religious instruction than the amending legislation had been intended to provide. The Ministry of Education would not agree to further concessions because to have done so would have meant that each transferred church school would have retained all its existing denominational characteristics and would not have become a 'public elementary school' as intended by the 1923 act. Some might argue that this is what should have been allowed to happen, as indeed Craig seems to have wished, but it was not how Londonderry and his ministry interpreted the law, nor was it how they wished to see the education system develop.

May and June 1925 witnessed intense lobbying of the ministry by the churches in order to obtain an agreed interpretation of the act. Following consultation between the minister, the churches and the teachers' unions the following agreement was reached, as set out in a memorandum of the ministry in July 1925:

... the Ministry is advised that notwithstanding the Amendment of Section 26 of the Education Act of 1923 by the Education Act this year, it is not open to Education Authorities to provide and pay for 'religious instruction' as defined in Section 26 of the Act of 1923. While the Education Authorities are bound by that Section of the Act to afford opportunities for catechetical instruction according to the tenets of religious denominations, the Minister is advised that an Education Authority may, if they so desire, adopt a programme of 'simple Bible instruction', to be given by the teachers in any or all of the provided and transferred schools under their management, in the period set apart in the time-table of the school for the purpose of religious instruction under Regulation 16 of the Ministry's Regulations in regard to religious instruction in public elementary schools, provided that such programme shall not include instruction according to the tenets distinctive of any religious denomination.

If any such programme of Bible instruction is adopted for any school or schools it shall be regarded as part of the ordinary course of instruction in the school and it shall be the duty of the teachers if so required by the Education Authority to give such instruction.[79]

This memorandum was very significant since, as far as the Protestant churches were concerned, the essence of religious instruction, i.e. Bible instruction, could now be provided as part of the ordinary school programme, although not during the hours of compulsory schooling, and teachers would be obliged to provide that instruction. On the appointment of teachers, school management committees, on which the churches hoped to be represented by virtue of their previous managerial and trusteeship roles, would be allowed to offer advice to the regional committees. The churches further expected, as events during the next few years would make clear, that they would be represented as of right on the latter as one of the major interest groups in education. It is now quite obvious, despite what the churches subsequently claimed, that the government had by virtue of the agreed interpretation of the Education Act given the Protestant churches all that they had sought in 1925. A form of religious instruction which Protestants regarded as quite acceptable and which teachers would be required to provide, albeit not during the hours of compulsory schooling, had been conceded together with a say in the appointment of the teachers themselves. The public elementary system had as a result become denominational in all but name, at least for the Protestant community. Notwithstanding this, one further round in the controversy remained to be fought before the Protestant churches were to be satisfied that what they sought was guaranteed in terms as absolute as it was possible to provide.

Forever Protestant

The agreement discussed above was reached between the ministry and the churches, but according to the act and as the memorandum itself made clear, the actual implementation of its terms lay with the regional committees. As events unfolded over the next year or so, not all of these committees were prepared to accept, as conditions of transfer, commitments in perpetuity to provide the kind of instruction agreed to, or to oblige teachers to provide it. Furthermore, the fact that some authorities did not nominate any clergymen to their education committees and that others did not nominate what the churches regarded as a satisfactory number of their representatives to serve on the regional committees, added to the agitation for firmer guarantees on both religious instruction and the role of churches in the administration of education in Northern Ireland. Matters came to a head when, in early 1928, the Armagh Regional Education Committee which had refused to accept transfer of a small number of schools on the terms being demanded by the intending transferors found itself embroiled in controversy with the ministry. The terms sought included a commitment, in perpetuity, to provide Bible instruction.

The Armagh committee had by this time concluded transfer agreements with over 50 schools and in no case had transfer deeds contained a commitment to provide Bible instruction.[80] Instead, as the committee pointed out in its correspondence with the Ministry of Education:

The Committee have no doubt that the giving of Bible instruction is more effectively secured by means of the clause in the teachers' service agreements than by a condition in transfer deed to which the teachers are not a party. . .[81]

The committee went on to point out that it had in mind the situation which would arise when it would be dealing with 'provided' schools:

There will be no transfer deeds in these cases but the Committee's arrangements will apply automatically, operating fairly and impartially in every case and preserving uniformity throughout the Education Area.[82]

This second point was of considerable significance since it highlighted a situation that was only emerging, but it was also one which was to engage the attention of the churches and for which quite an ingenious solution was to be found in further amending legislation in 1930.

In 1928, however, the ministry was very anxious to avoid any reopening of the issues surrounding transfer. There would appear to have been, as the Armagh correspondence reveals, almost a sense of desperation to ensure that transfers would proceed without any further hindrance. Referring to the agreement of 1925, Bonaparte Wyse, in his letter to the committee following protests by the Lurgan Clerical Union[83] about the former's stand on the terms of transfer, stated:

It was, of course, a necessary condition for the success of this agreed policy that education committees would be willing on their side to bind themselves in the transfer deeds to insist on the teaching of Bible instruction in the schools and it was evident that a refusal on the part of any authority to do so would revive the agitation against the Act in an acute form, would discourage everywhere the transfer of schools to public control and would to a large degree traverse and nullify many of the advantages expected to flow from the application of the Education Act to the conditions of elementary education in the province.[84]

Already the nationalist representatives in parliament had begun to refer to difficulties over transfer as evidence for their claim that the 1923 act was failing to meet the needs of the Northern Irish situation and, therefore, as strengthening *their* case for fresh legislation. If such was to happen, they would expect to see Roman Catholic grievances addressed as well as those of the Protestant churches.[85] Any further delay in having the legislation implemented would strengthen such demands, a situation the government clearly wanted to avoid.

Preventing such a situation developing was not easy in the conditions which pertained in Northern Ireland. William Corkey was once again prominent in seeking stronger guarantees and at the 1928 General Assembly of the Presbyterian Church sought guarantees, firstly, in the form of legislative provisions which would ensure that schools attended by Protestant pupils would be legally obliged to provide Bible instruction; secondly, that representatives of the churches would be given places on regional committees; and thirdly, that the Protestant churches would be adequately represented on the committee of Stranmillis Training College. On the first and second demand, Corkey argued with a sense of hurt about injustices done to the Protestant community and of fears of encroachment by the Catholic Church, that the people of Northern Ireland:

. . . never asked for a system of education from which the interest and help of the Protestant churches had been eliminated . . . The Protestant churches, which built most of the schools and which were transferring their schools and children to the Education Committees were not asked to nominate a single member [to these committees]. . .There was nothing in the transfer deed [with the Armagh Committee] to prevent any or all of those schools being used as secular schools or being used exclusively for the instruction of Roman Catholics.[86]

On the question of Protestant representation on the committee of Stranmillis College, which had recently been added to the list of demands, the claim was that the Catholic Church was being more favourably treated because of the grant to St Mary's College and the support for Catholic male students to train in London. Stranmillis, although a government college, was almost 100 per cent Protestant in its student members and since these students would be the future teachers of Protestant children their churches had a right, as Dr W. Strahan said at the General Assembly to 'be adequately represented on that College Committee'.[87]

Once again education was pushed to the forefront of public concern. Considerable stress was placed in this phase of the controversy on what the Protestant churches claimed was the more favourable treatment given to the Catholic Church for its educational work. In addition to the argument about teacher training, Protestant spokespersons pointed to the presence of Roman Catholics on some regional committees and claimed that their presence meant that Catholics had a say in the conduct of transferred Protestant schools, a say not matched in the case of Roman Catholic schools because none were being transferred.

Such claims totally ignored several points. One, no manager was compelled to transfer a school and Protestant managers who wished to retain the same autonomy as Catholic managers obviously had the choice not to transfer their schools. Two, since transfer carried with it the benefit of relieving the churches of any further expenditure on their schools, transferred and non-transferred schools were in completely different categories, financially as well as in managerial terms. Non-transferred schools were the responsibility of their managers, not of the local committees, as was the case with transferred schools. On all counts, the comparison was being drawn on very faulty bases, but that did not prevent the United Education Committee of the Protestant Churches claiming :

. . . since the Roman Catholic Church is retaining hold upon the education of her children everything possible ought to be done consistent with the principle of popular control to ensure that Protestant children are educated in an atmosphere of friendly relationship to the Protestant Churches and that those entrusted with the education of Protestant children should be men and women in whom members of the Protestant Churches immediately concerned should have the fullest confidence.[88]

It is quite clear from this statement that the Protestant churches were intent on ensuring that any schools catering for Protestant children, whether transferred, or provided, would be essentially 'Protestant' in character. However, the logic of their demand was never acknowledged, either by themselves or by any representative of the government, except rather obliquely by Craig in 1930.[89] That logic would have required an acknowledgement that Catholic schools could also transfer and retain their particular ethos and identity and that the same should pertain for all schools, no matter what their auspices. Such a situation would probably have created a dual system within the transferred and provided sector, one Protestant and the other Catholic. Its main advantage would, however, have been to have offered equality of treatment to the schools of all churches. Whether the Catholic Church would have found it possible to have accepted the offer would have been another question.

Standing firm

Concern about the failure, as the Protestant churches saw it, of local authorities to nominate any, or an adequate number of Protestant church representatives to the regional committees was the first of the issues to be directly taken up with the Minister of Education. In October 1927 a deputation from the Presbyterian Church sought to persuade the minister to have such representatives nominated, but his reply ruled out direct intervention by the ministry. The minister's parliamentary secretary pointed out that: 'It is not competent for the ministry to prescribe to these bodies how they should exercise their right of appointment'.[90] It was also pointed out that such powers had been given to the regional committees as part of the government's plan to place control of education 'in the hands of elected representatives of the ratepayers',[91] a reminder that the democratization of education which the Protestant churches had always stated they supported, meant that local authorities had to have control over such decisions as committee memberships. To obtain the guarantees they sought, it became apparent to the churches that fresh legislation would be necessary.

But resistance to further clerical encroachment upon what some within the Protestant–unionist community still wanted to see as a truly public and non-denominational system of education was more forthright on this occasion than it had been during the 1923–5 period. The Association of Education Committees, a body which had come into existence directly as a result of the 1923 act and which represented the collective voice of the new regional committees, was very anxious to protect what it regarded as the democratic gains achieved by that act. So, when demands from the churches for additional amendments emerged the association reacted very strongly in opposition to them:

. . . notwithstanding the growth of democracy and democratic methods the Government is being urged to set aside the representatives elected by the votes of the people for public duty and to disenfranchise the populace in favour of an autocracy of the clergy combined with additional bureaucratic power for the Ministry of Education [a reference to the possible imposition of church representatives on committees by the Ministry] . . .'[92]

Conceding to the demands of the churches would, in the opinion of the association, '(1) reintroduce the old individual and denominational control already repudiated by the majority of the population, (2) would put the teachers again under the control of the clergy and (3) would sectarianise education completely'.[93] The association was not, however, unmindful of Protestant fears about a Catholic influence over the education of Protestant children, but it argued that this problem '. . . could not be solved by reactionary methods or by attempts to prevent the people from choosing their own representatives'.[94] The principle of democratic control of school management was obviously seen by the association as under severe threat from the renewed campaign of the churches.

The main teachers' unions, the I.N.T.O. and the U.T.U., were also opposed to any amendments along the lines being suggested, the U.T.U. in particular being very hostile to any attempt to interfere with the 1923 act. In a public letter the president and general secretary of the U.T.U., declared that those who were campaigning for change were 'carrying on a war on three fronts: against the Ministry of Education, against the County Councils and Regional Committees and against the Ulster Teachers' Union'.[95]

Editorials in the *Belfast Telegraph*, while not opposed to some change, expressed anxiety about the need to have the democratic principles of the 1923 act maintained:

The Education Act now in force has worked for some years based on the system of popular control exercised through public authorities. It is highly regrettable that the present controversy has arisen, and that much vehemence has been introduced in denunciation of the existing system.[96]

The Minister of Education, Viscount Charlemont who had succeeded Londonderry in 1926, also defended the 1923 act claiming at an Orange Order meeting in 1929 that because of the act and '. . . in so far as an individual government could do such a thing, the Protestant faith in Protestant schools would be safe from attack'.[97] In other words, the case for further change based on a need to provide greater protection for Protestant children within the public system of education did not exist. Indeed, from the government's point of view, why the churches felt they had to seek firmer guarantees must have been very difficult to understand.

Northern Ireland had by the late 1920s achieved what appeared to be a considerable degree of political stability. Nationalist–republican armed resistance to the new order had been overcome, nationalist politicians had begun to play a more active role in public life, the border had been recognised in the Anglo-Irish Boundary Agreement of 1925 while unionist domination in government and in a majority of local authorities was beyond dispute. That the Protestant churches were not prepared to recognise the degree of protection which all these factors would provide for their educational concerns must have seemed difficult to comprehend to any clear-sighted observer.

Any apparent diminution in their power, control and influence was regarded with apprehension exacerbated by the belief that the Catholic Church was in a more privileged position. In taking this view, the latter simply failed to acknowledge that in order to retain complete power over its schools the Catholic Church was prepared to forgo the benefits which transferred and provided status would confer. So, in effect what the Protestant churches were demanding was the retention of their power, control and influence in addition to the financial and other benefits which transfer conferred. The means adopted to achieve their end was to portray the situation which had resulted from the 1923 act as one which posed a threat to Protestantism and not one which safeguarded Protestantism, as the government claimed.

A litany of demands

This threat was precisely the prospect outlined in a pamphlet prepared jointly by the Advisory Committee of the Protestant Churches and a Committee of the Grand Orange Lodge of Ireland. The pamphlet, entitled *Education Act Amendment* argued that the 1923 act had broken down because it had not been accepted by the Catholic Church and that the resultant situation was one in which only schools attended by Protestant pupils would be under public control:

An education system which places the education of Protestant children under the all but absolute control of public bodies which are by their constitution purely secular, and which over large areas are likely to be Roman Catholic or a combination of Roman Catholic and socialist and secular ought never to have been established.[98]

Such a portrayal touched basic sentiments regarding the very *raison d'être* of Northern Ireland as a separate political entity. It placed the onus on the government and on those who accepted the principles of the 1923 act to demonstrate to the satisfaction of the Protestant churches that their actions did provide safeguards and that could only effectively be demonstrated when schools were transferred. In such an argument those demanding safeguards needed only to reiterate the view that, as yet, the safeguards were not adequate in order to keep their opponents on the defensive and so gain additional concessions. This in effect is what the Protestant churches were to do in the final stages of their seven year battle with the government. The concessions sought on this occasion were set out in the same pamphlet. They included compulsory Bible instruction in public elementary schools if ten or more parents requested it, representation for church interests on the education authorities, representation for transferors on school management committees and, in the matter of teacher appointments, the right of school committees to submit three names from the list of applicants to the appropriate education authority.[99]

Further unconstitutional concessions

Clearly feeling that the pressure for amending legislation had to be responded to, the government sought the Attorney General's advice in February 1929. His advice was at first very negative. He pointed out that any change along the lines being suggested would be clearly 'ultra vires the Act of 1923'.[100] He went on to advise that the guidelines on religious instruction issued in July 1925 'were not warranted by law' and indicated that:

If legislation is contemplated to enable the education authorities to provide religious instruction and reverse the policy of the Act of 1923 which provides elementary education only, the instruction must be of such a nature and provided in such a way that will not be a breach of Section 5 of the Government of Ireland Act.[101]

Within two months, however, the Attorney General changed his position completely and advised that:

. . . I am now satisfied that such instruction can be given in a form which would not be contrary to the doctrines of any Christian Church and to this extent I wish to modify my former opinion. I still adhere to the view that this instruction cannot be given under the Act of 1923 as amended by the Act of 1925, and that further legislation will be required to enable the Ministry to give effect to the proposal.[102]

What precisely prompted this change of mind is unclear but can in part, be attributed to the fact that the two most important institutional supporters of unionism, the Protestant churches and the Orange Order had combined to exert pressure for change. Once again that pressure was being mounted at a politically sensitive time. There was, as in 1925, the imminence of a general election though on this occasion there was no great constitutional issue which would have required maximum unity within the Protestant–unionist community. There was only a small threat to the Unionist Party from independent unionists in a number of constituencies but hardly on the scale to threaten the party's dominance of northern politics.[103] Nevertheless, this may well have been the crucial factor in the government's decision to announce that it would introduce legislation to further safeguard religious instruction. On the question of providing representation for the churches on school and regional committees a more guarded approach was adopted. Craig indicated that more consultation would be necessary.[104] But why concessions were only made on the question of religious instruction has remained unclear. The very strong opposition expressed by the Association of Education Committees and the U.T.U. was most probably a factor. There was also the very real need to ensure that the main proposals of the 1923 act would not founder, i.e. that schools would be transferred to local committees.

While there had been a steady stream of transfers, particularly since 1925–6, there was still some concern that transfer was not proceeding fast enough, a fact confirmed, after fresh legislation had been passed, by remarks in the 1929–30 annual report of the Ministry of Education. In its comments on this legislation, the concessions it contained were claimed to have been necessitated in order to 'bring the interests which had hitherto controlled and managed the elementary school into closer touch with the local education authorities'[105] and because up until then school transfers had been going on 'steadily, if somewhat slowly'.[106]

A new bill

Reassured by his Attorney General's advice, the Minister of Education set about preparing the necessary amending legislation. The task was not an easy one. The difficulties facing Charlemont and his ministry as they tried to prepare a bill which would meet the demands of the Protestant churches while not infringing the constitutional prohibition on endowing religion, were underlined at a meeting in the Home Office in London in November 1929. There, representatives of the Northern Ireland government were advised of the British government's views on the proposed amendments in the following terms:

The Government would not recommend that the Royal Assent should be withheld, nor that the Bill should be referred to the Judicial Committee of the Privy Council under the Government of Ireland Act of 1920. If, after the Bill has become law, substantial representations were received against it from responsible parties in Northern Ireland they would refer the question to the Judicial Committee.[107]

Quite obviously the British officials were worried about the direction in which the proposed legislation was going. In particular they must have had in mind the possibility of 'substantial representations' being made by the Catholic Church. The latter was not likely to remain inactive if the Protestant churches were seen to be winning even further safeguards for their religious position within a system of publicly financed schools, while Catholic schools remained in receipt of very limited assistance.

Despite the Home Office opinion which was very similar to that expressed by the Duke of Abercorn in 1925, the ministry proceeded to prepare amending legislation to deal with religious instruction in public elementary schools and representation on school and regional committees with the intention of introducing it in the spring of 1930. It began to appear, therefore, that the Protestant churches were about to achieve a second, more notable victory than in 1925 but on this occasion they were not to be left as the only agitators on the field. The Catholic-nationalist community did not remain quiescent and gradually began mobilising its resources to demand a greater share, and in its own view a fairer share, of the public resources available to education.

4

Forging Compromises
in the North 1923–30

WHEN the Education Act of 1923 was passed the Catholic authorities made their rejection of it clear in no uncertain terms. In their view it was the kind of legislation which confirmed Catholic fears as to the treatment they would receive from a Northern Irish government established exclusively with the support of the Protestant community. In a joint statement the northern bishops of the church vigorously expressed their rejection:

... an education measure has been passed under which Catholic schools are starved unless indeed they go under a control that is animated by the dominant spirit towards Catholics . . . It is doubtful whether in modern times any parallel can be found for the way in which the Catholic minority in the North of Ireland is being systematically wronged under the laws of the Northern Parliament. This ever advancing aggression on Catholics is a grave menace to the peace of the whole community.[1]

The government's educational policies were presented by the Catholic bishops as part of a general policy of discrimination towards Catholics in which education, electoral law reform and the manner of appointment to positions within the public service were all linked in evidence.

What, it might be asked, did the Catholic Church expect of the new administration as far as education was concerned? In a phrase one could say 'to be left with the pre-1923 situation' or, in other words, that the system of school management be retained unmodified. This would have meant leaving the church virtually complete freedom to continue establishing and developing its own schools, though still expecting some financial support from the state. Inspection of schools to assess standards in the so-called 'secular' subjects, was the limit to public interference as far as the Catholic Church was concerned.

Technically the 1923 act did not attempt to deprive any church of the ownership, control or management of its schools. By allowing for the continued existence of the single manager voluntary school the act made it possible for the Catholic Church and indeed for any other agency, to establish and maintain schools which would be fully recognised as such by the public authorities. The terms of the act, however, by restricting very severely the level of public funding available to such schools, effectively only guaranteeing teachers' salaries and merely holding out the possibility of maintenance grants, placed them in a very unfavourable situation compared to schools in the 'provided' and 'transferred' categories. Transferred status, as set out by the terms of the 1923 act, the Catholic Church ruled out for two reasons. First, schools in this category were precluded by the original terms of the act from providing any form of religious instruction within the hours of compulsory schooling. This suggested that only a clear distinction between secular and religious education would be acceptable for such schools, a distinction which was incompatible with the traditional Catholic concept of education as an integrated process in which no area of the curriculum was free from the influence of religious beliefs and values. The second reason for the rejection of transferred status was the loss of ownership, management and control which transfer entailed, a loss which the church regarded as inevitably leading to the complete removal of religious influences from education. In the Northern Irish context this loss had a sharp, local political dimension as well because it could be construed as a gain for public authorities, most of which would be dominated by representatives of the Protestant–unionist community. Viewed from this political perspective the loss would be one from which nationalists would suffer and unionists would gain. While such a prospect only added to the church's general suspicion of any form of public encroachment into the educational sphere, it is probably true to say that its opposition to transfer would have been as strong as it had been only four years previously at the time of the MacPherson Bill, whatever the political or religious characteristics of public authorities.

Catholic opposition galvanised

During the early period of confrontation between the Protestant churches and the government, the Catholic Church remained relatively quiescent. Lacking any direct political input to the controversy because none of the nationalist members elected to the northern parliament had as yet taken their seats, the Catholic position was left to be articulated almost entirely by clerical spokespersons, mainly the bishops. While episcopal voices were frequently raised, the need for political action to add weight to these voices was soon recognised as essential if the Catholic case against the alleged discrimination was to be effectively advanced. So, from 1923 onwards, the bishops began urging that 'in view of what has already happened, after waiting very long in the hope of some approach to equal dealing, we consider the time has come for our people to organise openly on constitutional lines and resolve to lie down no longer under this degrading thraldom'.[2] Most notable in stressing the need for greater involvement by Catholics in public affairs in Northern Ireland was Cardinal Patrick O'Donnell, Logue's successor at Armagh. For him education was the matter which particularly required the attention of Catholics who would enter the political arena and once the boundary between north and south had been settled in 1925 he saw no further justification for nationalist abstention from the political process:

I know it is said that the Nationalists and Catholics gave no help in Parliament to keep things right for themselves. But what matters now is that the case [for Catholic education] be made in such a way as to be thoroughly well understood and that it be pressed by every legitimate means . . . The area of the Six Counties is now fixed as the area of Northern Ireland and everyone within it has to take account of that fact.[3]

The response from nationalist politicians to this call was less than whole-hearted to judge from the attendance of M.P.s at parliament. Joseph Devlin, the leading nationalist in Northern Ireland, did not take his seat until 1925 when he was accompanied by Thomas McAllister, M.P. for County Antrim.[4] However, once nationalist representatives did enter parliament they made education one of the major areas of government policy on which they spoke quite frequently. The effects of the 1923 act on Catholic schools and on the status of the Irish language and Gaelic heritage in the school curriculum were the aspects of education about which they expressed most concern. Of the two issues, the most pressing was the first, but jointly the manner in which both concerns were raised served to remind the government that no matter how it wished the situation otherwise, Northern Ireland contained two distinct communities whose needs and interests could not be effectively and justly served as if they were one.

Nationalist demands

Reflecting on the educational manoeuvrings of the government in the early months of 1925, the *Irish News* wryly commented that as a result of the amendments to the 1923 act 'denominationalism is firmly planted in the Six Counties by the legislative enactment of a Government and Parliament who have been shouting and shrieking against the denominationalism principle as an obstacle to progress and as a survival from barbaric ages'.[5] Nationalist members of parliament re-echoed these sentiments and in one of his first comments on recent educational developments Devlin claimed that the 1923 act had been amended 'to meet objections raised not by the Catholic school managers, or the Catholic authorities but by the Presbyterians . . . In my opinion there ought to be great consideration shown to the Catholic body in Ulster which constitutes thirty-five per cent of the population . . .'[6] Drawing attention to the question of minority rights and to the fact that the unionist case for separate treatment in Ireland rested on fears for their own rights as a minority in the whole island, Devlin went on to say:

. . . one would have thought that in the light of your experience, of your propaganda and of your success both as propagandists and as revolutionaries [in having established their own state] you would have given some consideration to the rights of the minority – larger in Ulster than you were in the whole of Ireland – in respect of educational matters.[7]

Claiming that the 1923 act left Catholic schools worse off than they had been under the previous regime when voluntary schools could receive up to two-thirds of their capital costs from the Board of National Education, Devlin appealed for consideration on the grounds that many Catholic schools were below acceptable health standards and that the government might be content to leave them so:

Does it mean let children stay in unhealthy schools, let us go on perpetuating the system by which those unhealthy schools will continue ? . . . This is not a question of whether managers are right or wrong. It is a question of what is just, and if voluntary schools give equality of education, if they come up to the common standards laid down by the government . . . on what grounds can you deny them the rights and privileges which are given to other schools, which are no more efficient and come up to no higher standards in educational efficiency.[8]

A determination not to accept what the church believed to be the terms of transfer was as emphatically stressed by nationalist politicians as it was by churchmen. The image of the persecuted Catholic community staunchly clinging to its religious faith was often invoked to underline this determination, together with a stress on the sacrifices which Catholics were prepared to make to maintain their own schools as the following comments by J.H. Collins, M.P. for Newry, illustrate:

. . . when we want to build or repair our schools we have to do so out of our own pockets. The reason for that is that under no circumstances will a Catholic Irishman give up religious teaching in his schools . . . They [the government] know that the Irish Catholic did without education for centuries and then was called an ignorant man, because he would not give up his religion.[9]

The government's response was to emphasise that the 1923 act did not seek to discriminate against or to favour any section of society. Its spokespersons argued that the terms of the act made it possible for all interested groups, Catholic and Protestant, to avail of the different forms of support which it provided. It was as open to Catholic managers to transfer their schools as it was to Protestant managers and if any manager or board of trustees chose not to transfer, that was their rightful decision. However, with a logic which attempted to ignore the principles underlying the 1923 act, nationalists proposed, in March 1927, that all non-transferred schools be considered for grant aid in the same manner as national schools had been prior to 1923.[10] In other words, the proposal asked that schools under voluntary management be entitled to capital grants of up to two-thirds of costs. In support of the motion the nationalist M.P., Patrick O'Neill, referred to the low percentage of transfer, a situation which continued to embarrass the government, as evidence that the act was repugnant not just to the Catholic authorities, but to other denominations as well.[11] Speaking on the motion, Devlin made a strong defence of the managerial system, carefully praising the work of clergymen of all denominations in establishing and managing schools:

. . . when laymen took very little interest in education . . . the clergymen of all denominations were mainly responsible for the building of schools for their respective denominations . . . they often sacrificed spiritual and religious interests to the fundamental necessity of having sound, efficient education . . . I think they are entitled jealously to guard what they have created and what they have built.[12]

Not surprisingly, the government firmly rejected the motion on several grounds, primarily because it was claimed that the 1923 act was fair to all sections of the community. Secondly, it was argued, that if Roman Catholic managers did not wish to transfer schools they could opt for 'four-and-two' status and thirdly, that the motion, if passed, would, by providing an excuse for not transferring schools, completely undermine the principle of democratic control. It was also pointed out that, prior to 1923, grants of two-thirds of costs had not been as liberally available as supporters of the motion and the Catholic Church had been claiming.[13] In the course of the debate the Prime Minister defended the act as being completely fair to all and bluntly stated that if the Catholic authorities did not wish to transfer, they should themselves accept full responsibility for the consequences:

If none of the Roman Catholic schools will be transferred I hope they will take the responsibility. Certainly that responsibility does not rest with Government. The door is open. If they do not walk in – very well, who is to blame ? Surely the charge cannot be made against the Government, who place every school upon an equality and who ask for nothing else than that local people should be in charge of local education . . . The door is open to every class and every body and every denomination to come along and make the Act a success.[14]

John Robb, the parliamentary secretary to the Minister of Education and the main speaker for the government, argued very trenchantly that if Catholic schools would not transfer then they should have no difficulty in accepting 'four-and-two' status as a small number already had:

. . . if they [Catholic managers] wish to preserve continuity of education policy which has been pursued in particular schools up to that date I cannot see that they have any grievance when the body that is to be set up to continue that management is to be one on which they are to have a two to one majority of nominees.[15]

The principle, as Robb reiterated, was that since school grants were derived from local rates 'the local authorities which supply these grants shall be given a modicum of control in the management of the schools. That is the person who provides the money shall have some say in the way which it is spent'.[16] This was not a principle which applied to the schools of any particular denomination but to all and so could not be discriminatory, at least not in the mind of the government.

Despite some interest in accepting the 'four-and-two' management structure and its actual adoption in a very limited number of parishes, neither the Catholic Church or nationalist politicians regarded it as the basis for a general compromise. Ignoring the fundamental distinction with respect to ownership and accountability between schools under public control and schools which opted to retain full voluntary status, both argued that the benefits which transferred schools would obtain meant that schools for Protestant children would be considerably advantaged as compared to schools attended by Catholic children. In other words, the leadership of the Catholic community was saying that the government, by introducing forms of school management which were known to be unacceptable to the Catholic Church, had effectively created a situation in which Catholic schools would be discriminated against. Whatever about the moral strength of this case, politically it was a hopeless one and given the strength of unionist representation in parliament the motion was roundly defeated.[17]

Extra-parliamentary pressure

The defeat of O'Neill's motion was to be expected but, despite this setback, outside of parliament the Catholic authorities continued to publicise their grievances with considerable vigour. Managers of schools in the Armagh diocese resolved at their annual meeting in 1929 to seek an amendment to the 1923 act which would restore the system of grant aid which the National Board had operated,[18] the defeat of the 1927 motion notwithstanding. Wider attention was drawn to the church's case during the centenary celebrations of the Catholic Emancipation Act held in Dublin in 1929 which brought an international audience of church representatives to the city. At a large public meeting held during these celebrations to discuss aspects of the church's work in the contemporary world, Dr Arthur Ryan, a priest and a well known lecturer in scholastic philosophy at Queen's University, Belfast, painted a stark picture of injustice directed at Catholic schools:

It is unfortunately true that we Catholics in the Six Counties do not enjoy the political and civil rights which are our due. We are once more the victims of ascendancy – less ruthless indeed, but more subtle than that which was shaken a hundred years ago. We have been unjustly treated with regard to primary education.[19]

Cardinal Joseph MacRory, then recently installed as Archbishop of Armagh, was even more forthright in his remarks during the same celebrations:

In the Six Counties the Ascendancy is fighting its last battle in the trenches carefully dug for it by Partition . . . We have grievances in the matter of appointments and preferments . . . Then we have a grievance in the matter of education . . . Before 1923 we could while retaining our managerial system get two-thirds of the expenses of a new school. Now we cannot get a penny since 1923 unless we abandon our managerial system and go under a committee . . . All we want is justice and that where Protestant schools are being supported we demand that Catholic schools be treated similarly.[20]

Not surprisingly, such comments evoked very angry responses in Belfast and cannot have helped foster any sympathy for the Catholic case in Protestant–unionist circles. To the editorial writer in the *Belfast Telegraph*, who had adopted a hostile attitude to the Protestant churches' demands for fresh amendments to the 1923 act:

The demand of the Catholic clergy is really for private control at public expense. The public are not to have control of their schools although they are to pay the teachers' salaries and the cost of erection and upkeep, while the Church is to retain the right to appoint and dismiss teachers at will.[21]

Indeed, just as Protestant clerics simplified the argument, so also did

Catholic clerics and their political supporters. Significantly, for example, they ignored the whole principle of democratic public accountability and, as Cardinal MacRory's remarks would suggest, appeared to have rejected it outright as far as education was concerned. In his Lenten pastoral letter in February 1930, the cardinal reiterated Catholic opposition to abandoning the managerial system and without explaining why, stated:

> The Catholics of the Six Counties, bishops, priests and laity are strongly opposed on religious grounds to having the management of their schools taken from the parish priest and handed over to a Committee and they justly complain that an Act of Parliament should seek to reinforce such a step upon them under pain of denial of all financial help for the building or enlargement of their schools.[22]

The terms of the cardinal's letter clearly indicated that he still perceived the provisions of the 1923 act as an 'attack' on Catholic schools, echoing the fears expressed by his predecessor Cardinal Logue when he declined Londonderry's invitation to nominate representatives to the Lynn Committee. Opposition to the 'four-and-two' system was a further manifestation of the church's suspicion of democratic institutions. The fact that under this system of management the four representatives of the trustees, i.e. church authorities in the case of Catholic schools, would be in a majority of two, thereby providing firm guarantees that Catholic interests could not be outvoted, did not seem to impress the church. Suspicion of any intrusion by public authorities was, in Northern Ireland, reinforced by distrust of the inevitable predominance of Protestants on the majority of local authorities. The prospect of a minority of two Protestants on school committees was, it seemed, just as objectionable as a majority of the same denomination on most of the education authorities.

Seeking a solution

As the pressure from the churches, in particular from the Protestant churches, began forcing the government to consider some modification to the sharp distinction between secular and religious interests in education contained in the 1923 act, it was hoped that any change could be contained within the basic framework of that legislation. Faced with very absolutist demands from the churches and, in the case of the Catholic Church, with demands of an exclusive nature, it would appear that the government had begun to consider the possibility of two separate sets of schools within the 'transferred' and 'provided' sector. Its thinking never became fully explicit in this respect but in a number of memoranda and later in public statements, it is clear that something along these lines was being tentatively explored. For example, one memorandum suggested that if 'provided' and 'transferred' schools were to be made 'safe for Protestant children' then:

> ... if precisely the same conditions are secured in the case of Catholic schools transferred to the education authorities, so that these schools are as safe for Catholic chil-

dren after transfer as they are for Protestants in the case of schools attended by Protestant children . . . how can it be alleged that this system gives a preference to one religion more than to the other.[23]

This suggestion must have occurred to the government as it became obvious that conceding Protestant demands would effectively mean retaining the Protestant character of any schools transferred by these churches. Had the suggestion been adopted, it would have led to a dual system of publicly controlled schools which, although separate would each have been treated on exactly the same basis. Although Londonderry had set himself against such a development,[24] it was not all that unusual an approach. In Scotland this is precisely what had emerged following the 1918 Education Act.[25] There the authorities in voluntary schools which transferred to local education committees retained a considerable voice in the conduct of those schools, both in terms of the curriculum and in terms of the appointment of teachers. However, in Northern Ireland the suggestion had really very little hope of success given, in particular, the distrust of local authorities which existed within the Catholic–nationalist community and the very firm stand taken by the Catholic Church in favour of the managerial system. Nonetheless, it was an approach which, if greater consideration had been given to it at the time, might have been the basis for a more satisfactory compromise than that which emerged in 1930.

There was also a second strategy which the government decided to use with the Catholic Church, namely to try to persuade its authorities that the 'four-and-two' management system held no threat to their basic position. It was an approach which received considerable attention, as is evident in several ministerial and cabinet memoranda one of which can be used to illustrate the extent to which it was being explored. Entitled 'Notes for reply to the Catholic case' the memorandum dealt first with the demands of the church for a return to the system of financial support to schools which operated under the Board of Commissioners of National Education. The memorandum firmly and unequivocally rejected this demand because it would 'cut right across one of the principles of the Education Act, delegation of responsibility for school buildings and maintenance to local authorities'.[26]

The memorandum further argued that the managerial system '. . . is in itself bad for education. It stifles all local interest in education on the part of the people, tends to foster the continuation of obsolete standards of educational progress and in many cases subjects the teachers to conditions which are degrading and derogatory to their position and standing in the community'.[27] These arguments would appear to suggest a clear determination on the government's part to stand by the principles of the 1923 act. This determination would also appear to be underlined by the attempt in the memorandum to present the argument as to why the Catholic Church should be encouraged to avail of the 'four-and-two' system, something, which the memorandum also noted, a small number of Roman Catholic managers had already done :

Why Catholic laymen should object to them ['four-and-two'] I cannot conceive as their effect when applied is to encourage the layman to take a share in the control of the education of his own children – that very parental control which the present Pope has claimed for parents in a recent pronouncement . . . Some Roman Catholic priests [Ballymena, Bangor] have already agreed to establish these committees so that the opposition to them is not universal.[28]

When these approaches were presented in public the first was immediately rejected but not the second. This was to happen in April 1930 and it would appear that some sections of the Catholic Church might have been prepared to enter the public system within the context of a modified 'four-and-two' system. The period of hope during which consideration would be given to such a development was to be, however, a very short one indeed.

A new act

Any resolution to the dilemma facing the government had to reconcile two competing and mutually exclusive claims about the effects of the 1923 act, an almost impossible task given prevailing attitudes amongst the different protagonists. For the Protestant churches, William Corkey summarised their attitude when he said:

We cannot be expected to view with equanimity the working of an Act which strips the Protestant cause of over half a million pounds worth of property [the value he placed on school buildings] and takes from the Protestant Churches all association with education, and at the same time endows the Church of Rome and entrenches her clergy more firmly than ever in the educational system of our country.[29]

Paralleling this Protestant reaction were the fears and suspicions of Catholics who claimed that very same legislation which Corkey saw as favouring Catholics was in fact discriminating against them in favour of the Protestant churches:

When non-Catholics get grants for their schools on conditions that they do no violence to their consciences does not equity demand that we Catholics get similar help on conditions that we may conscientiously accept? . . . This discrimination against Catholics is, we are convinced, unconstitutional, unstatesmanlike and unjust.[30]

The government's approach was to try to allay the fears on both sides by pointing out that the 1923 act did not pose the kinds of threats alleged. Then, as the pressure for amending legislation became irresistible, a bill was prepared which it was hoped would provide adequate safeguards without compromising the basic principles of the 1923 act. The bill, published in April 1930, proposed changes in the constitution and powers of school committees, in the representation of various interests on education committees and in the provisions governing Bible instruction.

With respect to representation on school committees and on educational authorities, the bill proposed that representatives of transferors should have not less than one half of the places on school committees with parents, teachers and the local education committee sharing the remainder. School management committees, rather than merely advising on teacher appointments, would have power to forward the names of three candidates from those considered to the local education committee which would then make the final decision. On these latter committees, the bill proposed that transferors' representatives would be guaranteed up to a quarter of the places. Finally, as far as Bible instruction was concerned, if ten or more parents requested it, a school would be obliged to provide Bible instruction and teachers obliged to teach it. Facilities for separate catechetical instruction would be provided as indicated in the 1923 act, but such instruction could not be required of teachers and would still have to take place outside of normal hours.

While it would appear from the nature of their presentation that these amendments had been introduced with Protestant demands more in mind than those of the Catholic Church, it was, nonetheless a hope at the outset that the latter could be persuaded to see merit in them. Speaking on the bill in parliament the Prime Minister began by emphasising how safe the amendments would make schools for Protestant pupils:

> To make provided and transferred schools safe for Protestant children is one of the legitimate objects of the Amending Act. This is done by enabling Protestant parents to require the education authority to provide for their children Bible instruction of a strictly undenominational character, such as is common to the beliefs of Christian denominations; by providing in addition, facilities and opportunities for religious teaching through the voluntary agency of the teachers . . . and by securing by means of the power of initiative in the appointment of teachers conferred on the school management committees in the Amending Bill, that the teachers shall be in harmony with the opinions of their former managers and trustees and the parents who actually make use of the school.[31]

However, as far as Catholic grievances were concerned Craig went on to argue that the very same conditions would apply in the case of any Catholic schools transferring. School management committees would consist of a majority of Catholics, 50 per cent transferors' representatives plus parent and teacher representatives, and this degree of representation for those most directly concerned with a school, trustees and parents, would provide the necessary safeguards in such sensitive areas as teacher appointments. On the matter of religious instruction, the form of Bible instruction could be based on versions of the Bible acceptable to the Catholic Church while further instruction could be provided on school premises by teachers, but outside of normal school hours. This, of course, was the argument which had been rehearsed in the memorandum 'Notes for reply to the Catholic case'. However, it was also an argument that ran straight up against that church's opposition to any transfer of its schools to public authorities or to any dilution of its total control over those schools.

Friendly and hostile reaction

Protestant–unionist political reaction to the bill was generally very favourable though, more generally, there were notable exceptions such as the

Belfast Telegraph, the teachers' unions and the Association of Education Committees. Within the Protestant churches it was recognised that the bill met virtually all of the objections which had been raised to the existing situation, a view warmly expressed in parliament by a brother of William Corkey, the Rev. Professor Robert Corkey M.P.:

I am bound to say that to me it gave great satisfaction, . . . I think it is calculated to create harmony throughout the Six Counties, at any rate as far as the majority of the population are concerned . . . the Clause in the Bill which appeals to me particularly is Clause 2 in which there is an Amendment of the principal Act as to the committees of management and in which these committees are given somewhat extended powers . . . the setting up of these committees will give security to people who wish to transfer.[32]

Another leading campaigner for the amendments, Rev. James Quinn of the Church of Ireland, also expressed satisfaction saying that 'this Amending Bill was making an honest effort to fully carry out the assurances he [the Prime Minister] had given the people of the Province before the election'.[33] Ominously, however, Quinn went on to refer to the question of the training of teachers which he claimed was not being satisfactorily dealt with in the proposed legislation:

There was one matter with which the Bill did not deal, and that was the training colleges for teachers. The Roman Catholic Church had been undoubtedly put in a privileged position in the arrangements at present in force for the training of Roman Catholic teachers. The Protestant Churches have asked for equality of treatment and he hoped before the Bill reached the Statute Book we would know just exactly what is proposed to remedy this defect.[34]

Satisfaction for the Protestant churches on the matter of teacher training was not forthcoming at this time but, as is discussed in chapter 6, in the face of renewed pressure, it was not to be very long delayed.

The reaction from the Protestant churches and from unionist politicians contrasted with that from sections of the teaching profession and from some local authorities. Speaking on behalf of the profession, the president of the U.T.U., Charles Wilson, in his address at his union's annual congress shortly after the bill had been published, expressed considerable concern about the powers which the bill proposed for school management committees suggesting that these powers were a step back towards denominational control:

It was an extraordinary demand to require such an extravagant increase in the powers of local school committees having the parochial constitution which the Joint Committee of the Protestant churches suggested. If that were granted the educational authorities would be shorn of all real responsibility and control; . . .[35]

It was this attenuation of their control which concerned local authorities, a concern which Armagh County Council expressed in a resolution declaring its opposition to the bill because 'it would deprive county councils, who provide the funds, of practically all powers to manage transferred and even provided schools built out of public funds'.[36] Several other county councils passed similar motions expressing their opposition to the bill's proposals.[37]

In a joint statement the I.N.T.O., the U.T.U. and the Principal Teachers' Union, strongly criticised many of the proposals and demanded that, if those transferring school were to be granted representation on school committees, then 'the same right should be conceded to teachers and other bodies specially interested in education'.[38]

Commenting on the bill's proposals, the Ireland correspondent of the *Times Educational Supplement* claimed that they had resulted purely from a desire to placate the Protestant churches '. . . in the innermost recesses of its heart the Ministry of Education must feel that in moving this Amendment of the act at this moment it has been moved by political pressure exercised by the Protestant clergy rather than by consideration of the educational needs of the province'.[39] As might have been expected, Roman Catholic reaction was almost uniformly hostile. In parliament, the opposition was led by Devlin who was quick to point out that the bill was brought in as a result of Protestant agitation in order to meet Protestant convictions and he refused to accept that the bill contained any safeguards for Catholic interests claiming instead that it was essentially discriminatory in its intent and effect:

That the Government should proceed to pass a law to meet the conscientious convictions of one section of the people of the Six Counties without at the same time making an effort to meet the equally conscientious convictions of another section, and that section which has the largest number of school-going children of any denomination, would at first blush seem outrageously impossible, but it is the outrageously impossible that continually happens in this unhappy portion of Ireland . . .We want a guarantee of Catholic teaching in Catholic schools and that is afforded us by the present managerial system.[40]

His colleague, Cahir Healy, reinforced this last comment pointing out that the government was moving to protect the Protestant churches against the decisions of democratic local councils because the latter had not appointed clerical representatives to their education committees, inferring thereby that the principle of democratic control so frequently quoted was not as inviolate as was being claimed. Equality of treatment for Catholics with Protestants was his plea, but to achieve it he too wanted what was clearly impossible, i.e. no change in the managerial system:

Protestants felt that education divorced from religion was not acceptable also. Now, if I may be allowed to point out this fact, I think the first opposition arose out of the failure of certain regional committees to appoint on their bodies clerical members. The position they took up was frankly anti-clerical. But whilst you took into consideration their views you entirely ignored the Catholic standpoint. I should like to quote for you in this connection what his Lordship the Bishop of Down and Connor recently said. . . . Are not Catholics citizens? Do they not shoulder their civic burden? Do they not pay their fair share of rates and taxes ? On what grounds are they to be ruled out of public benefit?[41]

Cardinal MacRory's reaction focused on the provisions for Bible instruction which to him denoted a Protestant approach to religious education and, as such, inadequate and unacceptable for Catholics:

Simple Bible teaching even simple Bible teaching from a Catholic Bible and in a Catholic school is directly opposed to the traditional and unchangeable doctrinal requirements of the Catholic Church. The Catholic Rule of Faith has ever been, not the Bible interpreted by private judgement, but the Bible plus tradition, the living voice of the Church controlling and interpreting both.[42]

To the cardinal, the bill was simply further evidence of a unionist government conceding the demands of the Protestant churches. Bishop Daniel Mageean of Down and Connor, in contrast, focused on management structures in an apparent attempt to discover if a modification of the 'four-and-two' system might be possible in order to make it more acceptable to his church. In his diocese a very small number of parishes had adopted this system, among them Ballymena whose parish priest at the time, Fr T. O'Donnell, had already been in correspondence with Bishop Mageean pointing out that such committees could be operated without fear that the church would lose control.[43] O'Donnell claimed that after four years experience he had 'not the slightest trouble' with his committee because 'the clerical manager has the right to nominate the four and if he is provident in his choice (there is no objection to his nominating four priests) he will always have a majority in his favour'.[44]

Drafts of various amendments to the bill prepared for Bishop Mageean[45] reveal that he was anxious to explore how a school committee system might be made more generally acceptable. On at least three occasions[46] the bishop publicly suggested that a two-tier management committee structure might be adopted, one tier of which would have responsibility for the care and maintenance of school buildings, the other being responsible for teacher appointments and the curriculum. The former committee would be the one to which education authorities would appoint representatives since public money would be spent mainly on buildings while the church authorities, he suggested, would control the second committee. If acceptable to the government, Bishop Mageean hoped that such a structure would allow Catholic schools adopting this management system to receive the same level of funding as Protestant transferred schools. He summarised his argument as follows:

The religious and secular aspects of education could not be separated without injury to both. That was not necessarily true of matters of administration such as sanitation, heating, lighting and so on which might be handed over to a committee under the Education Authority. But the question of religion must be reserved to the Church, to the Church authorities . . . the appointment of the teacher who has to do the religious and moral development of the child should be left to the Church . . . the same could be applied to the matter of textbooks.[47]

It is not clear how much support Bishop Mageean had for his proposals amongst the other bishops and clergy. His proposals emerged rather late in the debate at a time when less flexible positions had already been adopted within the church and by the nationalist community generally favouring a return to the system of financial support as it had existed under the National

Board. Nationalist representatives in County Fermanagh, for example, passed a resolution demanding that 'equal facilities be given to meet the conscientious difficulties of the Catholic body and that for this purpose such amendments be called for as will make it certain that grants for building, structural improvements and extensions of schools be given to schools under clerical management'.[48] The *Irish News* editorialised that the Minister of Education showed no understanding whatsoever of the 'inexorable Catholic demand for equality of treatment and management of our schools as conscience dictates'.[49] Some support for Mageean's proposals did emerge when, early in May 1930, a meeting of Catholic clergy from parts of the Down and Connor diocese passed a number of resolutions which incorporated the suggestions for modifying the 'four-and-two' arrangements,[50] but alongside them included proposals for a restoration of the two-thirds grant to schools retaining the managerial system, a move which seemed to indicate a clear preference for the latter.

Criticism of the government's attitude to the Catholic case did not emanate solely from the Catholic–nationalist community. A prominent academic at Queen's University, Professor R.M. Henry, a member of the Methodist Church, received considerable attention when he publicly condemned the Education Bill on the grounds that:

> . . . no community can maintain that it holds the balance evenly between Protestants and Catholics when it endows out of rates and taxes partly paid by Catholics, a form of instruction which is distinctive of Protestantism without at the same time making provision for similar teaching agreeable to Catholic members of the community.[51]

Henry's argument was identical to that advanced by many Catholics and served to underline the need for demonstrable equity in communal matters in a society as divided as Northern Ireland's was, a point which most Protestant and unionist commentators seemed to have missed in the course of the whole debate. It was a point which some within the Catholic community believed might have enabled an appeal to be mounted based on section 5 of the Government of Ireland Act alleging that provisions of the bill were discriminatory on religious grounds. At the end of March an approach was made by Joseph Devlin to the Labour Home Affairs Minister in the British government, J.R. Clynes, on this very point. Clynes replied in not very reassuring terms saying that 'there does not appear to me to be any grounds for invoking it [i.e. section 5]'.[52] Cardinal MacRory seems to have shared this view saying in a note to Bishop Mageean that he was 'not capable of forming a judgement as to whether the logicality of the amending bill should be challenged now'.[53] Perhaps had it been, the issue of equity might have been addressed more than a generation earlier than it was.

Placating Catholic demands

So, despite several months of public campaigning there emerged no sign of any change in the government's attitudes towards Catholic demands. A delegation led by Bishop B. O'Kane of Derry which included Devlin and Healy came away from a meeting with Lord Charlemont in early April with 'little hope that there would be any concession whatever'.[54] At the meeting the delegation argued the traditional case for church control of schools and frankly acknowledged that in seeking control 'they do not ask, therefore, for full equality of treatment with schools entirely controlled by the Minister and the local authority. But they do demand that they be put in a position equal to that which they occupied under the old National Board . . .'[55]

Nevertheless, faced with the fact that the bill was, by then, clearly being seen only as a set of further concessions to the Protestant case, the need for some compromise slowly began to be accepted by the government. So, despite the many firm statements to the contrary expressed in cabinet as late as mid-April 1930, it was decided to propose concessions to the Catholic Church. It was resolved to allow voluntary school managers to apply for building grants amounting to 50 per cent of the full costs for new schools, or for enlarging existing schools, without any prior requirement for the establishment of any kind of school management committee[56] and an amendment to the bill was prepared to make this possible.[57]

The decision to amend at such a late stage and to do so in order to accommodate Catholic demands was obviously one the government felt had to be carefully explained, especially to its own supporters who had been constantly reassured that no such concessions were being contemplated. Aware of possible opposition, Craig stressed that the amendment was intended to end strife in a major area of public life saying that the price required was generosity towards the 'minority' by going further than was strictly required to reach a satisfactory conclusion. Emphasising his government's generosity to a meeting of the Grand Orange Lodge of County Down, Craig was reported as saying that:

He recognised that an obligation rested on the government to go as far as possible – even beyond what might seem justifiable on strict grounds of equity – to settle the question on a basis satisfactory to every party in the State . . . the government had decided to make this concession after very full and anxious consideration of the whole question and in the hope that it would tend to promote that peace and harmony which are so necessary.[58]

In line with this approach and therefore muting its opposition somewhat, the *Belfast Telegraph* referred to the concession as:

. . . a wide departure from the lines on which the Ulster Government have so far proceeded in regard to educational reform. It can only be justified by its success in enlisting the support of all sections of the community in making the primary educational system of Northern Ireland that success which all patriotic citizens ought to desire.[59]

In parliament not all unionist M.P.s were quite so sanguine and one, echoing the views of several of his backbench colleagues said: '. . . with regard to the 50 per cent of costs of constructing schools I consider that the Prime Minister has no right at all to concede even half an inch . . . if they want a hundred per cent they have only to transfer their schools the same as we did'.[60]

In spite of such criticisms and of even more fierce attacks from nationalist members and from Catholic–nationalist opinion outside parliament still clamouring for equal funding with the transferred sector, or at least a return to the two-thirds funding alleged to have been available pre-1922, the government stood by the special resolution introduced to make its proposal possible.[61] However, it was also clear from the remarks of nationalist members that they were not going to reject completely what most regarded as a step forward. Nationalist opposition concentrated instead on the lack of balance which they claimed would continue between schools catering for Catholics and those catering for Protestants, but ignored, as they had before, the principle of democratic accountability.[62] By early June the bill was law. The government was congratulated by the General Assembly of the Presbyterian Church and by the Synod of the Church of Ireland[63] while nationalist members were congratulated by their church leaders for the staunch campaign they had conducted.[64]

Passing the legislation did not mean that peace and harmony descended upon matters educational. Even as the Presbyterian Assembly voted its congratulations, it also asked that the government proceed to make the conditions under which Protestant teachers were being trained 'as acceptable to the Protestant Churches as are the present conditions for Roman Catholic teachers to that Church'.[65] So, just as the protagonists were withdrawing to their respective corners, the bell for the next round of controversy was already sounding.

Effects of the 1930 act

The main effect of the 1930 legislation was to perpetuate the divisions and distinctions within the school system which had widened following the 1923 act. The system would continue to be divided, not just on denominational grounds, but on grounds of financial support as well. Transferred elementary schools which would be attended almost exclusively by Protestant pupils would, in addition to retaining their distinctly Protestant ethos, receive 100 per cent public funding. While schools to be attended by the vast majority of Catholic pupils could theoretically benefit from the same funding conditions, in practice they would not. The very fact that the government introduced amendments which could only have this result had created the clear impression that only Protestant concerns were being addressed. Then the hasty and belated introduction of a provision for capital grants for voluntary schools was, both in its timing and in its effect of maintaining a sharp difference in the level of public funding for the schools of both communities, inevitably seen by critics on all sides as a crude attempt to silence Catholic opposition, not the act of generosity which Craig tried to cloak it in.[66] An act of generosity was certainly not how the Catholic authorities viewed it. Bishop Mageean commented dismissively that 'what the Education Act of 1930 did was to reduce the grant from two-thirds to half for Catholics and to give full grants for their schools to non-Catholics. This is our grievance, deep-seated and well founded and it is aggravated by the fact that while we must pay half the cost of our own schools we are also bound to pay through rates and taxes our share for non-Catholic schools'.[67]

If the government misjudged the situation, what can be said of the churches? Perhaps little: they acted as history had almost pre-determined them to act. Armed with the strength of their moral and spiritual authority and with the influence deriving therefrom, they acted to protect the role and influence which they had developed for themselves within education, with little or no consideration as to how educational legislation might best be framed and operated within a divided society. The Protestant churches clearly won this round while the Catholic Church and the nationalist community generally, as yet unsure how to act, continued to nurse their grievances though satisfied that at least a not unimportant concession had been gained.

Culture and curriculum – but whose ?

Religious issues were not the only source of continuing conflict in education in Northern Ireland over this period. As pointed out in chapter 3, another area of contention was the recognition being afforded the Gaelic–Irish heritage within the curriculum since 1923. Few schools, other than those under Catholic auspices, had chosen to take account of any significant aspect of Gaelic–Irish heritage within their curricula before 1921. As a result the question of whether Gaelic culture would receive any recognition at all from the new northern authorities had been of concern to many teachers within the Catholic system and, more generally, to members of the Irish language movement itself. In some respects this concern was a very real one, but given the small number of Catholic schools in Northern Ireland offering Irish, the concern must also have been of more symbolic than real significance to the nationalist community in general. Out of more than 2,000 national schools only about one tenth, 242, or approximately one fifth of Catholic schools in Northern Ireland in 1923 offered Irish language courses.[68] At secondary level most of the 30 or so Catholic colleges also did. Interest in and participation in other aspects of Gaelic culture, such as Gaelic sports, Irish dancing and traditional music was much greater than for the language on its own. However, since learning the language depended, to a greater extent than the other activities, on opportunities for teaching it in school, there was a need for it to be at least officially recognised within the curriculum.

As has been pointed out in chapter 1, attitudes towards the Gaelic cultural revival generally and towards the revival of the language in particular, had so coincided with a nationalist outlook that within Northern Ireland hostility to the teaching of Irish had become intense for many unionists. The very idea that public money might be spent on teaching Irish had annoyed unionist members of parliament while in the unionist press editorials strongly attacked the value of teaching Irish. 'It cannot be argued that the acquisition of Gaelic has any practical value to the student' commented the *Belfast Telegraph* which went on to agree with Corkey's view that the teaching of Irish had fostered the 'blind hatred' of England which had been at the root of the recent troubles in the country.[69] The new Ministry of Education was obviously going to be under pressure from unionists to curtail the recognition afforded to Irish and to other aspects of Gaelic–Irish culture within school curricula.

Despite this the ministry did, upon its establishment, appoint an inspector for Irish and continued to conduct an examination for a 'certificate of proficiency' in Irish and made subsidies available for teachers wishing to attend Irish language summer schools. It was not until 1923 that the first major decision affecting the recognition given to Irish was announced. Circular 21[70] of that year implemented the recommendation of the Lynn Committee that Irish be no longer taught as an optional subject below standard 5.[71] The immediate effect of the ruling was a reduction in the number of pupils learning Irish and, to judge from the figures, this would seem to have led, at least indirectly, to a reduction in the number of elementary schools teaching Irish. From the figure of 242 in 1923 the number declined to 149 in 1927.[72] This regulation was followed, in 1926, by another which contained the decision to withdraw fees for teaching Irish as an 'extra' subject,[73] i.e. one taught outside of the normal hours of schooling, below standard 5, which entitled teachers to extra remuneration. In parliament, Devlin attacked these regulations claiming that they amounted to an attack on:

. . . the vocal sentiment of our people. You may not like it. We may be fools. It may be thought that it [Irish] is of no commercial value . . . I do trust that you will place the whole question of the Irish language on the same basis it occupied before this Education Act [i.e. the 1923 Act] was passed in Ulster.[74]

The parliamentary secretary to the Ministry of Education replied to Devlin using the same language as the Lynn Committee, that the ministry was only prepared to support the teaching of Irish 'at such times as the children may be able to profit by the teaching'.[75] However, as ministry papers reveal, this was not the full reason and nationalist fears for the future of Irish were not unfounded; there was more to these regulations than a judgement based purely on educational grounds. In a memorandum, in 1928, advising the Prime Minister how he should reply to a letter from the Loyalist League which had contained a resolution protesting against permitting Irish to be taught at all in Northern Ireland, Bonaparte Wyse discussed the situation regarding Irish since 1922:

It was felt desirable on the one hand to curtail opportunities for Irish teaching, but on the other it was believed to be more politic to allow its continuance as an optional subject to a modified extent. It was clear that any proposal to prohibit it altogether would give certain parties an opportunity of raising a grievance and at the same time intensify the desire of a section of the people to apply themselves to its study. It was decided to adopt a middle course and allow the teaching of Irish to continue with certain limitations.[76]

Such remarks indicate that it was hoped that by minimising support, enthusiasm for Irish would soon wane, at least in educational circles.

Further evidence of an attempt to curtail Irish can be inferred from the decision, discussed in chapter 1, to require that Irish be paired with history as optional subjects, a decision based on another recommendation of the Lynn Committee. Quite obviously, therefore, official attitudes towards Irish had been anything but sympathetic from the very establishment of the ministry. Only the fear of provoking greater opposition within the nationalist community had prevented the ministry from taking more radical measures to curtail the teaching of Irish. As the decade had advanced government and unionist sympathy generally was probably further eroded by the controversy in the Irish Free State regarding the intensification of the pressure to teach Irish at all levels of schooling. Adverse comment from unionist circles was frequent, in particular the claim that an injustice was being done to Protestants in the south because Irish had not previously been widely taught in their schools and that the same fate awaited northern Protestants should Ireland ever be united.[77]

Nevertheless, despite this climate of opinion amongst unionists, when a deputation from the Gaelic League in Northern Ireland did meet the Minister of Education early in 1927, it received a positive response.[78] The deputation made the case that since, under the Board of National Education, Irish had been allowed as an optional subject throughout the primary school, the same should be allowed by the new administration. The deputation also argued that Irish should not be treated like any other language since it was part of the cultural heritage of all of the people of Ireland. The minister replied that while he believed that Irish was not a very useful subject to teach, he would, nonetheless, allow Irish to be taught as an optional subject from standard 3, but as an extra subject only from standard 5. These new regulations took effect from March 1928[79] hence the representations by the Loyalist League referred to above.

If the new regulations brought some satisfaction to the Irish language lobby, concern about other aspects of Gaelic–Irish culture continued to be felt within the nationalist community. Nationalist members of parliament demanded a greater emphasis on Irish history in school curricula. They condemned textbooks for being 'British' in their orientation, particularly in history. J.H. Collins attacked the ministry for excluding any mention of Irish patriots like Wolfe Tone, William Orr, William Drennan or John Mitchel from textbooks:

... If the Parliamentary Secretary would take my advice and read up on some of these men ... who are Irish through and through, he would be doing much more good to the boys he is supposed to be educating ...[80]

Cahir Healy claimed that ignorance of their own country was a cause of emigration, since children were being educated to think of 'every country and the possibilities of every country in the world but their own'.[81] However, it is clear that just as unionist members were, at the same time, demanding greater efforts at inculcating a sense of Britishness,[82] nationalist members were seeking to foster a sense of Irishness, each apparently exclusive of the other.

The first decade of 'home rule' in Northern Ireland ended, contrary to the intentions of many reformers, with education being more firmly moulded than ever before by the conflicting beliefs, values and attitudes of its society. Compromises of a kind had been forged to address concerns of both communities, but there can be little doubt as to which community had benefitted most as a result. Consequently, despite the considerable deliberation about the nature of the reforms before their actual formulation, their main features are open to the assessment that they were naively conceived and then, insensitively implemented.

5

Freedom and Rigidity:
Educational Reform in the South 1922–30

TWO statements made within three years of the establishment of the Irish Free State together provide a succinct summary of what was intended and what was being achieved by the new state as far as education was concerned. The first was made by Professor Eoin MacNeill, then Minister of Education, in Dáil Éireann in 1924 when he said:

With regard to the general policy I said that my point of view is governed by certain main principles and one of these was that in education as administered by the state there should be as far as possible equality of opportunity for all those who are subjects of education. The second governing principle is that public education should have in view the general national interest and good of the nation in general and that this view should not be interrupted by the principle of the private and particular interests of individuals.[1]

The second statement was made a year later by the president of the Executive Council, or Prime Minister, William T. Cosgrave who spoke of what was being achieved in education:

Of the primary programme it may be said with truth that it reflects more profoundly than any other public service the far-reaching character of the changes brought about by the signing of the Treaty and the establishment of an Irish government, that as a result of its working the past three years have seen a revolution in Irish education the full import and significance of which is scarcely realized by the average citizen . . . a complete educational revolution has been effected by the putting into operation during the past year, of the new programme drawn up by the Secondary Education Commission of the Second Dáil. The nature of this revolution may be summed up in a sentence. Rigidity has been replaced by freedom . . .[2]

Taken together these statements indicate a firm conviction that education under the new administration was attempting and was indeed effecting significant and, in Cosgrave's words, 'revolutionary' changes. There was justification for at least some of the claims, but hardly for all. The curriculum initiatives taken in 1922 which were aimed primarily at the Gaelicisation of education were certainly 'revolutionary' in their intent. Furthermore, a single Department of Education to co-ordinate all aspects and levels of education had replaced the separate boards of commissioners, 'payment- by-results' at secondary level had been abolished,[3] reforms in teacher training to take account of the new school programmes at primary level had been introduced,[4] provision for additional scholarships to assist less well off pupils proceed to second level education had been made,[5] and a new and long sought for School Attendance Act to make schooling compulsory between the ages of six and fourteen, was just a year away.[6] Also, an outline framework indicating a pathway, or 'highway' as it was described in departmental papers, for the possible career of pupils from primary through post-primary to higher education, had been adopted within the Department of Education.[7] Essentially conceptual the path outlined did not indicate, except in the vaguest sense, a structurally integrated educational system. Perhaps the only practical implication which it held was the prospect that termination of compulsory education might soon be raised from fourteen to sixteen.

Overall, this list of reforms is not unimpressive, at least not at first sight, and would appear to justify MacNeill's reference to the 'national interest' and Cosgrave's to a 'revolution' as the motivation and context within which reform was being promoted. As MacNeill himself wrote, 'the chief function of Irish education policy is to conserve and develop Irish nationality . . .'[8] This function was precisely the one, as Pearse had so vehemently argued in *The murder machine*, which had been neither conserved, nor developed by the previous administration. The 'revolution' taking place in Irish education was intended to undo that wrong and it was precisely in those terms that one of those intimately involved in its formulation explained the policy. It was, wrote Séamus Ó Néill of the Department of Education, a policy aimed 'to redress the balance and to make compensation' for the neglect of Irish culture within the educational system in the past.[9] The 'revolution' was, therefore, in curriculum terms quite comprehensive and far-reaching in its intent.

The one major omission from the list of reforms was structural change. No detailed attention seems to have been given to such reform and the only evidence that the Department of Education was anxious to promote any form of structural change was revealed in a letter to Bishop Thomas O'Doherty of Galway indicating the department's concern about the physical condition of many school buildings and requesting advice as to how the bishops might wish the problem tackled.[10] The letter was accompanied by extracts from the report of the 1919 Killanin Committee of inquiry into primary education which contained the recommendations for local committees and the provision of rate support for the upkeep of schools. As might have been expected, the bishops did not find the implied suggestion that they might now agree to such committees any more acceptable within the new political context than they had within the old. On the more general issues of the control and provision of schools, the government was quite satisfied to continue with the procedures of the National Board and to provide financial support to schools conducted by voluntary agencies and was clearly not going to insist on any involvement in school management by public representatives, nor indeed insist that parents and teachers should be afforded such involvement either. Reforms directed at achieving democratically controlled management structures so evident in Northern Ireland were not going to be insisted upon by the new regime in the south, especially not when the major church in the state was totally opposed to the idea.

It was not simply a matter of church opposition which prevented reform in that direction. On several occasions MacNeill expressed himself against such change, obviously in answer to a demand that was still being pressed in several quarters, notably within the teaching profession itself. Presenting the estimates for his department in 1923, he quite explicitly rejected the need for legislative change in education, which any acceptance of 'democratisation' would have required, and laid down what was to become a deeply embedded procedural principle in the administration of education in the south for several decades:

I cannot venture to outline here any large proposals with regard to educational reform. I do not think that educational reform would require very much by way of legislation, but that a great deal of it will be possible by means of administration, and my object has been – and I hope that it will be found when I lay down the responsibility placed on me – I have endeavoured to leave such provision behind, that the people to whom we are all responsible, can rely on sound administrational progress and reform.[11]

So closely did successive governments adhere to this approach that education in the south has remained the area of public life least circumscribed by legislation. School management, in particular, was a matter over which the state did not, until relatively recent times, seek to exercise any direct control. Indeed, when the state did, in the mid-twenties, take the initiative to establish a small number of second level preparatory schools for potential teachers, these were immediately placed under the management of church agencies. MacNeill's approach was fully endorsed by his successor, Marcus O'Sullivan, who in an address to the Catholic Truth Society in 1926 spoke strongly in favour of the 'managerial system' and against state control of schools because, as he claimed, the latter fostered 'secularization'.[12] With some exaggerated modesty, O'Sullivan later explained to the Dáil what he regarded his department's role to be:

The Minister for Education and the Department of Education are not the people who educate the country. They have only a certain limited power to influence the people who educate the country . . . to help . . . to stimulate . . . to work for a certain amount of uniformity in aim in the educational system of the country.[13]

The major church and the governing party of the new state were, therefore, virtually at one as far as the nature and control of educational structures were concerned. It was also the case that no significant section of public opinion was campaigning to make things otherwise. When Fianna Fail first entered the Dáil in 1928 its declared educational policies did not differ in any significant respects from those of the Cumann na nGael governments. Like its predecessor, Gaelicisation was to be Fianna Fail's number one priority, the only difference being that Fianna Fail in government (1932–48) was to become even more insistent on progress being achieved in this area than Cumann na nGael. Only the small Labour Party, which provided the main opposition in the Dáil until Fianna Fail decided to take its seats, and the executives of the teachers' unions, expressed themselves in favour of democratising control over education. At the Trades Union Congress in 1923 the Association of Secondary Teachers of Ireland (A.S.T.I.) proposed:

That this Congress asserts the right to free secondary education for every Irish child capable of benefitting from it; that, further, it is the duty of the State to provide free secondary education, for such children, on a liberal and democratic basis . . .[14]

The resolution also called for the setting up of a committee to prepare a national plan for education, as a result of which a joint Labour Party and Trades Union Congress policy document was published in 1925 which contained proposals for the establishment of local education authorities in each county and an integrated school system making provision from nursery through to technical and higher education. According to the policy proposals, basic education should also be free with generous scholarship provision for those wishing to proceed to the post-primary sectors. Furthermore, the authors of the document felt it necessary to stress the essentially Christian dimension to education in Ireland, doing so in all probability to indicate that the Labour movement in Ireland intended no attack on the churches' role in education:

The aim of the national system of education should, in our opinion, be to produce men and women who are governors of themselves; whose object in life will be to become civilised Christian human beings, to be healthy, clean, alert, and responsible citizens of an Irish commonwealth; who will be efficient wealth producers not because, as the prevailing school of economists would have us believe, that the production of wealth is the essential object of all human endeavours, but because the production of more wealth will increase the comfort of all the people.[15]

Respect for the influence and authority of the churches, especially of the Catholic Church was difficult, if not impossible to circumvent. Although the endorsement of this policy document marked a shift in the Trade Union Congress' position on the role of local authorities in education from that encountered by Councillor Walker in 1907, it meant very little in real terms since congress had no direct influence over education while the Labour Party, with which congress was affiliated, was unlikely to be in a position to act upon its policies.

A further indication of the new state's desire to respect the Catholic Church's teachings on education has been highlighted by Dermot Keogh who has pointed out that when the constitution of the Irish Free State was being drafted the cabinet 'decided to consult the bishops on the wording of Article 10 concerning free primary education'.[16] The Catholic Church had always emphasised parents' responsibility for their children's education and there must have been concern that any commitment to make education free might have been interpreted by the church as an encroachment on that responsibility. In the event the wording was found acceptable, but the very fact that it was thought necessary to have what was by then a widely accepted policy elsewhere, i.e. free primary education, checked with the church, reveals that the authorities in the Free State were not anxious to adopt any educational policy which might not have had the full approval of that church.

While the new state disavowed any desire to directly control schools, in the terms of their ownership and management, it would be wrong to underestimate, as O'Sullivan's remarks appeared to do, the influence exercised by the Department of Education over what was actually taught in schools. If the involvement of public authorities in school management was not contemplated, then curriculum control certainly was and the extent of that control was quickly becoming very apparent in major innovations in primary and secondary school programmes. The new state's determination to exercise control over the curricula of Irish schools had been made emphatically clear by J.J. O'Kelly, the Sinn Féin Minister for Education, when he received a deputation from the I.N.T.O. to discuss the proposed programme being submitted by the National Conference in October 1921. While O'Kelly acknowledged the problems which the new programme might pose for many teachers, he strongly made the point that the teachers should 'realise that they are the servants of the nation, and that the nation who employs and pays them must have the right to specify the nature of the work which they are to do'.[17] Although this would not be how Catholic clerical managers to whom teachers were most immediatley and directly answerable, would have stated the latters' responsibilities, it was to a greater or lesser extent how the Department of Education was to view these responsibilities, at least on the question of implementing the policy of Gaelicisation. The new education authorities expected that this policy would be fully accepted by the teaching profession, whatever difficulties there might be in implementing it. Indeed, once full responsibility for education was handed over to the Free State authorities in 1922 those authorities lost no time in making clear what their number one priority was to be. Addressing the Board of National Education in February 1922, the person appointed chief executive officer for education, Pádraig Ó Brolcháin, told its members that:

In the administration of Irish education it is the intention of the new government to work with all its might for the strengthening of national fibre by giving the language, history, music and tradition of Ireland their natural place in the life of Irish schools.[18]

The first official step towards achieving this goal had already been taken with the decision in January 1922 to effect the previously mentioned regulation changes in the conduct and marking of examinations of the Intermediate Board to be held in June of that year.[19] In order to indicate the greater stress being placed on the study of Ireland, the board announced that candidates would be able to achieve full marks at junior grade in history and geography if they confined themselves to the section relating to Ireland; at senior grade 50 per cent of the marks would be allocated to a similar section. Secondly, to signal the new status being afforded the Irish language, candidates would be permitted to attempt papers wholly in Irish, partly in Irish and partly in English, as well as wholly in English.[20]

This announcement was followed in early February by the official adoption of the national programme recommended by the National Programme Conference and the announcement in Public Notice number 4 that it would be brought into effect from 1 April 1922.[21] The most significant aspect of this decision was that Irish would become a compulsory subject, to be taught for at least one hour each day in schools where there was a teacher qualified to do so. The notice stressed that '. . . a new starting point in the history of primary education in Ireland' had arrived with the introduction of the new programme.[22]

Other important early decisions relating to the policy of Gaelicisation included the requirement that teachers and student-teachers attend special summer courses in Irish[23] and the reform of the curriculum in the training colleges to take account of developments at primary school level.[24] The introduction of new curricula for the training colleges included Irish as a compulsory subject for the first time and the inclusion in the English syllabus of Anglo-Irish writers like James Clarence Mangan, Standish O'Grady and Patrick Pearse, presumably to familiarise student teachers with material which they could exploit in their future teaching since each had based much of their writings on Irish myths and legends. Another feature of this English curriculum was the inclusion of many authors in translation, e.g. Homer, Virgil, Plutarch, and St Francis, whose works replaced those of more familiar English writers,[25] an innovation designed to minimise contact with Anglo-Saxon literary influences and in keeping with the sentiments expressed in the report of the National Programme Conference.

As far as secondary school courses were concerned the first reforms were announced in July,[26] a notable feature of which was the very considerable degree of text choice which they allowed teachers in the literature courses, but once again the authors suggested for English indicated a bias against those of British nationality, Macauley being the only such author whose work was included. Further changes affecting the status of Irish in the secondary programmes were announced in 1924[27] when, to encourage the use of Irish as a medium of instruction, it was decided that students answering examination questions in Irish could qualify for bonus marks on a sliding scale from 10 per cent downwards. It was also announced that schools would not qualify for capitation grants unless 'a reasonable number of pupils' were following courses in Irish.[28] Schools offering subjects through the medium of Irish would qualify for additional capitation payments ranging from 10 to 25 per cent in accordance with the number of subjects offered through Irish. Schools operating on an all-Irish medium basis were classified as 'A' schools, those operating on a partially Irish medium, or bilingual basis were classified as 'B' schools and the rest as 'C' schools. Considerable attention was subsequently to be drawn to increases in the number of schools in categories 'A' and 'B', particularly, as might be expected, to increases in category 'A'. Such increases were to be interpreted by government spokespersons as evidence of the success of and enthusiasm for the Gaelicisation policy.

111

Other changes included the requirement that, in order to obtain an overall pass in the Intermediate examination, it would be necessary from 1928 to have obtained a pass in Irish.[29] This requirement was also made for an overall honours in the Leaving Certificate examination from the same year and was extended to the Leaving Certificate pass level examination in 1934.[30] One other feature of the regulations for secondary schools illustrates the manner in which Irish was being promoted. Up until 1927 Irish and English were grouped together in such a manner that candidates for the Intermediate examination could choose one or the other language, or both. Thereafter, Irish became a requirement by virtue of being the only subject in its group, while English was grouped in the modern languages section, thereby making it theoretically more possible not to choose it.[31] The likelihood of it not being chosen was, however, quite remote. Nonetheless, the 'demotion', as it were, of English to the modern languages group of subjects was clearly an attempt to signal its 'foreignness'.

Such regulations, taken in conjunction with the earlier matriculation regulation for the National University, had the effects of making Irish virtually complusory in all secondary schools and of encouraging the more enthusiastic, whether out of genuine interest or the desire for better grades and increased financial support, to adopt Irish as a medium of instruction. It is interesting to note that in taking these measures the department was very careful not to infringe the 'private' nature of secondary schools by directly imposing Irish upon them. Since secondary education was not compulsory and secondary schools were under voluntary control and even less directly subsidised by the department than primary schools, the department could not directly impose Irish. However, since the department did control the syllabus of both the Intermediate and Leaving examinations and since the department could attach conditions to the grants it disbursed, it did possess a very powerful, if indirect means of determining what would be taught in schools. This control the department chose to use to quite a considerable extent in order to promote the government's Gaelicisation policy. The option of not complying with the regulations remained available, but at the price of not receiving financial assistance and of depriving pupils of the opportunity of entering for the department's examinations.

The first attempts at educational innovation in the Irish Free State, apart from measures to ensure administrative tidiness, concentrated, therefore, almost exclusively on the curriculum of both primary and secondary education. At both levels the emphasis on Gaelicisation was marked by a determination to promote rapid linguistic and more general cultural change based on the conviction that schools could effectively achieve such a goal. The status of Irish was enhanced at secondary level, while at primary level it became a core element of the curriculum, almost *the* core element. Furthermore, in implementing the policy it is clear that some decisions were motivated not just by a desire to teach the Irish language and to inculcate a knowledge and understanding of Ireland's Gaelic heritage, but also by a desire to minimise, if not eliminate what were perceived to be sources of Anglo-Saxon influence, notably in literature, and in the teaching of history and geography. In effect the steps being taken by the Department of Education to Gaelicise Ireland also included measures to achieve what Douglas Hyde had termed the 'de-Anglicisation' of Ireland.

Reaction to curriculum reform

Reaction to the reforms outlined above had to take account of the profound political change that had occurred following the establishment of the Irish Free State and the adoption of a policy of trying to effect what would have amounted to a major 'cultural revolution'. By any measure this is in effect was what the new regime was aiming at when it decided to 'Gaelicise' education. It was clearly intended that this process of cultural change should not be confined to education, but that it should be extended as far and as quickly as possible to other spheres of life. Evidence of this extension was to be seen in many other initiatives, especially within the public services and in the symbolic presentation of the state. Bilingual street and place names appeared on road signs, bilingual forms were introduced throughout the public service, civil servants were encouraged to use Irish, and Irish became a necessary qualification for positions within the service. Underpinning and reinforcing all other initiaves, however, were the changes affecting education. If, as Corcoran and others hoped, the young generation could become Irish speaking and Gaelic in their outlook, then the next generation of adults would merely have to complete the revolution in order to have fully re-established a Gaelic nation in Ireland. As Professor Michael Tierney of University College Dublin, in an address endorsing the new state's language policy, put it , 'Irish was the most important education question for Irish teachers, parents and Government . . . [because] . . . if the Irish nation was to survive the restoration of the language was essential'.[32]

Many people shared the early hopes for this policy and the Gaelic League was confident that the new administration would succeed in achieving its aim. Reflecting this confidence its general secretary declared 'Ní bheidh oiread gá, i mo thuairim, feasta le múinteoireachta faoi scáth an Chonartha [In my opinion, there will be no further need for any teaching (of Irish) under the league's auspices]'.[33] Professor Corcoran believed that a three year period was all that was necessary for children to achieve fluency in the language, following which increasingly higher levels of use could be expected.[34] However, as has already been noted, Corcoran's basis for such hopes lay in situations quite different from those which pertained in Ireland. No one in the revival movement, and certainly not Professor Corcoran, or the Gaelic League seemed to appreciate the enormity of the task of displacing a language in a whole society, particularly when that language was English, a language which the Irish had made their own in so many respects and which also gave them so much access to other cultures and to other countries.

A clear political consensus as to the desirability of achieving the goal of Gaelicisation appears to have existed embracing both the pro and anti-treaty sections of Sinn Féin, now Cumann na nGael and Fianna Fail. Even the Labour Party, which was the only political voice clearly favouring a radical reform of educational structures, accepted the Gaelic League's goal of an Irish-speaking Ireland. According to its policy document, bilingualism should be the immediate aim with Irish ultimately becoming 'the dominant language of the country'.[35]

Such a radical policy required much more consideration in terms of its feasibility than it ever received in these early years of the new state's existence. It was not surprising, therefore, that when difficulties were encountered they tended to be attributed by enthusiasts for the policy to lack of effort on the part of those directly responsible for teaching Irish or to a lack of resources from government. The same difficulties, however, soon led others to question the very possibility of Irish being revived to anything like the degree aspired to by its supporters. As for the population at large, it was clear from its behaviour that most people in the state instinctively, if not consciously, rejected the proposition that Irish should ever totally replace English while, nonetheless, holding positive attitudes towards learning and using some Irish and towards becoming more familiar with their nation's Gaelic traditions. However, the failure to set out objectives which would have built upon these attitudes and which could have been realistically achieved, was to fuel the controversy which would surround the language policy, especially in education, over the next four decades.

Whatever misgivings can now be expressed in retrospect, it has to be acknowledged that there also existed considerable enthusiasm for reviving Irish in the immediate period after 1922, not least within the teaching profession. One national school teacher recalling this excitement and the commitment which it generated wrote, some 30 years later, how he and his colleagues had responded:

Fired by the impatience of a newly emancipated people the Ministry made the extravagantly courageous decision to teach teachers Irish overnight, and the teachers, no less patriotic, and unaware of the magnitude of the task, undertook to tackle it at once. Centres of instruction were established all over the land from Donegal to Kerry, instructors qualified and unqualified, were appointed to teach the thronging classes, in which grey-haired men and harassed matrons predominated, and the long summer holidays of 1922 were sacrificed to the forlorn hope of learning a difficult language before the schools reopened. How well I remember the mad enthusiasm of it all . . .[36]

The early enthusiasm did not, however, completely blind all to the need for the policy to be implemented with caution. In particular the I.N.T.O. was concerned, with the result that after only two years of the new programmes being implemented, the union asked that a second programme conference be convened to review the primary school curriculum. While the new programmes for Irish were not the sole reason for this request, they certainly were among the main reasons. The I.N.T.O. was of the view that the

Department of Education was urging a greater use of Irish as a medium of instruction than could be justified and teachers had also begun to react quite negatively to the pressures which they felt the new emphasis on Irish was making, as a resolution from a section of the I.N.T.O. in Kerry illustrates: 'The introduction of Irish has made such demands on the time and energy of both teachers and pupils as to render the remainder of the programme practically impossible without resort to cramming'.[37] The same teachers, somewhat like their northern counterparts' approach to religious instruction, stressed that they were not opposed to teaching Irish, only to it being made a compulsory subject. Indeed, as a past-president of the I.N.T.O. indicated, most teachers were not even opposed to making Irish compulsory provided there was 'no slave-driving' and he warned that 'the efforts of the idealists' would fail if the co-operation of the parents was not obtained.[38] The pressure for a second look at school programmes mounted so quickly and became so strident in the period 1923–25, that the Department of Education quickly accepted the need to convene a conference which became known as the Second National Programme Conference, the deliberations of which are discussed later in this chapter.

At secondary level, reaction to the curriculum reforms was quite mixed. There was a general welcome for the liberalisation of the curriculum which many believed resulted from the abandonment of set texts in the humanities.[39] Commenting on these changes Professor Corcoran hoped that they would mark a break with English educational traditions at secondary level and that they would lead to a restoration of the older more 'international' outlook which he claimed had, in former times, informed learning in Ireland.[40] The welcome afforded the new programmes was, however, tempered by a concern about Irish becoming a compulsory 'passing' subject in the Department of Education's certificate examinations. Initially, the main concern of the A.S.T.I., the principal union at this level, was to ensure that teachers would be in a position to fulfil the Irish language requirements. Like the I.N.T.O., the A.S.T.I. encouraged secondary teachers to participate in Irish language summer schools and throughout the rest of the decade organised several such schools itself.[41] Unlike the I.N.T.O., however, the A.S.T.I. does not appear to have taken any particular stand at this time on what became known as 'compulsory Irish' at secondary level.[42] Such concern and opposition as was expressed came initially and most forcefully from Protestant educational and church interests.

Protestant concerns

For one section of the population in the Irish Free State the government's apparent zeal for and commitment to a Gaelic revival was to provide special problems. For Protestants, the majority of whom had been staunchly unionist in their outlook and had only reluctantly accepted the break-up of the union with Britain, this policy became an early test of their willingness and capacity to adjust to the new political regime. Unlike their co-religionists in Northern Ireland, however, southern Protestants were not concentrated in particular geographical areas and so lacked the social cohesion and consequent political influence which such concentration had given their northern cousins. Within the overwhelmingly Catholic population the only concentration of Protestants in the south was to be found in the three Ulster counties and, even there, Protestants were but a small proportion of the population. In the larger towns and cities Protestants remained well represented in business and in the professions, but not in the population at large. Given their dispersal and with their overall numbers at less than 10 per cent of the population of the Irish Free State, they did not constitute a minority likely to pose any serious threat to the stability of the new state, in contrast to the position of the Catholic minority in the north.

Overall the situation in which Protestants found themselves at the creation of the new state was not a very happy, or secure one. It was only in the years immediately preceding independence that the leaders of southern unionism had accepted the inevitability of an end to the union with Britain, for their part of Ireland at least.[43] Having done so, they set about addressing the problem of the future of their community in what many feared might be quite daunting circumstances.[44] These fears were well grounded as the I.R.A.'s campaign developed and attacks on Protestants and their property featured in that campaign in several areas throughout the country. Later, during the early months of 1922, when pressure against the north was being orchestrated from the south and intercommunal violence broke out in Belfast on a large scale, many southern Protestants found themselves victims of retaliatory action. Following the murder of Catholics in Belfast in March 1922, for example, all non-Catholics in County Louth were threatened with reprisals by the I.R.A.[45] Protestants were ordered to leave parts of County Donegal and several Protestant ex-Royal Irish Constabulary members were murdered.[46]

Seeking some indication as to their future in the Irish Free State, a deputation from the Church of Ireland led by Archbishop John Gregg of Dublin met Michael Collins, representing the new Free State authorities, in May 1922 and asked 'if they [southern Protestants] were permitted to live in Ireland or if it was desired that they should leave the country'.[47] Collins answered that they were very welcome to remain and that the forces of the state would afford them whatever protection they could.[48] It was reassurance of a kind, but one which only had meaning if it was realised in practice. The poignancy of the Protestant situation in these early years of the new state was acutely expressed by a Church of Ireland preacher in a sermon delivered at a 1923 Armistice Day service:

. . . we imperial Irish are naturally feeling hurt and sore because these ideals of government which we valued and to which we were loyal have been allowed to be superseded. The flag which symbolised our loyalty to the Empire which our race did so much to build has been removed and another is substituted in its place . . .[49]

116

As Terence Brown has pointed out, Protestants in the south were indeed finding it extremely difficult to come to terms with their new circumstances because, as a community, they had not only not been part of the nationalist movement which had led to independence, but:

... ideologically ... apart from a few individuals who had been aroused by an enthusiasm for Gaelic revival made almost no effort to comprehend the nationalist cause. A dismissive contemptuousness had often reflected the offensive blend of insecurity and caste snobbery that characterized fairly commonplace Protestant reactions to Irish nationalism.[50]

It was not surprising, therefore, that the Protestant community was to experience a degree of discomfort and readjustment as a result of the new politico–cultural context in which it found itself. Ideologically unprepared for a number of the changes about to be introduced, the Protestant community also experienced a sharp drop in its numbers as many who had been part of, or closely associated with the British administration left the country.[51] Partition was a double blow, not only breaking the union with Britain, but also in separating southern Protestants from the majority of their co-religionists in the north. The one comforting factor for many Protestants was the Irish Free State's membership of the British Empire and Commonwealth. This was something to which they attached much deeper significance than did the majority of their Catholic–nationalist fellow-citizens and to those amongst them with strong unionist feelings, membership of the Empire meant that all had not been lost of their former links with Britain; it helped ease the 'pain' caused by the end of the union. Indeed, continued attachment to the British Empire was not motivated solely by sentiment since many from the Protestant community had served in the imperial services and these outlets for employment continued to be valued for many years after 1922. Hence some of the apprehension which developed that the new educational policies, because of their emphasis on Irish were likely to jeopardise such opportunities.[52]

As pointed out earlier, no official representatives of any section of Protestant education in the country had participated in the National Programme Conference of 1921, although some Protestants took part in other capacities. At the time the conference would have been seen by Protestants generally as an unofficial body motivated by nationalist concerns with no formal mandate to determine curricular matters. So, in a sense, analogous to Catholic non-participation in the Lynn Committee in Northern Ireland, official Protestant non-participation in the National Programme Conference had deprived that community of an input into the deliberations which had set out the basis for curricular reform at national school level. The same situation prevailed with respect to the deliberations of the Dáil Commission on Secondary Education. The latter had been established before the Anglo-Irish Treaty had been agreed, at a time when the majority of the Protestant community had not yet accepted the Dáil as an official parliament. However, the absence of significant Protestant participation in the deliberations of both bodies is difficult to assess. In the light of the pressures of the time and since the National Programme Conference made the very reasonable recommendation that Irish be taught only where qualified teachers were available, it is not easy to see how any official Protestant participants could have successfully pleaded for more special treatment for their community as far as the recommendations for Irish were concerned. So, despite the fact that there was no general tradition of teaching Irish in Protestant schools and that, as Jack White comments, 'Protestant educators had little sympathy with this development',[53] Protestant educationists generally did indicate a willingness to co-operate with the Department of Education in meeting the demands of the new policy. At teacher training level, for example, although Irish had not previously been included in the syllabus of the Church of Ireland College, instructors were appointed and syllabuses adopted to ensure that new teachers would be proficient in the language.[54] At school level, teachers were encouraged to attend the special in-service courses organised by the Department of Education.[55] Later, in 1926, when the Irish medium preparatory colleges were proposed the Church of Ireland was eager to ensure that one would be established to cater for Protestant students.[56]

This anxiety to co-operate with the new administration did not, however, prevent Protestants expressing their fears about the effects of the new emphasis on Irish once a degree of what was regarded as undue pressure began to be felt. In November 1924 at a meeting of Protestant school managers it was claimed that Irish was 'driving out other subjects' from the timetable[57] while Bishop Robert Miller of Waterford, speaking at his diocesan synod earlier in the same year, requested that Irish 'be one of the subjects taught in our schools, but do not make it compulsory'.[58] In a letter to William Cosgrave, a leading Protestant academic, Professor E.P. Culverwell of Trinity College, attacked the new educational policy as aiming 'to secure that the people of Ireland shall be a literary people saturated with the language and thought of the older Gael and in fact . . . a people out of touch with individual life as seen in other European countries'.[59] Culverwell was not opposed to Irish being taught and pleaded for the 'full and free opportunity to be given to the development of Irish studies' because he was confident that, as a result, there would 'be more bilingualism and more love of Irish studies a generation hence than there would be under the existing programme'.[60] At the Church of Ireland Synod in 1926 the Bishop of Limerick expressed his regret 'that the policy of compulsion had been forced upon the country without consulting the parents and teachers'[61] and went on to criticise the effects of compulsory Irish which he claimed would make Irish children 'among the most uneducated in Europe'.[62]

That resistance to the teaching of Irish was being practically expressed in some Protestant controlled national schools is evidenced by the case of Killoughter School at Redhills, County Cavan, where a number of parents signed a petition in 1924 indicating that they did not wish their children to be taught the language.[63] Since the principal of this two-teacher school knew no Irish himself and his assistant teacher had only recently begun learning the language, the department was obliged to accept a compromise by which Irish would only be taught in the lower classes, a situation which was allowed to persist until the early thirties and through its persistence demonstrated that compulsion did not always mean compulsion for all.[64]

At secondary level when the new syllabuses for the Intermediate and Leaving Certificate examinations were published together with new regulations requiring that Irish be passed in the certificate examinations, concerns were quite widely expressed within the Protestant community.[65] The headmaster of the High School in Dublin argued that 'schools cannot run ahead of public opinion' on the question of Irish and that when Irish had received the 'general approval that was given to the former compulsory subjects of the programme, its addition to their number would need no defence. But parents must first be convinced of its value'.[66] Bishop Miller, in remarks which recall the establishment of the Church Education Society in the 1830s in opposition to the Board of National Education, suggested that the Protestant community should consider providing all of the resources for the education of their children themselves.[67] Such a step would have removed Protestant schools from the jurisdiction of the Department of Education and, in such circumstances, they could formulate their own regulations regarding Irish. It would, however, also have had the effect of almost completely cutting the Protestant community off from the rest of the population and it was not seriously considered. Nonetheless, the very fact that it was proposed at all, particularly by a senior clergyman, underlined the depth of feeling that existed on the question of the Irish language policy amongst many Protestants. Only a few Protestants, such as Dr T.J. Irwin, headmaster of Wesley College, Dublin and Professor William Thrift of Trinity College and also a member of Dáil Éireann, criticised the Gaelicisation policy in principle as well as in practice. Irwin was opposed to the policy:

. . . from a cultural and educational point of view as well as from a utilitarian aspect . . . The intention to make Irish and other subjects compulsory did not leave enough room for Latin, French, music, drawing and those subjects the study of which make for culture and a liberal education.[68]

Fear that the promotion of Irish would encourage an isolationist mentality and cut Ireland off from the international community was invoked by a number of critics like Professor Thrift, who contested the claim that 'the development of Irish everywhere is necessary for the development of the national life' and spoke about the 'growth of internationalism' from which Ireland could be excluded as a result.[69] Since many aspects of national life in Ireland over the previous century at least, whether in its unionist or nationalist, Catholic or Protestant traditions, had developed through the medium of English, Thrift was reflecting no more than the truth of the situation as far as the immediate past was concerned. A more forthright but not widely expressed Protestant view was anonymously revealed in the *Church of Ireland*

Gazette by a correspondent who referred to the 'absurdity and hurtfulness of children having to waste their school time learning Irish and the fatuity and wastefulness connected with thrusting the Irish language on the public in general'.[70] There were also some real fears that the whole Gaelicisation policy was part of a general attack on the Protestant community in Ireland. Such fears were given some credance when one of the leading officials in the Department of Education, Seoirse MacNiocaill, declared in a public lecture that Gaelicisation aimed 'to drive'[71] English out of Ireland and to make the country wholly Gaelic speaking. Although MacNiocaill was rebuked by his minister,[72] the feeling persisted amongst Protestants that a 'learn Irish, or clear out' mentality was developing and Dr A.A. Luce of Trinity College forcibly expressed these fears saying:

Experience has already confirmed this contention in a small way and I venture to predict that in a hundred years half the Protestant population of the Free State will be converted to Roman Catholicism if the policy of compulsory Irish goes through.[73]

Fuelling these fears were regular attacks on aspects of Protestantism in Ireland from such platforms as that of the monthly journal the *Catholic Bulletin*. Although not an official church publication, prominent churchmen frequently wrote for it and views expressed in it were never repudiated. Protestant education was an issue which was often discussed in the *Bulletin*'s editorials during the 1920s with frequent attacks on the control and influence which it claimed Protestants continued to exercise over education:

We have exposed adequately the covert ways in which a Protestant ascendancy over Catholic education in Ireland is being maintained today and maintained to a great lowering of educational standards in our country.[74]

Referring to the concessions on Irish language qualifications granted to the Church of Ireland Training College when it was experiencing difficulties in recruiting an adequate supply of students, the *Bulletin* in rather denigrating tones wrote:

The problem of the Protestant Church in Ireland is to educate its teachers properly and to keep up the supply. It is their own problem. But let us hope that they realise that the day has quite gone when they can claim for their schools, their colleges, their University, any superiority of education.[75]

The frequent expression of such views together with reminders to Catholics of their church's prohibition on the attendance at Protestant educational institutions[76] cannot have been altogether reassuring to the Protestant community as to their place in the new Ireland. Perhaps the most telling political point made by Protestant spokespersons at this time about the implications of the Gaelicisation policy and, more so, the manner of its implementation was its likely effect on the case for Irish unity. The strong ties which southern Protestants had through their churches with their co-religionists in the north led many of them to judge the policy as quite negative in its likely effects on north–south relationships. As Dr Irwin stated in a speech to the Methodist Conference:

. . . It is clear that the goal of an Irish speaking Free State would never be achieved . . . it was a policy of fanaticism which sooner or later would have to be modified. One result would be the weakening of the affinity between them and their friends in the North and across the channel and an increase in emigration.[77]

In the north itself unionists were quick to exploit the same point and, by suggesting that the language policy was motivated by an anti-Protestant bias, claimed that the policy vindicated 'Ulster's' decision to remain politically apart from the rest of Ireland. As the *Belfast Telegraph* argued: 'If Ulster is ever to be brought into the Free State compulsory Irish will not hasten the day which Southern people profess to be longing for . . . It is a crying shame that Protestant children should be compelled to learn Irish at all. The government is deliberately thrusting Irish into all the Protestant schools by virtual compulsion, well knowing that it is most distasteful to Protestants and a knockout blow to many of the small schools'.[78]

That Irish did pose a particular difficulty for many Protestant pupils became apparent in examination results as the historian of one such school in Dublin points out:

By 1928 Irish had become compulsory for the Intermediate Certificate examination and thus began a series of reverses which have no parallel anywhere in the School's records for State examinations. In 1928, for example, all the entrants for the Intermediate failed because of the Irish language barrier, and in 1929 of the seven candidates presented only one succeeded in obtaining a qualifying mark and was the sole success. Had Irish not been compulsory, six of the seven entrants would have passed.[79]

It was this experience which led some Protestants to consider removing their children from schools in the south to have them educated in the north or in Britain, a fear that was greatest at secondary level. The Irish Free State correspondent of the *Times Educational Supplement* reported that 'pupils will go North or to Great Britain for education in which time and energy will not be spent learning a language which is useless outside Ireland and of doubtful value inside it'.[80] A suggestion that this may in fact have occurred is to be found in G.K. White's *History of St Columba's School*. St Columba's was a prestigeous Protestant boarding school near Dublin and White directly attributes the decline in numbers attending the college at this time to compulsory Irish:

Even among those Anglo-Irish parents who were themselves doggedly determined to make the best of a bad job there was from 1921 a widespread fear that the Ireland of the future would provide no livelihood for their sons. Happily this fear proved groundless but at the time it was real enough to impel people who were not die-hard Unionists to send their sons to school in England. The prospect of education in Ireland was made additionally uninviting to people of this sort by the knowledge that Ireland's new rulers were committed to the policy of making the Irish language compulsory in schools . . .[81]

White records that school numbers fell from 115 in 1920 to 62 by 1926. However, it would probably be more accurate to attribute the decline to a combination of factors including, for example, the withdrawal from Ireland of Protestant families associated with the British regime, civil and military, after 1921 rather than exclusively to any fears in the Protestant community about the quality of life and, in particular, of education in the new Irish state.

Despite difficulties with the policies associated with Irish, the leadership of the Protestant community was determined not to allow the language to become a barrier to Protestants playing their part in the new state. As Archbishop Gregg stated in a speech to his diocesan synod in 1927:

I want to see our young people holding Government positions and if the path to those positions is along the thorny track of Irish grammar, Irish cannot be altogether an uneconomic subject of study, when it makes the difference between employment and unemployment.[82]

It should also be borne in mind that there was a small, very pro-Irish lobby within the Protestant churches, in the Church of Ireland in particular, which fully supported the government's policies. Such Protestants were anxious to ensure that their community would not distance itself from the changes taking place in education but, on the contrary, would accept the case for their introduction. The Irish Guild of the Church of Ireland argued during the height of the controversy in 1926 that:

. . . it is essential that no distinction should be made between Irish Church children and those of other denominations with respect to subjects of the school curriculum and we protest against the attempt being made by certain members of the Church to approach the question of Irish in the schools from a sectarian rather than from a national aspect.[83]

Apart from a few, however, it was obvious that those within the Protestant churches concerned about Irish had generally attempted to make their case on educational and practical grounds rather than on political or sectarian grounds. Had the case been pursued in terms of the latter or in opposition to the teaching of Irish altogether, it is doubtful if they would have won any sympathy let alone any concessions whatever.

Concern about the educational effects of the Irish language policy was not confined to the Protestant community. However, at the outset, other voices, apart from those of the teachers which have been noted already, tended to be more muted. This absence of other protesting voices caused anxiety to the Protestant community by making it appear more isolated in its attitude than was really the case. An editorial in the *Irish Times* underlined this concern saying:

We have no doubt that the least excuse for the taunt of sectarianism would be removed if the authorities of the Roman Catholic Church and the Roman Catholic headmasters would make a frank statement of their views on compulsory Irish.[84]

Apart from the national teachers who were directly affected by the new policy, Catholic–nationalist opinion generally was slow to react in a negative sense for a number of reasons. First, there existed a broad consensus across the main political parties, whether pro- or anti-treaty, in favour of promoting the Irish language and Gaelic culture generally. Second, in the immediate aftermath of the civil war the language was an issue on which people could unite and to strongly challenge it would have been seen as unnecessarily divisive as well as being unpatriotic. Also, official Catholic Church opinion concerning Irish and the general trend of educational change remained quite positive. The earlier patronage of the language which the church had provided continued and as concern about the moral well-being of the Irish people came to be more and more stridently expressed in the decade after independence, the appeal of Gaelic culture as a form of moral shield increased as well.

Irish – a moral shield

Professor John Whyte in his seminal study, *Church and state in modern Ireland*, suggests that in the early 1920s the Catholic bishops appeared 'to have been deeply pessimistic about the state of their country'.[85] To the atrocities and outrages committed during the Anglo-Irish war were added 'evil' literature, modern dancing and the cinema. Lenten pastorals and sermons on the moral dangers posed by these 'evils' to a society in, as one bishop described it, 'a low level of degeneracy'[86] were frequent. Controls to curb the influence of these alleged evils were not delayed by the authorities of the new Irish state: legislation to censor films was enacted in 1923,[87] a committee of enquiry on evil literature was set up in 1926 and legislation followed in 1929;[88] an act to control public dancing reached the statute book in the early 1930s.[89] Like Patrick Forde a number of other Catholic clerics argued that the threat posed to the morals of the Irish people could be removed if the Gaelic revival succeeded. Linking the need to control the import of what he had previously described as 'salacious literature emanating from Britain'[90] with the campaign to revive the Irish language and Gaelic culture generally, the Jesuit writer, Fr R.S. Devane argued:

> We are at present engaged in a heroic effort to revive our national language, national customs, national values, national culture. These objects cannot be achieved without a cheap, healthy and independent native press. In the face of English competition such a press is an impossibility . . . Against such propaganda of the English language and English ideas the present effort at national revival looks very much like the effort to beat back an avalanche with a sweeping brush.[91]

The contrast between 'a cheap, healthy and independent native press' and the 'propaganda of the English language and English ideas' taken together with his reference to 'salacious literature', clearly implied the moral superiority of the former. On the significance of the Irish language and its cultural implications, the social theorist, Fr Edward Cahill, argued that the links between Gaelic Ireland and the Catholic faith of the Irish people were so intimate as be a justification, in themselves, for reviving the language:

> . . . the people of the Gaedhealtacht, besides being amongst the very best of the Irish race physically and morally, are of incalculable importance to the future of the Irish nation. Besides, the old Catholic Irish tradition of the Gaedhealtacht where alone the

Irish Catholic tradition now lives, is one of the nation's best bulwarks against the materialism of the English speaking world by which it is surrounded.[92]

With these claims Cahill virtually mythologised Gaeltacht people and their way of life just as Patrick Pearse, Michael Collins and others who claimed that only in the Gaeltacht did the real Irish nation persist, had done. To revive the nation necessitated extending Gaeltacht values and practices to the rest of the people of the island. Other Catholic spokespersons, like Dr Thomas Gilmartin, Archbishop of Tuam, praised the primary school curriculum, saying that 'Irish boys and girls must be taught to make Irish more productive, to buy and use Irish goods, to cultivate the Irish language, Irish games, Irish amusements'.[93] The popularity of this line of thinking probably explains the generally muted nature of criticism of the educational changes from official Catholic Church spokespersons.

There were, nonetheless, some voices within Catholic circles which did express concern. The president of St Colman's College Fermoy, Fr Thomas Tobin spoke about the threat which he claimed Irish posed for the classical languages and other subjects.[94] The Archdeacon of Cashel, Mgr Ryan,while careful not to directly criticise the new emphasis on Irish, condemned 'any method that would exclude the study of the English in our schools' adding that it was English which had helped 'to make Ireland an apostolic nation'.[95] In Dáil Éireann there were, even at this early stage members who were prepared to openly question the wisdom of the government's language policy for schools. Finian Lynch, who had been one of the ministers of education in the spring of 1922 when Irish had first become a requirement in national schools, was quite critical of his former department during the 1924 debate on the estimates for education:

I think I am entirely opposed to attempting to teach subjects through Irish where Irish is not the known language. You are killing Irish and you are not teaching the subject that you purport to teach . . . I therefore ask the education authorities to revise their attitude on the teaching of subjects in Irish when there are not text books available and when the students are absolutely incapable of absorbing lectures in Irish.[96]

During the same debate T.J. O'Connell also requested that the government indicate clearly what its policy was with regard to the national school programmes, whether it really was to render the country completely Irish speaking, because 'there is considerable doubt among people as to the value of what children are being taught in the schools'.[97]

Michael Heffernan, another T. D., also attacked the pressure for subjects to be taught through the medium of Irish and criticised the belief that Ireland could soon become an Irish speaking nation: 'we cannot have this country an Irish speaking country in two or three years. If we do it in twenty, twenty-five or thirty years we will be lucky'.[98] Such forthright questioning of what had quickly become almost national dogma was not, however, widely repeated in Dáil Éireann at this time.

Nonetheless, the volume of concern did mount, some even being expressed by persons involved in implementing the policy. In a special

Appendix to the report of national education for the year 1924–25, one inspector, L. Ó Fachtna, referred to the low percentage of teachers who possessed a certificate in Irish therefore implying how difficult it was to expect that Irish would be taught well in all national schools. More significantly he commented 'Ní measaim gur féidir a shéanadh go dtáining laghdú éifeachta . . . ar mhúineadh na nabhair eile ó tháinig an Clár Naisiúnta i bhfeidhm [I do not think it can be denied that there has been a decline in efficiency in the teaching of the other subjects since the introduction of the National Programme]'.[99]

Second National Programme Conference

Such was the volume of criticism being expressed, even by early 1924, about the manner in which the curriculum in national schools was being promoted by the Department of Education, that the executive of the I.N.T.O. adopted a resolution to reconvene the National Programme Conference.[100] Later that same year a deputation from the I.N.T.O. to the Minister of Education urged that the department should in fact become responsible for the conference.[101] To this suggestion the minister seems to have readily agreed and the notice convening the conference was published in June 1925. The terms of reference given to the Second National Programme Conference, as it came to be called, were:

To consider the suitability of the National Programme of Primary Instruction at present in operation in the national schools, to report to the Minister of Education thereon; and to make any recommendations to him as regards any alterations which may seem desirable.[102]

The membership of this conference, which was chaired by Fr Lambert McKenna S.J., was much more representative than its predecessor. Catholic and Protestant school managers were represented, as were the teachers themselves, the county councils, and the Gaelic League. Also invited were individuals drawn from a number of different sectors of public life, in particular from the Department of Education's own inspectorate and from the universities. Dr Kingsmill Moore was particularly pleased to have been invited to join the conference: 'it is with sincere pleasure that I say at once that from the first, in some inexplainable way, I found myself at home. High officials at the Ministry [as he referred to the Department of Education] had greeted my nomination with congratulations; . . .'[103]

Although instigated by the concerns surrounding the teaching of Irish the report dealt with the whole programme of instruction. It began by endorsing the national aims for education set out by P. Ó Brolcháin in January 1922, but, almost re-echoing O'Connell's concern, expressed the view that 'a clear statement of the conditions which they deemed necessary for the working of that ideally national system of education would stimulate the Government to establish those conditions by appropriate administrative measures'.[104]

The conference's list of recommendations commenced with a statement on the centrality of religious instruction in the school curriculum because it has 'as its subject matter, God's honour and service . . . [and] . . . We assume, therefore, that religious instruction is a fundamental part of the school course'.[105] This emphasis maintained the position of religion which had existed in the curricula of national schools since 1831. However, once the centrality of religious instruction had been emphasised, the conference's report left the details of the programmes to the relevant church authorities and passed on to outline programmes for 'secular' subjects.

While the scope of the recommendations was broad, Irish undoubtedly was the key issue. To address the concerns expressed, the conference recommended two courses, a higher and a lower course, each balanced, respectively, by a lower and higher English course. The higher course in each language was to be the more demanding and it was expected that only the higher Irish course would be taught in those schools where the teachers were very fluent. The introduction of the lower course was intended to meet the problems of those teachers who had previously had little or no knowledge of Irish.

The conference also endorsed, with only slight modification, the practice introduced in 1922, of conducting infant class work between the hours of 10.30 and 2.00 through the medium of Irish 'where teachers are sufficiently qualified'.[106] The word 'sufficiently' expressed the relaxation, but what it meant in practice still remained open to question. Bilingual, or higher certificates were mentioned as indicative of what a 'sufficiently' qualified teacher might be and it was to be left to inspectors to decide in the actual circumstances if a teacher was so qualified or not. The problem remained, therefore, that many teachers could be pressurised into trying to teach through the medium of a language in which they were not very fluent. So, while the conference can hardly be blamed for the kind of pressure which was subsequently to be mounted in order to promote the teaching of Irish, its failure to specify clearly the qualification necessary to teach Irish at each of the two levels could be said to have been a serious omission.

No concessions whatsoever were afforded those who complained about the effects which the enhanced status for Irish had on schools and their curricula at secondary level. The reason for this can only be a matter for speculation. It probably lay in the fact that the Department of Education was not convinced that the new regulations imposed any undue burden, examination results in some schools notwithstanding. To require students to obtain a passing grade in Irish was probably seen as the minimum that could be asked in order to ensure that the language would be studied seriously at secondary level. Indeed, it would also have been expected that following upon several years of learning Irish at primary level, no serious difficulties would be encountered by students at secondary level. The introduction of the requirement to pass Irish had been timed to ensure that the first cohort of students affected would have had some primary school experience of the language. So, after 1928 it would have been anticipated that the problem would have eased considerably, if not entirely disappeared.

Answering Protestant fears

As far as the new administration in the Irish Free State was concerned, it did not accept that it was in any way motivated by an anti-Protestant bias in its pursuit of its Gaelicisation policy. Indeed, it could point to the fact that one of the most enthusiastic ministers in the government in this regard was Earnán de Blaghad, a northern Presbyterian and that many other Protestants, like Douglas Hyde, had enthusiastically participated in the early days of the language revival movement.[107] The government was also at pains to reassure the Protestant community of its future in the new state and of its desire to facilitate it in whatever manner might reasonably be expected. One of the first specific issues on which Protestant educationists confronted the Department of Education was their concern over what they claimed was the very Roman Catholic flavour of Irish language textbooks. These Kingsmill Moore described as a 'possible danger to our faith'.[108] Following an interview between a delegation from the Protestant churches and Eoin MacNeill, Kingsmill Moore wrote that 'the Minister gave the most ample promises of plenary protection and we passed away . . . reassured'.[109]

Later, in 1923 when the requirements of the new Irish programme for training colleges were posing difficulties for students at the Church of Ireland Training College, the minister sanctioned a modified programme specifically for that college.[110] Also, when many applicants to the college failed to reach the required grade in Irish in their entrance examination, permission was obtained for a number who had fallen below that grade to be accepted.[111] Fourthly, when the establishment of an Irish medium preparatory college for Protestant students was proposed in 1925, it was warmly welcomed as a means of answering the problem of student supply.[112] Finally, when in 1926, as has already been discussed above, the Second National Programme Conference agreed that national schools could follow either a 'high' Irish course, or a 'low' course, the immediate concerns of Protestant teachers who considered themselves lacking in proficiency could be said to have been met.

The course is set

By the end of the 1920s education in the Irish Free State, in the eyes of its policy makers, had been set firmly on a course on which it was to remain for almost the next 40 years. One overriding national aim had been determined for education, i.e. in the words of Ó Brolcháin 'the strengthening of the national fibre by giving the language, history, music and tradition of Ireland their natural place in the life of Irish schools'. The means of so doing were prescribed in the national programmes of 1921 and 1926 and in the new programmes for secondary schools published in 1924. Training college programmes had been suitably changed and Irish medium preparatory colleges established to ensure that future primary teachers would be adequately prepared to meet the demands of the new programme.

Alongside this education renewal went a strengthening of Catholic Church influence over education and over national life generally. This was to be seen more obviously in the deference shown to the church's attitude to school management and, in an issue not discussed in detail in this study, in the understanding given to the Catholic Church that the new vocational schools established under the 1930 Vocational Education Act would not be in competition with existing secondary schools in terms of the curricula they would provide.[113]

It is difficult, therefore, to agree with the view expressed by some commentators that some weakening in church influence over education had been achieved by the end of the 1920s.[114] It is true, however, that state control had become more direct following the abolition of the two boards and the creation of a Department of Education determined to exercise a strong influence over curricular matters. State influence was increased, but that did not necessarily mean a weakening of Catholic Church influence. It is, on the evidence adduced in this study, more accurate to describe the situation as one in which a clear understanding of their respective roles in education emerged between the Catholic Church and the new political authorities in the south. Ministers MacNeill and O'Sullivan admitted as much and church and state were, in fact, complementing each other in matters of control, management, finance and curriculum. To both, the overall impression can only have been that education in the south was at last in very safe hands.

6

Consolidating Reforms: Education
North and South in the 1930s

Ideological certainty

FOLLOWING the reforms of the 1920s education in both parts of Ireland entered a period of consolidation. The dominant ideologies of both states were, by the beginning of the 1930s, firmly established and their exponents more confident and more assertive of their position than in the previous decade. Unionism and its religious ally, Protestantism, had become firmly entrenched in Northern Ireland while in the south, nationalism and Catholicism were strengthening ties which had been evolving over a long period creating as they did so a public ethos which contrasted markedly with that which had been dominant under British rule. David Miller's[1] treatment of this alliance in the generation prior to 1920 demonstrates its strength, a strength which enabled it to withstand the dramatic changes of 1918–22 when first one, then a second rupture occurred in its political wing. The further strengthening of this relationship together with an intensification of measures to achieve within it a revived, Gaelic Ireland continued to be the developments most influential on education in the south.

If the public ethos of the south was evolving along Catholic and Gaelic lines, it was paralleled in the north by a strengthening of the Protestant–unionist alliance in a 'Protestant state for a Protestant people'. The virtual end to educational controversy involving the Protestant churches and the government which was marked by the 1930 act, meant that the latter's attention could be concentrated on developing the elementary school system along the lines laid down in that legislation and, in particular, concentrating on that section of the education service which had been transferred to the control of the new regional authorities.

The one outstanding matter which did give rise to controversy in this period was the question of Protestant church representation on the board of management of Stranmillis College of Education. Given the successful demand for representation on school management and regional committees by these same churches pressure now mounted for representation on the board of the college. At first, the government did not see this demand as at all justifiable since Stranmillis was a government-owned and government-funded institution from the outset, not one which owed anything, in a direct sense at least, to the churches. Notwithstanding this fact, the churches were once again to be successful in forcing concessions in line with their demands. Thereafter, relationships between the government and the Protestant churches became very cordial and were not to be disturbed until further proposals for educational reform emerged in the 1940s.

The only source of challenge to this relationship came from the Catholic–nationalist community. However, since the 1930 legislation had succeeded, to some extent at least, in meeting its immediate needs, pressure from the Catholic Church and nationalist political leaders eased somewhat as far as educational matters were concerned, though neither was to completely neglect opportunities of reminding the government about the 'sacrifices' and grievances which they claimed were being borne by their community in order to maintain a separate school system. A timely reinforcement for the Catholic Church's stand on education was the 1929 encyclical letter of Pope Pius XI, *The Christian education of youth*. Its importance in the northern context lay in its definitive restatement of traditional Catholic teaching on education, in particular, the Church's claim to full control over the education of young Catholics and its criticism of what were called 'modern aberrations'. Among the latter the encyclical listed 'co-education', described as 'a promiscuous herding together of males and females on a completely equal footing',[2] a criticism to which the church in Northern Ireland would soon appeal during a clash with the government over school amalgamations in 1934.

Consolidation in Northern Ireland

The background against which these developments were to take place in Northern Ireland was one which saw the new state attaining a considerably greater degree of political stability than many would have thought possible at its establishment. The campaign of violence conducted by the I.R.A. against the very existence of Northern Ireland was long over and nationalist politicians were playing a somewhat more active, or at least less negative role as an opposition in the Northern Ireland parliament. Only the increasingly bleak economic situation seemed to pose any threat to Northern Ireland's stability, but this was a crisis which Northern Ireland experienced together with other parts of the western world, though perhaps to a greater extent than most. Unemployment was extremely high, 30 per cent of the registered workforce in 1930, and set to rise throughout the decade.

Relationships with the south remained cool and became even cooler following de Valera's assumption of power in 1932. This event filled many unionists with foreboding, especially since de Valera's government was committed to removing those aspects of the 1921 Anglo-Irish Treaty to which he and his party had taken exception, a move which unionists feared could bring Northern Ireland's constitutional position once more into question. Consequently, as de Valera embarked on a number of such measures, unionists began raising a chorus of criticism directed both at the south and at London which reached its climax when the 1922 constitution was replaced with one of de Valera's own making in 1937.[3] In reality, any external threat to Northern Ireland's stability was small and the state was left by both the south and by Britain to look after itself. The phrase 'a Protestant parliament for a Protestant people' generally attributed to Northern Ireland's first Prime Minister, James Craig,[4] summarised the situation as many perceived it, both within the Protestant–unionist community itself and within the Catholic–nationalist community which had still not accepted either the state, or its institutions with any degree of enthusiasm. Denied any positive involvement in the Ireland which had emerged from the 1920–25 settlements, the Catholic–nationalist community had virtually turned in on itself, thereby intensifying its sense of grievance and alienation. As a result, a kind of communal self-sufficiency evolved which was most manifest in the Catholic educational and medical services, in Gaelic sport and in cultural activities connected with the Irish language, music and dancing.

In terms of relationships with the Protestant–unionist community in this very non-ecumenical age, Catholics tended to be strengthened by a sense of religious 'superiority' derived from their church's claim to be the 'one, true Church of Christ' from which all others had deviated to a greater or lesser extent. This notion was probably nowhere more emphatically expressed at this time than in remarks by Cardinal MacRory in 1931 when he attempted to refute claims by the Church of Ireland to be in direct descent from the church established by St Patrick. In the course of his remarks the cardinal asserted, to the considerable applause of his audience, that 'the Protestant Church in Ireland . . . is not only not the rightful representative of the Early Irish Church, but it is not even a part of the Church of Christ'.[5]

Politically, the isolation of the Catholic–nationalist community was marked by the fate of its representation in parliament. There nationalist politicians continued to make their most notable impact when giving voice to the grievances and sacrifices which they claimed their constituents bore, however vain their protests. Education, the Irish language, traditional parades, Irish unity and the operation of electoral law were the issues on which they were at their most eloquent. A high point in the expression of nationalist grievances during the 1930s was the 'minority rights' motion moved by nationalist members in 1934. The substance of the motion, which alleged a systematic abrogation of minority rights in Northern Ireland included what Cahir Healy called 'penalties in education'.[6] Like all motions from nationalist M.P.s, it achieved nothing in practical terms and is most memorable because it was in his response to this motion that Prime Minister Craig made his oft quoted statement about a 'Protestant parliament serving a Protestant people'.

Hopes betrayed

If, at the beginning of the 1930s, relationships between the two main communities in Northern Ireland were distant, they still remained to be placed on a completely even keel within the Protestant–unionist community itself. Although Protestant church representation on the board of Stranmillis was not an issue with the same popular impact as those which had precipitated the 1930 act, the campaign to achieve such representation would once again demonstrate the political influence of these churches. The case of the Protestant churches was based on the fact that Stranmillis was *de facto* Protestant and that the churches were, thereby, entitled to representation, the legal status of the college as a non-denominational government-owned institution notwithstanding. Apart from a few Roman Catholics who had attended in its early years, Stranmillis was indeed overwhelmingly Protestant in its student body and the same was true of its staff. In practice, therefore, the function of the college was to educate the teachers who would serve in schools catering for the Protestant community. Consequently the Protestant churches argued that, as the Roman Catholic community had its own female college, St Mary's in Belfast and since Catholic male teachers were trained, at government expense, at a Catholic college in London, equity demanded a Protestant voice on the governing body of Stranmillis.

At first, Lord Charlemont agreed to this request[7] but later, under pressure from some cabinet colleagues he withdrew his offer for representation, dismissed the Committee on the Training of Teachers and placed the college directly under the Ministry of Education to remove the need for any intermediate management-type body upon which representation could be sought. The minister then offered the Protestant churches places on an advisory committee which would be consulted on matters pertaining to the religious and moral education of students, but the churches were not to be satisfied with anything less than a direct voice in the direction of the college.

Ministry of Education papers reveal just how carefully the case against granting the Protestant churches' demand for representation was prepared, once the minister had decided to adopt this stand. In a very detailed and cogently argued memorandum to the cabinet, Charlemont began with the surprising admission that, 'the Education (amending) Act, 1930, was in some respects a step back towards denominationalism . . .'[8] The minister feared that granting the representation requested by the churches would reinforce this development, arguing that representation could not be justified since the college was in complete public ownership. Another fear was that, should the Roman Catholic Church ever decide to permit attendance at Stranmillis for Catholic students, priests might have to be put on this committee. Then, revealing the constant government fear of what a reopening of fundamental issues might lead to, he argued:

. . . They [i.e. the Catholic Church] might make it the grounds for a review of the whole administration of the Education Act especially with regard to the alleged denominationalism of 'Simple Bible Teaching'.[9]

Charlemont's memorandum is remarkable in a number of respects. It reveals first of all a degree of very clear thinking about his government's stand on church–state relations in educational matters. Most significantly he admits that the educational structures of the public sector, i.e. the system of transferred and provided schools, in Northern Ireland had been 're-denomi-nationalised' as a result of the amendments to the 1923 act and that this exposed the government to the accusation that the schools serving the Protestant community were being more favourably treated than those serving the Roman Catholic community. Doing anything which might reopen this controversy should, he argued, be avoided at all costs. Charlemont's compromise to ensure against this, the recommendation that the churches be offered places on the proposed advisory committee, was rejected by the latter's Joint Education Committee as totally inadequate. In his reply on behalf of the committee, William Corkey claimed that proposing to restrict the Protestant churches to an advisory role amounted to:

. . . a fundamental change of policy from that which the Government has already adopted towards the Roman Catholic Church . . . To refuse the representatives . . . is to place the Protestant churches in a totally different relationship to the training of Protestant teachers from that which they occupied before the Northern Government was set up and to deny to them very much less than what has already been granted to the Roman Catholic Church.[10]

Once again Corkey's argument ignored the fact that the relationship between the Protestant churches and the government had been profoundly changed when the former agreed to transfer their schools to the regional committees. Their position was no longer comparable to that of the Roman Catholic Church which had not transferred any of its schools and by not doing so accepted that it had to raise a proportion of the capital expenditure for those schools. Basing his stand on a demand for parity of treatment he proceeded to attack the minister's offer of places on a restructured advisory committee on the training of teachers in the following terms:

In as much as it is intended that the Principal of the Training College is to give Bible instruction . . . the United Committee of the Protestant Churches wishes to know to what extent the work of the Principal of the College will be under the jurisdiction of the proposed enlarged committee and what voice the Representatives of the Committee will have in the appointment of a new Principal should a vacancy arise.[11]

Corkey went on, in his reply, to focus on the question of 'orthodoxy' in the teaching of history, a matter in which he had long taken an interest, particularly when it came to the question of Irish history:

. . . the United Education Committee wishes to know what relationship will obtain between the members of the teaching staff and the new enlarged committee. If a lecturer on History teaches his subject so as to weaken or undermine the loyalty of his class to those ideals for which the Protestant people of Ulster have stood in the past will this enlarged Departmental committee, in such a case, have jurisdiction and will it share in the making of appointments to the staff of the college and will these matters be dealt with solely by the officials of the Ministry.[12]

Corkey and his United Committee were, in effect, arguing for the closest possible relationship between the Protestant churches and the government in the provision of all major educational services in Northern Ireland. When direct representations to Charlemont failed to yield the desired results, the United Committee once again resorted to an appeal to the Orange movement and to unionist public opinion. The result was that the Prime Minister, who, at first, had responded to Corkey by rejecting his demands,[13] and another minister, J.E. Andrews, took the initiative over Charlemont's head and agreed with the United Committee to meet its demand for three places on a reconstituted management committee.[14]

The Stranmillis affair marked the high point of Protestant clerical influence over education in Northern Ireland. As a result not only was this influence present at local and regional levels through school and regional educational committees, but it was now present in the committee managing teacher education for the Protestant community. This was a clear indication, that unionism depended upon and needed organised Protestantism to sustain it.

Calmer waters

Following the Stranmillis concessions, relationships between the government and the Protestant churches entered a period of calm which endured until the early forties. As far as both were concerned, therefore, the educational record of the decade was one of gradual progress within the framework agreed to in the 1930 act. In urban areas, particularly in the eastern counties, schools were transferred at a fairly constant pace, new schools were built, curriculum development of a modest kind was attempted[15] and discussion began to focus on the needs of secondary education. Belfast, as the largest authority, gave a lead by providing sixteen new schools and by reconditioning and enlarging many more in the city in the period 1930–40. The vigour of the city's educational authority must have impressed the attractions of transfer on school managers because, apart from the Roman Catholic schools in the city, only eleven others had not been transferred by the end of the decade; this meant that over two-thirds of the city's schools were being managed by the local authority by 1940.[16] Elsewhere, the pace of transfer was much slower, particularly in the west, leading the ministry to comment in its annual report for 1932–33:

It is much to be regretted that voluntary managers in the north-west of the province do not take more advantage of the system of transfer. It is the considered policy of Roman Catholic managers to retain their schools as voluntary schools, but it was thought that the objections of other religious denominations to transfer had been removed by the Act of 1930.[17]

It is difficult to identify the precise reasons why schools were not transferred more rapidly in some areas. A natural conservatism amongst managers, an unwillingness to part with something which had been part of a particular community for generations and the absence of energetic educational authorities such as that in Belfast, rather than any serious differences of principle probably explain the reluctance to transfer. Whatever the precise causes, the effect was that by 1938, a considerable majority of the elementary schools remained under voluntary control; 1,074 as against 653 in the 'provided' and 'transferred' category.[18] It was to be a considerable time before the latter categories were to comprise the majority of schools serving the Protestant community .

Boys and girls still don't mix

While the disadvantages which the Roman Catholic Church saw itself enduring continued to be a focus for public comment by church and political leaders of that community, the one issue to renew open conflict between the government and the Catholic Church in the thirties arose following a decision by the Ministry of Education in 1934 to oblige the amalgamation of adjoining boys' and girls' schools where combined enrolments were less than 50.[19] Like the Board of National Education some 30 years previously, the ministry argued that such amalgamations made both educational and economic sense. However, once again these arguments were rejected by the Catholic Church and in October 1934, in the diocese of Down and Connor, school managers resolved to 'oppose by every means in our power all such attempts at amalgamating our Catholic Boys' and Catholic Girls' Schools'.[20] In parliament, nationalist politicians echoed the protest and argued that the policy of amalgamation was part of a more general policy of hostility to Catholic education. Speaking on behalf of those politicians Senator Thomas McLaughlin pointed out that amalgamation had been opposed and condemned by Pope Pius XI in his recent encyclical letter on education and pledged:

. . . that any action the managers of their Catholic schools may decide to take should the Ministry persist in their efforts to amalgamate Catholic boys' and girls' schools will have their entire and wholehearted support.[21]

It mattered nothing that the ministry claimed amalgamation would enable schools to be better organised and pupils better taught, or that Cardinal Patrick O'Donnell, when a member of the vice-regal committee in 1918, had accepted a similar recommendation.[22] Bishop Mageean dismissed the suggestion of any inconsistency in the church's approach[23] while an editorial in the *Irish News* quoted from the encyclical that 'false and harmful to Christian education was the so-called method of co-education' and added 'that for Catholics "when Rome has spoken the case is ended" '.[24] In a special address on the issue, Bishop Mageean argued that economy and efficiency were not the real reasons for amalgamation[25] and, accusing the authorities of discrimination, claimed that Catholics were already making sufficient sacrifices since only £75,000 had been spent on the Catholic elementary school population compared with £1,059,202 on pupils in the public (Protestant) sector. To the bishop, amalgamation was aimed at further reducing expenditure on Catholic schools by cutting the number of Catholic teachers who would be required.

This controversy which filled the pages of the nationalist press in the closing months of 1934, exemplified the continuing sense of grievance within the Catholic–nationalist community and how little it took to bring it to the surface. It was in the midst of this particular controversy that Cahir Healy tabled his minority rights motion in Stormont claiming that the Northern Irish government was systematically denying such rights, not least in matters of education.[26] In response, government and unionist members reiterated that if Catholics wanted to receive additional finances for their school they should avail of the 'four-and-two' management system, or else transfer their schools to local authority control. Since neither had become any more viable as options, as far as the Catholic Church was concerned, the argument continued in this ritualised fashion throughout the thirties and beyond. On the question of amalgamation itself, the ministry, faced with such concerted opposition, did not force the issue in the case of Catholic schools.

New focus

As the temperature lowered over matters affecting elementary education, attention focused on the situation at secondary level. Under the 1923 act, reform at this level had been minimal since neither structural, nor curricular innovation had been seriously recommended by the Lynn Committee. Beyond making it illegal to operate secondary schools for profit and encouraging local authorities to make a greater provision of scholarships for needy and promising pupils, nothing was done to interfere with the conduct of secondary education as it had been determined in 1879. As in the south a ministry had replaced the intermediate commissioners and the number of examinations offered at this level reduced to two, 'junior' and 'senior'. With the focus of attention almost exclusively on elementary education until the early thirties, the ministry felt it had enough concerns without having to also address the whole question of secondary education. So, when in 1926, the Board of Education's *Report on the education of the adolescent*[27] was published in England with its recommendations for extending opportunities for secondary education, the issue was not considered appropriate to Northern Ireland at the time, as the ministry's Advisory Committee on Education curtly and rather disingenuously stated, for reasons 'of finance'.[28]

It was not until the calm had settled on elementary education and significant increases in enrolments at secondary level were being noted that active consideration began to be given to reforming the secondary sector. The 1932–33 report of the Ministry of Education indicated that over the preceding five years the numbers entering for the 'senior' examination had trebled and those for the 'junior' had increased by 80 per cent[29] while four years later, the ministry's report revealed a very significant increase of 3,584 pupils in secondary schools, bringing the total enrolled in the 73 recognised schools to over 13,000.[30] As this increase became apparent and as education authorities in Britain began making wider provision for secondary schooling, the case for similar moves in Northern Ireland became more popular. Among those most enthusiastically advocating secondary education for all was the young and energetic republican socialist M.P., Harry Midgley whose political fortunes were eventually to turn 180 degrees bringing him into the Unionist Party and the post of Minister for Education in the early fifties. In the thirties, however, Midgley was entering his most socialist phase arguing, as far as education was concerned, that there was a need to make good 'the dearth of opportunity for secondary education'[31] and to provide direct support for families 'who are desirous of allowing their children to have the benefit of a secondary education and who are willing to make some sacrifice to achieve that'.[32]

1938 act

The government's response was a modest amendment to existing legislation whereby the school leaving age could be raised to fifteeen. The 1938 Education Act was generally welcomed as necessary in itself, but also because it was in line with the general unionist desire to keep developments in Northern Ireland in parallel with those in Britain where the school leaving age had been raised for England and Wales in 1936. As the parliamentary secretary to the Minister of Education, Dehra Parker, stated the act was intended to provide broad 'parity with England' while at the same time making some allowances for relevant local conditions.[33] The local conditions she had in mind related to the need for agricultural labour and the fact that not all parents might wish their children to remain on at school. Provision was therefore made in the legislation for 'half-time' attendance at technical or agricultural classes. In the event the act, which was scheduled to come into effect for the 1939–40 school year became a 'dead letter' because of the outbreak of war in September 1939.[34] Secondary reform was, as a result, postponed and when it eventually took place after the war, it was not merely to be a matter of raising the leaving age, it was also to involve a major reshaping of the whole educational system, an objective which, not unexpectedly, contained the seeds of considerable controversy.

Religious and political grievances re-emerge

Despite the relative mildness of the 1938 act, debate on it revealed the ease with which the ever strained politico-religious dimensions to education in Northern Ireland could surface. Although not reaching the level of earlier controversies, debate on the proposed legislation provided another opportunity for reminders that Catholic demands remained unsatisfied. Nationalist members of the Commons expressed concern at the additional costs which their community would have to bear to provide extra accommodation. Once again, proposed changes were represented as part of a general conspiracy to undermine Catholic schools with one leading nationalist M.P. rather bluntly stating:

This latest burden is rubbing salt into the sores and wounds already inflicted as a matter of deliberate statecraft on the voluntary schools of the Catholic people of Northern Ireland.[35]

The vehemence with which some of the views were articulated is again striking, revealing just how acute the sense of bitterness was and how absolute was the stand taken. As Richard Byrne M.P. for the Falls constituency, put it:

We have to suffer on account of our religion, but we will never surrender the right which Catholic children have to be taught in Catholic schools by Catholic teachers and under Catholic management. We will not surrender that right. It is unfair to penalise us because of our religion. Our religion is very near and dear to us, but we have no objection to other members of the community getting privileges provided they are suffering from any disadvantage.[36]

Renewed attack on Irish

Linked to the complaint about the financial treatment of Catholic schools was the continuing concern about the treatment of the Irish language and of Irish culture generally within the school programme for Northern Ireland, a concern which was heightened by a particularly petty decision in 1933. In that year the Minister of Education announced the withdrawal of the grant for the teaching of Irish as an extra subject in elementary schools because, as his parliamentary secretary, John Robb, stated:

. . . a comparatively insignificant number of those schools which might be expected to avail themselves of the privilege of studying Irish have done so, not more probably than one in every seven schools under Roman Catholic management.[37]

Nationalist politicians bitterly attacked the announcement and in his reply Robb made no attempt to hide what was a commonly expressed unionist attitude to Irish when he spoke about the 'considerations which influence the Ministry in drawing a distinction between Irish and *useful* [author's italics] modern languages such as French and German'.[38]

It is difficult to perceive what objective justification there was for the ministry's decision. The main aim of the decision, according to Robb, was to reduce expenditure but since it amounted to only £1,500 the saving was minimal, even at 1933 prices. Also, since the teaching of Irish was regularly commended by the inspectors for the high standards achieved, there did not appear to have been any pressing educational reasons that could be cited for withdrawing the grant. The 1928–29 report of the Ministry of Education, for example, had stated that 'Irish is taught in 77 schools as an extra and in many others as an ordinary subject. The teachers are interested in the subject and the work is earnest and efficient'.[39] The 1929–30 report stated that 'Irish is conducted with earnestness and with success'[40] while in the 1930–31 report, it was noted that 'Irish is a voluntary subject . . . the teaching is generally successful'.[41]

Welcomed by unionists, the withdrawal of the grant was inevitably seen by nationalists as another attack on the place of Irish and of the Gaelic heritage generally in the school programme. In the years that followed the issue surfaced regularly in educational debates, inside and outside parliament. One unionist politician rather dramatically illustrated unionist attitudes on the Irish language when he said, 'If I were to go up the Shankill Road and said I was going to learn Irish I would be excommunicated and shot. It would be looked upon as a terrible crime if I were to learn Irish'.[42] Another unionist M.P. claimed that 'the only people interested in this language are the people who are the avowed enemies of Northern Ireland'[43] while an editorial in the *Belfast Telegraph* was contemptuous of the value of learning Irish and supportive of the government's action in withdrawing the grant for teaching the language:

. . . it cannot be claimed that it confers any practical advantage upon the pupil in fitting him to take up a career in the world of business. It is one of the matters as to which the instinct of parents regarding the future of their children may be relied upon as a safe guide. The test as regards this province is conclusive . . . very little advantage has been taken of the privilege [of teaching Irish] . . . One of the worst features about the teaching of Gaelic in the primary schools is that it is likely to produce a number of boys and girls who have a smattering in two languages but are really proficient in neither . . . The action of the Ulster government must on the whole be held to be both necessary and justifiable.[44]

If unionists believed Irish to be a 'dead' language, one which did not confer 'any practical advantage' and one which should not be taught in 'our schools', and the learning of it an act of 'betrayal', nationalists held it to be part of their very birthright. To the latter the decision to withdraw the annual grant was a further injustice against their community. So, when government representatives argued that it was an economic measure and part of a general cost-cutting exercise affecting most areas of public expenditure, their arguments were dismissed as anti-Irish and the right of Irish children to learn their heritage pleaded instead:

Anyone who feels that Ireland, North and South, is his country takes pride in things appertaining to the Irish . . . if a child desires to be taught Irish, by all means let him use his discretion as to what value the language may be to him.[45]

In the southern state the pressure on schools to promote Irish was being intensified at this time and this may well have been a factor influencing unionists who were opposed to any association with a cultural programme now so intimately part of political life there. There was, therefore, no relenting in the face of nationalist opposition; £1,500 was saved and community relations suffered another blow.

'Catholicising' the south

In his treatise *Framework of a Christian state*, Edward Cahill pointed out that the 1922 Irish constitution had placed the state in a less than perfect relationship with the church.[46] Thus, he argued, '. . . any one of the fundamental rights or laws of the Church, such as on the question of divorce or birth control, may at any time be discussed and voted upon in the legislative body'.[47] This situation was, he went on to claim, 'manifestly not the ideal' and he feared that in addition to divorce and birth control becoming issues of church–state conflict, education could also give rise to friction.[48] Dealing with education in Ireland under the British regime he re-echoed many earlier Catholic voices, notably Cardinal Cullen's, in claiming that government policy had been essentially a 'secularising' one, 'the outcome of unChristian Liberalism'.[49] While Cahill conceded that the Irish educational system had improved over the years, he also argued that:

It would be an error to suppose that the system as it stands is perfect or free from danger. Neither the present system of primary education, nor the technical or vocational schools, nor (indeed much less) the Irish University system, nor even the Secondary system . . . realise the ideals of Catholic education . . . hence one may hope that they now be gradually refashioned in accordance with the full Catholic ideal.[50]

As events were soon to prove Cahill had no great need to worry as far as the south was concerned. The new Fianna Fail government appeared even more enthusiastic than its predecessor about upholding the importance of religion in education. Indeed, in front of an international audience during the World Education Conference held in Dublin in 1933, de Valera emphasised that:

. . . the beginning and end of true education, is the development of religious and moral character. It would be worse than useless to teach young people the nature and properties of material things around them if we fail to teach them to know and conform to the purpose that these things subserve . . . It is not force nor fear nor the sense of common material interests that bind man to man. It is the knowledge that they are children of one father, bound by the same law and destined to the same end.[51]

The constitution which de Valera was soon to prepare and which was adopted in 1937 stressed the point more emphatically by including virtually all Cahill's characteristics of the 'Catholic' state in some of its key articles. Catholic social teaching is most clearly in evidence in those articles of the constitution which set out fundamental law on *The family* (art. 41), *Education* (art. 42) and in the section entitled *Directive principles of social policy* (art. 45), as well as in the special position which the constitution as a whole afforded the Catholic Church (art. 44). On education, the constitution's provisions were formulated in very close parallel to the terms of the encyclical of Pope Pius XI. For example, art. 42.1 of the constitution recognises that :

. . . the primary and natural educator of the child is the Family and recognises the inalienable right and duty of parents to provide, according to their means, for the religious and moral, intellectual, physical and social education of their children.[52]

This bears close resemblance to para. 38 of the papal encyclical which states:

Parents are bound by a very grave obligation to care for the religious, moral, physical and civic education of their children to the best of their power, and also to provide for their temporal welfare.[53]

The sentiments are so similar as to suggest a very clear dependence of the former upon the latter. The same is true of the succeeding paragraphs of this article leading to the conclusion that careful note of the encyclical must have been taken by those drafting the constitution to ensure the kind of outcome for which Cahill was arguing. The political leadership of the south was obviously intent on ensuring that the principles underlying the state's school system would explicitly reflect as closely as possible those expounded by the Catholic Church.

Despite these very Catholic overtones to sections of the 1937 constitution, there remained within the church a number of prominent voices unhappy with the formal situation regarding church–state relationships in education. Their concern arose from the fact that, the constitutional position notwithstanding, legally schools were not regarded as formally denominational. Among those so concerned was the future Bishop of Cork, Cornelius Lucy, who claimed that while the state might be well disposed towards the Catholic Church's view of education '. . . this is due altogether to the goodwill of the personnel of the Department of Education, not to the letter of the law . . . What we want is a system giving us both the legal forms and the reality of Catholic education'.[54] Lucy reflected a concern very widespread within the Catholic Church of the time to limit state power and influence over education to the most minimal degree possible. The existing situation, he argued, left the church in control of school property, but not of the programmes provided therein,[55] a somewhat exaggerated point since the church also exercised complete control over the teaching staff and, presumably, also over the textbooks chosen in each school it managed. The likelihood of many ideas not approved of by the church being communicated to pupils in its schools was extremely remote.

Vocationalism and education

Dr Lucy was also closely involved in promoting the one major attempt to restructure public life in the south along lines even more central to contemporary Catholic social thinking than had been indicated in the 1937 constitution: the Commission on Vocational Organisation. It was an attempt which did not succeed because in the event the Commission's proposals were largely disregarded. Nevertheless, in the context of this study it deserves some mention, not least because of demands, which long pre-dated the commission, for a 'council of education' to which the commission gave some support and which were eventually to be conceded in the late forties.

The concept of vocational organisation, or corporatism, would, in its fullest sense, have meant the creation of new political structures alongside, or possibly in place of, those of the south's parliamentary system. A series of councils in which representation would be achieved on the basis of vocational organisations, rather than on the basis of a popular mandate would be established. Such councils would provide a means of giving formal representation to the major sectional interests in Irish society, e.g. agriculture, industry, commerce, education etc. The concept was one which had received considerable support in another encyclical letter of Pope Pius XI, *Quadragesimo anno*[56] because of the emphasis it placed on different sections of society, below the level of government, taking responsibility for their own affairs. 'Subsidiarity', as this form of responsibility was termed, had a particular appeal to a church opposed to what it saw as the growth of state power with its encroachments into such areas as education for which the church itself claimed a special responsibility.

Lucy was one of the Catholic churchmen in Ireland who strongly advocated 'vocationalism' and, in particular, its application to education through the establishment of a council of education[57] claiming that within a vocational structure the school system could become truly Catholic. He argued that 'every class, from chimney sweeps to golf professionals . . . has a right to a say in the education provided for their children' and a guild in which they would be represented as parents would give them this say.[58] A council of education, Lucy further claimed, would be 'a powerful intermediary between state and schools and would provide greater protection for church interests than the current arrangement does'.[59] Lucy's concern was not, therefore, confined to providing a voice for those whom he believed to be denied one. He was also concerned to ensure that the Catholic Church's role in education remained impregnable in the face of any attempt to infringe it by the state.

The considerable interest which vocationalism attracted in church and lay circles in the mid and late thirties resulted in the government 's decision, in 1939, to establish the commission referred to above. It was a commission chaired by Dr Michael Browne, Bishop of Galway and, as Whyte comments, its establishment was a further indication that 'Fianna Fail as well as other parties had been affected by the growing interest in Ireland in Catholic Social Teaching'.[60] The implications of its recommendations for education will be discussed in chapter 8.

By and large the Catholic Church was well pleased by what had been achieved in the thirties, certainly as far as education was concerned. The new constitution had entrenched the same basic educational principles as it held itself and, in practice, left the essential powers of managing Catholic schools in its hands. As Fr M. Brennan, a prominent commentator of the period, wrote, the system was 'almost perfect from the Church's point of view' and while the primary schools may be in principle 'undenominational', they were very much the opposite in practice.[61]

Intensely Gaelicising

If the case for promoting Irish fell on deaf ears in the north, it was the one issue to continually dominate educational debate in the south throughout the 1930s. While the policy of reviving Irish retained broad support across the political parties and very intense support from Fianna Fail, the decade was also to witness the emergence in several quarters of persistent criticism of several aspects of that policy. Not least to offer such criticism were the teachers. By the beginning of the decade it was being realised that promoting Irish to the point of it being widely adopted was an extremely difficult objective to achieve. Teachers, having been placed in the vanguard of this process were amongst those most loudly calling for a rethink as motions to their annual conferences were revealing. School principals too voiced their concerns, while the main Protestant churches again found themselves obliged to debate motions on the issue at their annual meetings. The Catholic Church remained generally sympathetic to the language with several more voices endorsing the belief that Gaelicisation held out the prospect of a society whose culture would be insulated from the malign influences of an increasingly materialistic world. As one contemporary Catholic writer, Michael Geraghty S.J. discussing the need to combat the 'idols of modern society' stated 'we look to our statesmen to devise a scheme of education that shall be true to the traditions of the Gael . . . '[62]

As for the Department of Education, working within the framework of the revival policy laid down since 1922, it continued to maintain an optimistic outlook which proclaimed that considerable progress was possible and was being achieved. In its report for 1931–32 the extent to which the policy of Gaelicising education had progressed was statistically highlighted: 40 per cent of teachers at primary level were reported as holding certificates attesting their competence to teach through the medium of Irish, while another 32 per cent, although not so certificated, were reported as claiming that they could.[63] To the department this was significant progress, given that a majority of teachers had commenced their careers before 1922 when no general requirement on teaching through Irish was in force. Progress at secondary level was measured, among other factors, by the increase in the number of schools classified as 'A' or 'B', the former being all-Irish medium and the latter offering some subjects through the medium of Irish. Their number had reached 34 and 71 respectively, a significant increase from the virtual non-existence of such schools in 1922. As an inducement to enter category 'A', schools now received an extra 25 per cent on their capitation while category 'B' schools could receive up to 10 per cent extra depending on the number of subjects offered through the medium of Irish. For schools not generally well endowed financially such additional funds were very attractive indeed and sufficient inducement to promote Irish. The increase in Irish medium schools was , as a result, probably not entirely motivated by a disinterested commitment to promoting the language.

The zeal and commitment of the department for promoting Irish can be gauged in the very pointed criticism directed at certain secondary schools, not directly named, which were not regarded as being as supportive of the policy as they were expected to be. Singled out for particular mention were what the 1931–32 report called the 'great' boys' schools for 'not committing themselves to teaching through Irish'. Such schools would have also been noted for their continued enthusiasm for 'British' games like rugby and cricket and would have included not just schools of the Protestant community but perhaps more significantly, certain Catholic schools from which more enthusiasm for Irish might have been expected. In order to encourage these schools to be more positive in their approach, it was recommended that they be specifically asked:

(a) How many of the teaching staff were qualified to teach through Irish.
(b) What were the subjects that could be taught through Irish by these teachers.
(c) What were the chief obstacles against the spread of such instruction.[64]

In the same year a Department of Education circular on *Teaching through the medium of Irish* spelt out clearly what was expected. The circular indicated :

. . . (a) that the aim of the programme is to secure the full use of Irish as the teaching medium in all schools as soon as possible; (b) that the use of Irish as the teaching medium is now obligatory when the teacher is competent to give the instruction and the pupils are able to assimilate the instruction so given . . .[65]

While the circular attempted to allay some of the apprehension which had arisen about the use of Irish as a teaching medium by pointing out that Irish should not be used unless both the teacher and the pupils were able to use and understand it, the main message was the desire to move as quickly as possible to a situation where Irish would be so used. In its implementation of government policy the Department of Education was adopting what might be described as a 'missionary' approach to the aim of 'Gaelicising' education, one that was to become even more obvious with Fianna Fail's advent to office the following year. That party's first Minister of Education, Tom Derrig, became noted for his zealous commitment to Gaelicisation, frequently emphasising that the ultimate objective as far as Irish in education was concerned was:

. . . an Ghaedhilg do chur in usáid i ndiaidh a chéile i múineadh na nadhbhar scríte, taobh amuigh den Bhéarla, go dtí go mbéadh ar chumas na leanbhaí uile ins na scoileanna teagasc na nadhbhar uile do ghlacadh tríd an nGaedhilg. [Irish to be gradually used in the teaching of the written subjects, apart from English, until the children would be able to receive instruction in all subjects through Irish][66]

He was convinced that '. . . the effort to revive Irish as a spoken language rests very largely with our schools . . . It is through their instrumentality that we hope to achieve success'.[67] This belief that education had to be the primary means by which Irish would be revived places him in the same school of thought as Pearse and Corcoran and, as Minister of Education, he believed that he had considerable power to influence the pace at which education could be made to carry out this task.

Fianna Fail's enthusiasm

Fianna Fail in office was only too anxious to build upon what had been achieved and to be seen to respond to the pressure which several Dáil members, keen supporters of the revival movement, were bringing to bear in the issue. T.D.s like Eamon Ó Néill and Donnchadh Ó Briain, the latter a former secretary of the Gaelic League, regularly expressed the view that not enough was being achieved and reminded their colleagues and the government that the ultimate object was the complete Gaelicisation of Irish society. Stressing the need for greater effort, Ó Néill claimed that despite ten years of effort the results had not been very significant:

Is é rud ata uaim ná Éire do Ghaolú agus is baol liom ná déanfar í do Ghaolú go deo mara ndeinimid brostú. Tá deich mbliana do mhor-shaothar caithte againn agus cad tá againn dá bharr? Gan an Ghaedhilg de bheith a lábhairt ach ag fíor-bheagán dos na leanbhaí nuair a bhíonn siad ag fagaint na scoileanna.[What I want is for Ireland to be Gaelicised and I fear that it will never be Gaelicised if we do not make haste. We have spent ten years of great effort and what have we to show for it but very little? Irish is spoken but by a very few children when they are leaving school.][68]

Ó Briain saw the revival of Irish as part of a language conflict in which English had gained the upper hand and felt that it was the minister's responsibility to reverse the situation:

Chaithfear chuimheamh i gcomhnuidhe go bhfuil an dá thangain ag troid i n-aghaidh a chéile, go bhfuil an lámh uachtar ag an mBéarla go fóill agus go bhfuil an Ghaedhilg i mbaoghal a caillte . . . [It must always be remembered that the two languages are in conflict against each other, that English presently has the upper hand and that Irish is in danger of its life][69]

and

Tá dualgas thar aon dualgas eile ar an Aire . . . sé sin an Ghaedhilg do chur in uachtar. Má theipeann air sin do dhéanamh is cuma cad eile a dhéanfaoi le oideachas . . . [There is one duty above any other duty on the Minister . . . that is to put Irish 'on top'. If he fails to do this it does not matter what else might be done with education][70]

Outside of the Oireachtas (Irish Parliament) pressure was maintained by the Gaelic League, a deputation from which in March 1933 argued that even if Ireland became politically and economically free, the historic Irish nation would be dead if the language died.[71] Spurred on by such pressure and claiming that he himself 'was not satisfied with the progress which was being made in Irish'[72] Derrig determined that efforts should be intensified in order to achieve more satisfactory results, overriding as he did the grave concerns of many teachers. A wide range of measures were adopted with the aim of creating more opportunities within the curriculum for teaching Irish. Among these measures was the withdrawal of the 'lower' Irish course introduced following the Second National Programme Conference in 1926,[73] thus reverting to the situation which had pertained from 1922–26 when Irish had been the required medium of instruction in infant classes. To create more curricular time for Irish the scope of the English programme for national schools was reduced and parts of the mathematics and rural science programmes rendered optional.[74] Non-curricular measures included special incentives for young people from Gaeltacht areas to apply for places in the preparatory colleges. Located in, or close to Gaeltacht areas, the preparatory colleges had been attracting students from these areas since their establishment in 1926. To increase this supply the Department of Education decided that the percentage of places reserved for native speakers of Irish would be raised from 25 to 40 per cent, while a further 40 per cent of the places was allocated to candidates fluent in Irish whatever their origin, but for which Gaeltacht applicants would obvioulsy have a distinct advantage.[75] An increase in candidates from Gaeltacht areas was also being encouraged by the introduction of grants to cover their travel and clothing requirements while the teachers of successful candidates in these areas would qualify for a special bonus.[76]

As a result of these measures a significant increase in the number of Gaeltacht candidates presenting themselves for the entrance examination to preparatory colleges was achieved, from 100 in 1931 to 329 in 1934 and an increase was also recorded in the percentage successful, 51 per cent in 1934 compared to 42 per cent in 1933.[77] The fact that a high percentage of the future supply of teachers was being sought from one kind of background and with one particular criterion in mind was not seen in any sense as unbalanced, or inimical to the most effective choice of student-teachers. The Gaelicisation of the teaching profession was further underlined by the new programme introduced into the teacher training colleges in 1932 requiring that Irish be the normal medium of instruction for all aspects of that programme and for all normal intercourse in the life of the colleges.[78]

The Gaeltacht was the focus for another initiative, quite innovative in terms of support for any language, the introduction of a direct annual payment, known in Irish as the 'deontas' (subsidy), for every child of primary school-going age in an Irish speaking family that was registered as such. It was an additional form of child subsidy, based not on economic need, but on the claim that the language of the home was Irish. The intention was to encourage families to continue using Irish and thereby to counter the process of Anglicisation in the remaining Irish speaking areas.[79]

At secondary level, the teaching and use of Irish were encouraged by extending the requirement to pass in Irish in order to be awarded the Leaving Certificate and by basing capitation grants on the number of pupils in a school following courses in the language.[80] Both regulations placed considerable pressure on schools to ensure that Irish was taught to all classes and to the highest level, since, on the one hand, parents would be anxious to ensure that their children would obtain a school leaving certificate and, on the other, school authorities would be anxious to obtain the maximum possible financial assistance from the department. A further practical incentive to the teaching of Irish was the decision to make some proficiency in the language a requirement for appointments in the public service.[81] Since most secondary schools regarded it as one of their responsibilities to prepare pupils for civil service examinations this regulation placed an additional importance on the teaching of Irish. In order to encourage secondary school teachers to teach their specialisms through the medium of Irish, the Department of Education suggested to the Registration Council for Secondary Teachers that competency in Irish become a requirement for all future registrations.

The council agreed and decided to include a test in oral Irish as part of the registration requirements of all entrants to secondary teaching from 1942.[82]

All these measures were attempts to ensure that Irish would be taught not just from a sense of patriotic fervour, but out of practical necessity – the necessity to obtain educational qualifications, to obtain a job or, as in the case of the 'deontas', to meet day-to-day family needs. Resorting to such material inducements may appear to fit uncomfortably alongside the rhetoric of patriotism and national renewal. However, behind their introduction lay a recognition that language change required some practical motivation. Practical need had contributed significantly to the abandonment of Irish and so it seemed logical to make practical need part, at least, of the motive for reviving the language. But logical as this might have seemed and however generous the inducements offered, the need for Irish was never likely to become so overwhelming as to outweigh the benefits which the people of Ireland continued to associate with English in their day-to-day activities.

While the language remained central to the whole Gaelicisation process, it was not its sole focus. As Ó Brolcháin had pointed out in his remarks to the national school commissioners in 1922, the intention of the new regime was to Gaelicise all aspects of the curriculum so as to create a truly Irish outlook, in particular one which would highlight the struggle against oppression down through the centuries. Emphasis on this aspect of the policy also intensified throughout the thirties, exemplified quite pertinently in the statement of aims for the teaching of history in the 'Notes for history teachers' circulated in 1933 by the Department of Education. These notes stated that among the specific objects for that subject '. . . is the study of the Gaelic race and Gaelic civilisation and of the resistance of that race and civilisation for a thousand years to foreign domination, whether Norse, Norman or English'.[83]

Another indication of the extent to which this aspect of educational policy was being effected can be gleaned from a brief perusal of textbooks published for use in Irish schools at this time which increasingly were replacing those in use since before 1922. An explicitly patriotic tone is evident in many. The *Irish world readers* published in 1935 for use in middle and upper primary classes, encouraged a positive attitude to the language and to Ireland's Gaelic heritage, as the following extracts illustrate:

I know them [the meaning of place names] because I am learning Irish at school, and Irish teaches you a great many things which you could not know without it. In learning the Irish language and Irish history, in reading the lives of the Irish saints, even in studying the Irish place-names in the geography lesson , you will often meet with stories of the olden times. And nowadays all the world admits that no other people told so many stories as the Gaels and that no other stories of any other nation are as wonderful as theirs.[84]

In the introduction to the *Senior book* in the series, the underlying message of the selection it contains is clearly spelt out:

In this little book Ireland is the chief point of view: the Irish OUTLOOK is the predominant feature. Our authors are representative of three great periods of literary output corresponding broadly to: the Young Ireland Movement; the Land League and the struggle for Home Rule; the Rising of 1916 and after.[85]

The content of textbooks in Irish not unexpectedly reflected a similar message:

Is í an Ghaeilg teanga na hÉireann. Do labhair óg agus aosta í fado. Bhi clú and cáil ar Éirinn an t-am úd. Táimid ag foghluim na Gaedhilge anois agus beidh sí againn go léir fós.
[Irish is the language of Ireland. Young and old spoke it a long time ago. Ireland was famous then. We are learning Irish now and we will all know it still.]
Tá Éire chomh folláin agus chomh háluinn le haon tír ar dhruim an domhain agus is beag tír ar an domhan mór atá chomh folláin no chomh háluinn lei.
[Ireland is as healthy and as beautiful as any country in the world and there are few countries that are as healthy or as beautiful as she is.][86]

It has to be borne in mind that patriotic and nationalistic as these sentiments are, their expression in school texts in the 1930s was not at all unusual when the wider context of the period is considered. It was a time of intense nationalism in many European countries. In Ireland's case, it was also a new state's attempt to inculcate a sense of pride and self-respect in its own distinctiveness. Missing, of course, from the concept of Irishness being promoted was any indication that there might have been another sense of Irishness on the island apart from that identified by Gaelic Christian–Catholic nationalism, the tradition which embraced those of a unionist and Protestant background for whom it would be necessary to find a place if Ireland was to really be as 'healthy' and as 'beautiful' as the textbooks claimed.

A resolute stand

Throughout the thirties criticism of the pressure mounted to promote Irish in schools had little immediate effect since the government remained resolute in its defence of both the policy and its implementation. It was not just the Minister of Education, but the entire government and, in particular, its leader, Eamon de Valera, who had to be persuaded of any need for change. De Valera believed what Patrick Pearse had preached, that language and nationality are so intimately linked that a non-Irish speaking Irish nation was a contradiction and would not survive. 'Nationality and language are mutually dependent . . . the seed and growth of the Gaelic people as a separate people would die if cut from its roots', he argued.[87] De Valera's argument ignored the capacity of people everywhere to mould and shape language after their own fashion, no matter what that language might be, as indeed Irish people had been doing with English for many generations, producing as they did so their own distinct varieties of the language and a literature in English distinctively Irish. Coincidentally, the same week that de Valera made the above remarks a Dr Howley of Trinity College addressed a meeting of the Library Association of Ireland on the same theme. Dr Howley's discussion of the relationship between language and nationality led him to quite a different conclusion, namely that 'language was not essential to nationality'.[88] Howley pointed to the manner in which the Swiss, with several languages, apparently found no difficulty in maintaining their distinct identity while people in the United States of America were no less distinct because they spoke a language not indigenous to America. He was not reported as referring directly to the Irish situation, though it offered another pertinent illustration of his case and may not have been far from his thoughts.

The main arguments against the government's policy were of a more immediate kind, concentrating as they did on the requirement to conduct all teaching in the infant classes through Irish and on the intention to extend Irish medium teaching to all classes as quickly as possible. By 1935 such criticism had reached a level of outspokenness and common purpose which had not been evident a decade previously. A central concern for many critics was the possibility that serious 'educational damage' was being done to young minds. Canon E.C. Hodges of the Church of Ireland Training College spoke of the decision 'to make Irish the medium of instruction in infant classes as a serious loss to the children'.[89] The leading Catholic newspaper, the *Standard*, asked: 'Can our children and our youth be educated in the full sense of the word in a language unfamiliar to their homes and unfamiliar to their teacher?'[90] Applying compulsion to Irish led even some previously dedicated supporters of the language revival like Professor Michael Tierney to ask if 'the insistence on Irish as the sole medium of instruction whether for infants or for adults might well mean the failure of the whole language movement'.[91]

National school teachers who were in the front line of the campaign to promote Irish were amongst the most vociferous in expressing concern. Their annual conferences were particularly noted for the volume of criticism expressed, with many resolutions calling for a fresh inquiry into policies on Irish. One resolution in 1930 called, 'for an educational assessment of the use of Irish as a teaching medium in schools in English speaking districts'[92] while at the 1931 congress a delegate described this 'as an educational outrage and is all the more outrageous because it is inflicted on helpless children'.[93] As public criticism mounted, a former president of the I.N.T.O., Mr Quin, queried the precise motives behind the language policy and wondered whether the policy was ultimately aimed at 'ousting English from the schools'.[94] For many Irish revivalists this was precisely what they were aiming for rather than the bilingual society which a majority of Irish people, if offered the opportunity, would most probably have supported. Quin, too, favoured the latter and endorsed the demand, now widespread within the I.N.T.O., for a committee of inquiry to examine the whole question of the language revival in schools.[95]

Towards the close of 1935, feeling within the I.N.T.O. was such that the organisation's Dublin branch adopted a motion calling upon the government to act on Quin's suggestion and address the general concern being expressed. This was the first formal step in what was to culminate in a full-scale I.N.T.O. inquiry into the use of Irish as a teaching medium.[96] Faced with the fact that the government itself was clearly not going to take such an initiative, the I.N.T.O. decided, at its annual congress the following year, to undertake its own in-depth study into the effects of the use of Irish as a teaching medium in non-Irish speaking areas[97] and set up a special committee to conduct it. The committee decided that the inquiry would be undertaken by means of a detailed questionnaire which would seek the views of teachers in non-Irish speaking areas.[98] It was to take almost six years before the results of inquiry were to be published (to be discussed in chapter 8), time which allowed a temporary lull to descend upon the attacks being directed at the government over the language issue.[99]

However, before that lull descended, strong counter-attacks had been launched both by the government itself and by organisations within the language revival movement. The Gaelic League, ever anxious to protect what it regarded as a major advance for the language, namely its use as an everyday medium in schools, reacted by describing all critics as either anti-Irish, or pro-British. The 'malign', so-called anti-Irish influence of Trinity College was often claimed to be at the root of the criticism launched against the language policy. Memories of Trinity academics like Mahaffy who had opposed the language and of others like Thrift and Culverwell who had criticised the new state's language policy in the twenties, no doubt still rankled. The Dublin national teachers' call for an inquiry was described by the league as 'in accordance with a campaign which is being carried on by Trinity College and other bodies opposed to Irish'.[100] Answering those who criticised the use of Irish and consequent non-use of English in schools, the Gaelic League argued an even more radical prospect than that then being promoted:

... for many years, aye decades, English can take care of itself in this country. It will have to become an optional subject in both national and secondary schools. Educationists in favour of revival have already urged this course ... [but] ... Just as change to an English speaking Ireland entailed the destruction of Irish so must the change back to an Irish speaking Ireland make the ultimate destruction of English in Ireland inevitable.[101]

Drawing a parallel between people's failure to understand and appreciate the 'sacrifice' of those who engaged in the 1916 Rising, the league argued that existing policies had of necessity to be maintained: 'if the people appear to lack appreciation of how necessary the language is to nationality and true freedom it should be remembered that in the years preceding 1916 they appeared to have lacked all appreciation of the necessity for freedom'.[102] Invoking such a powerful parallel illustrated how intimately the league linked the campaign for language revival with the struggle for national independence. The argument also suggested, though the league would probably not have wanted the point to be made too bluntly, that public apathy, indifference or lack of enthusiasm, justified a policy which included a high degree of coercion.

The government argued in somewhat similar terms, with Derrig reported as saying that 'there will be no regression in regard to the Irish language policy. They had made great sacrifices even to death, to make the country Gaelic, and not to make it an imitation of any other country'.[103] Behind such remarks one can detect a continuing determination to shape and mould Irish society into a distinct cultural community of which the Irish language would be its most distinguishing feature. Following the implementation of his new measures to assist and promote the teaching and use of Irish, Derrig also felt able to draw attention to the progress evidenced in the wider use of Irish in both primary and secondary schools as well as the success rate of pupils educated through the medium of Irish.[104] Furthermore, in support of its policies and their achievements the Department of Education, in 1939, prepared two quite lengthy documents outlining what had been done to promote Irish within the educational system since 1922. The first summarised the support provided in order to encourage teachers to learn Irish, the numbers of them who had attended summer schools and who had obtained qualifications in Irish, the financial inducements at secondary level for using Irish as a medium of instruction, and the regulation changes which required that Irish be taught in secondary schools and taken as an examination subject.[105]

In this first document, prepared specifically for de Valera, the department almost appeared to be saying that any lack of success in reviving Irish could not be attributed to a lack of attention, encouragement or means on its part, implying thereby that if there was failure it should be attributed to inadequacies, or lack of effort on the part of teachers. The second document, prepared in October 1939 after the department had received a copy of the interim report of the I.N.T.O.'s inquiry, was a detailed defence of teaching through Irish at primary level. Written by the secretary to the department, S. Ó Néill, it took as its key reference point the fact that the 'Policy of the government is to make Irish a living language in regular use amongst the people of the country'.[106] In it Ó Néill argued very strongly that education was possible through Irish, that many schools *were* achieving success and that to relent on the regulation requiring Irish at infant level 'is open to the grave objection that it might result in the widespread use of English in the majority of infant schools and even in the total elimination of Irish as the medium of instruction in a great many of them'.[107] In other words, according to the most senior civil servant in the department, only compulsion to use Irish could ensure its use. Ó Néill was even prepared to argue that, if there was a choice, the task of reviving Irish had to take precedence over general educational standards, saying that: 'it is probable that, during this generation at least, we can hardly avoid a certain amount of educational loss through the complete exclusion of English from infant classes in all schools'.[108]

There was to be no turning back at this stage from the school language policy, either in principle, or in implementation. Even if failure appeared possible, perhaps even likely, as de Valera himself seemed to concede from time to time when he claimed that it would be a shame and a disgrace if the language was lost,[109] no one was prepared to admit that change was necessary. The reason why no change was advanced seems to have been the absence of an alternative view of the relationship between language and nationality. It followed that if Irish nationality was essentially dependent on the Irish language, the promotion of the language was also essential and other matters had to be sacrificed in its favour. Anyone who attempted to advance a different view ran the risk of being branded as anti-Irish, or dismissed as part of the discredited pro-British lobby. The new orthodoxy was so well established and so well entrenched by the end of the thirties, that its critics could be virtually ignored, in public at least.

The thirties ended, therefore, for both parts of Ireland with the appearance of greater cohesion and tranquility on the educational scene matching that which seemed to exist at large in their respective societies, and much greater than that with which the decade had commenced. The calm so induced was not to remain unbroken for long, most particularly in the north where cohesion and tranquility were at their most tenuous.

7

Controversy Renewed:
Education in Northern Ireland 1940–47

A watershed

WORLD WAR II was a major watershed in the history of both parts of Ireland. Whereas the 1930s had witnessed a consolidation of the different socio–political ideologies which were shaping policies in each part of Ireland, World War II provided a very clear demonstration of the different destinies to which these ideologies pointed. In the case of Northern Ireland, linked as it was to Britain, it was destined to play an intimate part in the western allies' war effort. At the outbreak of hostilities Prime Minister Craig placed 'all Northern Ireland's resources at the disposal of the British government'[1] with the result that Northern Ireland was propelled from the status of an unimportant and under-developed area on the periphery of Europe to being a major military and indus-trial centre. Its ports became staging posts for North Atlantic convoys, its shipyards worked round-the-clock to meet the needs of the allied fleets while its engineering and textile industries were mobilised to make their contribution to the war effort. Later, construction and service industries boomed throughout the region to cater for the thousands of allied troops who came to be based there in preparation for the invasion of Europe.

One of the most immediate and obvious results of all of this activity was a very rapid decline in unemployment. From a figure of over 101,000 in 1938 the num-ber of unemployed declined to less than 18,000 in 1945. Beyond such a tangible effect there was the psychological boost which involvement in the war brought by inducing a sense of pride and importance amongst the people of Northern Ireland, most evidently so within the Protestant–unionist community. To the lat-ter, Northern Ireland was playing a very significant role in what came to be regarded as a world-wide crusade against fascist tyrannies. Political and military leaders in Britain and from Britain's allies acknowledged this role and many came in person to express their appreciation.[2] To unionists it was almost as if Northern Ireland's role in World War II was, in itself, a vindication of their stand against a separate all-Ireland state which would have deprived them of their British connections and of the only means by which they believed Northern Ireland could make the kind of contribution to world affairs which the war allowed it to make. The neutrality declared by the southern state was despised by unionists to the point where many felt justified in describing it as a betrayal of democracy and of the values which the allies claimed to be defending.

If involvement in the war brought prestige and an economic boom it also brought its share of suffering to Northern Ireland. Thousands of people were killed or injured and widescale destruction was caused in the course of several massive bombing raids on Belfast in the spring of 1941.[3] Hundreds more sacrificed their lives on active service with the British army. Gratitude for Northern Ireland's wartime sacrifices was widely acknowledged in Britain and as one of the more tangible marks of that gratitude the British government promised 'to transform its finances by conceding, in 1942, the principle of "leeway" by which Northern Ireland's services would be brought up to the British standards'.[4] In other words, no longer would Northern Ireland be a part of the United Kingdom only in a political sense, it would also be so on a basis of equal treatment with all other parts of the kingdom. Psychologically, this too was a very significant development as it distanced the north further from the south and in education it was to be paralleled by developments very closely modelled on those planned for England and Wales.

The period of reconstruction which followed the war also marked the experience of Northern Ireland off from that of the south. Reconstruction in Northern Ireland was pursued under the strong influence of developments in Britain. There a Labour government was determined to ensure the establishment of a welfare state and to that end social policy was based on the state accepting an increased responsibility for many services, particularly in health, education and social security. This approach became the model for Northern Ireland where a series of agreements with the British government ensured equality of treatment for Northern Ireland within the new welfare services.[5]

In contrast to the north, the south adopted a policy of military neutrality at the outset of hostilities and set about mobilising its resources in order to achieve as high a level of self-sufficiency as possible. The result was that the south lived out these years in a virtual state of siege with the provision of basic necessities and services being the first priority. The economy lagged in its general development as a consequence and there was no comparable investment such as the wartime needs of industry had made available to the north, while the maintenance of a vastly expanded army and security service added new burdens to public finances.[6] Neutrality, while respected by the western allies, was deeply resented in many countries, particularly in Britain where popular opinion was encouraged to believe that the use of Irish ports would have been of considerable assistance to the war effort in the Atlantic.[7] Furthermore, neutrality allowed the impression to be fostered that the south was, if not sympathetic to fascism, at least not as opposed to it as other democracies were.

As hostilities drew to a close another major contrast with the north became evident in the absence of detailed forward planning by the government for the post-war period. While some plans were prepared to reform the social services, including education, these were not accompanied by the commitment and determination necessary to ensure their implementation.[8] Unlike the north, therefore, the south was to emerge from the war years physically quite unscathed by its destructive forces, but also relatively untouched by the reconstructionist spirit which affected the former by virtue of its involvement in the war and of its membership of the United Kingdom. Sealed off from outside influences as the south was during these traumatic years, the values and attitudes of the 1930s persisted there into the late 1940s and beyond. It was only in the late 1950s, in the wake of a disastrous economic crisis, that a fundamental reassessment of many aspects of Irish life was undertaken, a reassessment that was to have significant effects on education.

Background to reform

Throughout the period under review unionist political control over Northern Ireland continued unabated. Appeals from the Belfast (Irish) Labour M.P., John Beattie, at the outbreak of the war for party representation in cabinet to be broadened, as had happened in Britain, were rejected out of hand.[9] The Prime Minister, John Andrews, Craig's successor, pointed to the fact that the Nationalist Party, the largest opposition grouping, had made it clear that, despite the war, 'partition' remained its first consideration.[10] Indeed, the attendance of nationalist M.P.s was so irregular and their attitude to the war such that it was impossible, according to John Andrews, to broaden his cabinet base and he declined to consider M.P.s from any other grouping.[11] Basil Brooke, Andrews' successor, in a rather mild gesture towards broadening the base of his cabinet, did include one non-unionist when, in May 1943, he appointed Harry Midgley, the maverick, independent Labour member, Minister of Public Security.[12] During the period under review in this chapter the Ministry of Education itself was in the charge of three ministers: John Robb (1937–43), Rev. Professor Robert Corkey (1943–44) and Lieutenant-Colonel Hall-Thompson (1944–50) while another prominent government voice on education was that of Dehra Parker, who served as parliamentary secretary to the Minister of Education.

The war's most immediate effects on education were essentially negative. The act raising the school leaving age to fifteen was suspended as was much of the building and capital development programme. Instead, attention focused on the evacuation of school children from Belfast and other large towns, and on the relocation of sections of the administration. Both the headquarters of the department and Stranmillis College were relocated to Portrush in County Antrim. Recruitment to teacher training itself was curtailed and in the case of male students was entirely suspended in 1939, though it was resumed in 1940 when a limited number of male students were again admitted to training.[13] However, since school rolls had been falling throughout the late thirties and continued to do so throughout the war years, dropping from a figure of 191,862 in 1938 to 185,470 in 1945,[14] this decline more than any wartime exigencies probably explains the curtailment.

In terms of education's direct contribution to the war effort, many teachers volunteered for service, at home and abroad, sixteen of whom were killed in action.[15] At home, education could also boast of other contributions to the

155

war effort. As Dehra Parker pointed out in the House of Commons in June 1941 there were '3,000 soldiers pursuing studies ranging from Spanish to woodwork' in technical schools throughout Northern Ireland and many schools had established junior sections of the armed services. The Air Training Corps, for example, attained a membership of over 1,700 from schools in Northern Ireland.[16] Directly as a result of wartime exigencies some important developments within the overall educational service did take place. The school meals service expanded to include, at a minimal cost, meals for 'non-necessitous' children as well as the 'necessitous'[17] while the school medical service was also considerably expanded, particularly in the Belfast area.[18]

As might be expected, none of the constraints imposed by the war, like the suspension of the school building programme, or the implementation of evacuation plans, were the cause of major controversy. Evacuation did give rise to serious problems of over-crowding and of inadequate resources in many of the rural schools which accepted evacuees.[19] However, such problems were generally accepted as unavoidable in the circumstances. There was also criticism of the overall evacuation plans when many children were taken back to Belfast because of the perceived absence of danger, only to be tragically caught up in the devastating raids of 1941.[20]

Wartime controversies

Such controversy as did arise in the early war years focused on matters much more deep-rooted in the Northern Irish psyche, like religious education or, more accurately, on the alleged absence or lack of emphasis on it at secondary level, or on the 'poorer' treatment of voluntary schools compared with public schools, or on the teaching of Irish and on why a greater sense of (British) citizenship was not being inculcated in young people. The most notable of these issues was religious education in secondary schools, which became controversial when questions were raised in parliament in 1940 alleging its neglect in prominent Protestant schools and colleges. It was an issue that was to remain high on the public agenda for the next seven years, reaching almost crisis proportions between 1945 and 1947 when a new education bill was being discussed.

Rev. Professor Robert Corkey M.P. was the first to raise the issue in parliament when he alleged that:

. . . in some of the secondary schools there is no conscious, no deliberate and no determined effort to provide education on Christian morals which lie at the base of our democracy, backed up by simple and credible notions about God and the world in which we live.[21]

Why the question arose precisely when it did is difficult to determine. Akenson offers the most plausible explanation, i.e. that Corkey wanted Northern Ireland to follow English and Scottish practice and have religious instruction specialists provided for secondary schools.[22] However, since secondary schools were almost completely outside the control of the Ministry of Education, all but 3 of the 70 secondary schools were conducted under voluntary auspices, the ministry could not dictate their curricula. Like its counterpart in the south, the ministry's influence was indirectly exercised through the syllabuses it set and the examinations it conducted. As independent institutions, most secondary schools were free to offer whatever curricula they considered appropriate and this included the freedom to offer, or not to offer courses in religious education. In accordance with this independence, religious education was not a subject which teachers could include amongst those hours which contributed to the eighteen hours weekly minimum which they were required to undertake in order to qualify for the ministry's incremental salary. Nonetheless, since most teachers taught considerably more hours than this minimum there was effectively no impediment to them teaching religious education and also qualifying for their increments. It was schools' failure to require them to do so that so upset Professor Corkey.

It was essentially the situation in Protestant secondary schools that concerned Corkey. The Roman Catholic schools were, by definition, committed to providing religious instruction and required no prompting from anyone to do so. The same was not true of all of the secondary schools attended by Protestant pupils and it would appear that a number of the latter made no clear provision for religious instruction at all; according to William Corkey only 17 of the 47 secondary schools catering for the Protestant community were providing any religious instruction and many of these were doing so for not more than one teaching period per week. Among them, he alleged, were some of the north's most prestigious schools.[23] It was clearly in an attempt to pressurise these schools into offering religious education or to offer it more regularly, that Corkey spoke out. The timing of his remarks is probably explained by the war which, by giving a special reason to invoke divine assistance, focused attention on religion and, as a result, on the kind of religious education provided in schools.

Pressure from within the Protestant churches gradually mounted over the next two years with the aim of persuading the government to recognise religious instruction as a subject which could be included amongst those hours formally accepted by the Ministry of Education for the purposes of incremental payments. The churches also requested that religious instruction be included on the examination syllabuses for the Northern Irish certificate examinations, as was the case in England and Wales. Following several requests, a deputation from the Protestant churches was eventually received by the Minister of Education, John Robb, in March 1942.[24] Robb pointed out that he had no power to impose religious instruction and that the most effective way of achieving the desired objectives would be by directly approaching the governors of the schools themselves. In making this point the minister would have been very conscious of the difficulties which could have arisen under section 5 of the Government of Ireland Act were he to accede to the churches' requests to impose religious education. The religious educational controversies of the 1920s and the doubts surrounding the legality of decisions taken at that time were still fresh to many people. Attempts to impose religious education in schools over which the ministry had no direct control at all could have reopened the whole issue and precipitated much wider controversy. The furthest the minister was prepared to go at this time was to commit himself to issuing a statement in which he invited the chairperson of each board of governors to:

. . . consider with your fellow governors and with the Principal of your school whether your present arrangements for the religious instruction of the pupils under your care are satisfactory and such as meet the wishes of the parents . . .[25]

This measure was, however, seen as falling far short of what the Protestant churches considered necessary to ensure religious instruction for Northern Ireland's secondary school students. As a result considerable dissatisfaction with the minister's reaction to the deputation's requests began to be expressed. A month after the minister had circulated his memorandum, the Methodist Church passed a strong resolution at its annual conference regretting 'the refusal of the Minister to grant the wishes of the joint deputation representing the Protestant churches in regard to religious instruction in schools'.[26] This was followed over the next two years by an ever increasing flow of resolutions condemning the minister's stand.[27] Several resolutions adopted by church bodies attempted to portray the minister as betraying the fight for civilisation to which Northern Ireland was contributing in so many other respects. The Clogher Diocesan Synod, for example, suggested that:

. . . it is incompatible with the sacrifices now being made in defence of Christian civilization, a civilization that cannot be expected to continue if boys and girls are not instructed in the Bible . . .[28]

Fuel was added to the controversy when Professor Corkey was dismissed from his position as Minister of Education early in 1944. His dismissal was linked with the stand against enforced religious education in secondary schools and was seen as evidence of the government's determination to deny the Protestant community a suitable form of education. The Derry Presbytery of the Presbyterian Church saw the two issues as grounds for threatening to 'withdraw its support from the present Government', a threat not new as far as matters educational were concerned.[29] As minister, Robb had made one concrete concession which did not, however, have the effect of diffusing the controversy. He announced in the Senate in November 1942 that only sixteen of the eighteen hours of a teacher's minimum weekly timetable needed to be devoted to recognised subjects, the remaining two hours 'to be spent on such other teaching duties in connection with the school as the Board of the School shall determine'.[30] With this modification, it became possible for teachers to include religious education within their minimum timetable and so have it counted for incremental purposes. There was, however, still no requirement on schools to provide religious education and it was the absence of this requirement which continued to concern the churches, just as had the same absence in the case of elementary schools in the 1920s. Once again the demand was for an explicit requirement of religious instruction rather than merely making it possible for this instruction to be provided. On this occasion it was a demand that was not acceded to.

The government's stand on this rather minor issue has some significance when viewed in the context of previous controversies involving it and the Protestant churches. Resistance to the demand marked the first time the government stood its ground in refusing to accede to demands made by these churches. While it can be argued that standing firm on this issue was not particularly difficult since the government's authority over secondary schools was quite restricted, nonetheless, a stand was taken, the significance of which is probably best appreciated in the light of the more important stand to be taken by government during the passage of the education bill over the period 1945–47.

Despite the government's refusal to make the concessions demanded, the Protestant churches continued to pursue the issue with considerable tenacity, again receiving support from unionist backbenchers at Stormont. One backbencher, James Brown, the M.P. for South Down, attempted, unsuccessfully, on several occasions to have a motion 'to ensure that boys and girls in all secondary schools in Northern Ireland receive religious instruction' debated.[31] Ironically, he was answered on one occasion by Corkey who as Minister of Education was obliged to point out that secondary schools could 'not be subjected to any legislative compulsion in regard to the provision of religious instruction'.[32] Brown eventually did succeed in having his point endorsed by the Commons in October 1943 when Professor John Renshaw, M.P. for Queen's University, proposed a motion calling for educational reform in Northern Ireland similar to that in Britain, and he (Brown) moved an amendment, which was accepted by the Commons, demanding 'the provision of the fullest possible facilities for religious education' as part of any reform.[33] While acceptance of the motion did not require any concrete measures, it was a sharp reminder to the government of the strength of feeling on matters pertaining to the relationship between religion and education.

Meanwhile, outside parliament, the Protestant churches continued to conduct their campaign with a vigour and vehemence that, once again, posed a political danger for Northern Ireland, a danger alluded to quite forcefully in a note to the Prime Minister from Dehra Parker:

I believe the road on which the Church is trying to force us is a most dangerous one which may do untold harm to our educational system over here, and which certainly cannot do any good and may reopen the whole elementary religious controversy with disastrous consequences. To me it looks as if the Protestant Churches feel as if they haven't got quite the authority over their people they once had, and that they want to re-establish and advertise their power by coercing the State.[34]

Their failure to win further concessions from the government eventually led some within the Protestant churches to recommend rather drastic measures. The Rev. William Hay, convenor of the Presbyterian Board of Education, demanded that religious education be made compulsory at secondary level, even if to do so required an amendment to the Government of Ireland Act. Such a step, he wrote, 'may well prove indeed the most satisfactory manner for dealing with the situation and the present is a most opportune moment for doing it'.[35] While the Prime Minister did no more than note Hay's advice, it was not to be forgotten. Dangerous as it was in terms of its constitutional implications, this very suggestion was to receive active consideration in both Belfast and London during the next phase of educational development in Northern Ireland between 1944 and 1947.

New context for old issues

By 1944 the focus of educational debate began to change as plans evolved for significant legislative changes affecting secondary and elementary schools in England and Wales, plans which envisaged the provision of secondary education as a right for all.[36] Anxious to keep abreast of developments in England, the government in Northern Ireland also felt obliged to plan for similar reform. However, when translated to the Northern Irish context, it was the plans' religious dimension, rather than any aims which focused on widening access to education which was to receive most attention. What the earlier debate over religious education had demonstrated was the firm determination of the leadership of the Protestant churches to ensure for themselves a continuing and influential role in educational matters in Northern Ireland. To this end they had been prepared to exercise considerable pressure on the government even if this meant asking for changes in the legislation which had established Northern Ireland.

In the next round of this campaign, the churches were again to find themselves in open conflict with that government and were to come close to achieving a victory similar to that which they had won in 1930. Their failure to achieve another victory has to be attributed to those constitutional dangers about which Parker had warned, dangers which had been recognised in 1925[37] and again in 1929–30,[38] but which had been ignored because of the pertaining political circumstances. The same risk would not be taken a third time.

Nationalist concerns

For nationalists, their seemingly unending quarrel with the government about the level of funding for Catholic schools continued to rumble on over these years together with their concern about the teaching of Irish and the recognition to be afforded Gaelic culture. Demands for change, for 'equality' of treatment with local authority schools and for more attention to be paid to Gaelic culture and to Irish history had become almost ritualistic. Comparisons were made with the south where schools serving all denominations were treated equally, albeit not very generously, from the public purse, in order to embarrass the government with the accusation that Catholic schools were being discriminated against in the north. Richard Byrne M.P., speaking during the education estimates debate in 1940, reiterated the demand that Catholic schools be treated on an equal basis to those for Protestant children, invoking as he did so the fact that the Catholic community had to bear an extra burden in terms of educational expenditure compared with their Protestant neighbours:

We want our children educated in Catholic schools. Owing to the penalty placed upon our people we have to curtail the equipment in the schools because we have not the necessary money to erect new buildings. We have been denied the rights to which we are entitled.[39]

On the teaching of Irish, the estimates debate of 1941 heard Patrick Agnew M.P. complain that:

... It is strange that though we call ourselves Irishmen the Government of Northern Ireland through their Department have a scheme for the teaching of Spanish, French and many other languages but that no provision is made for the teaching of the language of the country of which we are all natives.[40]

The government's response to Catholic demands for increased grant aid merely repeated that such aid was available to schools which accepted the 'four-and-two' management structure, but the church steadfastly refused to accept such a structure. On the question of the status of Irish the government's position was that Irish was being treated like French, Spanish and German and that what was being asked for was something more and this the Ministry of Education was not prepared to grant.

Wartime was not a period during which change could be realistically expected, nor did the Catholic Church go out of its way to seek the sympathy of either the government, or the Protestant–unionist community as a whole in order to achieve its desired change. In fact, it could be said that it did the exact opposite and alienated potential sympathy by its attitude to the war effort. When war broke out, the bishops identified discrimination against Catholics and partition as the greatest evils affecting their people in Northern Ireland and went on to:

... exhort the Catholic people in that area to face the difficulties with calm and patience in the confident hope that any just settlement must relieve them from the disabilities under which they suffer and restore them to that union with their country which they so ardently desire.[41]

The bishops' statement contained no reference to the evils of fascism, nor to the totalitarianism which lay at the heart of the conflict which had just broken out in Europe. To the unionist community it appeared that the Catholic community was pre-occupied with its own grievances to the exclusion of the wider concerns and dangers facing Europe as a whole. Taken together with a statement the previous year opposing the possible extension of military conscription to Northern Ireland,[42] the signals from the Catholic community were that the war effort in Northern Ireland was not going to receive either its political or moral support.

Adding to the ill-feeling caused by these statements amongst unionists, was the renewal of I.R.A. activity, first in Britain and then in Northern Ireland itself. In 1939, just before the outbreak of the war, the I.R.A. launched a bombing campaign in Britain to try to force a British withdrawal from Northern Ireland. This campaign, which claimed a number of lives and caused considerable anti-Irish feeling,[43] ended in 1940 but was followed by some minor I.R.A. activity in Northern Ireland throughout the war. The result of this latter campaign was the internment without trial of a number of nationalists, a measure which certainly did nothing for inter-communal relations whatever it about its contribution to security.[44] As a result Protestant–unionist sympathy for Catholic–nationalist demands during this period was, not surprisingly, almost non-existent and was typified by remarks from the Antrim M.P. Hugh Minford, about a request for funds for the teaching of Irish in convent schools:

In 1943 when we are fighting one of the greatest wars the world has ever known we hand over a sum of money to people, some of whom would rather see us in the hottest place in the next world.[45]

So, rather than being a means of creating unity and cohesion within a community, as wartime pressures frequently are, their effects on community relations in Northern Ireland tended to be negative. The ritual complaints of nationalist politicians and of the Catholic Church received ritual responses from their unionist and Protestant audience. Only in the context of the changes proposed for education towards the end of the war, did any thaw in these relationships appear.

Pressure for change

While developments in Britain in the early 1940s became a spur to reform in Northern Ireland, the desire to expand opportunities for secondary education had existed for quite a number of years, as the 1938 act had indicated. However, the scope of the changes being planned in Britain was much wider and more radical than merely raising the school leaving age. The aim was to provide 'equality of opportunity' for all to advance to second level education and, indeed beyond for those who would prove capable of doing so. Hitherto elementary education terminated at fourteen, while the few pupils who proceeded to secondary schools could transfer at any age after twelve. On behalf of the Northern Irish government Dehra Parker reflected a commitment to change as early as 1942 when she stated:

Every day the newspapers tell us of what must be done after the war. 'Equality of opportunity' has become the most well-worn cliche in education. For 'equality of opportunity' I prefer to use the expression 'equal opportunity in education for ability and intelligence' and in this realm we in Northern Ireland have still much to do and much that must be done after the war . . .[46]

Although it was still early days in the debate, it was clear that ideas were beginning to crystallise within the Ministry of Education in favour of a particular model for the provision of secondary education. That model was one which was premised, not so much on equality of opportunity as on the separation, at eleven or twelve years, of those who would be deemed most likely to benefit from an academic secondary education from the rest who would proceed to either a general, or a technical education. This desire to separate and divide the academic from the so-called non-academic was being reinforced by the Minister of Education, Col. Hall-Thompson, who quite obviously did not even believe that secondary education for all might be such a good thing. In October 1943, during one of the first major debates about future developments he argued that:

I am not in favour of every person having a secondary school education. I think it is much more useful in life for the average citizen to learn the so-called 3Rs properly and accurately and then to apply them in the after life rather than have a smattering of many subjects and a profound knowledge of none.[47]

The contrary approach was strongly articulated by Harry Midgley who urged change on the basis of what he claimed was a socialist interpretation of 'equality of opportunity':

Those, who like myself, stand for equality of opportunity stand for the recognition of the educational right of every person in the community on the basis of equality of opportunity. We have argued and we still argue that in Northern Ireland education is the big prerogative of those with the big bank balances and that, too often, many poor children are deprived of a full education simply through the poverty of their parents . . . We want to see an ever-growing development in the direction of placing within reach of larger numbers of children the right to have the education which they ought to have on the basis of equality of opportunity.[48]

Such remarks seemed to hold out the prospect that educational debate in Northern Ireland might move to a new basis, i.e. one which focused on educational issues *per se*. It was not, however, to be, as Northern Ireland's more traditional preoccupations with education's religious dimensions came to overshadow virtually all else in the debate.

Parity with Britain, but . . .

The October 1943 debate initiated by Professor Renshaw was the first to focus parliamentary attention on post-war prospects for education in Northern Ireland. Renshaw proposed that a scheme be prepared to provide 'for an educational advance commensurate, as far as possible, with that proposed for Britain'.[49] The debate which ensued highlighted the growing demand for secondary education, with speakers referring to large numbers of applicants failing to obtain places because existing schools were at capacity. Dehra Parker indicated that indeed it was the government's intention to introduce 'a scheme providing for an educational advance commensurate as far as possible with that proposed for Great Britain' adding, in what was surely an understatement, that in bringing in such a scheme account would have to be taken of local circumstances.[50]

Throughout the following year, 1944, discussion on educational reform gained momentum with considerable attention being focused on developments in Britain, where the education bill for England and Wales was receiving widespread publicity. Public comment, from within the Protestant–unionist community, on that bill was generally favourable, though some of the views expressed indicated the kind of opposition that was eventually to emerge when local proposals were published in December of that year. While Dr Stuart Hawnt, Director of Education in Belfast, pointed out that 'the outstanding feature [of the English bill] was the raising of the school leaving age to sixteen',[51] William Corkey's welcome for expansion rather ominously contained a reminder that 'the education system here had never been in all respects the same as in Great Britain'.[52] The extent to which it was not the same was frequently signalled, as expectations about the nature of anticipated reform increased. In 1944, the General Assembly of the Presbyterian Church emphasised the need to provide for religious instruction at least as effectively as in the English legislation, in a resolution which called for:

... a provision for religious education in secondary schools in Northern Ireland comparable to that provided in the Public Elementary School system and in the English Bill of 1944 along with such arrangements for the training of teachers in the subject, for its inspection and examination as may be necessary for its efficient teaching.[53]

These demands from the Presbyterian Church were supported by the Orange Order which ensured that resolutions of the following kind were passed by its county lodges:

... the Ministry of Education for Northern Ireland should make provision for the giving of Bible Instruction in all Secondary schools, subject to a conscience clause for teachers and parents, and also provide for the training in Bible knowledge of those teachers who are willing to give such instruction.[54]

Of further significance for developments in Northern Ireland, was the opposition of the Roman Catholic Church in England and Wales to certain aspects of the education bill there which did not go unnoticed in the Irish press. The official statement of the English and Welsh hierarchy which set out Catholic criticisms was widely reported, together with the efforts of Catholic members at Westminster to have the bill amended accordingly. Two particular points of criticism which were later to appear in the Irish bishops' attack on the proposals for Northern Ireland, were those about 'excessive state influence' and the 'financial burden on the Catholic community' which would result if the bill was to be enacted. To the Catholic Church any increase in state involvement in education was to be opposed on principle, while an increased financial burden to provide more school places would, ironically, oblige the church to seek more support from the state. The dilemma was how to avoid the former yet obtain the latter.

Other views

If traditional concerns about education were about to be stressed with the usual vehemence and vigour, other voices were also struggling to make themselves heard on the prospects for educational reform. Among the latter were the teachers' unions, but they would also include some of the political parties notably the Northern Ireland Labour Party (N.I.L.P.) and sections of the Unionist Party itself. The focus for much of the comment emanating from such bodies was the basis upon which secondary education would be structured and, even more significantly, the procedures by which pupils would be selected for the secondary schools.

The U.T.U. devoted considerable effort to drawing up its own plans for reform[55] among the key features of which were a rejection of selection at eleven and a recommendation that secondary education be organised along 'unilateral' or, in today's terms, comprehensive lines, instead of the multilateral proposal which had found favour in the English legislation.[56] The N.I.L.P., which was undergoing a revival and was about to enjoy some electoral success in the immediate post-war years, expressed a keen interest in education at this time. In January 1944 the party held a special conference to discuss educational matters[57] from which came recommendations proposing an integrated educational system, from nursery through to secondary schooling, with the school leaving age to be raised to sixteen. Like the U.T.U., the N.I.L.P. rejected the recommended selection at eleven, preferring instead the unilateral, or comprehensive approach for eleven to sixteen-year-olds. Broadly speaking these recommendations were in line with those being advanced by the British Labour Party and, historically, bear a number of similarities to those proposed by the Irish Labour Party in the mid-twenties.[58] Neither organisation carried the weight of influence in Northern Ireland which the churches did. So, inevitably, it was to be the latter's interests which would again dominate the debate over educational reform.

Church interests crucial

The emergence of these other voices into the debate proved no great distraction to a government keenly aware of the need to address the educational concerns of the churches as it prepared for an extensive measure of reform. Evidence of the government's concern to meet the arguments of the churches can be seen in several lengthy memoranda prepared in the Ministry of Education throughout 1944. The English bill with its provision for compulsory religious education and a compulsory daily act of common worship in all publicly aided schools was, initially, of considerable concern to the Northern Irish Ministry of Education whose view was that any similar provisions for Northern Irish schools would be in breach of section 5 of the Government of Ireland Act. Such measures could only be permitted if accompanied by an amendment to that act because as Hall-Thompson argued:

Without such an amendment we are really trying to reconcile the irreconcilable – on the one hand, a prohibition direct or indirect, on payment from public funds, and on the other, a desire to make religion by law obligatory in our schools . . . Incidentally, if the Imperial Acts are not amended when our new Education Bill is drafted we may find ourselves in added difficulties, apart from those which will confront us when it is learnt that we do not propose fully to meet the present demand. The Education Act of 1930 which prescribed . . . that Bible Instruction should be compulsory in schools directly managed by local authorities will have to be repealed . . . The net result will be that we shall have failed to meet the clamour for compulsory religious instruction in all schools and we shall have taken away the statutory provision for Bible Instruction in one class of school which has operated to the satisfaction of everybody concerned for the past fourteen years.[59]

Hall-Thompson's problems had been considerably increased because the Attorney General had given his opinion that the provision in section 4 of the 1930 act whereby local education authorities had been required to provide Bible instruction, was contrary to section 5 of the Government of Ireland Act so making it impossible, in Hall-Thompson's view, 'to even re-enact the substance of Section 4'. The Attorney General's view on section 4 was unambiguous stating that it:

. . . was a clear breach of the Government of Ireland Act of 1920 and it is difficult to account for this not having been challenged long ere this . . . I think it can be clearly shown that to give Bible Instruction in any school at a charge direct or indirect on public funds is to give a 'privilege or advantage on account of religious belief'.[60]

Nevertheless, despite the minister's apprehension, the government appears to have decided to adopt the main principles of the English bill as the basis for its own proposals. Cabinet minutes for the 22 June 1944 indicate that among the points agreed were the following: a collective act of worship and religious education to be compulsory in primary and secondary schools; teachers in local authority schools not to be required as a condition of appointment to give religious instruction; the Ministry of Education should endeavour to secure agreement on these matters with the churches.[61] Because these proposals would exempt teachers from a requirement to provide religious education the minister was not sanguine about the prospects for agreement with the Protestant churches. Cabinet minutes noted him saying that these churches would interpret any suggestion that legislation for Northern Ireland would be less favourable than that for England and Wales as:

. . . the basis of a claim that religious instruction should be treated as an ordinary subject in the school curriculum to be given by the teachers and to be brought within the ordinary arrangements for inspection and examination. He considered it likely that the Protestant churches would also press for access to the pupils by their clergy for the purposes of religious instruction and commented that no such provision was contained in the English Bill.[62]

In other words, proposals along English lines would only be the starting point for further demands by the local churches. The reasons for the minister's apprehension are not hard to find and they became only too clear as he set about consulting the various educational interests throughout Northern Ireland prior to publishing his white paper in December 1944. Meetings were arranged with several groups following the circulation of a letter in which the minister indicated the main points with which his new legislation would deal and on which he invited their views.[63] Several meetings took place between the minister and a deputation from the Catholic Church between May and October 1944, while a further set of meetings involved, among others, deputations representing Protestant school managers and the Association of Education Committees, a body whose members would be radically affected by the minister's new proposals.

Catholic-nationalist opposition

The meetings with the Catholic Church deputation concentrated on funding for voluntary schools[64] though this was not the only issue of concern to the church. Since the minister's letter had indicated that nursery education would be supported, although not made compulsory, the Catholic deputation made this proposal the first on which to differ with the ministry.[65] At the time any form of nursery schooling, but particularly nursery schooling provided by the state, was anathema because it signalled the state taking over a responsibility which, in the view of the Catholic Church, was exclusively one for the family and, in particular, for mothers. State provided nursery schooling smacked of a socialist–communist society and had been roundly condemned in several papal pronouncements, notably by Pius XI in his 1931 social encyclical *Quadragesimo anno*. The deputation made it clear that the church would not be providing any places for nursery education because the education of all children 'between two and five [should be] by their mothers in their homes'.[66] On the main plans for restructuring primary and secondary education, the deputation seemed to be in agreement with the minister although some misgiving was expressed at eleven-plus being the proposed age for transfer because of viability questions which this might raise for small schools and the problems associated with transporting large numbers of young people long distances in rural areas.

On the question of management, the deputation refused to consider the 'four-and-two' scheme to enable Catholic schools to receive additional public funds, though it was agreed that boards of management of some kind would have to be established for the new 'junior' secondary schools. On finance, the deputation pressed for grants of 75 per cent for capital costs and 100 per cent for heating, lighting and cleaning. The minister regretted that he could hold out no prospect of any more than 65 per cent unless a greater degree of public accountability was also accepted. Even an increase to such a level would be problematic, given the known attitudes of other interests.

The minister referred to the opposition of local authorities, who had responsibility for heating etc., and of other, i.e. Protestant, voluntary school managers. The latter were objecting on the grounds that, if Catholic schools were to receive signficant amounts of state funding, then transfer would no longer hold out any attraction and, in fact, should be reversed in order to return schools to the Protestant churches.[67] The series of meetings concluded with the minister and the church representatives almost as far apart as ever on the key issues of management and finance.

Outside the consultative process, the Catholic position was strongly supported by nationalist politicians. Once again a group of nationalist parliamentarians and local councillors in Fermanagh issued a statement supporting the main demands of the Catholic Church. The question of nursery education was one to which they too were particularly opposed, because they feared that 'it might eventually lead to mixed schools of children of different denominations . . . As Catholics we must ask that the Catholic children be educated in schools, primary and secondary, under the direct management of the Catholic clergy, who act for us in all matters concerning the education of our children'.[68]

Protestants and unionists also say 'no'

Meetings with Protestant and unionist interests prior to the publication of the white paper revealed considerable concern about religious education together with opposition to any increase in funding to voluntary schools in the absence of increased public representation in their management structure.[69] All Protestant interests consulted insisted that there should be no change in the provisions for religious instruction as set out in the 1930 act. It was also made clear that if grants to voluntary schools were to be increased to 65 per cent, the Protestant churches would express strong opposition. At one meeting[70] it was suggested to the minister that schools refusing to be transferred should 'be left at a decided disadvantage', i.e. receive little, or no state funding. In June 1944, the Presbyterian General Assembly adopted a resolution setting out a series of demands which became the basis for the Protestant churches' reaction to the government's proposals.[71] In addition to the points mentioned above, these included a request that an adequate number of teachers qualified to provide religious instruction would be available, the extension of compulsory religious instruction to all secondary schools and the highly controversial demand that the Protestant churches be represented on the boards of management of the new secondary schools.

A deputation from the unionist-controlled Association of Education Committees, which included Chancellor James Quinn of the Joint Education Committee of the Protestant Churches, had several meetings with the minister and his officials during 1944.[72] As a member of this deputation Quinn used each meeting as an opportunity to reiterate Protestant demands for 'safeguarding' religious instruction, for church representation on the new local authority junior secondary schools, and against increasing grants to voluntary schools. At one meeting Quinn quite bluntly told Hall-Thompson that 'the proposed absence of compulsion or disqualification [for religious instruction] would materially weaken the present position . . . [and] if a large number of teachers refused to give religious instruction a ridiculous situation would arise as the number of clergymen available to perform the duty would be inadequate'.[73] Teachers, therefore, had to be available to teach religion. Despite this argument, the Protestant churches did not declare total opposition to a conscience clause. In fact they accepted the need for such a clause, at least in principle. Not to have done so would have been rather difficult for Protestants, given their general attitude on 'freedom of conscience'. However, they did fear what might be described as a 'strong' clause, which many teachers could invoke to avoid teaching religion.

Small consolations

Consultation with other groups, like the teachers' unions, the Workers' Educational Association[74] and the parents' lobby[75] indicated that, outside the traditional interests, support was widespread for the general thrust of the minister's ideas for educational reform. The main points of difference related to the multilateral selective system at secondary level. Once again the teachers' representatives confirmed the stand on religious education they had taken in the 1920s, i.e. one of opposition to teachers being compelled to teach religion and they, therefore, welcomed the proposal to include a conscience clause as a defence of teachers' civil rights.[76] The support expressed by such bodies was, however, small consolation to a minister faced with the strength of church opposition to significant parts of his plans.

Final preoccupations

Since the consultation process did not remove many of the difficulties which Hall-Thompson had anticipated from the churches and their allies, it must have been with some trepidation that he proceeded to the final stages of drafting his white paper. In doing so the minister's major preoccupations were, on the one hand, how to meet the needs of the voluntary, mainly Catholic sector without upsetting the Protestant churches and the latter's unionist supporters while, on the other, allaying Protestant fears about religious instruction in public sector schools.

On the first issue, the minister was quite concerned to provide increased funding for Catholic schools. He was aware that many existing Catholic schools were suffering from lack of finances and, as he reported to his cabinet colleagues, were 'dirty, unhygienic and badly heated and the unfortunate child suffers though it is not his fault that he is in attendance at a voluntary school instead of at a transferred or provided school'.[77] The Catholic Church's opposition to any form of public representation on school management committees as the condition for increased funding remained an almost insuperable barrier to granting extra finance. It was a situation which was unlikely to change despite the fact that a small number of Catholic-controlled primary schools had successfully adopted the 'four-and-two' management structure.[78] Acknowledging this opposition, Hall-Thompson took a brave step and told his colleagues that he was 'fully satisfied that the Roman Catholic Managers should receive increased financial assistance for reconstruction; they will be put to very heavy expense and are entitled to something more than they have had hitherto'.[79] The cabinet remained, however, adamant on the principle of public representation and only agreed to an increase in maintenance grants to 100 per cent and capital costs to 65 per cent on condition that 'four-and-two' committees be established first.

A curious exception to the above requirement was to be allowed in the case of voluntary senior secondary schools, i.e. the existing secondary schools and colleges. In their case, it was agreed that grants of up to 65 per cent could be made for building and equipment without any requirement that their boards of management adopt a 'four-and-two' type structure.[80] It is difficult to avoid the conclusion that this exception was motivated by the fact that many of these secondary schools catered for the (Protestant) middle and upper classes and so had to be protected. The subsequent contradiction posed for those who attacked the increased level of assistance to (Catholic) voluntary schools did not seem to matter.

White paper

The proposals for educational reform were eventually published in December 1944.[81] As anticipated, the main proposals were to restructure education broadly along lines similar to those in England and Wales. Compulsory schooling would commence at five and last until fifteen, with provisions to raise it eventually to sixteen. Nursery education would be provided by local education authorities where needed and transfer to secondary school would take place at eleven. Senior secondary schools would receive pupils who were selected following a qualifying examination and would provide a traditional academic type education. Junior secondary schools would receive the rest, some of whom could transfer at thirteen to junior technical schools. On the vexed question of religion in education, all primary and secondary schools would be required to conduct a daily act of worship and provide religious instruction. Teachers' liberty of conscience would, however, be protected by the provision of a conscience clause.

The management of local authority primary schools would remain as it had been for public elementary schools and while the management structure for the new junior secondary schools was not specified, the white paper suggested that it would be appropriate to give the local authorities a greater voice than they had in the case of the elementary schools. As for the funding for voluntary schools, the condition for any increase beyond 50 per cent would be, as had been expected, the establishment of 'four-and-two' committees, senior secondary schools excepted. Stressing Northern Ireland's distinct character, the government, in its introduction to the bill, argued that there was a need to provide education of a standard equal to that in Britain, but not necessarily in precisely the same manner. To exactly parallel Britain 'would be to ignore local conditions and deny Ulster people the right to shape in their own way what is perhaps the most important of their social services'.[82] How true this statement would turn out to be!

Controversy relaunched

Like a calm before a storm, immediate responses to the white paper were either favourable or, if not, muted in the opposition expressed. The *Belfast Telegraph*, ever supportive of educational reform emanating from government, commented approvingly in an editorial on the day after the white paper's publication that:

There is plenty to bite on in this White Paper and it will be the duty of Parliament to discuss it thoroughly in order to clear the way for the preparation of a Bill which will make the broadest advance suitable to the needs of the people.[83]

First Protestant responses were also favourable with a spokesperson from the Church of Ireland, the Dean of Down and Connor, Rev. W.S. Kerr, saying 'I welcome heartily the provision for religious teaching in all schools, secondary as well as elementary . . . I do not anticipate any practical difficulties in this respect'.[84] His anticipation of no difficulties was to be short-lived. Within a week two articles in the *Irish Times* indicated that the Rev. Kerr's hopes were ill-founded.[85] These articles, which were generally favourable to the white paper, pointed out that while Catholic views had not been officially made known, it could be anticipated that they would be hostile to the key proposals on management and funding. The articles then went on to list the main points on which Protestant clerics would be likely to express at least some reservations and it was noted that already the Rev. William Corkey and the Grand Master of the Imperial Grand Chapter of the Orange Order were expressing opposition to the proposed conscience clause. The anonymous author defended the proposed reforms arguing that 'there is no fundamental contradiction in the White Paper; and there seems to be no reason why religious instruction should not be made compulsory in the schools without interfering with the teachers' liberty of conscience'.[86]

That was not how the churches officially viewed the white paper. The Boards of Education of the Protestant Churches issued a joint statement in which they singled out the proposed conscience clause, the proposed repeal of the 1930 act, the threat to many small Protestant schools which transfer at eleven contained, the new proposals for the appointment of teachers and the increase in public funding for voluntary schools, all as grounds for serious disagreement with the ministry's proposals.[87] In private correspondence with the Minister of Education, the Church of Ireland Archbishop of

Armagh, John Gregg, argued that since teachers in many voluntary schools were giving religious instruction and since their schools were in receipt of public funding, it should not be a problem to require teachers in public authority schools to do likewise.[88] Gregg seemed to fear that without a requirement to provide religious instruction, many teachers might be pressurised into not providing it!

Catholics enter the fray

As 1945 opened, opposition from the churches and from their traditional political allies hardened. Although the Catholic authorities had not as yet declared their position, nationalist members in parliament did not hesitate to anticipate what that position would be. Thomas Campbell M.P. strongly and sarcastically attacked the white paper saying to the minister:

Your discrimination against the Catholic voluntary schools continued and intensified in this White Paper scheme circumvents by craft worthy of Old Nick the prohibition contained in the Government of Ireland Act 1920 which you cling to as your charter against passing a law that would directly or indirectly impose a disadvantage on account of religious belief.[89]

Campbell was supported by his colleague, Michael McGurk M.P., who made the stark and absolute claim, in terms worthy of any prelate, that:

. . . not one Catholic manager of all the Catholic schools in Northern Ireland will transfer his school to a four-and-two committee . . . while grass grows and water runs the Cardinal Primate, or the Bishops, or the priests of Northern Ireland will never transfer their schools to a four-and-two committee.[90]

There was also little consolation for the minister in speeches by unionist members, not even when the Attorney General, John C. McDermott, made it clear that teachers could not be compelled to teach religious instruction and that to do so would be a breach of the Government of Ireland Act.[91] Tommy Henderson, the fiery independent unionist M.P., denounced this decision saying that:

The speech of the Attorney General will be received with great surprise by the Protestant denominations throughout Northern Ireland and I can assure the House that it will create a revolution in the ranks of the Orange Institution throughout this little province of ours . . . Greater men than you have been killed by the churches when Protestant teaching was opposed.[92]

Using dramatically vivid imagery, another unionist M.P. claimed that :

. . . while retaining Bible Instruction there is to be the right of a teacher to say that he or she is not prepared to give that instruction; in other words, the nail of Bible Instruction is to be handed to us without the assurance that a hammer will be provided to drive it home . . . I strongly oppose anything which takes away from the provisions of the 1930 Act.[93]

Reinforcing and re-echoing unionist opposition in parliament was a concerted campaign at local government level. The first two months of 1945 witnessed a series of resolutions being passed in unionist-controlled local authorities, each of which singled out particular aspects of the white paper for condemnation.[94] Transfer at eleven was condemned, as was increased funding for voluntary schools and the new provisions for religious instruction.

When the Catholic Church began to issue its response, it used the time honoured medium of Lenten pastorals. Bishop Neil Farren of Derry in his pastoral emphasised the church's determination to maintain its traditional stand on total control:

We are determined to keep control of our schools and to ensure that our Catholic children will get the type of education which their parents demand and have a right to claim . . . As Catholics we cannot accept either of the alternatives suggested in the White Paper, complete transfer of our schools or the installment transfer under a 'four-and-two' committee.[95]

Cardinal MacRory of Armagh appealed for equality of treatment for Catholics, implying that Catholics had to bear a form of double 'taxation' because of their support for church schools: 'All we want is that the education authority shall respect our consciences and allow us to share equally in the public funds to which we have equally contributed'.[96]

Some support

Only the teachers' unions, when they focused on the more pupil and classroom related aspects of the proposals, found much that was positive to say about them. The I.N.T.O., for example, praised the raising of the school leaving age, the intended progressive reduction in class size, the proposed enlarged scholarship scheme and the extension of the health and welfare services within schools.[97] As expected, like the other major union, the U.T.U., the I.N.T.O. was very critical of the proposed transfer at eleven and was concerned about the proposed level of funding for voluntary schools. The Principal Teachers' Union defended the proposals regarding religious instruction and the conscience clause saying that the 1930 act had been unnecessary and that its removal 'would restore to many of us the genuine enthusiasm which we had when co-operating with the clergy in the work of education in contrast to the compliance which comes from being compelled where no compulsion is necessary'.[98] Such voices of support were to be drowned in the crescendo of opposition emanating from the churches.

Conscience clause

The position of the Protestant churches on the conscience clause was a difficult one to argue, given that respect for the individual conscience was central to Protestantism and their spokespersons could not avoid publicly upholding that respect. Their difficulty was reconciling this respect with their demands that schools be obliged to provide Bible instruction and that teachers would have to provide it. Spelling out the Protestant churches' position the Rev. William Corkey wrote in the *Belfast Telegraph*:

The Protestant churches have made it abundantly clear that they do not desire to risk violence to the conscience of any teachers and should it be found possible would welcome a clause in the new Act appropriately safeguarding the liberty of conscience of the individual teacher while at the same time preserving to the full the liberty of the community to decide through Local Education Authorities who is to teach their children, and what these children are to be taught. These two principles are not inconsistent.[99]

In practice there was an inconsistency because the Protestant churches were claiming that while teachers should be able to have recourse to a conscience clause, the 1930 provisions had to be retained in order to ensure that this instruction would be given whether teachers wished to or not. According to the churches a conscience clause was incompatible with the retention of the 1930 legislation unless, of course, only teachers who did not sign such a clause were to be appointed, as Corkey himself seemed to be suggesting when he said that:

The primary demand made by the United Protestant Churches was that in schools where Bible Instruction was given in accordance with the wishes of the parents, those responsible for appointing the teachers should continue to take into account the competence and willingness of an applicant to give such instruction, when making an appointment.What the Protestant churches clearly wanted was legislation which would allow schools to continue as before and that no conscience clause should be allowed to interfere with existing appointment practices.[100]

Signs of flexibility

Despite the general intransigence of the churches initially, some signs of flexibility were to emerge within both the Catholic and Protestant positions. While these signs were not to prove significant in the short term, they did at least suggest that some within the churches were tiring of the old intransigence and inflexibility. It was within the Catholic Church that the first sign of possible movement appeared when, during the consultative process surrounding the white paper, some members of the clergy began indicating to Ministry of Education officials a desire to reach an accommodation whereby the 'four-and-two' management structure could be made generally acceptable to the church. The evidence for this development comes from Ministry of Education papers and from correspondence between the Prime Minister, Basil Brooke, and Sir Shane Leslie of County Monaghan, who was acting as a kind of intermediary on behalf of Cardinal MacRory of Armagh.[101]

Cardinal MacRory's attack on the white paper had, as has already been indicated above, concentrated on the injustice which he claimed Catholics were experiencing because they had to contribute twice to their schools, once through taxation and then through contributions to provide the 50 per cent which voluntary schools had to raise for capital projects. He was not, however, totally opposed to some form of public representation on management committees, a view shared by the clergy in contact with ministry officials. A Ministry of Education internal memorandum reporting on consultations with the latter noted that some of its younger members, 'would swallow the "four-and-two" principle if the Government would give them seventy-five per cent instead of sixty-five'.[102] One of the priests consulted was also reported as saying that 'the cardinal would agree wholeheartedly, but he is restrained by the bishops'.[103]

Confirmation of the cardinal's view is to be found in correspondence between Leslie and Brooke. Cardinal MacRory had apparently invited Leslie, a long acquaintance both of himself and Basil Brooke, to contact the latter on his behalf in order to explore the possibility of making the 'four-and-two' principle acceptable to the church. In the brief correspondence which followed from this request, Leslie indicated that the cardinal acknowledged, surprisingly in view of the church's long held position, that 'popular control must be safeguarded', but that the 'four-and-two' structure, as operated, 'would not work as it would lead to local canvassing [i.e. for teaching posts]'.[104] In the white paper the government itself had expressed concerns of its own about the extent to which canvassing of members of school committees was happening in the transferred and provided sector. However, the church's real objection was also bound up with the general nationalist mistrust of unionist-dominated local government in Northern Ireland. The cardinal's solution was for the minister himself to 'represent popular control' and, although he did not explicitly propose it, it would seem that he expected that in this capacity the minister, rather than the local authorities, would appoint the two public representatives to 'four-and-two' committees.[105] Leslie stressed in his correspondence that 'the old cardinal does want to offer an olive branch' and added his own perceptive plea 'I know you will not regret peace with the hierarchy. Bishops in all countries can be neutralised if they get a square deal on education'.[106] Further discussion of the cardinal's ideas was, unfortunately, interrupted by the publication at the end of March 1945 of the northern bishops' joint statement, a statement which expressed a very traditional church approach to the government's proposals.[107] Leslie then declined to act as intermediary any further.[108]

The bishops' statement reiterated the claim that the Ministry of Education was motivated to act against Catholic interests and indicated that a much harder line was being adopted than had been declared by the deputation which had gone to the ministry the previous year.[109] School committees were ruled out on grounds of principle, efficiency and, betraying current Catholic suspicions of state control '. . . fear that this attempt to deprive us of our voluntary schools is the initiation of a policy against our free institutions and our right of voluntary association which is a fundamental right of citizens in a free democracy'.[110] The proposals for a new system of secondary schools were also attacked since the provision of such schools would, because of their size, entail violating parish boundaries 'making it practically impossible to arrange for an equitable allocation of responsibility . . . and make it impossible for individual pastors to carry out their obligations as laid down in Canon Law to provide for the moral and spiritual formation of their flocks, especially the young'.[111] The most telling point in the statement lay in the contrast drawn between the amount of financial support received by Catholic and provided and transferred, i.e. Protestant, schools. Ministry figures quoted by the bishops showed that the former with a pupil enrolment of 70,000 received only £170,000 in grant aid, while the latter with 92,000 pupils received £2,785,000 in 1943–44. The statement concluded in terms which were hardly likely to make the ministry more favourably disposed to the bishops' arguments. Linking appeals to faith and nationalism, they accused the ministry of having 'once again surrendered to the threats of those brewers of bigotry, who by their unwise counsels, alien alike to Christianity and to patriotism, have brought so much misery on the land that we love'.[112] Nothing had changed either in the sentiments, or in the language in which the bishops' comments were expressed, the cardinal's desire for accommodation notwithstanding. Later in the year, a delegation led by Bishops Mageean and Farren met the Minister of Education to detail their opposition to the white paper proposals,[113] but apparently received no indication that any significant change would be made to meet their objections.[114]

To amend or not

As reaction to the white paper poured in to the Ministry of Education, officials began to examine possible options for dealing with the reservations expressed, foremost amongst which were those of the Protestant churches. Once again, to meet these objections consideration was given to the proposal that the British government should amend section 5 of the Government of Ireland Act. However, such consideration was short-lived when the Home Office in London indicated its objections in no uncertain terms[115] stating that an amendment would 'inevitably be liable to be represented as impairing the safeguards enacted in section 5 of the Government of Ireland Act for the maintenance of the principle of toleration and for the protection of minorities'.[116]

On the basis of this advice the Northern Irish cabinet decided in late January 1945 that there could be no question of changing its proposal to safeguard the liberty of conscience of teachers.[117] This did not, however, draw the debate to a close. Protestant-unionist discontent continued to simmer throughout the spring of that year and, as a general election was declared for June, this discontent again threatened unionist unity.[118] As in 1925 and in 1930, the leadership of the Unionist Party had no desire to face its supporters embroiled in a conflict with the Protestant churches and a section of its own party. Consequently, Prime Minister Brooke became very anxious to heal the growing rift and this anxiety afforded the Protestant clerics another opportunity to strengthen 'their leverage by striking hard as a general election approached'.[119] At the end of May, a series of meetings were hurriedly arranged between the government and backbench unionist M.P.s, between the government and the Orange Order, and between the government and representatives of the Protestant churches.[120] From the reports of these meetings it would appear as if the government had indicated a willingness to reconsider a number of the important points under dispute.

The cabinet report of the meeting with backbenchers suggests that guarantees that rights enjoyed under the 1925 and 1930 Education Acts would remain unaltered were conceded 'subject to an agreed conscience clause to be formulated to meet the objection to compulsion on the teacher'.[121] The meeting also agreed that the government would examine a proposal whereby the appointment of teachers might not have to be referred to the relevant local education authority. At the meeting with representatives of the Orange Order, the Minister of Education was faced with a resolution demanding that the conscience clause issue be settled 'as otherwise the churches would issue a questionnaire to election candidates and oppose any who failed to give them a satisfactory answer'.[122] Reporting the meeting with Protestant church representatives, the *Times Educational Supplement* highlighted two points which were apparently agreed at both that meeting and at the meeting with backbenchers:

1. It is the policy of the Government that the rights at present enjoyed by parents and school management committees under the 1925 and 1930 Education Acts will remain unaltered subject to an agreed conscience clause to be formulated to meet objections to compulsion on the teacher.

2. The question of the appointment of a teacher by a school management committee without recourse to the local education authority will be further examined with a view to improvement in the present basis of appointment.[123]

The *Irish Times* in its report also emphasised the retention of the principles laid down in the earlier legislation, noting, however, that a conscience clause would be provided to 'safeguard the rights of teachers who do not wish to give religious instruction'.[124] These reports suggested that the churches had, effectively, obtained what they were seeking: guarantees on compulsory religious instruction, an acceptable conscience clause and the likelihood of concessions on teacher appointments to preclude the possibility of nationalist-dominated education authorities interfering with appointments to schools in which the majority of pupils would be Protestant. The apparent understanding reached between representatives of the government and the Protestant churches dissolved the tension over the proposed conscience clause, at least for a short time.[125] The general election in June resulted once again in a convincing victory for the Unionist Party, a victory unsullied by dissension between that party and the Protestant churches.

The peace won in May was indeed short-lived. By July the Minister of Education was locked into a further dispute with the Protestant churches. Then, later in the year the question of the conscience clause was to return to haunt him, when it emerged that different interpretations were held as to what had been agreed at the end of May meetings. In July the question of how the new junior schools' management committees would be composed, precipitated sharp exchanges with the Protestant churches. Hall-Thompson proposed to a meeting with the Association of Education Committees that representation should be three-fold: one-third representing the management of contributing primary schools, one-third the local authority and one-third the parents.[126] This did not satisfy Protestant church interests who seemed to see in it a possibility that Catholics and communists could win control of junior secondary schools attended by Protestant pupils if 'transferor', i.e. church, representation was to be 'restricted' to one-third. Instead, Chancellor Quinn argued for one-half representation for 'transferors', even though, as the minister himself pointed out, there was 'no reason for transferors and ex-managers having such representation' since no schools existed to be transferred. Quinn persisted and indicated that one-half would be insisted upon.[127]

In effect Quinn was arguing the same point which had been argued in the 1920s in support of the demand for Protestant church representation on management committees of transferred and provided schools attended by a majority of Protestant pupils. At a later meeting with representatives of these churches to deal with this issue, the minister was presented with a vivid picture of Protestant fears as to what might happen were the churches not to be given significant representation on the boards of management of the new secondary schools. Using well worn arguments, the church representatives insisted that the minister's proposals 'would weaken the safeguard of Protestant teachers for Protestant schools; . . . would constitute a serious danger of giving power to Roman Catholics . . . Roman Catholics might take possession of a school . . . they would probably send sufficient children to the secondary schools to enable them to obtain control of the parents' representatives; . . . there was a small section outside the churches who were anxious to get control, largely persons of the communist type'.[128]

Nevertheless, these arguments must have prevailed, as the education bill was to reveal. Schools with no claim to be Protestant, other than a majority of their pupils being from the Protestant community, were to find that their management committees would contain a significant clerical presence from these same churches. Perhaps it was, that satisfaction for the Protestant churches on the question of representation was intended to offset the absence of any concession to them on the question of the conscience clause. On the latter issue the government stood by its decision.

Protestant consciences stirred

The Board of Education of the Presbyterian Church, prompted no doubt by the Rev. Corkey, in a resolution passed in November 1945 stated that it had:

. . . heard with amazement that the Minister of Education proposes in the case of children over eleven years to disregard the arrangement made on the eve of the last General Election.[129]

In almost identical terms, the Grand Lodge of the Orange Order also expressed its 'amazement' that the minister proposed 'to go back on the agreement arrived at on the 1st June between the Prime Minister, and other members of the Government . . . and the representatives of the Protestant Churches'.[130] Local sections of the order added their voices to that of the Grand Lodge. The Grand County Lodge of Tyrone, to express its distrust of the Minister of Education, wrote directly to the Prime Minister about the fears of Protestants in border areas which it claimed were greater in 1945 because of an alleged increase in the Catholic population. Hence, the lodge's letter went on, 'It is considered now is the proper time to safeguard against such an event so that no matter what happens the control of Protestant schools shall remain in Protestant hands'.[131]

These protests and representations elicited no immediate response from the government. So, during the spring of 1946 local presbyteries of the Presbyterian Church began passing resolutions, all similarly worded, demanding that:

. . . such powers as are now possessed by the Protestant people of Northern Ireland through the Education authorities to advertise for and appoint teachers to give Bible instruction shall remain unaltered subject to an agreed conscience clause.[132]

Further protests against additional funding for voluntary schools were expressed at the annual conference of the Unionist Party in February. One delegate, speaking in favour of the resolution opposing an increase said that 'sectarian' schools were not needed in Ulster and asked 'why should the voluntary schools get fifty per cent of the cost of new buildings to be devoted to one sect'.[133]

Then, almost as if not wanting to go unheard for too long in the continuing protest against the government's plans, Catholic voices also added to this clamour in early 1946. In his Lenten pastoral Bishop Mageean demanded that the legislation 'must give due recognition to our Voluntary School System which has the sanction of generations behind it and make such financial provision as will enable us to maintain and develop it'.[134]

Pressure was again mounting from all sides and it was hardly surprising that the government took its time in formulating its response. The Education Bill was not published until the autumn of 1946, but when it finally did appear it was still not of a kind to allay fears, nor to contain the fury which education was capable of generating in Northern Ireland.

Education Bill

The bill, published in September 1946, contained a lengthy and complex set of proposals, many merely of a technical kind. The main focus was the reorganisation of the elementary and secondary school system in order to provide access to a form of second level education for all and the financial, management and religious education provisions which would accompany that reorganisation. The key proposals for the restructuring of secondary education on a selective basis marked no change from those outlined in the white paper and as such were a disappointment to the teachers' unions in particular. Proposals for school management left unchanged what had previously been proposed for primary schools, for the senior secondary schools, now referred to as 'grammar' schools, and for the voluntary junior, now 'intermediate', schools. However, for the new local authority secondary intermediate schools, management committees were proposed consisting of 'not less than one half of the members nominated by the management committees of the contributing primary schools, not more than one quarter to be representatives of the parents and the remainder persons chosen by the local education authority'.[135] In other words, a significant concession was made to the Protestant churches which could now expect that their clergy, or other persons of an acceptable kind, would be nominated by the committees of the contributing schools. Significantly, on the question of grant aid to voluntary schools, the bill proposed that such schools should receive 65 per cent, without any additional requirements as to the type of management structures; in other words the 'four-and-two' structure was not to be required. The one condition attached to this proposal was that in order to receive such grants voluntary grammar schools would be required to reserve at least 80 per cent of their places for so-called 'qualifying' pupils, i.e. those who would pass the selection tests for entry to the grammar school sector.[136] On the controversial question of the 'conscience clause' the bill proposed a clause of the kind originally recommended in the white paper.[137]

Presenting the bill, the Minister of Education was careful to answer those criticisms which he knew would be directed at his proposals. He dealt with religious instruction by underlining the obligation on all schools to provide this instruction and, as if to answer those who had been critical of the absence of such an obligation on secondary schools in the past, he stressed 'that for the first time in our history we say definitely to the voluntary school, to the secondary school and to the junior technical school "You shall give religious instruction in your school" '.[138] and it would no longer be surrounded by the 'ifs' and 'provided thats' of the 1930 act. As for the conscience clause, the minister said its provision was a true mark of the Protestant, because it upheld a man's right 'to hold his own conviction and that if he does so he shall not be penalised'.[139] Justifying the grant of 65 per cent to voluntary schools Hall-Thompson pointed out that several hundred of the 966 non-transferred elementary schools were under Protestant management and that only 10 of the 76 secondary–academic schools (as he called the new grammar schools) were under regional authority control. He had therefore to be mindful of the needs of the children of all denominations in these schools and, so, he could not be accused of discriminating in favour of Roman Catholic schools.[140]

Reaction – negative

Even before the bill was published reaction was being prepared. An ultra-Protestant group, the National Union of Protestants, issued a letter to the

Prime Minister early in September calling upon the government to ensure that 'the provisions for Bible instruction in the 1925 and 1930 Acts be in no way diminished or abrogated'.[141] This was by no means the union's only intervention in the controversy that was to break out, but it did indicate the short yardstick by which many would be judging the bill. Even more significant in terms of an influential voice in Protestantism was the statement from the Imperial Black Chapter of County Down, issued in mid-October just as the bill was being debated for the first time in the House of Commons. In this statement the Minister of Education was attacked for not providing that 'only Protestant teachers would be appointed to Protestant schools, but on the contrary has opened the door to the appointment of Atheists, Agnostics and Roman Catholics to occupy those positions . . .'[142] Norman Porter, Belfast organiser of the National Union of Protestants, issued a public letter on the same day expressing similar sentiments. In it he attacked the proposal to increase grants to voluntary schools which he described as 'a sop to the withdrawal of Roman Catholic opposition' and as being 'at the expense of the tax payers of the six counties, the majority of whom are Protestant'.[143]

The Rev. William Corkey joined the attack two weeks later with a letter to the press in which he argued that the bill's proposals amounted to discrimination against Protestants. Protestants, he claimed, had transferred their schools, only to lose control, while Catholics, who had not transferred any school, were to receive a considerable degree of public funding.[144] The Church of Ireland Bishop of Derry and Raphoe, while acknowledging some positive points in the bill, referred to it as likely to have 'a discrediting rather than a stimulating effect upon education', because of the alleged dangers it posed to religious education.[145] Dr Gregg, Archbishop of Armagh, alleged that the bill 'made it possible for teachers in increasing numbers who were non-Christian or anti-Christian or agnostic to gain a footing on the teaching staff of primary as well as higher school and rank for promotion . . . even though their influence . . . might be altogether hostile to Christianity'.[146]

Within the Unionist Party, both in parliament and in the branches, protests mounted about the proposed grant to voluntary schools and the perceived threat to Protestantism from the conscience clause for teachers. At a meeting in the Wellington Hall in Belfast, the attendance of politicians, churchmen and general public, supported a motion condemning the 'threats to their Protestant inheritance contained in the bill' and another which protested against the proposed increase in grants for voluntary schools and in particular against the 65 per cent towards the building and maintenance of all voluntary schools which could only result in a further endowment to Roman Catholicism to the extent of about £2 million. The same meeting pledged that £20,000 would be raised to support the campaign against the provisions in the bill to which objection was being taken.[147] Similar public meetings were held in other towns and cities. A meeting in Derry's Guildhall heard a number of impassioned pleas to ensure 'that we shall have Protestant teachers to teach our children' and that 'A Protestant government elected by a Protestant people should maintain Protestant teachers for Protestant children . . . we shall never tolerate a Roman Catholic, an infidel or a Communist to teach in our schools'.[148]

The annual meeting of the Association of Northern Ireland Education Committees also opposed the conscience clause, adopting a motion which called for no 'interference with the provisions for religious instruction in the 1930 Act'[149] because, as one member argued, without these provisions, 'A teacher might be a Roman Catholic, a Jew, a secularist or an avowed atheist and be appointed to teach Protestant children under the provisions of the Bill'.[150]

An attempt by the Ministry of Education to summarise the advantages of the new proposals over the existing situation failed to influence those who believed that religious instruction and the appointment of teachers would, in the future, be to the disadvantage of the Protestant community. The ministry's statement pointed out that religious instruction would be even more firmly protected than under the 1930 act, that a collective act of worship would be obligatory and that the teacher's conscience would also be protected in a more satisfactory manner.[151]

In parliament, unionist attacks on the bill focused more on the increased grant to voluntary schools than on the conscience clause and its alleged effects on religious instruction in public authority schools. These attacks had a clear sectarian basis which, ironically, ignored the fact that many schools under Protestant management would also benefit from the increased grant. Several unionist members described it as a 'gift to the Roman Catholic Church', as a 'betrayal of Protestantism',[152] as a form of 'appeasement' and a 'concession' which was frustrating unionist hopes for education.[153] The inference was that Protestants in Northern Ireland were being asked to pay, or 'endow', as one member put it,[154] Catholic schools out of their taxes, as if the taxes were almost exclusively Protestant taxes. Harry Midgley, long an advocate of public education, who only reluctantly conceded any educational rights to denominational interests, was particularly forceful in opposing grant aid to denominational schools. He argued that those who wanted to provide denominational schools should be allowed to do so, provided they would make no demands on the public finances. Attacking the Catholic Church for seeking such aid, which he termed 'preferential', Midgley stated:

They are claiming preferential treatment to the extent that they are claiming exactly the same treatment as regards administration and upkeep of schools as the local authority and as accrues to other schools which have been provided by the public authority, schools which belong to the people as a whole which are nationally owned, nationally endowed, which are nationally administered, schools which are collective property belonging to all the people and have handed over all their liabilities and response to the public authority.[155]

Midgley's case was essentially a secularist one which argued that a form of education under secular control was the most appropriate for a modern democratic society. It was the same case that had been advanced and was being advanced by secularists in many societies. Its central weakness was that it assumed a political consensus and a degree of socio–political cohesion which were not present in Northern Irish society. Phrases like 'schools owned by the people', 'nationally owned' and 'collective property', suggested one nation and one collectivity, none of which even yet apply to Northern Ireland.

Catholic-nationalist reaction – firm but muted

Compared with the reaction from Protestant–unionist circles to the white paper, reaction to the bill from the Catholic–nationalist section of the community contained a mixture of positive and negative comment. Nationalist politicians praised what they saw as the bill's socially progressive provisions, in particular the widening of access to secondary education,[156] but despite the bill's concessions to voluntary schools on the question of grant aid, they claimed the concession had not gone far enough. From the introduction of the bill nationalist M.P.s argued that voluntary schools were still being discriminated against. The M.P. for Pottinger John Beattie, a Protestant himself, but of nationalist and socialist views, while praising many aspects of the bill also argued that, 'The children whose parents are Catholic have just the same rights to have the generous offer that the Minister has made to all transferred schools'.[157] Frank Hanna, another Belfast M.P., spoke about Catholic parents being penalised by the bill and that it 'is unjust and undemocratic and it is more undemocratic because in the last resort it works mainly against the poorer elements in the community'.[158]

The case made by these M.P.s and their colleagues was that voluntary schools should receive 100 per cent funding and that the government's insistence on public involvement in management structures was only an excuse to dismiss this demand. They claimed that if the government was satisfied that the existing management could be entrusted with existing grants, it could be entrusted with more. As Hanna stated: 'if the supervision of the expenditure of those moneys is possible, is it not equally possible and equally feasible to supervise it adequately and properly if there is a full one hundred per cent ?'[159] Nationalist M.P.s stressed that their case was not one of seeking favours or 'endowments', as Cahir Healy said, borrowing the terminology of section 5 of the Government of Ireland Act, but of upholding human rights and respect for the different approach to education taken by the Catholic Church to that of other churches.[160] To emphasise this difference, James McSparran M.P., arguing for that respect, provided the House of Commons with an outline of Catholic education principles which would have done credit to a theologian:

The question of religion and all those underlying principles of ethics and decency in life overlap the purely secular and the Catholic Church has taken up the attitude . . . that the parents and the Church are responsible for the education of the child; also that the spiritual aspect of the child's education is a primary aspect and that it is not subordinate to the State's interest in its education.[161]

Asserting the justice of their case and, at the same time, answering the accusation that it was the Protestant community which was being required to pay for Catholic schools, Hanna argued 'that all people in the community contribute a just share of taxation to the community, and if any section contributes in proportion to its numbers to a common fund, surely as a matter of elementary justice it is at least entitled to receive from any distribution of that fund in equal proportion'.[162]

As for the Catholic church itself, perhaps because it had already accepted that 65 per cent was as much as it could expect to obtain, it did not indulge in the same degree of polemical rhetoric as its Protestant counterparts. The growing willingness, within a section of the church at least, to accept that a greater degree of public accountability would have to be provided before any further increase could be obtained, may also explain this stance. It is signifcant, for example, that the Catholic bishops did not dwell on the bill in their Lenten pastorals issued in February 1947. Only Cardinal MacRory's successor, Archbishop William D'Alton, made education a central theme in his pastoral and his comments focused on suggestions for a common syllabus for religious instruction and criticised those who were saying that voluntary schools should not receive even grants of 50 per cent, but he did not launch any attack on what was actually being proposed.

The argument that equal treatment for all schools was the only just solution in the Northern Irish context was a strong argument, particularly given the manner in which the schools serving the Protestant community had come to be financed. However, when it came to practical politics, it is evident that none of the nationalist politicians held any hope that the case for 100 per cent funding for voluntary schools had any prospect of success. Although an amendment to this effect was tabled, it was done so in a manner which led to it being ruled out of order, something the M.P.s must have been aware was inevitable.[163] It would appear that they, like the Catholic Church itself were satisfied to accept the 65 per cent offer. Sixty-five per cent was, after all, 15 per cent greater than their counterparts in England and Wales were receiving under the 1944 act and was a significant advance on what they had been receiving since 1930.

Support – in and out of parliament

As on previous occasions there were those who voiced almost total support for the bill from the outset. In parliament, Dehra Parker was a consistent and strong defender of the changes proposed, pointing out that the grants would apply equally to schools under Protestant as well as Catholic management. She appealed for support for the increase for the sake of the children in the schools affected because, 'we must all recognise that it is going to make a tremendous difference to those schools if no consideration is taken of the increased cost of lighting and heating'.[164] Government ministers, like William Maginnis, re-echoed this concern saying that 'for the first time in the history of the children of Northern Ireland opportunity is given such as has rarely been granted to the children of any other country and certainly never exceeded'.[165]

Editorials in the *Belfast Telegraph* regretted the controversy which was surrounding the bill:

It has been difficult to reconcile conflicting interests in a Bill of such wide scope, but we believe that the Minister has made an honest attempt to meet various criticisms and that the House will support him in the view that in regard to the place of religion in the schools the Bill represents a great advance.[166]

Teachers' unions supported the conscience clause, though at least one, the small Incorporated Association of Assistant Mistresses (I.A.A.M.) which recruited in secondary schools, felt that the conscience clause did not afford the same degree of protection to teachers as was provided in England and Wales[167] and was very critical of the stand taken by the Protestant churches. The churches had not, the I.A.A.M. noted, appreciated 'the imperative need to safeguard the teacher's integrity of conscience [and] showed a disquieting apathy about the need for sincerity of belief and purpose on the part of those teachers who might agree to give religious instruction'.[168]

In the context of the controversy then raging, the most interesting of all the support which the government's proposals received, came from the Methodist Church and from a prominent ex-Moderator of the Presbyterian General Assembly. In October the Methodist Church issued a statement warmly welcoming the education bill.[169] In particular, the church supported the bill's conscience clause and condemned the kind of clause sought by the other (Protestant) churches. The statement emphasised the Methodist Church's belief 'in the policy of trusting the teachers', the very point which the teachers' unions had been making since 1923. Prior to this official statement, the President of the Methodist Conference, Rev. R.H. Gallagher, had praised the bill saying that it :

. . . would make a liberal education available to every child in the community. Opportunity will be offered to all, according to age, ability and aptitude. Another thing we rejoice at in this Bill is the place given to the teaching of religion . . . The State has come to realise that if its foundations are to be secure and permanent they must be Christian foundations.[170]

Ex-Moderator J. Waddell of the Presbyterian Church agreed with the Methodist Church and claimed that the Education Board of his own church was out of touch with the general opinion within the church.[171] He was unhappy with the criticisms coming from his colleagues about the increased grants to voluntary schools referring to them as 'a mere parrot cry to catch the ear of the mob'. Waddell concluded his statement with a strong warning that the churches would 'never be forgiven if they jeopardise by questionable methods of debate and objections that seem to most reasonable people trivial, a great measure of educational reform'.[172] It was a warning that would go unheeded for several more years.

Determination triumphs

Compared to earlier controversies, that of 1945–47, while dominated by similar protests phrased in similar rhetoric, was also marked by some slight but significant shifts, not least within the churches. These shifts were not very publicly apparent at the time and the louder voices of protest still dominated the debate. However, the government would appear to have been aware of the changes and they may well have encouraged Hall-Thompson to stand firm against the more strident demands of the period. Minor amendments were made to the bill, e.g. the right of school management committees to continue forwarding three names to the local authority when appointing teachers, but on the broad and central issues of its proposals the government stood firm. The bill passed all stages in the Commons in January 1947 and received royal assent following its passage through the Senate on 27 March. Despite the controversies which surrounded its adoption, the act was to provide the basis for a major advance in terms of access to secondary and later to higher education for many in Northern Ireland. Like its predecessors, however, its passage did not mark an end to the kind of controversy which had become characteristic of education in Northern Ireland. Nevertheless, while such controversy was to persist for some time yet, it is evident that after 1947 religious controversy of the very acrimonious kind witnessed from 1923–47 gradually moved to the margins of educational development in Northern Ireland.

8

Plans but no Action:
Education in the South 1940–50

Uncomfortable isolation

As in Northern Ireland, educational development of any significant kind in the south during the early 1940s was severely constrained by the exigencies of the time. The consensus which had very quickly established itself at the foundation of the state between the main educational interests continued to dominate, though some voices were beginning to question the means employed to promote those interests and, at times, even to question some of the state's fundamental educational aims. So, while little actually occurred by way of further reform, there is evidence that, inspired by developments elsewhere, some significant plans did at least reach the 'drawing board'. Towards the end of the decade the prolonged debate on the value of a consultative body concluded with the announcement that a council of education would be established. Failure to go beyond the planning stage meant that the forties and much of the fifties as well, became a period of no concerted development. The effect of this continuing failure to achieve reform from within the educational service itself made it all but inevitable that change would come from without.

Meanwhile Gaelicisation and its effects on education remained a major issue, if not *the* major preoccupation of educationists and of other commentators as well. The publication in 1942 of the I.N.T.O.'s investigation into the use of Irish in non-Irish speaking areas served to highlight how resistant official thinking was to any change in this respect. The findings of this report which indicated that many teachers were of the view that negative educational effects flowed from the use of Irish as a medium of instruction with children in such areas added immensely to the general unease which had begun to be expressed from the mid-thirties. To a Fianna Fail government strongly determined to maintain its approach to the promotion of Irish in schools, however, the report was most unwelcome and instead of proceeding to examine the criticisms and recommendations which followed, the Department of Education became very defensive and virtually dismissed the report out-of-hand.

Tilting at the managerial system

If controversies over the teaching and use of Irish held no implications for Catholic Church–state relationships in education, any attempt to interfere with the 'managerial system' certainly did. The first and rather hesitant challenge to this system to come from a southern government emerged during the mid-forties. It arose because the Department of Education attempted once again to persuade the Catholic Church to introduce changes in the manner in which the local contribution to school building and maintenance costs was made. Compared to the very gentle prodding of the church in the twenties this time the department was to be somewhat more persistent in its attempt to achieve change, but not any more successful. Faced with a growing backlog of school repairs and with a need to replace many delapidated school buildings, the department was anxious that in the post-war period greater progress might be made than had been possible previously. Proposals were, therefore, put to the Catholic bishops which, if adopted, would have led to the local contributions being made on a diocesan rather than on a parochial level. However, the changes proposed were to prove unacceptable to the church with the result that existing procedures were, by and large, retained.

The failure to obtain any change in the manner of meeting these contributions was another illustration of the jealousy with which the church guarded its traditional approach to school management. This failure was also indicative of the impotence, or at least lack of courage of the southern state when required to challenge the Catholic Church on the latter's interpretation of its role in education, even in situations where the state was convinced that children were suffering because of how the church insisted on that role being respected.

A third issue to be explored in this chapter concerns another failure, i.e. the failure to pursue plans for the extension of secondary education to all pupils in line with developments being undertaken in the post-war period in many other European countries, especially in Britain and in Northern Ireland.

Finally, the 1940s were to witness growing support for the long-canvassed idea that a council of education be established to provide a formal voice on educational matters for a variety of non-political interests. As already noted, a number of Catholic churchmen had become quite outspoken in favour of such a council, while at a political level, support was most keenly expressed by politicians of the main opposition party, Fine Gael. The idea became a very live one following the publication in 1944 of the *Report of the Commission on Vocational Organisation* which specifically dealt with the role of vocational interests in the public life of the state. It was not, however, until Fine Gael itself took office as the leading party in the coalition government of 1948–51, that the idea was implemented and a council of education was finally set up in 1950. On the council came to be pinned many of the hopes for educational reform in the south, hopes which, after a further decade's deliberations, would remain virtually unfulfilled.

Still Gaelicising

With respect to curriculum policy, insistence on the primacy of Irish and reaction to this insistence continued to exclude debate on most other aspects of curriculum development. Throughout the 1940s, the position adopted since

1922 that schools had to remain in the forefront of the campaign to revive Irish withstood mounting criticism from a wide range of sources. Tom Derrig continued to hold the office of Minister of Education throughout most of the period, explaining and defending government policy in the same forthright manner as when he first took the office in 1932. With time, his remarks began to acquire a sharper tone as criticism mounted and as he was obliged to admit that Irish might not be revived as rapidly, or as widely as he had earlier hoped.

A curious illustration of Derrig's determination to promote Irish can be found in the 1942 school attendance legislation for which he was responsible[1] and which seems to have been motivated more by a desire to compel all parents to ensure that their children would be taught the language rather than to improve their attendance at school.[2] Under the guise of a new schools attendance bill, the minister sought power to certify that the education received by children was 'suitable even if they were sent to schools outside the state'.[3] O'Connell of the I.N.T.O., still a member of the Dáil at the time as well as general secretary of his union, argued that this power was sought because it was intended 'to apply to parents who had sent their children to schools either in Britain or in Northern Ireland'.[4] He went on to claim that 'there was something more than a suspicion that a knowledge of Irish would be an important factor in the test for the necessary certificate'.[5] De Valera confirmed this suspicion when he stated in the Dáil that the bill was aimed at parents who might wish to deprive their children of the opportunity of learning Irish and of 'fitting themselves to be useful members of the community; and if we take it that Irish is part of state policy, and if we regard it as part of the equipment necessary for a good citizen – and if there are people who are likely to do that – then I think the minister would be entitled to say that we are going to close that gap'.[6] In other words there was to be no escape from learning Irish wherever Irish parents might choose to have their children educated.

This extraordinary measure to ensure that Irish would be taught to all Irish children was passed by both houses of the Oireachtas, but was referred by President Douglas Hyde to the Supreme Court which declared that it was repugnant to article 42 of the constitution. The grounds for this decision owed much to the entrenched position which the 1937 constitution had granted to the family by acknowledging '. . . that the primary and natural educator of the child is the Family and guarantees to respect the inalienable right and duty of parents to provide . . . for the religious, and moral, intellectual, physical and social education of their children'.[7] The bill was then withdrawn and since no attempt was made to produce an amended version, it must be assumed that the government had accepted that it could not extend its remit beyond the state, at least not on matters educational.

A new debate

If the School Attendance Bill was a further indication of an aggressive dimension to the language policy in education, the government's reaction to the long-awaited I.N.T.O. survey of teachers' attitudes towards the use of Irish as a medium of instruction was to reveal its defensiveness and its determination to maintain its established position, whatever the evidence and whatever the criticism. Nonetheless, this defensiveness and determination were also signals that a new and more intense phase of debate over the language issue was emerging, not just in educational circles, but in the wider Irish society.

Following a number of delays in its preparation and a period in which the Department of Education was allowed to consider its contents, the report was eventually published in 1942.[8] In it considerable attention was given to the views of teachers of infant classes, because the use of Irish in these classes had been made virtually compulsory in all schools. A majority of the teachers surveyed were negative in their assessment of the effects of using Irish. In the words of the report 'their pupils did not derive benefit from instruction through the medium of Irish, equal to that which they would derive, were English used'.[9] A report published by the Church of Ireland Board of Education at the same time and based on a survey of teachers in that church's schools contained similar findings.[10] Commenting on the latter's findings the board stated, in terms similar to those of the I.N.T.O., that 'the use of Irish has retarded progress without increasing interest in the language'.[11] It further noted that opposition to the use of Irish as a medium of instruction had resulted in some parents in border areas sending their children to school in Northern Ireland, a factor which, as O'Connell pointed out, seems to have motivated the unconstitutional School Attendance Bill.[12]

Speaking about the effects of teaching through Irish at infant level, the president of the I.N.T.O., J.P. Griffith, with his union's report very much in his mind, said at the 1942 congress:

In our infant departments we have, in excluding the home language and contrary to all hitherto accepted principles of educational practice, placed each child – each little budding sensitive soul – straight into a linguistic strait-jacket in which he cannot reveal the mysterious workings of his opening mind. We have tried this strange experiment but I fear it has not yielded the results claimed for it.[13]

At secondary level, strong union criticism was also being expressed at this time. The annual A.S.T.I. publication Schools and colleges year book of 1940–41 commented 'we feel that after the experience of twenty years the time is ripe for stock taking and we demand an enquiry into the position of Irish in the curriculum'.[14] Echoing the sentiments of his secondary colleagues, Griffith called for 'a complete survey of national education by some competent and independent body that would be advisable and profitable'.[15] Such a survey, he went on to say:

. . . would help us define and restate our aims which tend to become blurred and dimmed with the years . . . But probably the greatest good would be to effect, if possible, some measure of reconciliation between the national and utilitarian ideals whose apparent conflict has created some uneasiness.[16]

It was this latter point which went to the heart of the issue as far as many people were concerned, i.e. the fact that concentration on Irish was felt to be inhibiting other desirable developments, notably literacy in English which was regarded as essential for employment at home and also abroad.

Despite these comments and the I.N.T.O.'s report, the Department of Education remained belligerently defensive as its very hostile comments on the report reveal . The chief inspector criticised the committee which conducted the investigation for its composition and for aspects of its investigation's design.[17] The committee contained no women teachers and so, according to the chief inspector, lacked experience in infant teaching; witnesses, he pointed out, were not interrogated, merely asked to respond to written questions while the committee's understanding of infant teaching betrayed a lack of familiarity with the most recent thinking in the area. The chief inspector also argued in terms which by then had become commonplace within the department, namely that it was the teachers themselves who were to blame for not abiding by official regulations and recommendations:

If the Department's instructions and advice in the matter of deciding when to use Irish as a medium of instruction are kept in mind, if the Department of Education's Programmes are properly interpreted and if the 'Notes' for teachers in the various branches are studied and followed everything is to be gained by using Irish as a medium.[18]

In his conclusion, the I.N.T.O. report was rather dismissively described as representing 'the views of middle-aged, somewhat tired and not too well linguistically equipped teachers . . . who will not make the additional preparation and study needed in using Irish as a medium'.[19] Younger teachers, it was argued, were more at home with Irish as a medium. So, by implication, as the latter advanced through the profession and were followed by others who would be even more fluent in Irish, the complaints and criticisms would no longer be heard.

These comments formed the basis of the department's reaction to the report and to similar criticisms at the time on the teaching and use of Irish. Whatever substance these criticisms had, it is impossible to avoid the conclusion that in the department a firm attempt was being made to dismiss as unfounded an unease which was widely shared, however adequately, or inadequately it was being expressed. Irish had to be restored, that was the agreed national policy and schools had a crucial role to play in its restoration. To relent on this role or even to modify the manner of its implementation was seen as tantamount to abandoning the very policy itself. The determination to press ahead in face of the odds was, perhaps, nowhere more strongly expressed than when the same chief inspector remarked that:

If we are to wait until Irish is the language of the homes, until the girls leaving our schools have sufficient power over and interest in the Irish language to speak it to their children, the restoration of the language is a long way ahead. The next twenty years are likely to be critical ones. Utmost use must be made of school hours and all our efforts concentrated on giving the children the power to speak Irish as their national language.[20]

In effect, the department chose to regard the report not as information of a kind to be used in reassessing the language policy and its implementation, but rather as a dishonest attack on that policy and as an attempt to subvert a key national objective.

Derrig used the occasion of the education estimates debates in the Dáil and Senate in 1942 as opportunities to mount a strong defence of the language policy and of the manner of its implementation. In his speeches, he reminded his audience of the I.N.T.O.'s role in formulating the language policy for schools through the National Programme Conferences of the 1920s and insisted, despite I.N.T.O. claims to the contrary, that teachers were not being compelled to teach through Irish.[21] Echoing his chief inspector's comments Derrig was also quite critical of what he regarded as a lack of effort and enthusiasm on the part of teachers to extend the use of Irish beyond the infant classes and of their failure to use Irish for ordinary intercourse among themselves and with their pupils. Finally, when touching on the I.N.T.O. investigation, he dismissed it, saying that 'remarks made in this report about the infant schools are an entirely unjustifiable and wrong account of actual conditions in infant schools'.[22] A strong attack on the I.N.T.O.'s investigation was also launched by the Gaelic League which suggested that the former's conclusions did not reflect those of the majority of teachers. 'Ní fiú an Tuarascabháil aon tsuim dáiribh . . . [the report hardly merits any interest at all . . .]' was how it attempted to dismiss its significance in a pamphlet prepared, nonetheless, especially to counter its findings.[23]

Support for the I.N.T.O. came from many opposition members of the Dáil and Senate, a number of whom argued that the government should itself institute an investigation. The main opposition spokesperson on education was Richard Mulcahy of Fine Gael, himself a future Minister of Education. Speaking in the Dáil he claimed that the language policy had acquired such a status that 'people are afraid to discuss certain aspects of the teaching of Irish lest it react on them politically'[24] and he argued that the department should respond positively to the report, a point on which he was joined by the former Minister of Education, Professor Marcus O'Sullivan.[25] A future colleague of Mulcahy's in government, James Dillon, was one of the most outspoken politicians critical of the language policy and speaking in the Dáil in 1944 he pressed again for a government inquiry, asking that a special commission on Irish be set up.[26] In Dillon's opinion any attempt to replace English with Irish should be opposed. 'I will fight any such policy with all the resources at my disposal', he said, while at the same time proclaiming his love for Irish and his desire to see it taught effectively.[27] Twelve months later he repeated his criticism claiming that existing policies for reviving Irish were being viewed with growing cynicism and hostility.

An attitude is growing up in this country which instead of being friendly towards and solicitous of the Irish language is becoming hostile to it. It is coming to be regarded as the hallmark of mediocrity in that mediocre persons seek to use it in order to get positions and preferment in the life of this country, not on the ground that they are the most highly fitted people for the position they seek, but on the ground that they are good enough to do the job and that they have Irish.[28]

Despite the growing volume of criticism, the government could not be moved. Derrig continued to argue forcibly for determined efforts to Gaelicise education completely, especially at primary level. In Derrig's view Irish was not the same as other school subjects because:

I cannot see how the language is to be restored without very intensive effort on the part of the teachers in the schools. It would be quite impossible, if we are not going to concentrate on the language in the schools, to make up for the serious inroads that the English speaking atmosphere all around them must have on the children.[29]

The continued absence of any comparable effort to Gaelicise life outside of school meant that the schools operated in a vacuum, a fact that gave considerable weight to arguments that their pupils were not being prepared for living in the real world of an English speaking society. Comments highly critical of the language policy were also beginning to intensify outside of educational and political circles. The noted literary journal, *The Bell*, which flourished in the forties and early fifties frequently turned its editorial comment to the language question to which it linked what it also claimed was the impoverished state of intellectual life in Ireland generally. Such comment was usually quite scathing of the language revival campaign, described in one editorial as 'the non-revolutionary revolution which brought the state into being'.[30] The implication was that the attempt to Gaelicise Ireland, or at least the manner in which this was being attempted, was having the effect of turning Irish society away from the more fundamental concerns of the contemporary world and, rather than opening up intellectual life in the country, it was, in fact, having the opposite effect. In a frequently quoted comment contained in an editorial in July 1945, *The Bell* suggested that Ireland's insular preoccupations, among which it would have had in mind the attempt to revive Irish, had starved its people of 'interests in all the ideas and problems which the rest of the world is still straining to solve . . .'[31] This particular perspective had also been expressed by a previously enthusiastic supporter of the revival movement, Professor Michael Tierney, who argued that Irish was unsuited as a vehicle of communication in an urbanised industrialised society:

To suppose that you can restore it merely as a language and at the same time make it a vehicle of an urban, mechanical, materialist way of life for which English is infinitely more suited is to indulge in the most futile and unattractive of day dreams.[32]

While most linguists would utterly reject this view, the absence of scientific texts in Irish and the virtual absence of an urban literature in Irish, must have conveyed the impression that the language was almost exclusively confined to a rural culture and that it enshrined values of the past, rather than of the present and even less of the future.

Yet, for de Valera and his government the complete revival of Irish remained a central and essential national aim because upon the successful revival of Irish depended the full achievement of Irish nationhood. De Valera, in particular, was still convinced that language and nationality were so inextricably linked that he warned:

If we failed to restore the language we never would be the nation that those who had died for it wanted. Unless we are prepared to make every effort we cannot save the language. The foundation has been laid by the work of the schools, but what is needed is a spark that will kindle that enthusiasm for speaking the language on all occasions. We must decide whether we want an English speaking Ireland or an Irish speaking Ireland.[33]

De Valera was obviously reflecting on what had been said over the previous few years about the progress of the language revival and in particular about its relationship with education. The goal to which he aspired remained the exclusive one of 'an Irish speaking Ireland', not the more realistic one of an Irish and an English speaking country. The failure to achieve the former goal simply called for fresh efforts, even if he was unclear as to what form they should take.

Despite all the criticism and the foreboding, it has to be acknowledged that signs of some progress existed, at least in the direction of the more realistic goal of a bilingual Ireland. As Terence Brown points out[34] a new generation of enthusiasts was coming to the fore, many of whom had begun to broaden the base of the revival movement. The establishment of the periodicals *Inniu* and *Comhar* in 1943, of *Feasta* in 1948, and of the *Club Leabhar* (Book Club) also in 1948, were all examples of this new enthusiasm and of new outlets for Irish which it produced. None of these initiatives would have been possible without a public sufficiently literate in Irish to provide a readership, a point cited both to justify the language policy in schools and to indicate how necessary it was to establish a broader approach to its revival. Brown suggests that 'a watershed in the fortunes of the Irish language'[35] seemed to have been reached, one which held out hope of a brighter future. Unfortunately, that watershed was slow to make itself apparent within the country's education system and however hopeful its portents, they were limited in their impact and could not be taken as indications of the kind of breakthrough for which de Valera longed, nor could they contain the continuing stream of criticism directed at the language policy as it affected education.

In the Dáil, the education estimates debates of 1947 contained several very strong attacks on the whole approach to Irish from opposition members. One T.D., Joseph Hughes, claimed that 'the whole thing has been brought to such a state of absurdity that the young people who have been compulsorily over-dosed with Irish are revolting against the whole system'.[36] Brendan Corish of the Labour Party asked 'could not the Fianna Fail government admit that there has not been any serious advance in the revival of Irish and change their policy regarding it ?'[37] Outside of the Oireachtas the I.N.T.O. continued to press its case for change. The organisation's vice-president, J. O'Kelly, claimed at the 1947 congress that 'the present Irish policy has failed completely over the past twenty-five years. The department had put up an iron curtain around the Gaeltacht and it would only be a matter of time until the Gaeltacht would be extinct'.[38] In the press, the *Irish Times*, whose editorials continued to ridicule many aspects of the language policy, claimed that 'Irish is the altar upon which is sacrificed essential general knowledge . . . The fanatical insistence on the desirability of a national language has had deplorable results and has set a high premium on ignorance'.[39]

Obviously worried about possible concessions officials advised Derrig there should be no compromise on the language policy and urged that the *status quo* be maintained: 'Either we are serious in our efforts to revive Irish or we are not. There can be no reversion to a state of affairs where those who wish to despise and reject the language may be free to do so . . . it is inevitable that once the principle of reviving the language is accepted, compulsion in some degree must be employed'.[40] Such advice suggests that, at times, it may have been senior officials in the Department of Education rather than their ministers who were the more determined to adhere to the language policy and to the manner of its implementation. From an official perspective the argument for not changing either policy or tactics with respect to Irish must have seemed a strong one. Schools provided a captive audience and on a number of measures the use of Irish could be seen to be having desirable results. The number of pupils pursuing all or part of their studies through the medium of Irish in secondary schools had increased quite dramatically since the early thirties.[41] The increased use of Irish in schools had resulted in an increase in the number of publications in Irish, mainly school texts, but, as has been discussed above, with a public more literate in Irish a small but growing contemporary literature in Irish was also emerging together with several examples of popular journalism. A small number of government departments conducted their business through Irish, most notably of course the Department of Education itself. Such achievements must have seemed significant given the previous circumstances of the language, thus strengthening rather than weakening the case for a relentless pursuit of the policies which seemed to have made them possible.

Tentative reform

Nevertheless, pressure for reform was such that it was likely that some account would have to be taken of it. So, when the change of government took place in 1948 the first tentative step was taken by way of an amendment to the regulations governing the use of Irish at primary level. The conviction, which the I.N.T.O. survey had reinforced, that the extensive use Irish at infant level was educationally unhealthy for many pupils led to a commitment being given by Richard Mulcahy, the new Minister of Education to have the matter reviewed.[42] The review which Mulcahy caused to be undertaken proved to be of a very limited kind: four inspectors were assigned to conduct it which they did by visiting 26 schools in several areas, rural and urban. Providing details in the Dáil as to their findings[43] Mulcahy indicated that hardly any school fully implemented the regulations regarding the use of Irish in infant classes; in other words some instruction was being carried out in English in these classes. The outcome was a slight modification in the wording of the regulations regarding the use of Irish to mitigate its compulsory tone and the granting of permission for English to be used for one half-hour per day in any school where this was thought desirable by the manager.[44]

Managerial system unassailable

If some modification to the regulations governing Irish was achieved, no change at all was to be effected on the matter of school management, even when this was linked very directly to the physical conditions in which young children were being taught. Because of their deteriorating condition, the need to replace and refurbish many hundreds of national schools through out the country had become a critical matter. In 1939 officials from the Department of Education had met with members of the Office of Public Works to prepare a six year plan 'to clear off arrears as regards condemned schools'.[45] Nothing further seems to have been done on this matter until 1942, probably because of the outbreak of war and the diversion of resources to meet the needs created by the emergency situation which ensued. In that year a further meeting between officials of the same two departments was held, the minutes of which reveal that out of a total of approximately 5,000 school buildings for which the department and the Office of Public Works were responsible, 464 required urgent attention, 550 were described as unsuited while a further 1,500 were in need of some improvement or enlargement.[46]

Discussions as to how the work might be expedited raised the problem of having to deal individually with each local school manager. It would appear that not all managers were as diligent as the department's officials would have wished in replying to correspondence, or in meeting their obligations regarding the condition of school buildings. Furthermore, quite a number of managers seemed to be experiencing difficulties in raising the local contribution which, officially, had remained unchanged since pre-independence times, at one-third.[47] Despite these difficulties Derrig defended his department's record claiming that it had not been miserly where applications for maintenance grants were concerned but that the initiative lay with the local school manager.[48]

As a result of the meetings between officials, a number of recommendations were made which the Minister of Education put to the Catholic bishops. The recommendations were contained in a lengthy letter from Derrig to Bishop James Staunton of Ferns, then secretary to the Catholic hierarchy.[49] In his letter Derrig outlined the steps being taken by his department to implement a school building and refurbishment programme. He indicated that over £5 million would be needed and that such a sum would require considerable local contributions. He proposed, therefore, that the hierarchy consider changing the method of raising such contributions by creating diocesan funds which would share the burden across all parishes. To administer such funds and to assist in co-ordinating building programmes the minister suggested that diocesan committees be established on which school managers would sit. The minister claimed that such committees would also make for administrative efficiency and would encourage 'some managers to give adequate attention to the maintenance of the buildings and to have the sanitation properly supervised'.[50] Derrig also took the opportunity to point to further weaknesses in the manner in which the managerial system operated. Over 350 schools had not received any heating or cleaning grants during the financial year of 1941–42 because their managers had failed to apply for such grants.[51] A diocesan committee would help to obviate such problems because the department would be able to pay such grants directly to the committees for disbursement to the local managers.

The changes proposed were not major changes since they did not entail any serious restructuring of the system. At most, they probably would have meant some slight curtailment of the discretion enjoyed by managers, but since any such curtailment would have been exercised by a committee of the church, it could not have amounted to any major infringement of traditional managerial rights. Nevertheless, the recommendation for a co-ordinating committee of the kind proposed did not find episcopal favour. The October 1943 meeting of the bishops considered the minister's letter and agreed that diocesan committees could indeed be set up, but with a much more reduced role than that proposed by the Department of Education. In the letter outlining the bishops' response Dr Staunton indicated that diocesan committees should only operate to co-ordinate building programmes by establishing priorities within a diocese, but that they should not 'take from the manager his prime and basic responsibility with regard to the school as any lessening of the final responsibility of the manager would defeat the end of the Committee's formation'.[52] Staunton's letter went on to indicate that each bishop would be free to determine the financial arrangements which should apply in his own diocese. However, he rejected the idea that financial contributions should be shared, saying that parishes which had 'good' schools would be 'unwilling to contribute to their neighbours what they had provided for themselves',[53] a curious interpretation of the Christian message that the strong should help the weak!

The willingness of the bishops to set up diocesan committees, even on the very modified basis indicated in Staunton's letter, would not appear to have been at all whole-hearted since no steps were taken to act on the proposals. Apparently still anxious to obtain a positive response Derrig used the opportunity of the 1944 debate on the education estimates to highlight what was being done and what remained to be done by way of school refurbishment and replacement. Commenting on the situation he claimed that 'tá áiteanna ann ina gcuirtear fíor-bheagán suime i mbail na dtithe scoile nó na fo-thuithe bhaineas leo [there are some places in which very little interest is taken in the condition of school buildings or in their out-houses]'.[54] Still there was no response and, after a long period of waiting for developments, Derrig wrote again to Dr Staunton, in January 1945, pointing out that only one or two dioceses had supplied information on their committees of managers.[55] As if to underline the need for progress, he also pointed out that managers in many dioceses were failing to make any significant local contribution to building funds. Less than one-sixth of the total estimated cost of the work carried out in thirteen dioceses had been raised locally, while in only one diocese was the required one-third raised.[56]

The matter would appear to have ended with this correspondence since the relevant file contains no copy of any reply from Bishop Staunton. However, at the I.N.T.O. congress held in Galway in 1945, the local bishop, Dr Michael Browne, launched a strong attack on suggestions that any change might be made in the managerial system saying that 'the managerial system has been the legal safeguard of the freedom of Catholic education in this land for a century'.[57] Browne was obviously giving the bishops' response to the minister's proposals and in view of the general inaction on the bishops' part to implement their own decision, Dr Browne would appear to have been expressing their continuing fundamental opposition to change of any kind in the managerial system as it then operated. The problem of unfit schools remained and at that same congress in 1945, T.J. O'Connell while denying that the I.N.T.O. was involved in any plans to end the managerial system, pointed out that 2,500 school buildings were defective, 1,000 of them seriously so and that an obligation lay upon managers and the Department of Education to deal with the problem.[58]

Given the attitude of the bishops, the department was left to deal with the problem on the same slow basis as before, a situation which was clearly exasperating to some members of the government, the minister in charge of the Office of Public Works, Patrick Smith, in particular. He summarised the dire situation in many schools when he wrote to Derrig in July 1945 urging him to try again to persuade the bishops that some changes were needed to facilitate improvements. Quoting one example from a long list of complaints about the failure of managers to take their responsibilities seriously, he remarked in rather trenchant terms:

The manager may be old or be very young for all I know. What I am sure is that there are kids crammed into this derelict building on which we made a report six years ago recommending a new school. Surely the age, energy and enthusiasm of the manager should not be allowed to come into it. Isn't the bishop of the diocese one of the trustees?[59]

It was indeed a curious situation in a state where a high level of consensus existed between the main source of religious influence and the government as to how each should operate, that the Catholic Church should still harbour suspicions that it could have lost influence by making the changes suggested. The managerial system so treasured by the church was not under any threat from the Department of Education's proposal. No change had been proposed in the basic arrangements between the department and school managers as far as ownership of the schools was concerned. Only a minor administrative change, which would have assisted managers, had been suggested; the threat to the managerial system, such as it was, was more a figment of the bishops' imagination than anything else. Indeed, the government frequently appeared only too anxious to support the managerial system. Derrig was often at pains to underline how much he valued it. Even when, as during the education debate in 1944, he seemed to be making some mild criticism of managers who did not always fulfil their managerial responsibilities, he added the reassuring words that 'we have the happy position that we have church and state working hand in hand ... and in regard to any development which may be considered necessary ... we shall not have those very critical questions confronting us which divide nations so sharply ... Thank God we are all united in these fundamental matters in this country'.[60]

Defending the managerial system on another occasion, Derrig made it clear that the government was not contemplating a complete reorganisation of the school system as was being planned elsewhere. He went on to say that he did not think that it was necessary claiming that 'our system had been praised as specially suited to our conditions. It has indeed been described as almost ideal'.[61] Such words could well have been spoken by any Catholic churchman, so close were their sentiments to those of the church itself. They certainly contain no sense of the frustration with the managerial system which Derrig seems to have felt within the privacy of his department.

What is interesting about this failed attempt to modify, however slightly, the managerial system, is the illustration it provides of just how dependent the southern state was on the will of the Catholic Church in matters of educational development. Notwithstanding the fact that the Department of Education was responsible for subsidising church schools, frequently at levels above the statutory amounts required, its influence could be reduced to a minimum, simply because the church judged its vital interests to be threatened, whether they actually were or not. Furthermore, the inability of the government in the south to persuade the Catholic Church to adopt changes intended to ensure hygienic and suitable accommodation for school children, stands in marked contrast to the firm approach being adopted at the same time by the government in Northern Ireland in face of the much more public opposition from the churches there to its plans for educational reform. The southern state's deference to the church was once again underlined, a deference to be further exemplified in the next initiative to be examined, the proposals for structural reform designed to facilitate access to second level education.

New structures proposed

The extension of educational facilities to all beyond fourteen years was not a matter to which the Department of Education had given much more than aspirational consideration before 1945. It would appear that the policy prior to then was to allow the kind of 'natural' growth that was already taking place in the system to continue. Speaking on the issue when presenting the estimates for his department in 1944, Derrig said that 'our ultimate policy aims at the extension of continuing education until provision is made for the attendance of all young persons between fourteen and sixteen years of age at suitable courses of instruction'.[62] Derrig seems to have had in mind that the vocational and technical schools which were already providing continuing education for fourteen to sixteen year olds would provide many of the places in such a development.

By late 1944 when it was obvious that governments elsewhere, especially those in Britain and in Northern Ireland, were intent on a carefully planned restructuring of their education systems in order to make second level education available as of right, de Valera decided it was time for his government to act. So, notwithstanding his very nationalist views, he recommended to Derrig, in a memorandum written only a few days after the publication of the white paper *Educational reconstruction in Northern Ireland*, that the latter take note of such developments:

Fé mar is eol duit ta pleananna áirithe foillsithe ag rialtas na Breataine Móire agus ag an Rialtas sna Sé Conntaethe . . . b'fhéidir go mbeadh smaointe sna paipéirí bána a foillsíodh nár mhiste iad do breithniú féachaint an bhfeadfaimis aon tairbhe a bhaint astu . . . [As you are aware certain plans have been published by the British government and by the government in the Six Counties . . . perhaps these white papers contain ideas which we should examine in order to see if they might be useful to us . . .][63]

De Valera was not the only person in the south to pay attention to these plans. They made a particular impact in Protestant circles where concern began to be expressed that provision for secondary education in the north would soon be considerably greater than that in the south. Perhaps a renewed fear that Protestant parents might choose schools in Northern Ireland lay behind some of the concern expressed. The *Irish Times*, in an editorial on the northern white paper, gently chided Derrig about his frequent remarks that education in the south was equal to that anywhere else, saying that 'Irishmen who can see as far as the other side of the border will think differently'.[64] The headmistress of a leading Protestant girls' school, Miss L. Staunton, argued that 'we cannot afford to have children less well equipped for life than the children in Northern Ireland'.[65] The Church of Ireland Archbishop of Dublin, Dr A.W. Barton, speaking at the A.S.T.I. convention in April 1945, made similar points, saying that the south would lag behind the north if it did not expand opportunities for secondary education, a view echoed on the same occasion by the president of the A.S.T.I.[66]

Already, and perhaps urged on by de Valera's memorandum, the Department of Education had begun to consider what developments might be possible with the result that early in February 1945 Derrig set up a departmental committee with the brief:

To examine the existing educational system, primary, secondary, technical, vocational and the provision available for university education and to make recommendations to the Minister as to what changes and reforms, if any, are necessary in order to raise the standard of education generally and to provide greater educational facilities for all our people.[67]

This was a very wide brief indeed, but, in the event, the committee focused its deliberations on the changes thought necessary to facilitate an extension of second level education and the consequent effects this would have at primary level. This was not the first official committee to investigate the same issue. In 1926 the Government had included a provision in the School Attendance Act whereby the leaving age could be raised to sixteen while the Commission on Technical and Vocational Education (1927) had recommended that the school leaving age be raised to fifteen and later to sixteen[68] and in 1935 an inter-departmental working-party had also examined the need for any change in the school leaving age, but had not recommended that it be changed.[69] The need to re-examine the question in the mid-forties was justified not only by the plans being formulated elsewhere but also by the steady increase in the numbers attending secondary schools and in the numbers availing of some form of full-time education beyond fourteen years in vocational and national schools. Figures for the period from 1929–30 to 1943–44 indicated an increase in secondary school enrolments of more than 10,000 (29,000 to 40,000) and an increase of 80 in the number of such schools, from 290 to 377.[70] There were also 186 vocational or technical schools with an overall enrolment of 13,000 full-time pupils, aged fourteen plus. Furthermore, a large number of pupils, 19 per cent of those in full-time education between the ages of fourteen and sixteen, were enrolled in national schools;[71] in other words, many thousands of pupils were remaining in full-time attendance in national schools beyond fourteen years and were receiving a form of full-time education from teachers who were essentially only trained to provide elementary education. This latter phenomenon was no doubt mainly created by the lack of opportunity to attend a secondary school, most probably from lack of finance and/or availability of a convenient school.

After almost two and a half years' deliberations the departmental committee made its report available to the minister in June 1947. Although no action was ever taken on the basis of the report, it is, nonetheless, of considerable interest for a number of reasons. It was, to begin with, the first full-scale review of educational structures conducted by the Department of Education in the south since the state had been established and the first to recommend significant changes in those structures. The educational principles upon which the report's recommendations were based closely paralleled those adopted in Northern Ireland and in Britain. The kind of secondary education suggested was one 'which in addition to literary courses would include practical subjects and activities'.[72] Pupils would, however, have to be selected at twelve years of age, on the basis of psychological evidence, for one of two types of secondary schools, one providing 'combined literary and practical education', the other 'a more literary or academic type'.[73] In other words, a selection procedure such as was being adopted in Northern Ireland was recommended. Such recommendations, as in the north, would have necessitated a complete restructuring of the system at national school level together with the provision of a network of new secondary schools to provide a combined literary and practical type education, although it was recognised that existing vocational and technical schools could contribute to this provision. However, when it came to discussing who should provide and manage the schools, the sensitivities of the department's officials to the perceived views of the 'ecclesiastical authorities', as the report describes them, became paramount. It was apparently hoped that at least some of the new type of secondary schools would be provided by religious communities and if this was to happen the committee recommended that 'there should be no question of setting up rival schools under the local authorities',[74] though how pupils of denominations other than Catholic might be catered for did not seem to be a problem. Furthermore, although the new schools would have to be large and, in many places, cater for areas more extensive than a single parish, it was agreed that they should be 'under a system of management and control similar to, or based on, that which prevails in the national schools at present and it would be up to the ecclesiastical authorities to state what their views may be as to the government and management of post-primary schools which would probably cater for considerably wider areas than single parishes'.[75] Obviously, there was no intention to break with the managerial system unless with the prior approval of the churches, particularly the Catholic Church.

On the question of co-education the committee also deferred to the Catholic Church in a manner which undoubtedly would have caused considerable extra public expenditure had the recommendations been implemented. 'Co-education should be avoided as far as possible' was the succinct recommendation made by the committee.[76] The recommendation was no doubt made because any suggestion that co-education should be the rule, rather than the very occasional exception, would not have been acceptable to a church, one of whose leading theologians in Ireland at the time, had written of a girl's education in the following terms:

... while studying the same subjects as man, she must study them in a different way and for another purpose. For her the study of letters and sciences must be more directly cultural; it should lack the competitive note. It is moreover desirable that in the curriculum of girls' courses of study there should be a decided bias towards the practical arts and accomplishments called into play in the management of the home.[77]

Any implementation of plans to restructure the system would have only been possible with the full co-operation of the Catholic Church. The plans were never published, nor were any steps taken to implement them.

I.N.T.O. proposals

The department's consideration of possible changes in the system are not the only evidence of attention being devoted to extending access to secondary education at this time. The I.N.T.O. had conducted its own study of the need for major reform of the system and this resulted in the publication of its *Plan for education* in 1947.[78] Its recommendations are interesting because of the very clear commitment to equality of opportunity which they contained. In line with advocates of social change elsewhere the I.N.T.O. stressed the need for 'equality of educational opportunity' which, it claimed, '. . . is still denied to the majority of our people and both secondary and university education which are in practice denied to the vast bulk of the population are financed on a much more generous scale than primary education'.[79] Based on this premise, the *Plan for education* attacked the academic bias of education and, like the Department of Education's own recommendations called for a much broader curriculum which would include an emphasis on practical subjects. With echoes of earlier reports, the plans also called for a fully integrated educational service catering for primary, secondary, technical and adult education, and a greater involvement on the part of the local community in schools. The proposals also reiterated longstanding demands from the I.N.T.O. for a review of Irish in the curriculum and for the establishment of a council of education.

Promising change

The growing sense that the education system was in need of radical reform and development was clearly evident when commitments to change appeared in several manifestoes issued by the main political parties contesting the 1948 general election.[80] This election was to prove one of the most interesting since the foundation of the state. It not only led to the creation of the first non-Fianna Fail government in sixteen years, but it also witnessed the emergence of a new party, Clann na Poblachta, led by Sean McBride, a former republican leader. From an educational point of view Clann na Poblachta was also interesting because it enjoyed considerable support amongst teachers, especially among many national teachers who had become disaffected with Fianna Fail as a result of several salary disputes over the preceding years and the protracted Dublin teachers' strike of 1946. Following the election, Clann na Poblachta joined with other opposition parties, notably Fine Gael and Labour to form a coalition government.[81] Educationally, therefore, much was hoped for from an administration composed of parties committed to extending access to education and to creating a council of education which would provide a strong professional and lay input into education policy making. It was only on the creation of a council that any of the promises were to be fulfilled.

The council panacea

Throughout the forties demands that a council of education be established became quite persistent. No longer were these demands coming from the teachers' unions and prominent individuals, they had also gained the support of the Commission on Vocational Organisation and from the main opposition party, Fine Gael. Even within the Department of Education, which previously had been totally opposed to the idea, a role for a council was being accepted and proposals were put to the minister as to how it might be composed and how it might function.

However, the nature of a council and, in particular, whether it should be an executive council with powers like those advocated by Bishop Lucy, or merely an advisory council to provide the Minister of Education with both lay and specialist views, was a matter on which there was no general agreement. Not surprisingly, in a submission by the private secretary of the Department of Education to the Commission on Vocational Organisation, it was recommended that a council of education should be purely advisory taking 'wide and long views of education'.[82] The department was willing to allow its own officials to be summoned to give evidence to such a council and to have its activities reviewed on an annual basis, but expressed opposition to a council having any policy making role, though it might comment on the government's own educational policies.[83] As far as the composition of a council was concerned, the department was not in favour of a representative body such as the teachers' unions sought. Instead, it recommended that council members be selected from 'outstanding personalities' in various professions.

The teachers' unions argued for a council with considerable powers. The A.S.T.I. which had long campaigned on the issue, was to adopt a motion at its 1948 convention outlining an elaborate structure for a council of education.[84] What the A.S.T.I. sought was a two-tier council, one tier of which would consist of committees to deal with each sector of education, with the second tier being representative of the first. To the first tier of such a council the A.S.T.I. sought the right to nominate its own representatives. The I.N.T.O., likewise, advocated a strong council and had done so from as early as 1924.[85]

Political views as to the role of a council were not always very clear. In the Senate, Professor Michael Tierney moved a resolution in 1941 calling for the establishment of a council on lines similar to the Board of Education in Britain[86] and, in doing so, regretted the abolition of the Boards of Commissioners claiming that as a result the south had 'a more completely bureaucratic system of education, primary and secondary, than exists in almost any other country in the world'.[87] For him, a council of education would be an effective antidote to the ills which he saw in such control. However, when it came to being precise as to a council's functions, Tierney seems to have favoured a body with an advisory role only, albeit one with a very wide remit, rather than a council with executive powers analogous to those of the Boards of Commissioners. A council, he argued, could be 'sitting continually, continually engaged in examining questions put before it from time to time by the Minister'.[88]

Fine Gael, despite its general support for a council, was also not always sure of what kind. At first it seemed to favour an executive rather than an advisory council. Then, prompted by the publication of the *Report of the commission on vocational organisation* in 1944, the party put down a motion in the Dáil calling for a council to be established which would consist of representatives of parents, of bodies directly involved in education, and of agriculture, industry and commerce.[89] Although Mulcahy and his colleagues tended to describe the kind of council they sought as being representative of various interests, it became clear that in terms of its functions they displayed a reluctance to propose a council with decision making powers. Instead, Mulcahy stressed the need for a council to be answerable to the Dáil and in his speech on the above motion asked that an all-party committee be charged with determining membership of the council.[90] Not surprisingly, the government was unwilling to concede such a responsibility exclusively to the Dáil and since it was not, itself, yet convinced of the need for a council the motion was defeated.

Nonetheless within the Department of Education, opinion did begin to shift somewhat towards a more favourable view of a council, even before Mulcahy's motion was tabled. While there is little doubt about Derrig's own very strong reservations, by early 1945 he was anxious to put some plans to the government which would be seen as a positive response to the pressure for a council. A Department of Education memorandum in February of that year made clear this anxiety, containing as it did comments about a council's possible composition and remit, which the department was anxious should not include any close supervision of its own work.[91]

Nothing happened, however, and in 1947 Derrig was of the view that because in Ireland there was not the 'the same urgency . . . with regard to educational rehabilitation or reconstruction' as elsewhere in Europe, the need for a council also lacked urgency.[92] So, in the final year of Fianna Fail's long period in office, Derrig decided to drop the whole question. Speaking in the Senate to a motion calling for a statement on the I.N.T.O.'s *Plan for education*,[93] he argued that a council was not necessary because 'the policy of the Department has been to consult and to confer with the other educational interests'[94] and thus it should continue.

The final stage in the story of setting up a council had to await the change of government in 1948. In his first major pronouncement on educational policy, the new minister, Richard Mulcahy, declared it his intention to establish one. It would not however be a representative body as Mulcahy himself had previously advocated, but 'a council of men and women with experience and standing in the educational world'.[95] Outlining one of the functions which he suggested that the council might have, the minister was anxious to assure traditional interests that they would be fully protected:

One of the foremost functions I would think that the council would perform would be to emphasise the rights and responsibilities of parents in the matter of education, to make clear the field of authority that belonged to the Church, to make clear that whatever the function of the State was, it had no power to interfere either with the rights of the parents or with the authority of the Church and that the main part of its function was to help to provide in the general economic, social and political interest of the country, the machinery that could be provided only by the State to serve parents and Church and people generally.[96]

While Mulcahy did seem determined to press ahead and meet his commitment, it took some considerable time to translate into reality. During his first eighteen months in office the minister frequently referred to his intention to proceed with the council's establishment and explained his delayed announcement as arising from his need to gain experience of the Department of Education. Early in 1949 he announced that it would be in place by the autumn of that year and a motion to the effect that a council be established 'as a permanent advisory body to the Minister of Education' was passed in the Dáil in February.[97] The date of its announcement was later put back to the end of 1949, but it was not until March 1950 that the Council of Education was formally established with a brief: 'To advise the Minister, in so far as pertains to the powers, duties and functions of the State, upon such matters relating to educational theory and practice as they see fit and upon any educational questions and problems referred to them by him'.[98] In terms of its composition the council of 32 members was essentially an establishment body. Catholic Church influence was guaranteed by the appointment of a prominent clergyman, Canon Denis O'Keefe, to chair the council together with seven Catholic religious as ordinary members.[99]

Despite the feeling and pressure in favour of widening access to secondary education evident over the preceding few years, the first task of the council was not directed at that objective but rather to advising the minister as to (i) the function of the primary school and (ii) the curriculum to be pursued in the primary school up to twelve years of age. Only this second task which set the upper limit to the primary curriculum at twelve years instead of fourteen, suggested that any restructuring of the system might still have been in the minister's mind. Logical as it might have appeared to have commenced with an examination of primary education, it is clear that the council was not in fact addressing the most important and pressing educational issue of the day. By deciding the council's priorities as he did, the minister ensured that the question of general access to post-primary education would not be considered for some time. This delay contributed in no small measure to the fact that when second level education did undergo change in the south it was to do so quite rapidly in a very uncontrolled and, in the judgement of many, not very satisfactory manner.

A disheartening scene

Examined in isolation from other aspects of life in the south, education in the 1940s presents a rather disheartening picture, especially from the middle of the decade when an awareness of the need for change seemed to be accompanied by a real desire and intent to take action, at least on the part of some of those concerned at policy making level. The general direction in which reform should go was identified: at primary level, school building and school refurbishment were priorities, while at secondary level widening access was accepted as a necessary objective.

Failure to act on these objectives can be difficult to understand at this remove. A desire not to precipitate a clash with the Catholic Church clearly frustrated plans to expedite the school building programme. As for secondary level, the failure to bring forward plans already formulated is difficult to explain given the favourable state of the economy in the immediate post-war years and the general desire within political parties to make access available to all. Was this reluctance due to almost innate fears arising from the challenge to some aspects of church interests in education which the plans contained ? In the light of the evidence surrounding the very mild proposals for dealing with school buildings it is likely that these fears did exist and were influential, but to what extent it is difficult to determine. As the decade drew to a close and a deepening economic crisis developed, the lack of finance became an understandable excuse, but by then the will to change had, it would seem, evaporated as interested parties awaited what the new Council of Education might propose.

9

Effecting and Anticipating Change:
Education North and South 1950–65

Extreme diversity

It is probably no exaggeration to state that the period from the late 1940s until the early 1960s was the time of greatest divergence between the two educational systems in Ireland. This divergence reflected the almost inevitable widening of divisions which had been developing since partition and which had been considerably intensified by the very different experiences of both parts of Ireland during World War II. In F.S.L. Lyons'[1] terms, cultural diversity in the two states of Ireland in this period was to effect its greatest sense of distance and distinction between north and south. In Northern Ireland the reforms heralded by the 1947 act, although at first slow to be implemented, gradually began reshaping popular concepts of education. Secondary education did eventually come within the reach of all as both sections of the restructured secondary system became fully operational. At least four years of secondary education came to be freely available, in either grammar or secondary intermediate schools, while for those who wished to remain in full-time education beyond this period, grammar and technical schools provided appropriate opportunities.

In the south, unlike the north, the education system was to remain virtually unreformed throughout this whole period. The same beliefs, values and attitudes continued to influence those who controlled education as in the preceding decades thus ensuring quite effective resistance to the kind of change which a growing number of people had begun to recognise as necessary. Within the southern school system itself pressures for change were mounting as the number of pupils remaining in full-time education beyond the statutory leaving age of fourteen continued to rise, but while the Council of Education deliberated over possible reforms in primary and secondary education and produced two lengthy reports, neither was to be seen as adequate to the needs and pressures affecting both levels. Both reports would underline the need to increase opportunities for secondary and technical education and to co-ordinate primary and post-primary education more effectively, but the timidity of their recommendations was to leave the initiative for educational change to other forces in Irish society. Unfavourable, indeed almost disastrous economic conditions in the south reinforced official resistance to change until the late fifties when the first signs of economic improvement emerged. In effect, education remained unchanged until external pressures, the product of rapid and quite dynamic economic development, gradually built up to the point where reform within the system became unavoidable. Only then did the system itself respond. Change came quite quickly and for a while education appeared to be undergoing another 'revolution', this time one that was to effect significant structural, as well as curricular reform.

Northern Ireland – reconstruction and deconstruction

The 1950s and early sixties witnessed considerable change in many aspects of life in Northern Ireland. As part of the United Kingdom, Northern Ireland began to enjoy the benefits of the 'welfare state' as the social and medical services were restructured to provide a comprehensive range of services to the whole community. In the same period infrastructural development resulted in improved road communications and the first major attempt to address the appalling housing conditions of many lower-income families. Also, as shipbuilding, linen and their allied engineering industries declined, investment in new industries, particularly in the man-made fibre industry, increased to make Northern Ireland a major European centre for the latter. The effect of all these developments was to further emphasise the progressive, forward and outward looking character which Northern Ireland had, at one level, acquired during World War II and to set it even more apart from the south which was struggling with its deep economic crisis during the early part of this period. However, all was not positive or progressive in northern society. Large pockets of unemployment and poverty persisted; unemployment figures by the late fifties and early sixties were, at 6–9 per cent, still twice those of the U.K. average, while emigration hid the full impact of declining job opportunities.[2] Furthermore, and potentially more dangerous, many of the old socio–political antagonisms and grievances still smouldered, refusing to go away and remaining impervious to the modernising processes of post-war reconstruction. Nationalists and unionists were politically as far apart as ever, and it was likewise with their associated churches.

In politics, Northern Ireland remained trapped in this unionist-nationalist divide. The general election in 1949 was fought by the Unionist Party as a response to the decision in the south to formally declare itself a republic and by nationalists as part of the anti-partition campaign then being orchestrated by an all-party committee in Dublin.[3] In the fifties, the re-emergence of the I.R.A. with its campaign of cross-border attacks, its bombings and its involvement in Westminster elections through its political wing, Sinn Féin, brought the latter to an influential, if still essentially negative, role in political life at the close of that decade[4] inhibiting prospects of a rapprochement between the two major political traditions.

Within the churches, Protestants and Catholics continued to see themselves less as fellow members of the Christian community than as mutually hostile ideologists, each proclaiming themselves to be the 'true' exponents of God's message. To many Protestants, Catholicism at this time was typified by its emphasis on 'Marianism' as exemplified by the declaration of the 'Assumption' dogma in 1950 and the celebrations which marked the 'Marian' year in 1954.[5] To Protestants, this dogma and the whole range of Marian devotions only underlined the extent to which the Roman Church had 'strayed' from 'true' Christianity. To Catholics, Protestants were still less than fully Christian, were in need of conversion and, above all, were people with whom it was not advisable to mix too much.

Not until the end of the 1950s, when a new generation of political activists began to emerge within both traditions were the first seeds of a possible political rapprochement sown. By then a sense of openness between different Christian traditions was also beginning to express itself in Europe generally. Ecumenical contacts began to be developed between the churches, while in Roman Catholicism, the election of Pope John XXIII in 1958 gave that development a new emphasis, one that was to be especially underlined in the deliberations of the Second Vatican Council which he was to convene.

The close of the 1950s was also marked in western society by the easing of social tensions as the economic benefits of post-war reconstruction resulted in rising standards of living, greater spending power, increased travel and improved educational opportunities. All of these developments were to have their effects in Ireland and in Northern Ireland in particular, such that the prospect for a new era of understanding and respect between the communities there began to appear quite favourable. From within the Catholic–nationalist community, this prospect was most publicly indicated for the first time at the Social Studies Conference held in Garron Tower in 1958. At that conference, one participant argued that Catholics had a duty 'to co-operate with the de facto authority that controls . . . life and welfare'.[6] Coming in the middle of an I.R.A. campaign it was a brave statement, but it was, nonetheless, one that was to find an echo amongst many from the same community some years later when the civil rights campaign developed in the mid and late sixties.[7] Education, too, was also to reflect aspects of that prospect, although much less spectacularly.

Against this evolving background, discussion of educational developments commences with the early stages of the implementation of the 1947 act and traces reaction to it throughout the period until the mid-sixties when it became subject to a major review.

Protestant unease foments

The government's success in resisting pressure to dilute the conscience clause of the 1947 act together with its decision to make a higher level of public funding available to voluntary schools would seem to have been interpreted as a double defeat by some sections of Protestant–unionist opinion. An indication of this feeling was strongly reflected at the the

Presbyterian General Assembly in June 1947, when it adopted a resolution critical of many aspects of the act.[8] The resolution claimed that, because of the conscience clause, the act would deprive 'appointing bodies of the right . . . to prefer for teaching posts the duly qualified candidates whom they consider most suitable'.[9] Protestant schools, the same resolution claimed, 'have been stripped of their defences' and went on to ask 'how are our schools to be protected in view of the rising tide of Romanism in many parts of Northern Ireland'.[10] The resolution demanded that the act be amended to provide acceptable safeguards particularly over the appointment of teachers.

In a pamphlet entitled *Defence of Ulster*, published by the committee established at a public meeting in the Ulster Hall in 1946 during the protest campaign against the government's proposals, similar arguments were made.[11] The pamphlet claimed that the Catholic Church was the only beneficiary of the 1947 act while Protestants had been deprived 'of the security' provided by the amending acts of 1925 and 1930. As with the assembly's resolution, the pamphlet demanded appropriate amendments to the legislation.

Extra-parliamentary agitation against the act found strong echoes in parliament itself where a number of members tried, unsuccessfully, to have the legislation amended. The government's determination not to tamper with the conscience clause meant that most Protestant–unionist opposition was focused on the advantages which voluntary, i.e. Catholic schools were alleged to have gained from the 1947 act. So it was that over the next decade or so, but particularly in the years immediately following the passing of the legislation, several attempts were made to limit, or even reduce, the level of funding available to voluntary schools. Because it touched raw nerves within the northern Protestant psyche, such a strategy was the one most likely to win wide support. Should this strategy succeed, its proponents believed that an opportunity would have been provided in which the other issue of more direct concern to the dissatisfied Protestant–unionist lobby, i.e. the conscience clause, could again be brought to the fore with some hope of success.

First crisis

The implementation of the 1947 act had hardly begun before the Ministry of Education and, indeed, the government as a whole, was faced with a crisis which had little to do directly with education, but all to do with more general relationships between the communities in Northern Ireland. The outcome was to be the resignation of Hall-Thompson, the minister who had withstood the campaigns against sections of the 1947 act. He was to be replaced by the still energetic, but by now quite unapologetically anti-Catholic Harry Midgley who had been particularly prominent in the attacks on grant aid for voluntary schools, inside and outside parliament.

The crisis which forced Hall-Thompson's resignation developed when he proposed that since the Ministry of Education paid, in full, the salaries of teachers in voluntary schools, that it should also pay the employer's national insurance contribution for those teachers.[12] As Akenson points out the proposal 'resurrected all the parliamentary hostility to augmenting grants to voluntary schools which had fumed forth during the debates on the 1947 Act'[13] and many unionist members demanded that not only should the government not pay the employer's contribution in full, but that it and the basic grants to voluntary school be reduced to 50 per cent. A recently elected M.P., the future Prime Minister, Brian Faulkner, declared 'I did not agree with the increase of the grant in the recent Education Act, nor do I agree with it in this Bill'[14] while Harry Midgley, even more bluntly, turned his criticism of the proposal into a scarcely veiled attack on what he saw as the ultimate motives of the Catholic Church:

I think that at the present time there is enough infiltration going on in Northern Ireland. Not only are our properties and undertakings being acquired, but institutions are being set up which will be seats of power in the future, and now they are increasingly looking to public funds for the support of those institutions. At the same time they repudiate their right to recognise the public authority in any way.[15]

In Midgley's eyes Catholic school buildings were almost 'stolen' properties, presumably because they were being built for the exclusive use of one church with a considerable amount of public money. The matter came to a head in December when, following a series of crisis meetings involving the Grand Lodge of the Orange Order and backbenchers of the Unionist Party, Hall-Thompson tendered his resignation and the government promised to review the 1947 act.[16] As for the matter of national insurance payments it was eventually decided that the department would only pay 65 per cent of the employer's contribution, a percentage in line with that payable by way of capital grant to voluntary schools.[17]

The controversy was quite unnecessary and, because of its sectarian overtones, quite nasty. It was unnecessary because the Ministry of Education had been paying the national insurance contributions in full for the previous two years.[18] It was nasty because the attacks on the bill and on the minister for introducing it, were also directed unashamedly at the Catholic Church. In the course of the debates no mention was made of the fact that the same provision applied in the case of voluntary schools under Protestant management, of which there was a still a considerable number, especially in the grammar school sector, and governors of the latter had no intention of ever transferring their schools to local authority control. Furthermore, the controversy revealed once again that attitude of mind within sections of the unionist community which suggested that, somehow, all public money belonged to it and that grants to Catholic schools and to other Catholic agencies, such as hospitals, were expressions of special generosity. Even the *Belfast Telegraph*, which was normally anxious to avoid any overt indications of intolerance, could not avoid making this point at the height of the 1949 controversy:

. . . the 'other sort' [i.e. the Catholics] want it both ways, no control but its [i.e. the state's] benefits. That is their record not only here but the world over. It is the same in regard to their hospitals, under the Health Scheme. Also when generous treatment is meted out to them it would be foolish to expect it . . . to be recognised as such . . .[19]

As expenditure on public services increased over the following decade this particular note of resentment was to be sounded more and more frequently in unionist comments upon Catholic demands for financial support.

For its part, the Catholic–nationalist community responded with the claim that, in fact, it was really subsidising public, i.e. Protestant, schools. This claim was made on the basis that, while contributing 100 per cent of the taxes for which it was liable, the Catholic community only received in return 65 per cent of the capital expenditure on its schools and so had to raise the remaining 35 per cent itself. The Protestant–unionist community, on the other hand, had to make no contribution to its schools beyond that which it paid through general taxation and rates. Supporting the Catholic–nationalist case an *Irish News* editorial claimed:

The consideration and just treatment that should be accorded to voluntary schools should never be in doubt. The vast majority of the 900 voluntary schools are under Catholic management and Catholic pupils on the rolls of public elementary schools are a good first in the religious groups . . . If the many bigots succeed in their agitation they will be victimising the voluntary school children who number approximately one half of those receiving an elementary education.[20]

At issue were questions affecting minority and parental rights in education. On the one hand, those who argued against special treatment for Catholic schools or who only grudgingly conceded it, ignored the claims of the Catholic-nationalist minority for equality of treatment with the majority community so that its children could avail of educational services which it would regard as supportive of its Catholic faith and nationalist culture. The unionist offer of equality of treatment within publicly controlled schools, the church continued to regard as unacceptable since it implied the transfer of its schools to public ownership. Transfer was still totally unacceptable and, even if possible, schools catering for both Catholics and Protestants could not, without considerable planning, have been neutral on many issues relating to cultural identity, much less accommodating of the cultural differences concerned. Given the spirit of the times, unionist majorities on most educational authorities would have been likely to have insisted that public schools continue promoting values inimical to the nationalist identity in Northern Ireland. On the Catholic–nationalist side therefore, the overriding concern was the need to continue defending the right to be educated in Catholic schools where their own community values would be fostered, whatever the financial cost to their community.

A recurring theme

The controversy over national insurance payments was not the only controversy affecting Catholic schools which arose as a result of the 1947 act. The claim that (Catholic) voluntary schools might be 'privileged' in a manner unacceptable to some unionist politicians had been foreshadowed by the less publicised question of boarding school fees and travel payments to some

Catholic pupils, especially in rural areas, necessary in order to ensure access to second level education. One such pupil from Garvagh in County Derry who qualified for grammar school applied to have his boarding fees paid in addition to the normal amount awarded to cover fees to grammar school pupils. The pupil's parents argued that the nearest suitable school was in Derry City, some 40 miles from his home, but the unionist-controlled Derry County Education Committee refused the request on the grounds of 'unreasonable expenditure of public funds'.[21] In the view of the committee the pupil in question should have been availing of a grammar school in either Coleraine or Limavady, which, although not Catholic, could be attended from home on a daily basis.[22]

Cabinet memoranda on such cases reveal that 'strong Protestants' objecting to special payments to Catholics and other political motives lay, in the Ministry of Education's opinion, at the root of the decisions not to award special boarding or travel payments.[23] Because legislation enshrined the principle that pupils should be 'educated in accordance with the wishes of their parents' legal opinion advised that non-payment of the additional funds requested would probably not be upheld in court.[24] The cabinet, therefore, decided that payment would not be unreasonable in the Garvagh case and this decision appears to have become a precedent for those that followed.[25]

However, if the government upheld the conscientious rights of the Catholic community as enshrined in legislation, in some respects, the same was not true for all. Several practical matters arose as the 1947 act was being implemented, on which decisions were made at ministry and cabinet level which reflected a considerable degree of antagonism towards Catholic education. Harry Midgley's own very personal feelings can, perhaps, explain a number of these decisions although his was not the only voice involved since some of these decisions were made before he took office, others after his death. Many were preceded by pressure from unionist sources inside and outside parliament and usually related to what was judged to be unwarranted additional public funding for voluntary (Catholic) schools.

One very early decision in which the needs of a local Catholic community for a grammar school were not met for fear of offending local Protestant–unionist interests was that taken by Hall-Thompson, in 1949, not to support the establishment of a Catholic grammar school in Maghera, also in County Derry.[26] This decision was taken despite the evidence from the Ministry of Education's own officials that a grammar school was justified,[27] a view not shared by the County Education Committee which stated that it was 'not satisfied that the case for the building of a grammar school in Maghera is established'.[28] The committee also noted the provision of grammar school facilities at the Rainey Endowed School in nearby Magherafelt. Rainey was not a Catholic school but, in the absence of a local alternative, many Catholic pupils were in attendance there. It was this latter point which seems to have been most influential in the minister's decision, rather than whether or not Catholic pupil numbers justified a new grammar school.

Representations were made by Dehra Parker, M.P. for the area, who expressed concern about the possible competition from such a school for the Rainey Endowed School. Later applications were also turned down when Midgley became Minister of Education.[29]

Persistence by the Catholic clergy in Maghera with their application may well have begun to embarrass Midgley because, when in 1955 the application was again renewed, the matter was taken to the cabinet. There it was once more turned down, despite the fact that Midgley informed his colleagues that 'detailed inquiries by his officials indicated that there were enough pupils in the area to justify the establishment of a grammar school'.[30] Nonetheless, the most the cabinet was prepared to support was 'a grammar school stream in the new intermediate school'.[31] Maghera never got its Catholic grammar school and instead, two secondary intermediate schools, one for boys, the other for girls, were provided.[32]

Midgley attacks Catholic system

The minister himself seems to have lost few opportunities to give vent to his very critical views of the Catholic Church's approach to education. A rather blatant example was in the course of a speech to the Ulster Teachers' Union when he stated with characteristic bluntness that:

Those responsible for such a policy [i.e. the Catholic ban on attendance at public authority schools] must feel increasingly unhappy in their minds as they contemplate a future in which their chosen policy of segregation will result in the perpetuation of animosities which will not aid the development of a community spirit.[33]

To place all blame for the 'perpetuation of animosities' on the Catholic Church was quite an extreme and one-sided view, bearing in mind the hostile attitudes towards that church so frequently expressed by leading Protestant and unionist spokespersons and the educational controversies over which they themselves had been in conflict. Midgley's views must have encouraged those who wanted to see steps taken to make it as difficult as possible for the Catholic Church to develop its school system at this crucial period. Whenever Catholic Church spokespersons, or nationalist politicians sought to excuse the very slow provision of Catholic intermediate schools by reference to the burden which raising 35 per cent of the capital was placing on their community, they were either reminded of the 'generosity' of the government, or obliged to listen to demands for the reduction of their grants to former levels. In 1956, the unionist M.P., Nat Minford, moved a resolution in the House of Commons demanding that 'no education grants to voluntary schools should in future exceed fifty per cent of the approved expenditure unless such voluntary schools adopt a four-and-two committee basis of management'.[34] If passed, the resolution would have had the effect of seriously delaying the provision of new intermediate and additional grammar school places for the Catholic community.

Seconded by Norman Porter, by then an independent Protestant–unionist M.P., the resolution immediately threatened to reopen the whole controversy which had surrounded the same issue in 1947. On this occasion considerable bitterness was injected into the debate when, in order to strengthen the case for greater public accountability in voluntary schools, Porter alleged that some Catholic school managers were conspiring with contractors to obtain more money from the ministry than their 65 per cent grants entitled them to.[35] Midgley himself obviously sympathised with those who moved the resolution when he acknowledged that there was 'a general feeling throughout the community, justified or unjustified, that the control of voluntary schools was not what it should be'.[36] The minister was, however, astute enough to realise the problems which would be caused if the amendment was to be passed. A circular to all Catholic school managers from the Archbishop of Armagh, Cardinal William D'Alton had underlined this danger[37] with the claim that the resolution was 'aimed chiefly at the Catholic schools' and that if it was to be passed 'it will serve to confirm the opinion widely held not only among Catholics but among non-Catholics, that government policy is in the last resort being dictated by a body whose chief desire seems to be the resurgence of the strife and disorder in this part of Ireland'.[38] In the face of this danger Midgley felt obliged to admit that no evidence existed to substantiate Porter's allegations and he supported an amendment which called for a review of grants to voluntary schools.[39] The amendment was passed, a full-scale renewal of controversy with the Catholic Chuch was avoided and, as Midgley probably anticipated, no review ever took place.

Failure on this occasion did not dissuade those who resented the level of grant aid to voluntary schools as their opposition to Midgley's later proposal to provide 65 per cent of the salary for clerical assistants in such schools would again demonstrate.[40] One unionist parliamentarian, Captain O.W. Henderson M.P., argued his opposition to the proposal with the claim that so much public money was being given to voluntary schools that 'these schools are being maintained and run entirely on such funds'.[41] Henderson's claim was quite inaccurate based as it was on the same insinuation made by Porter that the management of Catholic schools was somehow defrauding the public purse.[42] The unionist-dominated Association of Education Committees added an extra-parliamentary voice to oppose the proposal saying that an additional burden would have to be borne by local authorities should a decision be made to grant-aid such salaries. Faced with this opposition Midgley withdrew his proposal again using the excuse that the whole question of grants to voluntary schools was about to be reviewed, though once again no review took place.[43]

Midgley died quite suddenly soon after this[44] and his successor, Morris May, tried unsuccessfully to have the proposal to meet the cost of clerical salaries from departmental funds reintroduced the following September. In cabinet he argued that there were no grounds for any objection to publicly funding, in part, clerical assistants in voluntary schools, saying that 'in principle and equity there was a strong case for making available grants in aid of clerical assistants in larger voluntary schools . . . that the right thing for me to do is to proceed to make the necessary regulations.'[45] Unstated 'political considerations', which can only have referred to backbench and extra-parliamentary opinion, were the reasons given in the minute of the same cabinet meeting for the decision that 'further action should be postponed and that grants in aid of clerical assistants in voluntary schools should not be made available at present'.[46]

Catholic system's slow development

This series of what were, in effect, rather petty decisions, inevitably fuelled the existing Catholic sense of grievance at not receiving a greater level of funding than 65 per cent. Had these new sources of grievance not been added, it might have been possible to have overcome the former, given the church's willingness to work the 1947 act. Instead, the sense of grievance seems to have been further intensified when it came to the practical task of providing Catholic intermediate schools. The figures for the provision of intermediate schools indicate that by 1955–56 only 7 Catholic intermediate schools had been provided, as compared with 43 in the county, or public authority sector.[47] Midgley occasionally seemed to blame the Catholic authorities for not submitting plans, but then, when they did so, as for example, for increased grammar school provision in Maghera, they ran the risk of having their plans turned down.

Why there was this slow rate of development is difficult to determine. Some of the Catholic dioceses had detailed plans before the Ministry of Education by late 1948, or early 1949 and by mid-1950 all dioceses had submitted their plans.[48] Bishop Neil Farren in Derry, for example, had plans not only submitted, but revised by December 1949, following discussion with ministry officials[49] and in several dioceses, Catholic planning was ahead of that by the relevant local educational authority.[50] The evidence available suggests that difficulties in obtaining suitable sites was a major cause of delays, but the extent to which such difficulties may have arisen because of anti-Catholic feelings is not easy to determine. A meeting with the Minister of Education and his officials in 1952 highlighted the problem of obtaining sites especially in Belfast and in Counties Antrim and Down, but with no obvious resolution to such difficulties recorded.[51]

Catholic churchmen and nationalist politicians continued to make the argument that the level of funding they were receiving remained inadequate, that it was a form of discrimination and effectively was the main reason for their system's slow development. As Harry Diamond M.P. said, 'it was very unfair that the government should make any distinction or discrimination with regard to the grants for voluntary schools' since between 40 and 50 per cent of the school population was in voluntary schools.[52] However, knowing the degree of opposition it had provoked on such relatively minor matters as national insurance payments and clerical salaries, the government must have felt quite justified in saying, through the Minister of Education, that there were no circumstances 'by which the amount of grants would be increased'.[53] The Minister of Education added that the government felt 'quite genuinely and sincerely that we are making the maximum contribution we can make to the equipment and the expenses of maintaining schools where such a degree of independence is retained by the managers'.[54]

When the decision was taken in Britain in 1959 to increase to 75 per cent (from 50 per cent) capital grants to voluntary schools,[55] the temperature was again raised over the matter in Northern Ireland. On this occasion the Minister of Education was able to point to the increased level of public representation on school committees required as a prior condition for obtaining the new level of public funding in Britain.[56] He sugggested that an increase could be obtained by the church in Northern Ireland if it too would be prepared to accept the 'four-and-two' committee system.[57] The answer to his suggestion remained negative.[58]

Although controversy continued it gradually lost some of its more bitter overtones following Midgley's death. Tributes from Midgley's successors to the Catholic Church for its efforts to increase the number of intermediate school places became noticeable, where previously they had been absent.[59] By 1960–61 36 voluntary intermediate schools were operating, a figure that was almost doubled five years later.[60]

Despite the slow thaw in some ministers' attitudes, nationalist members of parliament persisted with their demands for increased grants and in 1965 moved a motion seeking a review of the 'state grants for building and maintenance of voluntary schools'.[61] Harry Diamond, in proposing the motion, pointed out that since almost 50 per cent of the school going population was in voluntary schools (140,000 pupils as compared to 145, 000 in local authority schools) the voluntary system merited equal treatment to the public system.[62] Diamond referred to an improving climate in community relations in the country and seemed to hope that it would assist their case. Seconding the motion his Belfast colleague, Gerry Fitt , called for 100 per cent funding for all voluntary schools. Arguing that not to do so was discriminatory, Fitt claimed that 'in denying the Catholic minority what I consider to be their just rights in the field of education the Government are only creating a legacy of bitterness'.[63]

Despite the changing climate to which Diamond referred there was no hint of compromise from the Catholic Church on school management structures and the government would not move unless a greater degree of public accountability was first accepted through the establishment of 'four-and-two' committees. Herbie Kirk , the then Minister of Education, put the matter beyond dispute at this time when he said that 'the Government could not agree to any change in respect of schools which continue to reject the principle of four-and-two'.[64] The motion was rejected, but the matter did not rest for very long because within two years the Catholic Church did change.

'Four-and-two' committees, once apparently insurmountable barriers to the church, were finally accepted and under the terms of the Education Act of 1968 voluntary schools had their capital grants increased to 80 per cent, with all current expenditure being met from public funds.[65]

School texts and cultural conflict

The persistence of the political and religious divide on education also continued to be marked, during the 1950s, in approaches to cultural issues in the curriculum. Nationalists persisted with their demands that the teaching of Irish and of Irish history be encouraged, while some unionists became vociferous insisting that nothing was being done in schools to inculcate any appreciation of the Ulster–Protestant heritage. Harry Diamond complained in parliament that 'by depriving pupils of the opportunity of learning the language we are depriving them of a knowledge of the past and of their background'[66] while unionists continued to oppose Irish both for its alleged 'uselessness' and its 'subversive' influence. Terence O'Neill, Minister of Finance, betrayed not only his attitude to Irish, but his view of Catholics' prospects of employment at home, when he criticised the 'waste of time' in learning a language which was of no use because those who learn it 'then go over to England and get a job'.[67] Nat Minford called for strict supervision of the teaching of Irish, presumably to ensure that it would be free of any undesirable overtones[68] while other unionists called upon the Minister of Education to provide school texts 'so that our young people would be right up to date on the background of . . . Irish Protestantism'[69] and denounced the use of textbooks published in the south.[70]

Despite these demands and protests, the Ministry of Education took no action to modify the curriculum. Indeed there was little it could do, given the freedom which schools enjoyed as to whether Irish would, or would not be offered and as to which topics in history would be included in their curriculum. However, the ministry did have power to sanction expenditure on school textbooks and, in 1956, it chose to use this power to withhold approval for an Irish language text, one picture in which caused offence to some unionists. Considered retrospectively the incident appears almost comical. It concerned an illustration in the text *Cosán an Óir*, published in Dublin, in which a small boy was shown with an Irish tricolour in his hand. Unionist opposition to the display of the tricolour in Northern Ireland was almost endemic and their protests about the use of this particular text because it pictured the tricolour, led to directives being issued to schools by education authorities for the return to them of all copies.[71] In the House of Commons, Midgley stated that the 'book was regarded as unsuitable because of its pictorial content, namely the display of the tricolour' and such books could not, in the minister's words, be paid for from public funds because 'we are not going to subsidise this disloyalty'.[72] To Norman Porter the book 'was provocative because it insults the flag of our country, by show-ing the tricolour of Eire'.[73] Nationalists attacked the minister for censorship, a sensitive point because of Midgley's frequent criticisms of the Republic of Ireland for its censorship of publications legislation. Cahir Healy pointed out in mocking tones that the minister was 'censoring the colours on a little flag carried by a little boy'[74] while Harry Diamond sarcastically asked whether the minister was 'aware that any standard atlas in the primary schools con-tains a page showing the colours of the nations of the world, including the Republic of Ireland, and whether he proposes to continue this policy of ban-ning every document giving any knowledge in connection with another part of this country'.[75]

Despite the protests, the ban on the textbook in question, at least as an approved item for public expenditure, stood and the decision served as fur-ther evidence to nationalists that unionists were intent on circumscribing expressions of nationalist culture as much as possible. Nothing in the period covered by this study was to seriously alter that perception. More generally and in a more subtle manner, unionist values were being promoted within the curriculum, though not in the overt manner demanded by Porter and Minford. In 1956 a new *Programme for primary schools* was published. In conceptual terms, the new programme further exemplified the extent to which education in Northern Ireland was being shaped along British lines, even more firmly than in the past. In line with educational developments in Britain, the approach to the curriculum outlined in the new programme was decidedly child centred. Quoting the pre-war Hadow Report which had rec-ommended such an approach, the programme stated that the curriculum should be conceived 'less in terms of departments of knowledge to be taught and more in terms of activities and interests to be broadened'.[76] The multi-faceted nature of a child's personality was stressed and teachers were advised to develop curricula which would respond to the child's physical, emotional, social, moral and spiritual, as well as intellectual needs. Yet, within the new framework of thinking about the curriculum, there was no hint that primary education in Northern Ireland was taking place in a society with significantly different traditions. Indeed, in stark contra-diction to the principle of children learning from experience, which the programme claimed to uphold, Northern Ireland's cultural heritage was completely ignored. At a more general level and in a rather oblique fashion, the programme reiterated the same concern to promote 'loyalty' which was expressed in the Lynn Report in 1922–23. In that section of the programme dealing with citizenship, it was again suggested that citizenship in Northern Ireland implied an exclusive kind of loyalty.[77] Pupils, it was pointed out, 'should be brought to realize that they enjoy great benefits at the hands of the community and that this entails on their parts certain duties and responsibilities which they must loyally undertake'.[78] However oblique, it was an exhortation which could only have appealed to one section of that 'community'.

Progress despite all

It would be churlish, however, to suggest that the 1947 act did not mark a considerable change in the educational opportunities available to young people throughout the north. Change was at its most obvious in terms of the numbers availing of secondary education and the scale of provision in the new secondary intermediate schools which were being built throughout Northern Ireland. By 1964 when the government published a review of developments since 1947, 129 new secondary intermediate schools were in operation, 2 new grammar schools had been added to the pre-existing 80 while many of the latter had been extended to cope with increased enrolments; total pupil numbers in second level schools had increased from just over 27,000 in 1947 to almost 95,000 in 1963,[79] evidence that many thousands of young people were now gaining access to secondary education. So, in terms of providing access to second level education, considerable progress had been made as a result of the structural reforms introduced by the 1947 act, progress which stood in marked contrast to the failure to reform in the south.

'Nothing startling' in the south

While education in Northern Ireland was beginning to experience the reforms heralded by the 1947 act, the 1950s in the south marked a further period of almost no change, a situation that was accurately described in a Minister of Education's remark when introducing the annual debate on his department, 'I have nothing startling to record'.[80] An accurate statement which did not, however, imply that nothing needed to be done. If neither structural, nor curricular change was the order of the day, nonetheless, a kind of natural development did take place, most notably in the form of increased, voluntary participation in second and third level education. The consequent pressure on personnel, accommodation and on other resources only served to underline the urgent need for a planned approach to education. The extent of this development can be most immediately gauged in the continuous growth in the number of pupils attending secondary schools. The figures reveal an increase from 48,559 in 1950–51 to 76,843 ten years later in 1960–61, together with an increase in the number of secondary schools from 424 to 526 in the same period.[81] Even at primary level significant increases were being registered throughout the fifties with national school numbers increasing to over 500,000 by 1960. Increases on such a scale were bound to create their own momentum for change.[82]

However, when change came, it was not to be effected, as many at the beginning of the fifties had hoped, as a result of the Council of Education's investigations, but almost in spite of them. Change was to come as the result of much wider influences, some of which were beginning to make themselves felt in Irish life from the late 1940s. As these influences coalesced, they formed an amalgam of national and international economic, social, political and religious forces which were to have the effect of very rapidly transforming important aspects of Irish life, among them education.

Before that more hopeful and positive phase in the south's development in the late 1950s, a sense of stagnation and near despair was to grip the country. So pervasive was this feeling that it was not uncommon to hear voices raised proclaiming the actual eclipse of the Irish nation, a feeling highlighted by an Irish American author in a publication entitled *The vanishing Irish*.[83] Other more local voices, like that of Bishop Lucy of Cork, claimed that 'rural Ireland is stricken and dying. The will to marry and live on the land is almost gone'.[84] The source of this despondency was the very severe economic crisis which the state experienced in the immediate post-war period. Inflation took hold from 1947 which, when compounded with low levels of industrial and agricultural production, led to very high rates of unemployment and emigration.[85] The crisis deepened in the following years and it was not until about 1956–57 that it was arrested.[86] Only then did the south begin to share some of the benefits which post-war reconstruction had brought to the rest of Europe. The measures taken then, and in the years immediately after, were to launch the south on its most significant period of economic and social development since the state's establishment.

Ever so Catholic Ireland

Alongside the absence of economic and social development went an increasingly stronger role for the Catholic Church in public life in the south, giving to outsiders the impression that the church was contributing to, or even was the causal factor in that absence. The extensive publicity which church events received at the time can only have reinforced this impression, pilgrimages, religous processions and other celebrations being widely reported in the media. The church's Marian Year of 1954, for example, was celebrated with almost the same fervour by the state as it was by the church.[87] As one commentator described the decade: 'The 1950s were remarkable for urban church-going. Churches in suburb and city centre parishes often allowed for the celebration of six masses on a Sunday to accommodate the vast numbers who flocked to fulfil their religious obligations and daily masses were required to meet the demands of the faithful'.[88] In a more significant sense, the influence of the Catholic Church was to be seen in the manner in which it continued to set the parameters for social policy in the south. This was most clearly and dramatically underlined in the controversy over the government's plans, in 1950, for a comprehensive medical welfare scheme, commonly known as the 'Mother and Child Scheme'.[89] Catholic Church objections to some features of this plan led to the resignation of the Minister of Health, Dr Noel Browne and, consequently, of the coalition government itself.[90] This controversy, the first major church–state conflict since the establishment of the state, was a clear warning to politicians that the Catholic Church would not hesitate to exercise its considerable influence in opposing any attempt to introduce social legislation of a kind which it judged to transgress its own teachings.

Two issues lay at the heart of the church's opposition to the scheme. First, it was concerned about possible violations of its own teachings on medical ethics.[91] Secondly, the church viewed any scheme for 'socialised' medicine as an unnecessary and unwarranted encroachment by the state into an area for which the individual and other agencies had prior and more fundamental responsibilities.[92] The spectre of socialised services such as were being developed in other western countries and more comprehensively in communist countries, was one which seemed to haunt the Catholic Church in Ireland resulting in frequent condemnations of such state control by leading churchmen at this time.[93]

Liberal-minded people and the Protestant community in the south, in particular, were very shaken by the stand taken by the church over the Mother and Child Scheme, but, even more so, by what was perceived to be the abject compliance by the government with the church's demands. The Taoiseach, John Costello, was seen to have epitomised this compliance when he said in the course of one of the many Dáil debates on the matter: 'I am a Catholic first'.[94] It was not surprising that some people in the south viewed the church, in the words of an *Irish Times* editorial, 'to be the effective government of this country'.[95] Obviously, any southern government which might have wished to put forward comprehensive plans for the reform of education had a cautionary example of the fate which might befall it, should those plans not conform to the wishes of the Catholic Church.

For northern unionists, the Mother and Child Scheme controversy was one which seemed to prove once again their wisdom in resisting an all-Ireland state. As an editorial in the *Belfast Telegraph* commented '. . . this controversy shows how partition is a wise recognition of fundamental differences which are criss-crossed we believe by a radical difference of outlook between north and south in social reform'.[96] Conveniently ignored were the many close parallels with recent conflicts between the Protestant churches and northern governments in which the former had scored notable victories.

Throughout the 1950s many actions and statements by Catholic Church leaders only served to reinforce this perception of the south as a Catholic dominated society. The prohibition on Catholic students attending Trinity College, Dublin, reiterated annually in the Lenten Regulations for the Dublin diocese, further strengthened this perception[97] while Dr William Philbin, Bishop of Clonfert and, later, Bishop of Down and Connor, added his reinforcement when he warned against the kind of concessions which he claimed were being demanded of Catholics in Ireland in order to reconcile 'a dissident minority [i.e. northern unionists]'.[98] He claimed, quoting no firm evidence to support his case, that non-Catholics were attempting :

. . . to secure a dominating position in our public life . . . a leadership in thought and ideals . . . this is an explicit challenge to a Catholic nation which it would be unwise to overlook . . . We may have reached a stage when calling Ireland a Catholic nation will itself be regarded as a challenge and even deplored by some Catholics.[99]

However, despite the church's warnings and the measures taken to protect its members against what it perceived to be anti-Catholic influences, for most Irish people the challenge to the Catholicism with which they were familiar was to come, in the first instance, from within the church itself. The death in 1958 of Pius XII, a pope who had vigorously upheld the traditional teachings of the church as understood in Ireland, was followed by the election of a pope of quite a different style. The very amiable Pope John XXIII was to display an unexpected anxiety to 'modernise' the Catholic Church. His decision to summon a council of the church to examine and assess the role of Roman Catholicism in the modern world was to be the means whereby a very significant challenge was to be made to traditional Irish Catholicism.

Nationalism – slightly militant

If Catholicism marked the most notable expression of continuity in Irish life during this decade, continuity was also marked by one of the darker forces in Irish life, militant nationalism. The fifties were to witness another doomed attempt by advocates of 'physical force' nationalism to end 'British' rule in the north through a campaign of violence, a campaign which was to belie one of the main aims behind the decision by the government to declare a republic in 1949. The formal declaration in 1949 that the south was a republic, together with its withdrawal from the Commonwealth, were probably the most nationalist initiatives taken by a southern government in the immediate post-war period.[100] Essentially symbolic, the declaration of a republic was motivated as much by a desire on the part of the first coalition government to upstage the rival Fianna Fail party, as by any meaningful gain which the initiative could achieve.[101] Taoiseach John Costello claimed that as well as clarifying the status of the southern state, one of its other effects would be to take 'the gun out of Irish politics'.[102] The activities of the I.R.A. in the 1950s and early sixties soon proved this conviction to be quite erroneous.

A number of southern I.R.A. activists became quite prominent in this campaign and, following the deaths of some of those involved, the extent to which emotions could still be stirred by partition were strongly revealed. The huge crowds, including some public representatives and Catholic clergy, which attended the funerals of southern members of the I.R.A. killed in action in the north was testimony to this emotion.[103] That emotion had been sustained and fostered, not just in the political rhetoric of the preceding decades, but, to some extent at least, through the pressure for a Gaelic Ireland which had been placed on the educational system.

Nonetheless, it has to be also pointed out that despite this emotional response, militant nationalism received no widespread political support in the south at this time[104] and both southern governments which held office during the I.R.A.'s campaign felt sufficiently confident to take strong measures against the latter's activists and to do so, to a certain extent, in co-ordination with the government in the north.[105]

Signs of change

This co-ordination on security was a sign of the 'thaw' taking place in north–south relations during the 1950s and can also be seen as part of the more general change about to overtake the south. These changes can be described as the product of a gradually emerging pragmatism on both sides which led to co-operation with respect to such practical matters as the fisheries on the River Foyle, the Great Northern Railway and River Erne hydro-electric scheme.[106] Co-operation found explicit political expression in the approach articulated by Sean Lemass, the Fianna Fail leader who succeeded de Valera in 1959. In a widely reported speech to the Oxford Union in September 1959, Lemass made it quite clear that no southern government would endorse the use of force to achieve unity.[107] North–south co-operation was Lemass' preferred route to better relationships and increasing such opportunities was to become a hallmark of Lemass' period in office. For a time, this pragmatically based co-operation gradually began drawing both parts of Ireland into a new and more cordial relationship. Some of the distance which had been growing between north and south since 1922 was reduced and the groundwork laid for the brief period of friendly relations which was to emerge in the mid-sixties.[108]

Stirrings in other spheres of Irish life can also be seen as harbingers of change, notably those that were developing a network of international contacts for the south. Amongst these were membership of the Council of Europe and of the O.E.C.D.,[109] both affording government ministers and officials, for the first time since League of Nations days in the thirties, opportunities to come directly abreast of contemporary ideas for economic and social development. At a more general level, the gradual expansion in communications, especially through radio, television and air travel also had the effect of slowly opening avenues of contact for the general population. By the mid-fifties, many Irish homes listened regularly to British radio stations and by the end of the decade a rapidly increasing number of homes in the east of the country were receiving British television broadcasts.[110] Air travel gradually made destinations abroad, other than in Britain, accessible for business and holidays.[111] The cumulative effect of such access to the rapidly changing cultures of the western world could not fail to hold profound significance for a small English speaking society such as Ireland's. Challenge and change were becoming evident in virtually every area of Irish life, not least in education.

The kind of profound challenge posed both by a serious economic crisis and a rapidly expanding access to wider influences inevitably meant that the ideological twins dominating southern society, Roman Catholicism and Irish nationalism, were themselves to become subject to much more intense examination as this period advanced. However, before the effects of such influences could make themselves felt in education, hopes for change resided in those to whom responsibility for mapping out the future had been given in 1950, namely the members of the Council of Education. Unfortunately, they were in no great hurry to complete their work and so, while the country waited, public debate continued to focus on the same issues which had pre-occupied educational interests in the south since 1922. The language question continued to receive its, by now, ritual attention. Those who had been critical of the government's educational policy for reviving Irish because of its alleged intensity remained critical, while those who believed that not enough was being achieved maintained their pressure for even greater efforts. Amongst the former, in the Dáil, the prominent Fine Gael politician, James Dillon was still proclaiming his love of the language while decrying that it had been made 'an instrument of base corruption'[112] while Eamon de Valera, to whom the revival of Irish seemed to mean as much as political independence, claimed that what was needed most in order to promote Irish was 'devoted teachers – teachers who love the language and who desire to hear the language spoken in later life by the children whom they are now teaching'.[113] But for the absence of such teachers, de Valera seemed to be saying, 'we ought now to have arrived at a stage in which the children will realise when they are using Irish that they are using the language of the nation . . . and that it is the mode of expression most characteristic of our nation had it not been for historical accidents which deprived us of having it as the general speech'.[114]

In effect, de Valera's comments were virtual admissions of the impossible nature of the task of bringing Irish back into 'general speech'. On the one hand he acknowledged that the kind of teachers needed were not there and, on the other, his argument that Irish could only be the 'most characteristic mode of expression' of the nation if it was the 'general speech', implied accepting that it was not characteristic because it was not 'general speech'. However, de Valera was not one to openly admit failure believing, as he also said during these years, that 'a thorough examination now can lead to a general improvement directed mainly towards the use of the language in speech'.[115] In these remarks can be seen the seeds of the Commission on the Irish Language which was to be established later in the decade.The inter-party government's Minister of Education continued to be Richard Mulcahy who espoused an extremely minimalist approach to government intervention in education. As to the role of schools in reviving Irish, he seemed to take consolation from the fact that by then almost half of the 447 secondary schools were offering some Irish medium instruction, 91 of them being completely Irish medium schools[116] and so was content to leave 'well enough' alone .

However, more pressing and immediate needs were emerging, especially with respect to school accommodation. The need for additional and replacement school accommodation was becoming more and more obvious, but here patriotic effort was less than enthusiastic. Dublin apart, the attempts to establish a formal and co-ordinated approach on the part of the Catholic Church to meet this problem do not seem to have achieved any real success. In Dublin, where large sections of the inner-city's population were being rehoused in new suburban estates, a committee of departmental and diocesan officials was already planning school provision for these estates from the late forties.[117] Elsewhere, school accommodation remained the responsibility of individual parishes, a matter that continued to cause concern to the Department of Education. Sean Moylan, the Minister of Education in the 1951–53 Fianna Fail government, expressed his anxiety several times and mildly suggested the very approach to which the Catholic Church had not been at all responsive in the past, namely that local people should become involved in the maintenance of schools:

I see no reason why publicly minded citizens should not take sufficient interest in schools to band themselves into a local committee and see that the schools are properly kept.[118]

A similar view was expressed by many other politicians such as the Labour Party member for Cork, Daniel Desmond, who argued that 'the parents themselves as well as the manager, should realise that they must take their share of responsibility and play their part, themselves, in their own localities'.[119] The I.N.T.O. was also becoming increasingly concerned about school accommodation and, in order to detail the situation, it had, in 1950, requested information from its members throughout the country as to conditions in their schools.[120] As O'Connell points out, the widespread dissatisfaction expressed by teachers encouraged the organisation to obtain support for its long-standing proposal that the state should take full responsibility for the erection and maintenance of school buildings.[121] Not surprisingly, the Catholic Church remained firmly opposed to such a proposal and urged the I.N.T.O. to withdraw this demand. In a letter to the I.N.T.O., Cardinal D'Alton claimed that the bishops' opposition was motivated 'by their determination to guard the foundation of the managerial system and the system of denominational education which it ensures'.[122] For the bishops, guarding the managerial system still required the retention of complete control of Catholic schools within the institutional church, whatever the consequences for the children in their charge from being taught in physically unfit buildings.

Pressure for action did have some slight effect. Statistics for 1957 revealed that an average of approximately 100 new schools, extensions and major repair contracts were being completed each year.[123] However, this progress has to be seen against the continuing need to replace between 1,000 and 1,500 schools,[124] figures which meant that it would take some considerable time before school accommodation in the south would be satisfactory. The I.N.T.O. refused to be impressed and continued to press for increased maintenance, cleaning and heating grants. Several deputations were organised to meet with officials of the Department of Education, but these failed to hasten the improvements requested.[125] The department reiterated the need for local contributions in addition to the funds provided by government, thereby underlining a key principle in the whole concept of the managerial system which dated back to 1831, but which church officials seemed to conveniently overlook at times.[126]

At secondary level, where government had no responsibility for capital expenditure, accommodation was also becoming a critical issue as enrolments increased. Writing in 1953, T.J. McElligott, a secondary teacher himself, was bitterly critical of the lack of investment arguing that Christian Ireland was failing to meet its responsibilities when compared with totalitarian countries:

We must defend the Christian tradition in education, but the best way of defending it is by making our school buildings at least as good as those of countries in which the state has usurped all rights in this field.[127]

Christian Ireland was, however, not yet ready to take up this challenge.

The council reports

In educational terms the highlight of the early fifties was the publication in 1954 of the Council of Education's first report entitled *Report on the function and curriculum of the primary school*.[128] While the title suggests a wide ranging discussion, the report itself was confined almost exclusively to curricular issues. Discussion of the structures of education, much less of education's relationship with the wider socio–economic context of the state, was quite limited. Before discussing the curriculum, however, the council made one very significant recommendation regarding the very nature of schools in the south. Pointing to what it claimed was the failure to have the denominational basis to the aims and management of national schools formally recognised, the council recommended an amendment to the *Rules and regulations for national schools* in order that their denominational character be so recognised.[129] This recommendation was implemented when the rules were eventually revised in 1965.[130]

The amendment was significant because, in itself, it represented a triumph for a 'campaign' the origins of which are to be found in the opposition to the national system at its very beginning from church leaders like Archbishop McHale of Tuam.[131] Later, when the demand for denominationalism was fully endorsed by the Irish Catholic hierarchy at the Synod of Thurles in 1851, Cardinal Cullen had campaigned vigorously but unsuccessfully for a formally recognised denominational system.[132] Voices in favour of such recognition had occasionally been raised in the years following political independence, but the matter never became one of major importance because the majority opinion in the church had held that the system was as close to perfect as it was legally possible to make it and so it was neither thought necessary or desirable to seek such formal recognition.[133] It was a curious recommendation at a time when no threat existed to the role of the churches in southern education and reflected the very legalistic approach frequently articulated in Catholic Church circles in the thirties and discussed earlier in chapter 6. The recommendation, for all its 'Catholicity', completely ignored parental rights since, if all national schools were to be regarded as 'denominational', the possibility of establishing schools whose patrons might not wish to uphold particular denominational principles or any at all was rejected, at least implicitly.[134]

Philosophically, the whole report was based upon a very traditional Christian–Catholic concept of childhood with little or no evidence that its authors were familiar with, let alone sympathetic to, contemporary or alternative views. According to the report a child is born in a state of sin and must, therefore, be trained in the 'right' way. Schools exist to 'train their children in the fear and love of God'[135] and the duty to so train children 'is fulfilled through the religious and moral training of the child, through the teaching of good habits, through his instruction in duties of citizenship, and in his obligations to his parents and to the community'.[136] Any sense that education might play a creative role in shaping the future of society was summarily dismissed. Indeed, as if to answer those who believed that schools might play a 'reconstructionist' social function the council argued that 'it is not the function of the Primary School to establish a new social outlook'.[137]

As such comments indicate education was viewed as a very prescriptive process, one in which children would be 'formed' according to clearly defined precepts for clearly defined ends. Any suggestion that children might be creative themselves, that they might have talents for which education would provide outlets is virtually absent. When it came to i ndicating the aims of the curriculum, the report stated them as follows. The child 'should leave primary school with a clear conception of his dignity as a creature of God and the duties that he owes to his Creator, of his final destiny and the means at his disposal to attain it, of the duties he owes to his fellow men'.[138] To these aims of serving God and one's fellow men, was added the specific national aim of reviving the native language which, according to the report, had been a national aim 'even before the establishment of native government'.[139] The only comment on this aim was one of complete endorsement for the existing role of the primary school in that revival. The report quite firmly stated that 'no argument is necessary to prove that such an aim could not be realised unless Irish should find an important place in the primary school'.[140] Complementing religious education and the learning of Irish, was the study of history which, the council argued in words reminiscent of earlier documents, illustrated 'the best characteristics of our people, their esteem for spiritual things, their love of culture, their fidelity to ideals, their willingness to sacrifice, their desire for freedom'.[141]

Stating the fundamentals of education in such terms placed the report within the same conceptual framework as that which had informed the First and Second National Programme Conferences. Christianity and nationalism remained the twin pillars upon which the curriculum should be built. No desire to innovate can be detected across its more than 200 paragraphs, still less any awareness of fresh thinking about the nature of education, or of the kind of general changes in thinking and policy that were taking place elsewhere in primary education.

With respect to the different curriculum areas, it was not surprising that religious instruction received first mention, although no actual details were prescribed. In accordance with the council's strong denominational bias, detailing the syllabus for religious education was a matter for the churches themselves. However, as a reminder of its basic educational principles, the report once again stressed that:

Of all subjects of a school curriculum Religious Instruction is by far the most important, as its subject-matter, God's honour and service, includes the proper use of all man's faculties, and affords the most powerful inducement to their proper use. Religious instruction is, therefore, a fundamental part of the school course.[142]

Discussing the place of Irish in the curriculum the council accepted that the underlying aim of the revival campaign was 'the extension of its use as a vernacular language, as a vehicle of communication in the ordinary life of the country'.[143] No attempt was made by the council to clarify what might be meant by 'the extension of its use as a vernacular language'. Instead, the ideal that Irish might replace English was adhered to, even though the council itself admitted that 'the certainty of its survival within existing limits and under present circumstances seems to be unassured'.[144] Such confused thinking suggests that many, if not all of the council's members, had some sense of the educational problems posed by the official approach to Irish, but felt under no obligation to clearly identify what these problems were, much less suggest a solution to them. The council merely rejected any suggestion that the school could be blamed for the lack of progress in reviving Irish and asked, with considerable justification on this point at least, that it be given 'encouragement and support in its work for Irish'.[145]

The only forthright comments on the language issue made by the council were in the argument that, unless the language became a medium of communication within other major institutions of society in the country, then the aim of its revival would not be achieved.[146] These comments, although couched in less than direct terms, could be described as the first tentative criticism of the language revival policy to emanate from an official body since the foundation of the state. It was, however, criticism of a very mild nature and did no more than repeat what many people had been saying in other contexts for a long time. A further slight indication of change was evident in the discussion about English. In the report, English was not relegated to the apparently minor status in which some Irish language enthusiasts, like Professor Corcoran, had tried to have it placed in the twenties.[147] The council acknowledged that it was the language of the vast majority of Irish children and that 'even if the revival of Irish were to be achieved within a short time, it is likely that English would continue as an important second language in our schools'.[148] So, instead of the two languages being set virtually in mutual antagonism, as Corcoran had tried to do, the report recommended that learning and developing each language should be seen as complementary and overlapping processes.[149] This was an enlightened approach and one which would still be recommended by language specialists today.[150] In addressing the contentious issue of the use of Irish in infant classes, the council seemed to ignore the I.N.T.O.'s 1942 survey report and merely endorsed the slight modification introduced by Minister Mulcahy, namely that while Irish should continue to be the language of instruction in these classes, English could be 'taught for half an hour daily in all Infant classes in schools outside the Irish-speaking districts'.[151]

A minority view

If the majority of the council's members remained broadly faithful to the language policy as laid down since 1922, there was a minority on the council that was prepared to be more critical. Three members entered a lengthy reservation in which they critically analysed the policy on the language adopted since the 1920s.[152] In their view 'the introduction of the Irish language in the infant schools and in at least the earlier stages of the primary standards and still more its use as a medium of instruction is a serious limiting factor in the width and quality of our primary education'.[153] Instead of its early introduction, these members recommended that Irish not be introduced until pupils were 10–11 years of age.[154] Such a step would be, they believed, 'in accordance with what is regarded as sound educational practice'.[155] Psychological evidence as well as the I.N.T.O. survey of 1941 were also quoted in support of this recommendation,[156] one that was to gradually attract considerable attention over the next few years.

Structural matters

Since the main focus of the council's deliberations had been curricular, it was able to avoid detailed discussion of the structure of primary education, though it was impossible for it to avoid the issue entirely. However, when it did turn its attention to structural issues a similarly conservative attitude was displayed, just as in its discussion of the curriculum, essentially endorsing existing structures as well suited to the Irish context. Secondary education was outside its brief, and the council's main recommendation in its regard was to propose an increase in the number of scholarships.[157] That apart, the report offered nothing by way of recommending wider access to second-level education, despite the fact that this was a major issue in all western countries at the time. On the question of raising the school leaving age the council felt that the time was not yet ripe for such a move notwithstanding the many representations it had received urging such a recommendation. The council's approach was cautious in the extreme stating that 'there would be the difficult and invidious task of enforcement, finally by legal powers. Apart from the question of parental rights, it was most doubtful whether the strain, both economic and social which would be imposed on the public would result in a compensating educational benefit'.[158] Such a judgement betrayed an outlook which failed to appreciate any close link between education and economic progress, not to mention any appreciation of the value to society, in general terms, of a more educated population. It was, in essence, an elitist view and one that was at odds with the growing conviction in many countries that access to second-level education for all was a necessary concomitant to economic progress and in some that it was a right which could not be denied.

Widespread disappointment

Public comment on the council's report was full of disappointment, itself a clear indication of the desire for reform. The disappointment was, perhaps, best expressed by an editorial in the *Irish Times*:

Is it the Report for which the public had been waiting and hoping ? Surely one of the first questions for the Council to ask itself and as far as possible answer, was whether the existing system . . . has been a success. The Council has been content to accept the existing system wholesale and confines itself to the suggestion of respects in which it might be improved . . . Such bland acceptance of the status quo, in our opinion, impairs the value of the Report.[159]

The I.N.T.O. claimed that the report provided no answers about the effect of using Irish.[160] In fact, the council's failure to even refer to the I.N.T.O.'s own investigation into the effects of the use of Irish was very pointed. The I.N.T.O. also criticised the council's concept of education for ignoring 'one of the most vital aims of all education – the desirability of training children to educate themselves through the correct use of text-books and the development of the powers of initiative and self-independence, which is such a valuable result of self-education'.[161]

Writing in the *Irish Ecclesiastical Record*, Fr Peter Birch, a lecturer at Maynooth College and later to be Professor of Education there, criticised the report for the very few real changes it recommended.[162] He agreed with those who claimed that the council had not adequately dealt with the Irish language question, nor had it considered properly the needs of urban schools which were undergoing very rapid expansion at the time. He also criticised the failure to make firm proposals for co-ordinating primary and post-primary schooling. Fr Sean Ó Catháin, a lecturer in education at University College, Dublin and later also to be a Professor of Education, in a highly critical commentary of the report, singled out what he regarded as a number of its most significant failures.[163] Among these he instanced its failure to recommend that the school leaving age be raised to fifteen and, reflecting some of the arguments of the minority reservation, what he regarded as an unsatisfactory discussion of the place of Irish in the curriculum. On the former, he accused the council of being overly cautious in the weight it had given to the difficulties which lay in the way of extending compulsory schooling. The difficulties instanced by the council were, he claimed, essentially temporary and could be overcome. On the question of Irish he was very critical of the council's stand on the use of Irish at infant level, for which he claimed there was no supporting evidence.

The Minister of Education invited comment from all interested parties, but apart from that appeared to take no immediate action on the basis of the report's recommendations. Indeed two years later the same minister claimed that he was still considering the report and the comments he had received.[164] Because of this, he himself would offer no comment as to the likely nature of any changes that might be introduced. Indeed, it was in the same context that the minister described his role as that of 'a dungaree man, the plumber who will make the satisfactory communications and streamline the forces and potentialities of the education workers and education management in this country'.[165] His and the Department of Education's reaction to the council's report only served to underline such a passive concept of the state's role in developing and extending educational provision.

Curiously a number of years later, when in opposition and when he was criticising the Fianna Fail government for inaction, Mulcahy claimed that in November 1956 certain decisions had been made by his department on the basis of recommendations contained in the council's report but had not been implemented by his successor.[166] However, these were essentially decisions regarding the need to increase the supply of teachers and hardly a sign that Mulcahy had been about to introduce major reform. A more significant step forward, though still a relatively minor one, was the decision to increase the number of scholarships available to pupils wishing to pursue second-level education and effected in the 1961 Local Authorities (Scholarships) Act .[167] The increase while welcomed was not of a size to widen access to second-level education to all who sought it and who could not afford it, but it did at least signal a move in that direction.

Until the close of the decade the pace of change in southern education remained very slow. In 1957 the new Fianna Fail Minister of Education,[168] Jack Lynch, made no reference at all to the council's report during his contribution to the annual Dáil debate on education, nor to the likelihood of any change.[169] In his early years as minister, Lynch continued to express the same complacency and satisfaction about the education system as his predecessors had. Speaking to the A.S.T.I. congress in 1958, he described the system as 'sound' and once again argued that the state's role was merely 'to allow the conductors of schools the widest possible freedom compatible with the protection of the State's interests arising from expenditure undertaken by it'.[170] Complacency was, however, more evident in government and other establishment circles than it was in Irish society at large. Public debate was intensifying and by focusing on the need for change in terms which went beyond traditional concerns, it was beginning to force reform to the point where it could no longer be delayed.

Pressure on Irish

The timidity of the council's recommendations regarding Irish and the government's unwillingness to change can be judged against the background of rising criticism of education throughout Irish public life. Dissatisfaction with official approaches to the revival of Irish intensified considerably in the 1950s, both before and after the council published its report on primary education. The government-appointed Commission on Youth Unemployment, in its report in 1951, had commented that 'in view of the criticism received . . . we consider there is a grave need to examine the content of primary education, more particularly the content of Irish and the treatment of that language'[171] A representative of the Archbishop of Dublin, Fr S. Ó Cuív, told the A.S.T.I. congress in 1956 that 'children must not be sacrificed on the altar of any language',[172] a clear reference to Irish, and warned against attempts to suggest 'that only in the Irish tradition was the supernatural and Christian mentality to be found'. In 1958 another priest, Fr E. O'Doherty, a lecturer in psychology in University College, Dublin, pointed to scientific evidence which seemed to suggest that using a second language, i.e. not a language naturally acquired or generally in use in the child's environment, as a medium of instruction was likely to have retarding effects on children's educational development, the very point made in the Council of Education's minority report.[173] From another academic, R.H. Breathnach of University College, Cork came the very strong criticism that pressure and preferment of an inappropriate kind were being used to promote Irish. These forces, together with the attempt to claim as 'an objective reality' what was merely an ideal, i.e. that Irish was the national language, were, Breathnach argued, all damaging to the very prospect of revival.[174]

In a series of articles, published intermittently from 1951 and later as a collection in 1958,[175] Fr Ó Catháin developed a critique of approaches to the teaching of Irish, particularly at secondary level. On the existence of Irish medium education at this level, he acknowledged the 'very high level of ease and competency in speaking Irish' attained as a result, but claimed that there were negative factors, notably because 'the standard of the teaching given . . . has been called into question'.[176] Ó Catháin made the very radical suggestion that Irish, as a secondary school subject, be 'put outside the examination system altogether'[177] and that an essentially oral approach to it be adopted. He argued for the need to 'get rid of the compulsion of threats and punishments and failure and bring in the compulsion of love and esteem'.[178]

The nature of the criticisms now being raised and the credentials of many of the critics, a number of whom were obviously sympathetic to Irish, were such that the government felt obliged to respond. This it did by establishing a commission whose task it was to examine the role and place of the Irish language in Irish society. Formally entitled the Commission on the Restoration of the Irish Language, its deliberations were to mark the first comprehensive study of how the revival of Irish might be approached, what its precise aims might realistically be and how agencies other than the school could play a role in that revival.[179] The very establishment of such a commission, almost 40 years after the state had adopted a policy in favour of reviving Irish using the schools as the main instrument to implement that policy, was an indication of how critical the language issue had become and just how necessary it was to reassess approaches to it in the light of all the other emerging pressures both on education and on other aspects of Irish life.

Secondary education

As the general debate on education gathered pace, the need to reform secondary education, where the pressure of numbers was becoming quite acute, began to receive more and more public attention. Most of the initial attention focused on the curriculum, a review of which had already been embarked upon by the Council of Education in 1954,[180] but since it was not to publish its findings until 1962, its views were not available as the more public debate got under way. Meantime, Ó Catháin's articles containing far reaching proposals for curriculum reform were influencing a wide audience. He was particularly critical of the narrowly academic mould in which secondary education was cast, its dominance by an examination system which he regarded as out-moded and suited mainly to the needs of the small number of students who advanced to university education. No attempt was being made, he claimed, to take account 'of the varieties of abilities in pupils and of the conditions necessary for good learning'.[181] There was much, Ó Catháin also wrote, that Irish education could learn in these respects from recent developments elsewhere, especially in such areas as the teaching of science, and of European languages.[182] The teaching of science was notable for the complete absence of any requirement within the department's syllabuses for the study of biology, while the chemistry syllabus was described as 'so stagnant . . . that a student trained in 1880 or even earlier would have a good chance of passing the science examination papers in the present day matriculation examination'.[183] Modern European language teaching was constrained by the fact that all pupils were required to study Irish and most also studied Latin, or Greek. This was particularly the case in boys' secondary schools where modern European languages suffered from a very low priority, a tradition that reflected the fact that many boys' secondary schools were regarded by their church managers as preparatory institutions for the priesthood and religious life for which knowledge of the classics was particularly important.

Pressure for curricular change at secondary level did have some desired effects. By the end of the decade the first steps had been taken to improve standards in both science and language teaching: an increase in laboratory grants to secondary schools was announced and, to encourage a greater oral competency in language teaching, a decision taken to recognise service by modern language teachers in countries where their languages were spoken.[184]

On the need for more general reform in the education system many voices were also being raised particularly focusing on the case for widening access to secondary education. In 1952, the Commission on Youth Unemployment had recommended that the school leaving age be raised, arguing that use be made of the provisions within the Vocational Education Act of 1930 whereby the school leaving age could be raised in different areas at different times as the required accommodation became available.[185] McElligott severely criticised the Council of Education's very cautious approach to the question, saying that 'secondary schools must open their doors to all'.[186] Limited access to second level education was, in his view, socially divisive in Ireland because 'we . . . continue to regard primary and secondary education not as successive stages of education but as alternative kinds of education meant for different social classes'.[187] What was required, he argued, was '. . . a Minister of Education who will accept the inescapable truth which has long been accepted in Northern Ireland, that primary and secondary education are stages in a single process through which all should normally pass'.[188] McElligott had taught for a time in the north and seemed to view the changes there as much more progressive than the situation which continued to prevail in the south.

Professor John O'Meara, a classics scholar at University College, Dublin was, perhaps, an unusual voice in the growing public debate. From 1957 when he first voiced his concerns in public O'Meara became a trenchant critic of what he perceived to be the 'the stagnant pond which is the Department of Education since the State was founded'.[189] His pamphlet *Reform in education* received considerable public attention and did much to raise the temperature and level of the debate. Like Ó Catháin, O'Meara attacked what he regarded to be an antiquated school curriculum, particularly at secondary level.[190] Quoting figures published by U.N.E.S.C.O. he also attacked the low levels of public expenditure on education in the south. Compared with England and Northern Ireland, where the annual expenditure on education was approximately £2 per head of the population, O'Meara pointed out that the equivalent figure in the south amounted to no more than 50p.[191] Furthermore, as the Council of Education was to indicate, government grants to secondary schools had been reduced by 10 per cent between 1957 and 1959 at a time when other countries were significantly increasing their expenditure.[192] Commentators also pointed to the small size of many secondary schools, a factor which severely constrained curriculum choice: in 1956–57, 398 secondary schools out of a total of 480 had enrolments of 200, or less.[193]

A commitment to change

Debate over the need for educational reform had reached such a pitch by the end of the fifties that Noel Browne, by then a member of the small National Progressive Democratic Party, moved a resolution in the Dáil urging that the school leaving age be raised to fifteen.[194] The debate provoked by this motion can well be said to have elicited the first official signal of the changes which were to overtake education in the south during the 1960s. On this occasion, education was debated with explicit references to people's daily lives and to their practical aspirations as far as schooling was concerned. This was most clearly indicated by the fact that, for almost the first time in an educational debate, the Irish language was not a main talking point. Browne spoke of the barriers which lay in the way of many families who wished that their children might have access to second-level education. He instanced the large number of candidates, 3,100 in 1959, competing for a mere 690 secondary scholarships as an indication of this desire.[195] Like O'Meara, he referred to the U.N.E.S.C.O. figures on educational expenditure which placed the southern state amongst the very low spenders in the western world. Summarising his case Browne spoke of the need to reassess the whole provision of education, 'the curriculum whether it is suitable, whether there is overcrowding, the influence of learning the language [Irish], the overcrowding of classrooms, bad school buildings, indifferent teaching methods and corporal punishment . . .'[196]

The chief government spokesperson, the Minister of Education, Patrick Hillery, adopted the traditional approach of defending the system claiming that the 'picture was much better than many of our critics would appear to believe'.[197] Hillery referred to increased facilities, increased numbers and the promise of an increase in the number of secondary scholarships. Mindful of church interests in education, the minister reiterated the traditional reference to the 'harmonious co-operation' which existed between the state and 'minority and majority churches',[198] but while Hillery acknowledged that progress had still to be made in a number of respects, he made no commitment to the substance of the resolution.

The matter did not rest there, because in what Randles describes as an extraordinary intervention in a debate on educational matters, the Taoiseach, Sean Lemass, committed the government to raising the school leaving age, saying that 'the aim of the government is to bring about a situation in which all children will continue their schooling until they are at least fifteen years of age. We intend to strive to achieve that situation with the least possible delay'.[199] Reinforcing this approach Lemass, in an address to the A.S.T.I. some three days later, made the point that there was a great deal to be done to extend and improve facilities for secondary education.[200] Such an admission was a long way from the self-satisfaction expressed by his Minister of Education though the latter did join Lemass in stating that 'if we are to overcome the degree of underdevelopment at which we find ourselves we must have more and more education. A large part of the State's responsibility was to foster the country's economic interests and the first essential in this regard was that the system of education should, as far as possible, fit the pupils to face the modern world by, for example, promoting the teaching of science'.[201]

A redefinition of the aims and priorities in the south's education seemed to be taking place almost overnight. Inadequacies were being openly acknowledged and reform promised. It was no surprise, therefore, that Browne's resolution, which did not commit the government to any timetable, was passed without a division.[202]

Fuelling educational change

By the close of the 1950s, change was very much in the air throughout the state. The Fianna Fail government under the leadership of Sean Lemass who had replaced Eamon de Valera in 1958, when the latter had retired from active politics to be elected to the ceremonial role of President, had initiated a programme of economic reform. In many respects this reform was one of the first major effects to flow from the gradual opening of the south to international influences. The main aim of the reform programme was to prepare for the free trade conditions of the European Economic Community by modernising Irish industry and agriculture and as well by encouraging foreign investment in the south. Details of the changes introduced under Lemass' leadership have been well documented elsewhere, the basic thrust of which were outlined in the policy document *Economic development* adopted by government in 1958 and which, in Lyons words, was 'a five-year plan for expansion'.[203] The re-orientation of economic development away from a protectionist philosophy towards free trade which was required by this policy meant that, to succeed, Irish business would henceforward have to compete on equal terms with foreign business. To be Irish would no longer be a guarantee of economic advantage for the indigenous enterprise. To meet this challenge also meant that the education and training available in the south had to possess the capacity and means of educating and training Irish people in intellectual and technical skills to the standards of Ireland's competitors. Hence the new light in which both education and training began to be viewed by policy makers at this time.

Secondary education was the area which was seen to be in most urgent need of change, for many of the reasons already discussed in this study. Not surprisingly, therefore, more and more hope came to be placed in the Council of Education's investigation into the secondary curriculum, but once again hopes were to be sadly dashed. When the council did eventually publish its report, another wave of disappointment was registered. The report was given to the Minister of Education in 1960, but was not publicly released until 1962. By then it was already being seen as belonging to a different age, reflecting as it did, a very conservative approach to educational planning.[204]

In the light of the changes which were overtaking Irish society from the late 1950s, the council can be accused of having confined itself to an overly narrow interpretation of its brief to examine the secondary curriculum. By being so narrow the council chose to ignore the wider socio–political influences which affect education. Even within the interpretation with which the council operated, it can be accused of undervaluing significant curriculum developments. The report began by again stressing an essentially religious aim for education , saying 'it is only just that we should emphasise the paramount educative value of this historic religious purpose in the schools and realise the advantages our people have compared with others in modern times'.[205] By keeping its aim almost exclusively directed on the next world the council failed to take adequate note of the changes and needs of the new world which Ireland was entering in the late fifties and early sixties. Throughout, the report was virtually a vote of confidence in the existing system. It expressed no need to broaden the curriculum in order to include 'practical' subjects, a development which any move to provide wider access to secondary education would necessitate.[206] Nor did it recommend any need to formalise 'vocational guidance'.[207] It recommended that small schools continue to be supported, even though they might not be able to provide 'a full science programme with science laboratories'.[208] The idea that children might be transported to larger schools did not appear to enter the council's thinking. The need for close co-ordination between first and second-level education was not seen as problematic as many commentators had been arguing,[209] nor did the council feel that any need existed for a standard age of transfer to secondary school.[210]

As to the details of the curriculum, the council had few major recommendations to make. On Irish, the council again adopted a complacent attitude. Indeed, reading the council's comments one would imagine that most students were leaving secondary schools with at least an adequate command of the language and that it was only because of the lack of its wider use that more progress had not been achieved in its revival.[211] True as this may have been in the case of some students, it hardly justified the council's failure to critically examine the syllabus, or its naive hope 'that additional time may be devoted to oral practice and to showing the reasons why the language is studied and the wealth of national tradition, oral and written, behind it'.[212]

In discussing other language syllabuses, the council also endorsed, in general terms, the need to attend to oral language, but declined to recommend that it be assessed, thereby virtually undermining its own recommendation.[213] The importance of experimental science was recognised, but this did not persuade the council that it should be become a required subject on the curriculum throughout secondary school, nor that an experimental as opposed to a demonstrative approach be used in its teaching,[214] residual effects, perhaps, of a long humanist tradition often hostile to scientific methods. The generally conservative approach to the curriculum was only abandoned with respect to one subject area, the classics. Only when discussing these subjects did the council allow itself to talk of a need for 'a radical reform of aims and programme',[215] a reflection, perhaps of the strong clerical presence in the council and, again, further evidence of a preference for the humanist tradition.

239

General access – 'utopian'

When discussing the demand for general access to second-level education the council portrayed itself at its most conservative. The recommendation adopted was precisely that which the council had made in its first report, i.e. that while access to secondary education should be facilitated for those who could be deemed to benefit from it, general access was rejected.[216] The council argued that on educational grounds there were objections to widening such access because 'only a minority of pupils would be capable of profiting by secondary [grammar school] education, as is attested by the experience of other countries'.[217] However, despite being in line with some contemporary thinking as far as secondary–grammar school education was concerned, the council argued against general access to secondary education. Without adducing any evidence, it claimed that 'the unqualified scheme of "secondary education for all" is utopian'.[218] Instead, the council argued that an enhanced scholarship scheme, together with improved grants to the schools themselves, would be the best means of assisting those who would benefit from secondary education.

While these recommendations may, to some extent, have been defended on economic and educational grounds, one cannot fail to detect the influence of very traditional Catholic social teaching with its stress on individuals making as direct a contribution as possible towards the services they wished to avail of. The council's report virtually said as much, arguing that such measures 'would preserve the principle of contribution on the part of the parents in proportion to their means, a principle desirable on general social grounds and also because it preserves in both parents and children a sense of the value in education'.[219] On this issue the council's recommendation had been clearly overtaken in principle, at least, by Lemass' assurance that the government had accepted as policy that the school leaving age would be raised to fifteen.

On almost all of the major issues the council argued, at the most, for what can only be described as a 'tidying-up' exercise, rather than any significant change. No evidence can be found in the report to suggest that the council was in touch with educational thinking elsewhere, a surprising fact in view of the intensification of educational debate in other countries. Instead, a deep sense that fundamentally all was fine with secondary education in the south, both philosophically and practically, pervades the report.

Another 'dead letter'

Reaction to the report was strongly critical and dismissive with the result that it quickly became a dead letter. In the words of an *Irish Times* editorial the report 'has missed a singular opportunity to give a new direction to the cultural and commercial orientation of Irish secondary education'.[220] In essence, the council's thinking was judged to be rooted in the past. The approach to education which directed its thinking was of a very traditional

Christian and Catholic humanist kind which displayed little awareness of the actual needs of the society that was emerging in Ireland during the period of the council's deliberations. The report appeared to assume that this model of secondary education was beyond question and required little more than minor adjustments to maintain its relevance. Little wonder then, that in the very same year of the report's publication, steps were already being taken to initiate the study that would, more than any other, reveal what needed to be done in order to reform education in the south. The pace of change, both within and without the world of education, had overtaken whatever relevance the council's report might have had. Within the Department of Education considerable attention was being given to the kind of thinking that was influencing educational change abroad. Officials of the department, together with other educationists, had been attending various international conferences dealing with curriculum and educational reform generally and had become aware of the need to assess education within a much wider framework of thinking than that which had guided the Council of Education.[221]

The first significant sign of fresh thinking was revealed in July 1962 when the Minister of Education, with assistance from the O.E.C.D., established a team of experts to survey Irish education.[222] In marked contrast with the membership of the Council of Education the steering committee and its survey team were composed not of educationists, but of senior civil servants from a number of departments, leading academics, economists and business people. The terms of reference indicated a desire to frame 'educational targets, including provision for research in relation to the assessments to be made of overall needs for skilled manpower according to field of study, level of skill, for the next 10–15 years . . ., and to assess future essential demand for educational facilities at different levels based on present trends and international experience and having regard to any other factors likely to influence such demand'.[223]

Such terms of reference indicated an intention to place the development of education in the south within the wider framework of the state's general economic and social development. The more planned approach to the latter which had been introduced by the Lemass government in 1958, was now to be extended to education. Such an approach implied, however imperceptibly at first, educational aims which would challenge the Christian–Catholic and nationalist aims which had shaped education in the state since 1920.

10

As One Sows

The 40 years of educational development in both parts of Ireland examined in this study reveal the extent to which that development very rapidly became bound up with and determined by the rival beliefs, values and attitudes north and south and the manner in which together they were shaping the political landscape in both parts of the country. Within a relatively short period following the establishment of both new political entities essential characteristics of education had been replaced, reshaped or reformed to accord with the visions of the mutually exclusive forces which had brought those two states into existence in 1921–22. Unionists in the north and nationalists in the south, now politically dominant within their respective domains, were able to set about moulding their respective educational systems according to their distinctive and exclusive visions for the societies of which they had charge. As we have seen, the political leadership of both traditions set about the task with considerable enthusiasm and no little determination. However, the extent to which success in pursuit of these visions was achieved is highly questionable while the price to both parts of the country invites interesting speculation.

The aims which were derived from the respective visions of education were undoubtedly ambitious. A non-denominational, democratically controlled system which would foster local pride in schools and community involvement in education was the essential characteristic of the vision espoused in the north. In the south, an education system fostering Gaelic culture and the Irish language in particular, was to be the principal means by which the reGaelicisation of Irish society generally was to be achieved and thereby, the complete vindication of the struggle for political independence.

For unionists, a modern, forward-looking and democratic state which the ideal stated was to be the hallmark of Northern Ireland, required the extension of popular control over education. Furthermore, since the rest of the United Kingdom was already embarked upon this road it was the direction which Northern Ireland had to follow as part of a general policy of maintaining parity with the rest of Britain. In the south, a determination that education should play a leading role in promoting essentially Irish cultural values and practices in order to remove what were understood to be the destructive influences of centuries of British domination seemed fully in keeping with the independent era which the new state was then entering.

242

These visions had been signalled for quite some time before both states were established and, as this study has pointed out, moves to achieve them had already been attempted, though with limited success. The political arrangements reached in 1921–22 seemed, therefore, to provide unparalleled opportunities for their attainment which neither state was slow to grasp. There were, however, other critical realities apart from political power which required consideration by those charged with developing and implementing new educational policies. Firstly, since the political context in Ireland was strongly influenced by religious considerations and since education itself was very directly a church concern, any developments required sensitivity to the churches' long established role in this area. Secondly, given that in both north and south there existed politico–religious minorities whose aspirations were not those of the dominant group in each, educational policy determined exclusively by the latter could not be automatically assumed to conform with the views of the former, a reality that was to be much more critical in the north where the minority composed one third of the population and where aspirations and traditions were most sharply divided. Thirdly, in the south, the goal of a Gaelic revival on the scale contemplated was being adopted in the context of an almost completely English speaking society whose sense of a distinctly Irish identity and whose support for Irish freedom had not been dependent to any considerable extent on a knowledge of the Irish language, much less on its use. Any measure, therefore, by which the implementation of educational policies adopted in both parts of the country may be evaluated needs to take account of how these significant realities were addressed.

A brief reflection on key features of the politics which had determined the systems of education inherited by the two Irish regimes, discussed in the opening chapter may be helpful. Educational development over the 90 years before partition had depended to a crucial degree on the role of the churches. For the British authorities in Ireland in the early nineteenth century, the political issue to be resolved, as far as education was concerned, was not so much how to ensure the co-operation of the churches in the provision of schools as to how a Protestant state could support schools in the control and management of which the Catholic church would be deeply involved. Support for church schools was not a problem in principle since prior to 1831 a denominational system controlled by the Church of Ireland and a variety of associated agencies had long been supported by the state while Catholic schools and those of other Protestant denominations had been deliberately denied such support. Extending the principle of state support to include schools of denominations other than those of the Church of Ireland was not yet an acceptable prospect to British governments in the early nineteenth century. Hence the compromise that became the 'national system'.

Once the compromise had been decided and a viable degree of church, especially Catholic Church support anticipated, it was possible to appeal to virtue, i.e. to the notion that through schools open to pupils of all denominations, understanding and tolerance might be fostered. The hope that national schools would be religiously mixed, or 'integrated' to use today's terminology, was never realised on any significant or meaningful scale and it can be questioned if it was ever seriously expected to be. None of the churches, in particular not the Catholic Church, accepted it with that end in mind. What the national school system achieved in the first instance was an arrangement whereby the British (Protestant) state was able to provide public funds to schools managed by churches and agencies other than the Church of Ireland, especially the Catholic Church. The fact that the other churches were slower to fully enter the system or that some sections of the Catholic Church itself remained outside the system, was not a major concern. The church of the overwhelming majority of the population did, for the most part, agree to work the system and that was the crucial factor in ensuring its success.

As a result, a degree of structural harmony eventually settled over Irish education and it persisted until the country was partitioned. This harmony was considerably strengthened as the main Protestant churches entered the system allowing thereby a form of co-operation to evolve between the state and all of the churches, which was quite unique to Ireland. This is not to say that the co-operation which was realised through the workings of the National Board, later paralleled in a much looser manner in the Intermediate Board, was as fruitful or as free from acrimony as the term harmony suggests. Catholic attitudes in the second half of the nineteenth century gradually became more belligerent towards the national system, just as Protestant attitudes were becoming more friendly, while the emergence of cultural nationalism with its demands for significant policy and curriculum reform only added to the hostile pressures on the system. Nonetheless, in spite of these pressures the system did survive, affording equity of treatment in terms of funding at least, to those who built and managed Ireland's schools and to those who taught in them, consequently laying the foundations for the orderly development of education throughout the country. Furthermore, it can be argued that by bringing together on their boards the major interests in Irish education, the two systems did mitigate some of the more extreme religious and political tendencies attempting to influence education in Ireland in the 90 years before partition. In other words, the boards of commissioners provided a simple, some might say a crude form of checks and balances over the administration and development of Irish education throughout that period.

The inadequacies of both systems, of which there were many, lay to a considerable extent in the level of funding which could be made available, a matter effectively outside their boards' direct control. Secondly, the general policy of promoting the Anglicisation, or at least the deGaelicisation of those parts of Irish society which had been Gaelic, led to the whole system of education being condemned as anti-national by revivalist movements which believed that education in Ireland should sustain and promote distinctly

Irish cultural patterns and who wished to reverse the process of encultura-
tion which the educational system appeared to promote. In addition to these
inadequacies, the boards suffered one major structural weakness, a weakness that became increasingly apparent as the new century dawned.
Centralised and essentially elitist in their memberships the two boards were
unable to directly involve local interests in education nor, indeed, any interest deemed unacceptable to the British administration in Ireland. In effect
they lacked a popular, democratic base. So, as pressure mounted to develop
a local input into educational development and as the boards came increasingly under attack for their role in deGaelicising Irish society, it became clear
that they would not long survive the political changes imminent at the end
of century's second decade.

However, when it came to addressing these weaknesses and inadequacies
in post-partition Ireland and to directing educational development in accordance with the visions identified earlier, the evidence examined clearly suggests that appropriate checks and balances were not effected in either
jurisdiction as part of the subsequent reform process. With party political
interests in almost complete control of educational policy and of its implementation, and amenable only to influence from those on whom they
directly depended for that control, i.e. their own electorates and the institutional interests associated with those electorates, it is understandable how
other interests could be minimised, if not ignored.

While not wanting to suggest that the boards of commissioners should
have been maintained, the establishment of fora, representative of the major
educational interests, to discuss and advise both administrations as to the
implications of their policies, might well have avoided some of the problems
which have been discussed in this study. The advisory committees and com-
missions established in both jurisdictions either lacked broad representation,
as was the case in the north, or else were established so occasionally and
were so circumscribed in their remit, as in the south, as to be almost totally
ineffectual .

In the north, might not a greater understanding by the churches of what
the new administration had been attempting and, as a result, a more comprehensive compromise avoiding separate and unequal systems have been
achieved, had a broadly representative body charged with giving regular
and considered attention to educational development been established?
Such a body rather than the ad hoc Lynn Committee could have built on the
tradition established by the boards and while the Catholic Church may well
have boycotted it in 1921, just as it had the Lynn Committee, it may have
found it possible to participate later when, as from 1923–24 onwards, it
began to campaign for what it regarded as its just share of public funds. In
such circumstances might it not have been possible to address issues of
school management and funding as well as curriculum policy in a manner
conducive to general compromise? In the south, would Gaelicisation have
been so contentious had there been a regular forum for the exchange of views

between policy makers and those who controlled and taught in the schools in which policy had to be implemented? Would the issue of school maintenance and repair have been resolved more expeditiously and might access to second-level education have been more effectively planned?

Questions such as these are, of course, unanswerable. Posing them, however, only highlights the fact that, in the absence of effective consultative mechanisms, the interests which influenced and determined the direction of education in Ireland exercised a much greater degree of freedom than they might otherwise have had. In neither jurisdiction did parliament offer an effective check on the administrations in power. In the northern parliament, nationalists were ignored not simply because of their small numbers, but even more so because they were viewed as the 'enemy' and their views on education, as on any other matter, as hardly worthy of comment. In the Dáil, the consensus behind the general thrust of educational policies extended across party lines with the result that until the late 1950s, successive administrations only tended to be severely criticised on educational issues for their alleged failures to more effectively achieve the national aim of restoring Irish as a widely spoken language. When voices were raised critical of aspects of the language policy in itself, they tended to be ignored.

Unfettered power – almost

The major feature common to education north and south was the manner in which the churches sought to maintain their role in education; one of almost complete control in the case of the Catholic Church and of partial control in the case of the Protestant churches. From this role the churches were to prove virtually immovable. Indeed, as this and other studies have shown, so immovable were they that such major measures to restructure the national system as those proposed in the 1919 MacPherson Bill before partition and the 1923 Education Act in Northern Ireland were either completely or partially frustrated. At secondary level the influence of the churches was no less powerful. In the south for all of the period studied, they remained as they had been from the outset virtually the sole and unchallenged providers of traditional second-level education. In the north, church influence was considerable both in the traditional grammar sector of secondary education, particularly in Catholic schools, and for all of the churches in the new secondary intermediate sector after 1947.

What is most striking about church attitudes towards education is their suspicion and hostility towards a direct role for local communities in developing their educational services, communities which in both parts of Ireland not only provided the finances for these services but which were also very loyal and faithful to their churches. While the Protestant churches were, in principle, not opposed to this role and rhetorically welcomed it, their determination to so circumscribe it even in circumstances where it was highly unlikely that their influence would not be seriously reduced, as in the north, betrayed a considerable lack of trust in the political representatives of their own community. The same can be said of the attitudes of the Catholic Church, especially in the south where the introduction of the very mild forms of local democracy into education suggested from time to time could hardly have posed any serious threat to the church's role and influence.

This direct church influence and control over the schools attended by the overwhelming majority of Irish pupils at primary and secondary level was probably unparalleled elsewhere in the western world. The fact that it could be achieved on such a scale was, in itself, testimony not just to the institutional churches' political influence. It was also a reflection of the very deep commitment of Irish people to their churches and of their confidence in them as providers and guardians of the education of Ireland's youth. Without this commitment it would have been almost impossible for these churches to have maintained the degree of control and general influence over education which they did.

In the south the argument has been made that church control had an economic advantage which suited a state whose governments seldom embraced social policies entailing considerable outlays of public funds. Certainly the extent to which the Catholic Church invested in education was considerable. This is not an argument which has been seen as central to this study, though it is one which deserves attention because the principal factor underlying the close dependence on the churches in south as providers of education was the latters' influence over the people of Ireland and, hence, over their representatives. This is particularly borne out by the confidence of the Catholic Church in the north that it could sustain a viable system of schools when it refused to accept both the proposals for the transfer of its schools to local committees and the 'four-and-two' management structure before 1968. It knew it could rely on its own members to provide the necessary funds.

The final point to be made about church control and influence is the extent to which it served to sustain and reinforce divisions and antagonisms between Christians in both parts of the country, but especially in the north where religion overlapped so much with politics. There is no evidence in the sources consulted for this study of any educational initiatives by the churches aimed at removing, or even mitigating these divisions and antagonisms. On the contrary many church leaders seemed more intent on their maintenance than the reverse. The less contact between children of the different churches the better, seemed to be the preferred option.

At curriculum level, the study has revealed similar tendencies. In this respect policies were devised and implemented which had the effect of widening existing communal divisions by, on the one hand, the attempted Gaelic 'cultural revolution' in the south and, on the other, the emphasis on Britishness and loyalty to the crown in the publicly controlled and Protestant sector of education in the north. In the manner in which they were implemented both approaches reinforced alienation between the majorities in both parts of Ireland and, more immediately, from their own respective minorities, though to a much lesser extent in the south than in the north.

The particular cultural emphases in question cannot be deemed invalid in themselves. The desire to foster a distinctly Irish identity which drew upon the country's Gaelic heritage and which had never been officially celebrated to any significant extent in schools during the British regime was a goal which can be judged as worthy. Likewise, a desire to promote a sense of Britishness and pride in their own identity on the part of unionists can be regarded as a worthy aspiration. Such aims, promoted in a strident and exclusive manner as they tended to be in both parts of Ireland over the period reviewed, immediately lose their wider appeal as well sowing seeds of discontent in those who do not share the same cultural values. In the north, where deep-seated communal tensions and suspicions have existed for centuries, hostile attitudes by unionist administrations towards the status and value of the Irish language in school curricula together with an antipathy towards the Catholic Church, only served to promote such discontent. In the south, the relentless and almost exclusive pursuit of Gaelicisation through the school system undoubtedly sowed seeds of discontent not only in southern society itself, but also between north and south, reinforcing thereby the partition of Ireland to which all southern political parties claimed to be opposed. The sense of Irishness associated with that policy was not one inclusive of all Irish traditions, celebrating as it did only those elements of Irish culture and history which conformed to a narrowly nationalist view of what it meant to be Irish.

If the period began on notes of high optimism inspired by ideals which were in themselves very worthy, it ended with their implementation, as well as many of the attitudes which they had fostered, being exposed to close and critical scrutiny. Reform was very much in the air by the mid-sixties. Educational structures which had escaped virtually untouched in the south throughout the previous 45 years were being challenged by the sheer pressure of expansion in the numbers enrolling for second-level education as well as new and powerful social and economic forces. These structures would soon undergo change in a manner that would, for the first time in the state's history, raise serious questions over the church's dominant role within them. Expansion was also bringing in its wake demands for curriculum reform which would broaden the debate beyond an almost exclusive concern about how schools should assist and promote the Irish language. In the north, the growing concern about civil rights and community relations was soon to broaden the educational debate there away from its exclusive preoccupation with structures and funding to how schools should address some of these wider issues and contribute to a healthier, more inclusive society. There were signs too of renewed and positive contacts between educationists north and south for the first time since partition to address common issues. However, before education could contribute in a positive manner, darker forces were at work overshadowing more hopeful developments and reaping the harvest which some of the educational seeds sown in Ireland over these 45 years had helped to produce. The story of how education in both parts of Ireland has responded to the trauma of what followed will make for an extremely interesting study.

Notes

Chapter 1

1. The annual reports of the Commissioners of Intermediate Education contained lists of intermediate schools and their respective managements.
2. The Board of Commissioners of National Education was formally established in 1831, but its status remained somewhat uncertain until it was granted a charter of incorporation in 1844. D.H. Akenson, *The Irish education experiment, the national system of education in the nineteenth century* (London,Routledge and Kegan Paul, and Toronto, University of Toronto Press, 1970), pp 133–5. (Hereafter cited as Akenson, *Irish education*).
3. Intermediate Education (Ireland) Act, 1878, 41 & 42 Vic., ch. 66.
4. Akenson, *Irish education*, ch. 4.
5. The Intermediate Board did not make grants available either for the construction of school buildings, or, initially, for the payment of teachers.
6. An inspectorate was eventually established in 1909.
7. Annual reports of both boards contain a full listing of their respective memberships.
8. Akenson, *Irish education*, pp 301–94, discusses the background to the changes in numbers and representation on the National Board.
9. At its establishment the Board of Commissioners of National Education consisted of seven members: two established church (Church of Ireland), two Roman Catholics and one Presbyterian and one Unitarian. The Intermediate Board consisted of four Roman Catholics and three Protestants at its establishment.
10. Stanley's letter to the Duke of Leinster on the formation of a Board of Commissioners for Education in Ireland. Akenson, *Irish education*, presents two versions of this letter. This quotation is taken from version 'A'.
11. Ibid. and quoted in the statement of aims contained in *Rules and regulations of the Board of Commissioners of National Education*, published annually.
12. The eighth and ninth reports of the commission of inquiry 1824–6 contain several references to questions put to representatives of the Catholic Church regarding the jurisdiction and authority of the Pope as well as their loyalty to him on matters of a political nature. S. Ó Canainn, 'The education inquiry of 1824–1826 in its social and political context' in *Irish Educational Studies*, 3, no. 2 (1983), pp 1–21 provides a useful summary of prevailing attitudes towards Catholics expressed at the inquiry.
13. Ibid.
14. Akenson, *Irish education*, p. 190.
15. A. Hyland and K. Milne, *Irish educational documents, volume 1* (Dublin, C.I.C.E., 1987), pp 83–7. (Hereafter cited as Hyland and Milne, *Irish ed. doc. v.1*).
16. Akenson, *Irish education*, p. 93.
17. Timothy Kelly, 'Education' in M. Hurley (ed.), *Irish Anglicanism* (Dublin, Allen Figgis, 1970), pp 51–64.
18. Ibid.
19. Ibid.
20. John A. McIvor, *Popular education in the Irish Presbyterian Church* (Dublin, Scepter Books,1969), ch7.
21. Ibid.
22. Akenson, *Irish education*, pp 185–7.
23. Ibid.
24. Ironically, in view of its earlier stand, the Presbyterian Church frequently passed resolutions in favour of what it termed 'united education'. As early as 1864, at its General Assembly, res-

olutions to this effect were endorsed as a reaction to the Catholic Church's attacks on the national system. Parliamentary papers, 1864 (285), xlvi, 411.

25. Akenson, *Irish education*, pp 202–4.

26. Ibid.

27. The Christian Brothers at Archbishop Murray's encouragement experimented with the national system in the 1830s. See J.D. Fitzpatrick, *Edmund Rice, founder and first superior general of the brothers of the Christian schools of Ireland* (Dublin, Christian Brothers, 1945), pp 249–51.

28. The Catholic bishops' pastoral letter on the occasion of the Synod of Thurles 1850. See Battersby's *Catholic Directory, 1851*.

29. Memorial of the Catholic bishops of Ireland, November 1859. See Battersby's *Catholic Directory*, 1860, pp 237–41.

30. *Reply of the Chief Secretary for Ireland to the memorial of the Roman Catholic prelates of Ireland*, H.C. 1860, (26), liii.

31. Archbishop Paul Cullen in evidence to the commission of inquiry into primary education in Ireland (Powis Commission), 22 Feb, 1868.

32. E. Larkin, *The consolidation of the Roman Catholic church in Ireland 1860–1870* (Dublin, Gill and Macmillan, 1987), pp 158–62.

33. Recommendation 44 of the Powis Commission effectively removed the prohibition on the display of religious emblems in schools catering for children of one denomination. *Report of the commissioners appointed to inquire into the nature and extent of the instruction afforded by several institutions in Ireland for the purpose of elementary or primary education; also into the practical working of the system of national education in Ireland, etc.* 1870 (C. 6) xxviii, 1.

34. Paul Cullen, pastoral letter, St Patrick's Day 1861 in P. Mac Suibhne, *Paul Cullen and his contemporaries,volume 2* (Naas, Leinster Leader, 1961), p. 222.

35. Ibid.

36. Statement by the Catholic bishops, May 1862.

37. B. McSweeney, *Roman Catholicism: the search for relevance* (London, Blackwell,1980).

38. Timothy Corcoran, evidence to the vice-regal committee of inquiry into primary education in Ireland. Evidence, memoranda etc. in [Cmd. 178], H.C. 1919 xxi.

39. Mgr Denis Hallinan, 'State aggressiveness in education III' in *Irish Education Review*, 1, p. 409.

40. S.J. Curtis, *History of education in Great Britain* (London, University Tutorial Press, 1948), pp 166–7.

41. Rules 127b, 186 and 194 in *Rules and regulations for national schools 1904* (Dublin, Commissioners of National Education, 1904).

42. *Irish Catholic Directory 1905*, p. 446.

43. *Report of the Commissioners of National Education, 1919–20*.

44. *Rules and regulations of the Board of National Education, 1919–20*.

45. Commissioners of National Education in Ireland *New rules and regulations for 1900–1901* [Cmd. 251], H.C. 1900, lxvi, 131 and [Cmd. 601], H.C. 1901, lviii, 1.

46. Ibid.

47. Ibid.

48. Ibid.

49. Ibid.

50. John Coolahan, *Irish education, history and structure* (Dublin, Institute of Public Administration, 1981), p. 35.

51. *Report of F.H. Dale, H.M.I. on primary education in Ireland* [Cmd. 1981], H.C.xx, 947. (Hereafter cited as Dale, *1904)*

52. *New rules and regulations for 1900–1901*.

53. Akenson, *Irish education,* ch. 7.

54. Ibid.

55. Explanatory document on Stanley's letter issued by the Commissioners of National Education: appendix to the commissioners' eighth report.

56. Akenson, *Irish education*, p. 351.

57. *Report of the Commissioners of National Education, 1919–20*, pp 8–10.

58. Liam MacMathúna, 'The potential for Irish-English dual-medium instruction in the primary school' in *Oideas*, 32 (1988), pp 5–21. See S. Ó Buachalla, 'Educational policy and the role of the Irish language from 1831–1981' in *European Journal of Education*, 19, 1 (1984), pp 75–92.

59. J. Kavanagh, Inspector, quoted in *Report of the Commissioners of National Education, 1850*.

60. Chief Secretary's correspondence, 1884 (81), lxi, 617. Gaelic Union's plea for Irish.
61. Akenson, *Irish education*, pp 381–2.
62. T. Ó Fiaich, 'The great controversy' in Seán Ó Tuama (ed.) *The Gaelic League idea* (Cork and Dublin, Mercier Press, 1972), pp 63–75. (Hereafter cited as Ó Fiaich in Ó Tuama).
63. This was a period when many parallel language movements were being established in Europe, e.g. in Scotland and Wales, in Hungary, in Norway. For example, the Scottish equivalent to the Gaelic League, An Comunn Gaedhealach, was established in 1891.
64. Douglas Hyde, 'The necessity for de-Anglicising Ireland' in B. Ó Conaire (ed.), *Language, lore and lyrics, essays and lectures of Douglas Hyde* (Dublin, Academic Press, 1986), pp 153–70.
65. Fr P. O'Hickey, *The nationalisation of Irish education*, Gaelic League pamphlet 27 (n.d.). O'Hickey was an early member of the Gaelic League and wrote several of its pamphlets.
66. Census returns from 1881 revealed that the number of people claiming to know Irish had declined from 18.2 per cent in 1881 to 14.4 per cent in 1901. Census returns for 1911 revealed a further drop in the number of Irish speakers in the population.
67. D.P. Moran, *The philosophy of Irish Ireland* (Dublin, James Duffy, 1905).
68. An Púicín, 'Naisiúntacht agus Oideachas' in *Irish Education Review*, 1 (1907–8),p. 30 & p. 291.
69. William Rooney was a journalist very much in the mould of D.P. Moran. A collection of his articles from the *United Irishman* was published posthumously: *Prose writings* (Dublin and Waterford, Gill and Son,1909).
70. T.J. O'Connell, *History of the I.N.T.O.* (Dublin, I.N.T.O., 1969). (Hereafter cited as O'Connell *I.N.T.O.*).
71. *Irish Catholic Directory, 1906*, p. 443.
72. W.F. Mandle, *The Gaelic Athletic Association and Irish nationalist politics 1884–1924* (London and Dublin,Croom Helm and Gill and Macmillan, 1987), ch. 5 (Hereafter cited as Mandle, *The G.A.A.*).
73. Ibid.
74. Neither in P. Puirséal, *The G.A.A and its times* (Dublin, Purcell,1982), nor Mandle, *The G.A.A.*, is any evidence provided that Gaelic games enjoyed popularity in Protestant schools. Both contain an abundance of evidence as to the games' popularity in Catholic schools.
75. Mandle, *The G.A.A.*
76. *The Sinn Féin manifesto for the 1918 general election*. Copy in National Library of Ireland.
77. Michael Collins, *The path to freedom* (Cork, Mercier Press, 1968), p. 100.
78. P. Forde, *The Irish language movement – its philosophy* (Dublin, Gaelic League pamphlet 21, 1899).
79. Ibid.
80. From *What Sinn Féin stands for* quoted by Senator Duffy, Seanad Éireann, vol. 33, col. 1979 (18 June 1947).
81. The education programme of the Gaelic League adopted in November 1918. See A. Hyland and K. Milne, *Irish ed. doc. v. 1*, pp 190–91.
82. Dáil Éireann was convened by the Sinn Féin M.P.s elected at the general elections of 1918. Only Sinn Féin M.P.s attended and when they did their first formal act was to declare Ireland to be an independent republic. See Dáil Éireann, *Minutes of the proceedings of the first parliament of the Republic of Ireland 1919–1921* (Dublin, Stationery Office).
83. Ibid., p. 172.
84. Ibid., pp 21–3. Democratic programme presented to Dáil Éireann by J.J. O'Kelly on the occasion of the Dáil's inaugural meeting, January 1919.
85. Timothy Corcoran, 'The Irish language in Irish schools', in *Studies* (1925), pp 377–88.
86. Evidence from many sources indicates that by the end of the eighteenth century most of Leinster, east Ulster and east Munster were English speaking and that Irish was mainly a rural language, predominant outside the towns in the rest of the country. Maureen Wall, 'The decline of the Irish language' in B. Ó Cuív (ed.), *A view of the Irish language*, (Dublin, Stationery Office, 1969), pp 81–90.
87. Patrick Pearse, 'The murder machine' in *Political writings and speeches* (Dublin, Talbot Press, 1962), p. 47.
88. Ibid., p. 7.
89. Ibid., p. 16.
90. E. Martyn, *Ireland's battle for her language* (Dublin, Gaelic League pamphlet, n.d.).

91. Intermediate Education Act (Ireland),1879.
92. *Report of the Commissioners of Intermediate Education, 1919–20.*
93. Ibid.
94. *Report of the vice-regal committee on intermediate education in Ireland, 1919.*
95. Ó Fiaich, in Ó Tuama, p. 67.
96. Ibid., p. 69.
97. Ibid., p. 70.
98. Annual reports of the Commissioners of Intermediate Education, 1899–1901 and 1902–3.
99. T.J. Morrissey, *Towards a national university, William Delaney S.J., 1835–1924* (Dublin, Wolfhound Press, 1983), ch. XVIII.
100. Ibid.
101. *Report of the Commissioners of Intermediate Education, 1919–1920.*
102. Ibid.
103. Ibid.
104. *Times Educational Supplement (T.E.S.),* 24 Apr. 1919.
105. Speech by J. Thompson of the High School, Dublin. *T.E.S.,* 13 May 1920.
106. T.J. McElligott, *Secondary education in Ireland 1870–1921* (Dublin, Irish Academic Press, 1981), p. 122. (Hereafter cited as McElligott, *Secondary education*).
107. *Report of Messrs Dale and Stephens on intermediate education in Ireland* [Cmd. 2546], 1905, xxviii, 709. (Hereafter cited as Dale and Stephens, *1905*).
108. R. Wilkinson, 'Educational Endowments Act (Ireland) 1885 as part of nineteenth century educational reform' in *Irish Educational Studies,* 3, no. 2, (1983), pp 98–121.
109. Ibid., p. 58.
110. *Report of the Commissioners of Intermediate Education, 1919–20.*
111. E. Brian Titley, *Church, state and the control of schooling in Ireland 1900–1944* (Dublin, Gill and Macmillan and Kingston and Montreal, McGill-Queen's University, 1983), p. 53. (Hereafter cited as Titley, *Church state*).
112. Dale, *1904.*
113. Dale and Stephens, *1905.*
114. Statement of the Irish bishops, *Irish Catholic Directory, 1905,* pp 458–61.
115. A. Hyland, 'The Treasury and Irish education 1850–1922: the myth and the reality' in *Irish Educational Studies,* 3, 2 (1983), pp 57–82.
116. *Bill to provide for the establishment and functions of an administrative council in Ireland,* 1907 (18) ii, 481.
117. *Bill to provide for the heating of national school houses in Ireland,* 1907 (255) ii 523–1908 (161) ii, 1049–1099.
118. *Irish Catholic Directory, 1910,* pp 513–5.
119. General report of the Belfast circuit contained in the *Report of the Commissioners of National Education, 1911–12.*
120. D.J. Phenix in evidence to the vice-regal committee of inquiry into primary education (Ireland), 1918.
121. Motion to the Belfast Trades Council, 1901, quoted in 'Public opinion and educational reform in the North of Ireland 1900–1954'. Unpublished M.A. dissertation by E. Holmes, Q.U.B., 1969.
122. Ibid.
123. Ibid.
124. Ibid.
125. Ibid.
126. Ibid.
127. Ibid.
128. *Belfast Education Bill (1919),* 'to make better provision for primary education in the city of Belfast'.
129. Hansard (Commons), v. 114, col. 1477 (3 Apr. 1919).
130. Ibid.
131. *Irish News,* 3 Mar. 1919.
132. *Church of Ireland Gazette,* 25 Jan. 1918.
133. Ibid. 17 May 1918.
134. *Report of the vice-regal committee of inquiry into primary education (Ireland)* [Cmd. 178], H.C.1919, cxi.
135. *Report of the vice-regal committee of inquiry into intermediate education (Ireland)* [Cmd. 66], H.C. 1919, xxi.

136. Ian MacPherson, Chief Secretary for Ireland, had established a committee to draft an education bill for the whole of Ireland. The bill was entitled: *Education Ireland Bill*, 10 Geo. V, H.C. 1920, i, pp 563ff.
137. *T.E.S.*, 18 Dec. 1919.
138. Ibid., 1 Jan. 1920
139. O'Connell, *I.N.T.O.*, pp 307–9.
140. *T.E.S.*, 18 Dec. 1919.
141. McElligott, *Secondary education*, p. 132.
142. 'Statement of the standing committee of the Irish bishops on the proposed Education Bill for Ireland, December 1919' in *Irish Ecclesiastical Record* (Jan. 1920), pp 504–7.
143. 'Statement by the Catholic hierarchy of Ireland, January 1920' in *Irish Ecclesiastical Record* (Feb. 1920), pp 150–1.
144. Hansard (Commons), v. 126, col. 1505 (11 Mar. 1920).
145. 'Statement of the standing committee of the Irish bishops' in *Irish Ecclesiatical Record* (Jan.1920).
146. *T.E.S.*, 8 Jan. 1920.
147. Titley, *Church state*, p. 68.
148. Hansard (Commons), v. 126, col. 1504 (11 Mar. 1920).
149. Ibid.
150. O'Connell, *I.N.T.O.*, p. 305.
151. John Coolahan, 'The education bill of 1919, problems of educational reform' in *Proceedings of the Educational Studies Association of Ireland conference 1979* (Galway, Galway University Press, 1980), pp 11–31. (Hereafter cited as Coolahan, *Proceedings*).
152. Ibid.
153. Hansard (Commons), v. 125, col. 1019 (19 Feb. 1920).
154. *Church of Ireland Gazette*, 12 Dec. 1919.
155. *T.E.S.*, 15 Apr. 1920.
156. O'Connell, *I.N.T.O.*, p. 307.
157. *T.E.S.*, 29 Apr. 1920.
158. Hansard (Commons), v. 125, col. 1019 (19 Feb. 1920).
159. Coolahan, *Proceedings*, p. 26.
160. D. Miller, *Church, state and nation in Ireland* (Dublin, Gill and Macmillan, 1973), pp 436–42. (Hereafter cited as Miller, *Church, state and nation*).

Chapter 2

1. Education Act, 1902, Edw. VII, ch. 42.
2. Articles of agreement for a treaty between plenipotentiaries from Dáil Éireann and representatives of the British government were signed in London 6 December 1921.
3. Dáil Éireann, *Official report of the debate on the treaty between Ireland and Great Britain*, 7 Jan. 1921.
4. The civil war commenced in June 1921 and ended in May 1923 when anti-treaty forces ceased hostilities. See M. Hopkinson, *Green against green: the Irish civil war* (Dublin, Gill and Macmillan,1988). (Hereafter cited as Hopkinson, *Green against green*).
5. Following the split in Sinn Féin over the treaty the two major political parties which have dominated southern politics ever since were formed: Cumann na nGael (later Fine Gael), the pro-treaty party, and Fianna Fail, anti-treaty.
6. The first reforms were introduced in the spring of 1922 within two months of the southern government taking over full responsibilities for education.
7. P. Buckland, *Irish unionism 1885–1923: a documentary history* (Belfast, H.M.S.O., 1986), p. 119. (Hereafter cited as Buckland, *Irish unionism*).
8. Archbishop C. D'Arcy, *Belfast Newsletter*, 6 June 1921.
9. Section 5, Government of Ireland Act, 1920.
10. Ibid.
11. Ireland (Confirmation of Agreement) 1925, 15 & 16 Geo. V, ch. 77.
12. *Belfast Newsletter*, 10 June 1921.
13. P. Buckland, *A history of Northern Ireland* (Dublin, Gill and Macmillan,1981), pp 35–50. (Hereafter cited as Buckland, *History of Northern Ireland*) .

14. According to authorities like Hopkinson, *Green against green*, and E. Phoenix, *Northern nationalism* (Belfast, Ulster Historical Foundation, 1994) Michael Collins was the minister most responsible for encouraging nationalist resistance to the new administration in the north; education minister, Eoin MacNeill, was also active in encouraging this resistance.
15. N.I. Senate debates, v. 1, col. 24 (23 June 1921).
16. The committee was established in August 1921 and officially announced in the Senate by Londonderry 21 September.
17. *T.E.S.*, 31 Mar. 1921
18. The Belfast Co-ordinating Conference had endorsed proposals for local authority control and rate subsidies for primary schools.
19. *Irish News*, 5 Sept. 1921.
20. Londonderry to Lord Lieutenant of Ireland. 4 Sept. 1921. N.I. Cabinet papers 1921.
21. Logue to Londonderry, 2 Sept. 1921. N.I. Cabinet papers 1921.
22. *Belfast Telegraph*, 5 May 1921.
23. St John Ervine, *Craigavon* (London, George Allen and Unwin, 1946), p. 194.
24. *Belfast Telegraph*, 25 June 1920.
25. *Irish News*, 23 Sept. 1921.
26. Statement by the (Catholic) Clerical Managers' Association, *T.E.S.*, 29 Nov. 1921.
27. *Irish News*, 30 Aug., 1921.
28. In July 1921 a truce between the I.R.A. and British forces was arranged in order to allow negotiations to commence between Sinn Féin and the British government. These negotiations took place over the following months and concluded with the Anglo-Irish Treaty in London in December.
29. Hopkinson, *Green against green*, p. 20.
30. *Irish News*, 1 Oct. 1921.
31. *Irish News*, 5 Sept. 1921.
32. While nationalist M.P.s boycotted the new northern parliament and several nationalist controlled councils refused to recognise the authority of the new administration in Belfast, nationalist opinion was not unanimous on the question of non-recognition. See E. Phoenix, *Northern nationalism* (Belfast, Ulster Historical Foundation, 1994), chs 4 & 5.
33. Londonderry to Logue, 10 Sept. 1921. N.I. Cabinet papers, 1921.
34. Londonderry to Lord Lieutenant of Ireland, 4 Sept. 1921. N.I. Cabinet papers, 1921.
35. N.I. Senate, v. 1, cols. 48–49 (21 Sept. 1921).
36. S. Ó Snodaigh, *Hidden Ulster – the other Ireland* (Dublin, Clodhanna Teoranta, 1977).
37. W. Corkey, *The Church of Rome and Irish unrest: how hatred of Britain is taught in Irish schools.* Publication details not known.
38. N.I. H.C., v. 1, col. 521 (23 June 1921).
39. Ibid.
40. N.I. H.C., v. 1, col. 5211 (9 Dec. 1921).
41. Commissioners of Intermediate Education to Ministry of Education (N.I.), 26 Jan. 1922. N.I. Ministry of Education papers.
42. *The Freeman's Journal*, 5 Feb. 1922.
43. D.H. Akenson, *Education and enmity: the control of schooling in Northern Ireland 1920–1950* (Newton Abbot, David and Charles, 1973), p. 46. (Hereafter cited as Akenson, *Education and enmity*).
44. The establishment of a special commission to examine and determine the precise boundary between Northern Ireland and the Irish Free State was one of the matters agreed to in the Anglo-Irish Treaty. Nationalists had expected that such a commission would recommend the transfer of large areas of Northern Ireland from the exisiting border counties, where they were in the majority, to the Irish Free State. Such transfers would, they also hoped, leave an economically non-viable entity for Northern Ireland with the result that unionist opposition to unity would soon end.
45. Hopkinson, *Green against green*, ch. 10.
46. A boycott of northern businesses and of northern products throughout Ireland as well as the non-involvement by nationalists in the operation of the new administration etc. Such a boycott had already been operating in southern counties to a greater or lesser extent since early 1921 in response to loyalist attacks on Catholics in Belfast and in other parts of the north. In the spring of 1922 it was planned to intensify and strengthen it. See Buckland, *History of Northern Ireland*, p. 35.
47. Akenson, *Education and enmity*, p. 44.

48. E. Phoenix, 'Teachers rejected pay from Belfast' in the *Irish Times*, 2 Jan. 1988.
49. Akenson, *Education and enmity*, pp 44–6.
50. M. Harris, *The Catholic Church and the foundation of the Northern Irish State* (Cork, Cork University Press, 1993), pp 119–24. (Hereafter cited as Harris, *Catholic Church*).
51. E. Phoenix, *Irish Times*, 2 Jan. 1988.
52. S. Farren, 'Teacher education: the collapse of its all-Ireland dimensions in 1922' in *Irish Educational Studies*, 7, 2 (1988), pp 20–34.
53. Akenson, *Education and enmity*, p. 52.
54. Ibid.
55. Education Act (Northern Ireland), 1923.
56. Ministry of Education, *Interim report of the departmental committee on educational services in Northern Ireland* (Belfast, H.M.S.O.) [Cmd. 48], 1923, p. 11.
57. Ibid.
58. Ibid.
59. The evidence presented on behalf of the Methodist Church, for example, recommended that school principals should be Protestant or Roman Catholic according to the religion of the majority of the pupils. Minute book of the departmental committee on educational services in Northern Ireland available in the P.R.O.N.I.
60. *Final report of the departmental committee on educational services in Northern Ireland.* (Belfast, H.M.S.O.) [Cmd. 15], 1923.
61. Ibid., section VI, para. 136–42.
62. *Belfast Telegraph*, 15 Oct. 1921.
63. *Final report of the departmental committee on educational services in Northern Ireland.* (Belfast, H.M.S.O.) [Cmd. 15], 1923.
64. Ibid., para. 198.
65. Memorandum to Londonderry on the teaching of Irish, 22 Nov. 1921. Ministry of Education papers.
66. *Final report of the departmental committee on educational services in Northern Ireland* (Belfast: H.M.S.O.) [Cmd. 15], 1923, para. 208.
67. N.I. Senate, v. 1, cols. 48–58 (21 Sept. 1921).
68. Ministry of Education, Ed 32/1/2, 16 Mar. 1922.
69. Ibid.
70. Minutes of a meeting between representatives of the Board of the Church of Ireland Training College and of the Ministry of Education, 3 April 1922. N.I. Cabinet papers, 1922.
71. L. McQuibban to H. Kingsmill Moore, 13 Jan. 1923. Ed 13/1/989.
72. Ibid., Kingsmill Moore to McQuibban.
73. The files of the Ministry of Education (N.I.) contain copies of correspondence to training colleges in the south requesting that they provide suitable courses for northern students. The Church of Ireland College apart, the other colleges either declined or did not reply.
74. Harris, *Catholic Church*, p. 216.
75. *Annual report of the Ministry of Education (N.I.) 1924–25* H.C. 80.
76. *Report of the Department of Education 1924–25* (Dublin, Stationery Office, 1925).
77. O'Connell, *I.N.T.O.*, p. 342.
78. Ibid., pp 342–5.
79. *Irish Schools Weekly* , 23 Oct. 1970.
80. *T.E.S.*, 12 Aug. 1920.
81. National Programme Conference, *National programme of primary instruction* (Dublin, The Educational Company, 1921), p. 3.
82. Ibid., p. 4
83. Ibid., p. 5
84. T. Corcoran, 'The new secondary programmes in Ireland: classical studies' *Studies*, 11 (1922), p. 359.
85. Titley, *Church state*, p. 97.
86. Ibid.
87. *T.E.S.*, 31 Aug. 1921.
88. Ibid., 24 Sept. 1921.
89. Ibid.
90. The commission's report was not published in a single volume but in parts which appeared in *Irish Schools Weekly* from December 1921.

91. *T.E.S.*, 31 Aug. 1921.
92. *'Misneach'* 21 Eanair [January], 1921 quoted in A. Ó Muimhneacháin, *Dóchas agus Duainéis* (Corcaigh, Mercier Press, 1974), p. 17. (Hereafter cited as Ó Muimhneacháin, *Dóchas*).

Chapter 3

1. Education Act (Northern Ireland),1923.
2. Ibid., section 2 (2).
3. Ibid., section 14.
4. Ibid., section 14 (4).
5. Ibid., section 3 (2).
6. Ibid., section 15.
7. Ibid., section 15 (2).
8. Ibid., section 7.
9. Ibid., section 26.
10. Ibid., section 66 (3).
11. Ibid., parts III, IV, VIII & IX.
12. *Belfast Telegraph*, 29 Sept. 1921
13. N.I. Senate, v. 2, cols 148–60 (4 June 1923).
14. Ibid.
15. N.I. H.C., v. 3, cols 114–27 (14 Mar. 1923).
16. Ibid.
17. N.I. Senate debates, v. 2, cols 148–60 (4 June 1923).
18. N.I. H.C., v. 3, cols 114–27 (14 Mar. 1923).
19. Government of Ireland Act, 1920.
20. N.I. Senate debates, v. 2, cols 148–60 (4 June 1923).
21. Lord Londonderry, 'Public education in Northern Ireland: the new system' in *The Nineteenth Century* (Mar. 1924), pp 328–34.
22. N.I. Cabinet papers, 4/77, 16 Apr. 1923.
23. Ibid., 4/61, 15 Dec. 1922.
24. Ibid., 4/86, 2 Oct. 1923.
25. N.I. Cabinet conclusions in Ed 32/1/3, 16 Apr. 1923.
26. Evidence presented by the Presbyterian Church in Ireland to the Lynn Committee. Minutebook of the departmental committee on the educational services in Northern Ireland.
27. Ibid.
28. *T.E.S.*, 21 Apr. 1923.
29. N.I. H.C., v. 3, cols 341–60 (17 Apr. 1923).
30. Ibid.
31. N.I. H.C., v. 3, col. 709 (8 May 1923). The amendment was moved by the parliamentary secretary to the Minister of Education.
32. N.I. H.C., v. 3, cols 375–7 (17 Apr. 1923).
33. N.I. H.C. (9 May 1923).
34. Ibid.
35. Akenson, *Education and enmity*, p. 68.
36. Minutebook of the departmental committee on the educational services in Northern Ireland.
37. W.Coote, N.I. H.C., v. 3, cols 1603–6 (25 Oct. 1923).
38. Ibid.
39. *T.E.S.*, 2 June 1923.
40. N.I. H.C., v. 3, col. 916–8 (16 May 1923).
41. *T.E.S.*, 2 June 1923.
42. *T.E.S.*, 7 Apr. 1923.
43. *Belfast Telegraph*, 10 Sept. 1923.
44. N.I. H.C., v. 3, cols 921 (16 May 1923).
45. *Belfast Telegraph*, 16 June 1923
46. Ibid., 18 Sept. 1923.
47. Ibid., 26 Oct. 1923.
48. Hugh Pollock quoted in *T.E.S.*, 22 Dec. 1923.
49. N.I. H.C., v. 3, col. 1483, (16 Oct. 1923).
50. N.I. Senate, v. 3, col. 162, (4 June 1923).

51. *Belfast Telegraph*, 26 Oct. 1923.
52. Ibid., 13 Oct. 1923.
53. *T.E.S.*, 3 Nov. 1923.
54. Ibid., 3 Jan. 1924.
55. Ibid., 26 Mar. 1924.
56. Ibid., 7 June 1924.
57. Presbyterian Church in Ireland, *General Assembly of the Presbyterian Church in Ireland and the Education Act (N.I.) 1923* (Belfast, Presbyterian Church in Ireland, 1924).
58. *Belfast Telegraph*, 10 Oct. 1924.
59. United Education Committee of the Protestant Churches, 1925. See W. Corkey *Episode in the history of Protestant Ulster*, p. 39. Publication details unknown. (Hereafter cited as Corkey, *Episode*).
60. A meeting of representatives of the Protestant churches presided over by Archbishop D'Arcy demanded an amending act. *Belfast Telegraph* 26 Mar. 1924.
61. Ministry of Education, Ed 32/2/1, 16 Oct. 1923.
62. *Belfast Telegraph*, 25 Jan. 1924.
63. *T.E.S.*, 7 Mar. 1925.
64. *Irish News*, 10 Mar. 1925.
65. *Belfast Telegraph*, 13 Feb. 1925.
66. N.I. H.C., v. 4, col. 346 (26 Mar. 1924).
67. N.I. Cabinet papers, 4/86, 28 Sept. 1923.
68. *Belfast Telegraph*, 24 Apr. 1924.
69. Ibid., 16 Feb. 1925.
70. Ibid.
71. *Belfast Telegraph*, 5 Mar. 1925.
72. Akenson, *Education and enmity*, p. 83.
73. Corkey, *Episode*, p. 87.
74. *Belfast Telegraph*, 23 Apr. 1925.
75. N.I. Cabinet papers, Abercorn to Prime Minister Craig, 9D/1/8, 13 Mar. 1925.
76. *Irish News*, 10 Mar. 1925.
77. The *Annual report of the Ministry of Education 1925–26* contains a section which details the ministry's case.
78. Corkey, *Episode*, p. 47.
79. *Annual report of the Ministry of Education 1925–26.*
80. *Correspondence between the Ministry of Education and the Armagh Regional Committee on the subject of Bible instruction in transferred schools* (Belfast, H.M.S.O., 1928) [Cmd. 84].
81. Ibid.
82. Ibid.
83. Ibid.
84. Ibid.
85. The nationalist M.P. Joseph Devlin was prominent in articulating Catholic grievances and in pointing to the lack of support for the 1923 Education Act, e.g. N.I. H.C. 13 May 1926 and 3 May 1927.
86. Address to the General Assembly of the Presbyterian Church in Ireland, *Belfast Telegraph*, 9 June 1928.
87. Ibid.
88. Statement in reply to the Association of Education Committees, *Belfast Telegraph*, 6 Apr. 1929.
89. N.I. H.C., v. 12, col. 725 (9 Apr. 1930).
90. N.I. H.C., v. 9, col. 811 (29 Mar. 1928).
91. Ibid.
92. *Belfast Telegraph*, 6 Apr. 1929.
93. Ibid.
94. Ibid.
95. *Belfast Telegraph*, 24 Apr. 1929.
96. *Belfast Telegraph*, 6 Apr. 1929.
97. *Belfast Telegraph*, 13 July 1929.
98. This pamphlet, as its title indicates, was a joint publication of the United Education Committee and a committee of the Grand Orange Lodge of Ireland. Copy in N.I. Cabinet papers, 9D/1/8.

99. Ibid.
100. N.I. Cabinet papers, 9D/1/8, memo dated 21 Feb. 1929.
101. Ibid.
102. Ibid., memo dated 19 Apr. 1929.
103. Buckland, *History of Northern Ireland*, p. 67.
104. *Belfast Telegraph*, 23 Apr. 1929.
105. *Annual report of the Ministry of Education (N.I.) 1929–30.*
106. Ibid.
107. Report of interview at the Home Office, London, 26 November. N.I. Cabinet papers, 9D/1/8.

Chapter 4

1. *Belfast Telegraph*, 13 Oct. 1923.
2. Ibid.
3. *Belfast Telegraph*, 15 Feb. 1926.
4. They both entered parliament on 28 April 1925 following the general election earlier that same month.
5. Editorial, *Irish News*, 12 Mar. 1925.
6. N.I. H.C., v. 7, col. 1244 (13 May 1926).
7. Ibid., col. 1245.
8. Ibid., v. 8, cols 1532–3 (3 May 1927).
9. Ibid., v. 10, col. 140 (27 Feb. 1929).
10. Ibid., v. 8, col. 543 (30 Mar. 1927).
11. Ibid., col. 544.
12. Ibid., col. 559.
13. Ibid., col. 550.
14. Ibid., col. 567.
15. Ibid., col. 550.
16. Ibid., col. 556.
17. The vote was 24–6 against the motion. N.I. H.C. 30 Mar. 1927.
18. John Tierney, secretary of the Armagh Provincial Council of Catholic Clerical Managers, to Lord Charlemont, 6 Aug. 1929. Down and Connor, E11/30.
19. 'The emancipation struggle' address delivered in the Mansion House, Dublin. *Belfast Telegraph*, 22 June 1929.
20. *Belfast Telegraph*, 22 June 1929.
21. Ibid.
22. *Irish News*, 22 Feb. 1930.
23. N.I. Cabinet papers, 9D/1/8. Memorandum headed 'Roman Catholic managers – proposals for amendment'.
24. Londonderry's parliamentary speeches on the 23 June and 21 September make clear his preference for a single comprehensive system of elementary education.
25. Education Act (Scotland), 1918.
26. N.I. Cabinet papers, 9D/25/1.
27. Ibid.
28. Ibid.
29. Speech to the General Assembly of the Presbyterian Church in Ireland, 1928.
30. Pastoral letter for Lent, *Belfast Telegraph*, 3 Mar. 1930.
31. N.I. H.C., v. 12, col. 725 (9 Apr. 1930).
32. Ibid., col. 740.
33. *Belfast Telegraph*, 10 Apr. 1930
34. Ibid.
35. Ibid., 23 Apr. 1930.
36. Ibid., 16 Apr. 1930.
37. Down County Council, for example, followed quickly with a resolution in opposition to the bill.
38. *Belfast Telegraph*, 19 Mar. 1930.
39. *T.E.S.*, 12 Apr. 1930.
40. N.I. H.C., v. 12, col. 715 (10 Apr. 1930).
41. Ibid., col. 785.

42. *Belfast Telegraph*, 14 Apr. 1930.
43. O'Donnell to Mageean, 2 Oct. 1929, Down and Connor, E11/29.
44. Ibid.
45. Down and Connor, E11/29.
46. *Belfast Telegraph*, 22 Apr., 3 and 17 May 1930.
47. Ibid.
48. *Irish News*, 29 Mar. 1930.
49. Ibid.
50. *T.E.S.*, 17 May 1930.
51. *Irish Independent*, 8 Apr. 1930.
52. Down and Connor, E11/30.
53. Ibid.
54. Report of meeting, Down and Connor, E11/30.
55. Ibid.
56. N.I. Cabinet papers, 4/258, 15 Apr. 1930.
57. Ibid., 4/260, 7 May 1930.
58. *Belfast Telegraph*, 9 May 1930.
59. Ibid., 14 May 1930.
60. Minford, N.I. H.C., v. 12, col. 1426 (21 May 1930).
61. The bill passed its third reading with a comfortable majority, 27–10.
62. Healy, N.I. H.C., v. 12, col. 1417 (21 May 1930).
63. *Belfast Telegraph*, 7 June 1930.
64. *T.E.S.*, 28 June 1930.
65. Ibid.
66. Akenson, *Education and enmity*, pp 111–18.
67. *T.E.S.*, 12 Apr. 1930.
68. N.I. Cabinet papers, 9D/44/1 entitled 'Teaching Irish in public elementary schools' contains memoranda and copies of circulars to schools dealing with Irish 1921–8.
69. *Belfast Telegraph*, 5 May 1926.
70. Ministry of Education, *Irish in primary schools in Northern Ireland*, P.C. 21, 1923.
71. Lynn Committee report.
72. Cabinet papers, 9D/44/1.
73. Ibid.
74. N.I. H.C., v. 7, col. 1255 (13 May 1926).
75. Ibid.
76. Wyse to Blackmore, secretary to the cabinet, 28 May 1928, N.I. Cabinet papers, 9D/44/14.
77. Editorials in *Belfast Telegraph* frequently attacked the policy of Gaelicisation in the south, e.g. 9 Sept. 1922, 25 Sept. 1924, 4 May 1928, 4 Mar. 1929, 25 Apr. 1930.
78. Ministry of Education memorandum 'Ministry of Education and Gaelic League deputation', 1 Feb. 1928.
79. Ministry of Education, P.C. 133, Mar. 1928.
80. N.I. H.C., v. 9, col. 1363 (3 May 1928).
81. Ibid.
82. Several unionist M.P.s made a point of stressing this need, e.g. Captain Henry Mulholland, 23 June 1921 and Samuel Kyle, 3 May 1928.

Chapter 5

1. Dáil Éireann, v. 9, col. 545 (7 July 1924).
2. Dáil Éireann, 11 June 1925.
3. Intermediate Education (Amendment) Act, 1924.
4. Department of Education, *Clár i gcóir macléinn ins na coláistí múinteoireachta 1924–25*.
5. Local Government (Temporary Provisions) Act, 1923.
6. School Attendance Act, 1926.
7. Review of the activities of the Department of Education, 1923–27, Irish state papers, S5360/6.
8. *T.E.S.*, 31 Oct. 1925.
9. Ó Néill to Cosgrave, 1925, Irish state papers, S7801.
10. Copy in O'Donnell files, Armagh.

11. Dáil Éireann, v. 3, col. 1390 (31 May 1923).
12. *T.E.S.*, 23 Oct. 1926.
13. Education estimates debate, Dáil Éireann, v. 23, col. 2052 (24 May 1928).
14. John Coolahan, *The A.S.T.I. and post-primary education 1909–1984* (Dublin, A.S.T.I., 1985), p. 67. (Hereafter cited as Coolahan, *A.S.T.I.*).
15. Irish Labour Party and Trades Union Congress, *Policy on education* (Dublin, Irish Labour Party, 1926). (National Library of Ireland, P1626).
16. Dermot Keogh, *The Vatican, the bishops and Irish politics 1919–1939* (Cambridge, Cambridge University Press, 1986), p. 90.
17. *Irish School Weekly*, 28 Jan. 1922, report of the October meeting with J.J. O'Kelly, Minister of Education.
18. *Report of the Commissioners of Intermediate Education, 1922–23.*
19. Intermediate Education Board for Ireland, 26 Jan. 1922, Ministry of Education papers, Ed 13/1/38.
20. *Report of the Commissioners of Intermediate Education, 1922–23.*
21. Public Notice no. 4, Irish state papers, S855.
22. Ibid.
23. *Report of the Department of Education, 1922–23.*
24. *T.E.S.*, 22 Apr. 1922.
25. Ibid., 3 June and 11 Nov. 1922.
26. Ibid., 15 July 1922.
27. *Rules and regulations for secondary schools, 1924–25.*
28. Ibid.
29. Ibid.
30. *Rules and regulations for secondary schools 1931–32.*
31. *Rules and regulations for secondary schools 1927–28.*
32. *T.E.S.*, 3 May 1924.
33. Sean Ó Muirthile, secretary of the Gaelic League in Ó Muimhneacháin, *Dóchas*, p. 18. (Hereafter, Ó Muirthile in Ó Muimhneacháin, *Dóchas*)
34. Timothy Corcoran, 'How the Irish language can be revived' in *Irish Monthly* (Jan. 1923), pp 26–30.
35. Ó Muirthile in Ó Muimhneacháin, *Dóchas*, p. 18.
36. J. O'Connor 'The teaching of Irish, testament of a pioneer' in *Capuchin Annual* (1949), pp 205–20.
37. *T.E.S.*, 5 Sept. 1925.
38. Ibid.
39. Coolahan, *A.S.T.I.*, pp 71–72.
40. Timothy Corcoran, 'The new secondary programmes in Ireland: classical studies' in *Studies*, 11 (1922), p. 359.
41. Coolahan, *A.S.T.I.*, p. 72.
42. Coolahan's detailed history of the A.S.T.I. notes no major adverse criticism of the new administration in the latter's early years.
43. P. Buckland, *Irish unionism I: the Anglo-Irish and the new Ireland 1885–1922* (Dublin, Gill and Macmillan, 1972).
44. Ibid.
45. Denis Kennedy, *The widening gulf: northern attitudes to an independent Irish state 1919–1949* (Belfast, Blackstaff Press, 1988), p. 115. (Hereafter cited as Kennedy, *Widening gulf*).
46. Ibid.
47. G. Seaver, *John Allen Fitzgerald Gregg, Archbishop* (London, Faith Press, 1963), p. 121.
48. Ibid.
49. Rev. G.A. Chamberlain speaking at an Armistice Day service in Dublin in 1923, quoted by M. O'Callaghan, 'Language nationality and cultural identity' in *Irish Historical Studies*, 24, 94 (1984), pp 226–45.
50. T. Brown, *Ireland a social and cultural history 1922–1979* (London, Fontana, 1981), p. 106. (Hereafter cited as Brown, *Ireland*).
51. The 1926 census revealed that the Protestant population in the south had declined from 308,000 in 1911 to 202,000. Fatalities during W. W. I together with the departure in 1922 of large numbers associated with the British administration as well as the forced departure of others who felt intimidated during the violence of 1919–22 were among the main factors contributing to this decline. See Ireland, *Irish Free State Census of Population 1926* (Dublin, Stationery Office, 1927).

52. *Church of Ireland Gazette*, 26 Nov. 1926.
53. Jack White, *Minority report* (Dublin, Gill and Macmillan, 1975), p. 140.
54. *Annual report of the Church of Ireland Training College, 1921–22*.
55. Ibid.
56. Kingsmill Moore, *Reminiscences and reflections* (London, n.d), p. 293.(Hereafter cited as Kingsmill Moore, *Reminiscences*).
57. *T.E.S.*, 15 Nov. 1924.
58. Ibid., 5 May 1924.
59. Culverwell to Cosgrave, 6 Aug. 1925, Irish state papers S7801.
60. Ibid.
61. *T.E.S.*, 21 June 1924.
62. Ibid.
63. Department of Education files (National Archives): letter dated 29 May 1924 from the district inspector reported the survey of parents' wishes.The general situation in the division as revealed in the departmental report for 1926–7 was one of 'little enthusiasm for the language'.
64. Further correspondence and reports contained in the same file record the attempts to encourage more teaching and use of Irish in the school over the next few years.
65. *T.E.S.*, 28 June 1924.
66. Ibid., 5 July 1924.
67. Ibid. Under existing regulations schools could, theoretically, operate without any approval from the Department of Education, provided they did not seek financial support from the latter.
68. *Church of Ireland Gazette*, 17 Dec. 1926.
69. Dáil Éireann, v. 8, col. 595 (7 July 1924).
70. *Church of Ireland Gazette*, 5 Mar. 1926.
71. Ibid., 5 Mar. 1926.
72. Ibid.
73. Ibid., 3 Dec. 1926.
74. *Catholic Bulletin*, Jan. 1925.
75. Ibid., Dec.1925.
76. The *Catholic Bulletin* was particularly vituperative in its frequent comments about the 'Protestant ascendancy' and in particular the influence of the latter over such institutions as Trinity College and the College of Surgeons.
77. Address to Methodist Conference, Belfast, June 1926.
78. *Belfast Telegraph*, 9 Sept. 1922.
79. J.F. Burns, *Shop window on the world, Masonic Boys' School 1867–1967* (Dublin, Board of Governors Masonic School, 1967), p. 108.
80. *T.E.S.*, 21 June 1924.
81. G.K. White, *History of St Columba's College* (Dublin, Old Columbian Society, 1980), p. 146.
82. Susan Parkes, *Kildare Place: history of the Church of Ireland Training College* (Dublin, C.I.C.E.,1984), p. 151.
83. *T.E.S.*, 11 Dec. 1926.
84. *Irish Times*, 4 Dec. 1926.
85. John Whyte, *Church and state in modern Ireland* (Dublin, Gill and Macmillan, 1971). (Hereafter cited as Whyte, *Church and state*).
86. Ibid., p. 24.
87. Censorship of Films Act, 1923.
88. *Report of the committee on evil literature* (Dublin, Stationery Office, 1927). This was followed by the Censorship of Publications Act, 1929.
89. Public Dance Halls Act, 1935.
90. Fr R.S. Devane, 'Indecent literature' in *Irish Ecclesiastical Record* 25, (1925), pp 182–204.
91. Ibid.
92. Edward Cahill, *Framework of a Christian state* (Dublin, Gill, 1932), p. 666. (Hereafter cited as Cahill, *Christian state*).
93. *T.E.S.*, 2 Jan. 1931.
94. Ibid., 8 Dec. 1924.
95. *Irish Times*, 15 June 1926.
96. Dáil Éireann, v. 8, col. 430 (7 July 1924).
97. Ibid.

98. Dáil Éireann, v. 8, col. 559 (7 July 1924).
99. *Appendix to the annual report of the Department of Education 1924–25.*
100. O'Connell, *I.N.T.O.,* p. 355.
101. Ibid.
102. National Programme Conference, *Report and programme* (Dublin, Stationery Office, 1926).
103. Kingsmill Moore, *Reminiscences.*
104. National Programme Conference, *Report and programme.*
105. Ibid.
106. Ibid.
107. Earnán de Blaghd (Ernest Blythe) was an enthusiastic member of the language movement who became a Sinn Féin activist and eventually served in Cumann na nGael governments in the 1920s. His three-part autobiography *Trasna na Bóinne, Slán le hUltaibh* and *Gaeil ar Mhúscailt* was published by Sairseal and Dill 1957,1970 and 1973. See also D. Greene 'The founding of the Gaelic League' in *The Gaelic League idea,* edited by Seán Ó Tuama, (Cork and Dublin, Mercier Press, 1972), pp 9–19.
108. Kingsmill Moore, *Reminiscences,* p. 287.
109. Ibid., p. 288.
110. *Annual report of the Church of Ireland Training College 1923–24.*
111. Ibid., 1925–26.
112. Ibid.
113. Whyte, *Church and state,* p. 37.
114. Ibid., p. 34–9.

Chapter 6

1. Miller, *Church, state and nation.*
2. Pope Pius XI, *The Christian education of youth* (London, Catholic Truth Society, 1970). (Hereafter cited as Pius XI, *Christian education.*)
3. Kennedy, *Widening gulf,* ch. 13.
4. Buckland, *History of Northern Ireland,* p. 35 and p. 32.
5. *Irish News,* 18 Dec. 1931.
6. Ibid.
7. Akenson, *Education and enmity,* p. 125.
8. Memorandum 'Stranmillis Training College: demand of the Committee of the Protestant Churches', 27 July 1931, N.I. Cabinet papers, 4/289/15.
9. Ibid.
10. Corkey to Craig, 19 Aug. 1931, N.I. Cabinet papers, 4/270/15.
11. Ibid.
12. Ibid.
13. Craig to Corkey, 21 Aug. 1931, N.I. Cabinet papers, 4/290/16.
14. Akenson, *Education and enmity,* p. 132.
15. A new primary programme was introduced in 1932, *Programme of instruction for public elementary schools* (Belfast, H.M.S.O., 1932).
16. Norman McNeilly, *Exactly 50 years: the Belfast education authority and its work* (Belfast, Belfast Education and Library Board, 1973), ch. 6. (Hereafter cited as McNeilly, *Exactly 50 years.*).
17. Ministry of Education (N.I.), *Annual report of the Ministry of Education (N.I.), 1932–33,* H.C. 294.
18. Ibid., 1937–38, H.C. 440.
19. Ibid., 1933–34, H.C. 315.
20. *Irish News,* 30 Oct. 1934.
21. Ibid., 13 Nov. 1934.
22. Ibid., 9 Nov. 1934.
23. Ibid., 14 Nov. 1934.
24. Ibid., 9 Nov. 1934.
25. Ibid., 15 Nov. 1934.
26. Ibid., 13 Nov. 1934.
27. Board of Education, *The education of the adolescent* (Hadow Report), (London, H.M.S.O., 1926).
28. Advisory Committee on Education, June 1926 (P.R.O.N.I.).

29. Ministry of Education (N.I.), *Annual report of the Ministry of Education (N.I.) 1932–33*, H.C. 294.
30. Ibid., 1936–37, H.C. 410.
31. N.I. H.C., v. 18, cols 1224–26 (30 Apr. 1936).
32. Ibid., v. 19, col. 1316 (6 May 1937).
33. Ibid., v. 21, cols 1472–80 (11 Oct. 1938).
34. The act was due to take effect in 1939, but was postponed and never came into effect.
35. T. Campbell, N.I. H.C., v. 21, col. 1529 (12 Oct. 1938).
36. N.I. H.C., v. 21, col. 1544 (12 Oct. 1938).
37. Ibid., v. 15, col. 1077 (25 Apr. 1933).
38. Ibid., v. 15, col. 919 (16 Mar. 1933).
39. Ministry of Education (N.I.), *Annual report of the Ministry of Education (N.I.), 1928–29*, H.C. 180.
40. Ibid., 1929–30, H.C. 211.
41. Ibid., 1930–31, H.C. 242.
42. T. Henderson, N.I. H.C., v. 15, col. 960 (21 Mar. 1933).
43. W. Grant, N.I. H.C., v. 15, col. 772 (9 Mar. 1933).
44. *Belfast Telegraph*, 26 Apr. 1933.
45. J. Beattie, N.I. H.C., v. 15, col. 1095 (25 Apr. 1933).
46. Cahill, *Christian state*, p. 611.
47. Ibid.
48. Ibid., p. 353.
49. Ibid., p. 376.
50. Ibid.
51. Address to World Federation of Education Associations Congress. *T.E.S.*, July–August 1933.
52. Bunreacht na hÉireann (Dublin, Stationery Office, 1937).
53. Pius XI, *Christian education*, p. 18.
54. C. Lucy, ' Making the school system of Ireland Catholic' in *Irish Ecclesiastical Record*, 52 (1938), pp 405–17.
55. Ibid.
56. Pope Pius XI , *Quadragesimo anno*, 1931.
57. *Irish Ecclesiastical Record*, 52 (1938), p. 116.
58. Ibid.
59. Ibid.
60. Whyte, *Church and state*.
61. M. Brennan, 'The Catholic school system of Ireland' in *Irish Ecclesiastical Record*, 52 (1938), pp 257– 72.
62. Michael Geraghty S.J., *Idols of modern society* (Dublin, Irish Messenger Press, 1931).
63. *Report of the Department of Education, 1931–32*.
64. Ibid.
65. Department of Education, 'Teaching through the medium of Irish', Circular 11/31.
66. Dáil Éireann, v. 43, col. 1090 (15 July 1932).
67. Ibid., v. 51, col. 1604 (11 Apr. 1934).
68. Dáil Éireann, v. 46, col. 2318 (5 Apr. 1933).
69. Ibid., v. 51, col. 1591 (11 Apr. 1934).
70. *T.E.S.*, 1 Apr. 1933.
71. O'Connell, *I.N.T.O.*, p. 363.
72. Ibid.
73. The withdrawal of the lower course was announced in the department's *Rules and regulations for national schools, 1934*.
74. *Rules and regulations for national schools, 1935*.
75. Derrig, Dáil Éireann, v. 55, col. 1850 (3 Apr. 1935).
76. Ibid., v. 55, col. 1919 (4 Apr.1934).
77. Ibid.
78. Ibid.
79. Ibid.
80. *Rules and regulations for secondary schools, 1934* .
Irish language tests were gradually introduced and extended throughout the public service
m 1922. Even positions requiring quite low general educational standards became sub-
an Irish language test.

82. Coolahan, *A.S.T.I.*, p. 111.
83. Department of Education, *Notes for teachers: history*, 1933.
84. *Irish world readers: middle book* (Dublin, Brown and Nolan, 1933).
85. Ibid., *Senior book.*
86. *Léitheoirí Inse Fáil* (Dublin, Educational Company, n.d. 1931?).
87. *T.E.S.*, 6 June 1936.
88. Ibid.
89. Ibid., 25 May 1935.
90. Ibid., 13 July 1935.
91. Ibid., 6 May 1935.
92. *Belfast Telegraph*, 24 Apr. 1930.
93. Ibid., 9 Apr. 1931.
94. *T.E.S.*, 7 Aug. 1935.
95. Ibid.
96. Ibid., 14 Dec. 1935.
97. O'Connell, *I.N.T.O.*, p. 366.
98. Ibid.
99. Although an interim report was made available in 1939, the full report was not published until 1941. In the meantime criticism was somewhat more muted although not entirely silenced.
100. *T.E.S.*, 14 Dec. 1935.
101. 'Torna', *You may revive the Gaelic language* (Dublin, Gaelic League, 1936).
102. Ibid.
103. *T.E.S.*, 4 Jan. 1936.
104. Ibid.
105. Department of Education, paper prepared for An Taoiseach, Jan. 1939, Irish State papers, S 7801.
106. S. Ó Néill, Secretary of the Department of Education, *Statement on the development of the position as regards teaching through Irish in the national schools*, 13 Oct. 1939, Irish state papers, S 7801.
107. Ibid.
108. Ibid.
109. *T.E.S.*, 6 June, 1936.

Chapter 7

1. Buckland, *History of Northern Ireland*, p. 82.
2. Many allied leaders like General Eisenhower visited Northern Ireland and expressed appreciation of Northern Ireland's contribution to the war effort. See J.W. Blake, *Northern Ireland in the second world war* (Belfast, H.M.S.O., 1956).
3. Ibid.
4. Buckland, *History of Northern Ireland*, p. 83.
5. Unionist M.P.s at Westminster opposed the British Labour Party's social welfare legislation, but the government in Northern Ireland decided that it would be wise to follow Britain's example in order to maintain parity with the rest of the U.K. See F.S.L. Lyons, *Ireland since the famine* (London, Fontana, 1971), p. 739.
6. Ibid., p. 557.
7. Ibid., p. 555.
8. Plans were prepared by the Fianna Fail government to expand health and social welfare services and, as will be discussed in chapter 8, plans were also prepared for the restructuring of the education system.
9. N.I. H.C., v. 23, cols 1652–57 (28 May 1940).
10. Buckland, *History of Northern Ireland*, p. 84.
11. N.I. H.C., v. 23, col. 1666 (28 May 1940).
12. *Belfast Telegraph*, 7 May 1943.
13. T.H. Ellis, *Noisy mansions: reflections on a career in Ulster schools* (Lisnaskea, The Whitethorn Press, 1983), p. 29 provides a personal account of a student teacher's life at this time. (Hereafter cited as Ellis, *Noisy mansions*).
14. *Annual report of the Ministry of Education (N.I.), 1945–46* H.C. 783.
15. Ibid., 1946–47 H.C. 822.

16. *T.E.S.*, 15 Feb. 1941.
17. McNeilly, *Exactly 50 years*, ch. 10.
18. Ibid., chap. 11
19. Ellis, *Noisy mansions*, p. 44.
20. Akenson, *Education and enmity*, pp 148–52.
21. N.I. H.C., v. 23, col. 1304 (29 May 1940).
22. Akenson, *Education and enmity*, p. 163.
23. Corkey, *Protestant Ulster.*
24. Minutes of a meeting with a deputation to the Ministry of Education, 4 Mar. 1942, Ed 13/1/2025.
25. Ministry of Education Cir., 18 May 1942.
26. Copy in Ministry of Education file, Ed 13/1/2025.
27. Synods of Derry and Raphoe, 28 Nov. 1942, Armagh, 29 Oct. 1943, Presbytery of Ards, 8 Mar. 1944. Copies of resolutions in Ministry of Education file, Ed 13/1/2025..
28. Ibid., Synod of Clogher, 25 Sept. 1942.
29. *Belfast Telegraph*, 8 Mar. 1944.
30. N.I. Senate, v. 45, col. 258 (10 Nov. 1942).
31. Brown, N.I. H.C., v. 25, col. 3046 (24 Nov. 1942).
32. N.I. H.C., v. 26, col. 454–5 (11 May 1943).
33. N.I. H.C., v. 26, col. 1752 (19 Oct. 1943).
34. Parker to Andrews, 3 Dec. 1942, Ed 13/1/2026.
35. Ibid., Hay to Prime Minister, 25 Dec. 1943.
36. Proposals which were to lead to the famous Butler Act in 1944 were being widely discussed in Britain in 1942–3 and were, of course, reported in Northern Ireland.
37. See note 75, ch. 3.
38. See note 107, ch. 3.
39. N.I. H.C., v. 23, col. 1306 (29 May 1940).
40. Ibid., v. 24, col. 1008 (30 June 1941).
41. *Belfast Telegraph*, 26 June 1940.
42. *Irish News*, 2 May 1939.
43. B. Bell, *The secret army, a history of the I.R.A.* (Dublin, Academy Press, 1979).
44. Buckland, *History of Northern Ireland*, p. 84.
45. N.I. H.C., v. 26, col. 1705 (1 June 1943).
46. Ibid., v. 25, col. 808 (30 June 1942).
47. Ibid., v. 26, col. 1778 (19 Oct. 1943).
48. Ibid., v. 25, col. 1716 (19 June 1942)
49. Ibid., v. 26, col. 1705 (19 Oct. 1943).
50. Ibid., col. 1761.
51. *Belfast Telegraph*, 5 June 1944.
52. Ibid.
53. Ibid., 10 June 1944.
54. Ibid., N.I. Cabinet papers, 9D/1/11.
55. *U.T.U. Bulletin*, Oct. 1945.
56. Ibid.
57. Erskine Holmes, *Public opinion.*
58. N.I.L.P., *Education policy* (Belfast, N.I.L.P., 1944).
59. N.I. Cabinet papers, 4/586/11, 24 May 1944.
60. Ibid.
61. Ibid.
62. N.I. Cabinet papers, 9D/1/10, 15 Nov. 1944.
63. Circular letter to the managers of all voluntary elementary schools, Apr. 1944, Ed 13/1/2125.
64. Meetings were held 22, 31 May, 5 June and 25 Oct. 1944, Ed 13/1/2127.
65. Meeting of 22 May, Ed 13/1/2127.
66. Ibid.
67. Ed 13/1/2125.
68. Copy of statement in Ed 13/1/2127.
69. Meetings with Protestant voluntary managers, 9 June and 11 Aug. 1944, Ed 13/1/2128.
70. Ed 13/1/2127.
71. Meeting with Protestant voluntary managers, 11 Aug. 1944, Ed 13/1/2125.
72. Meetings held 15 May, 11 June, 31 July and 13 Oct. 1944, Ed 13/1/3130.

73. 31 July 1944.
74. The W.E.A. issued an education policy in June 1944 advocating the provision of a state assisted education system from nursery to secondary level with a school leaving age raised to sixteen.
75. Copy of correspondence from the N.I. Parents' Council in Ed 13/1/3134.
76. Deputation representing the U.T.U., I.N.T.O., W.T.U. and P.T.U., 18 Oct. 1944, Ed 32/3/24/11.
77. N.I. Cabinet papers 4/601, 12 Oct. 1944.
78. Ibid., 9D/25/1.
79. Ibid., 4/601, 12 Oct. 1944.
80. Ibid., 9D/1/10, 7 Nov. 1944.
81. Ministry of Education (N.I.), *Educational reconstruction in Northern Ireland* (Belfast, H.M.S.O., 1944).
82. Ibid.
83. *Belfast Telegraph*, 11 Dec. 1944.
84. Ibid., 12 Dec. 1944.
85. *Irish Times*, 20 and 21 Dec. 1944.
86. Ibid.
87. *Belfast Telegraph*, 25 Jan. 1945.
88. Ed 13/24/13.
89. N.I. H.C., v.27, col. 2792 (24 Jan. 1945).
90. Ibid., col. 2961 (1 Feb. 1945).
91. Ibid., col. 2844–55 (25 Jan. 1945).
92. Ibid., col. 2967 (1 Feb. 1945).
93. Ibid., Quin, cols 2817–8 (25 Jan. 1945)
94. Ministry of Education file Ed 13/1/2177 contains copies of resolutions passed by various local authorities such as Derry and Antrim County Councils, Coleraine Union and Rural D.C., Lisnaskea and Larne R.D.C.s, Belfast Education Committee, Cookstown Regional Committee, Association of N. I. Education Committees. The association's resolution stated: 'That the present system of religious instruction in provided and transferred schools should continue and that in the secondary and technical schools to which scholarships are awarded by the L.E.A.s should not fall below the standard at present provided and given in provided and transferred schools'.
95. *Irish Times*, 12 Feb. 1945.
96. Ibid.
97. Copy in N.I. Cabinet Papers, 9D/1/11.
98. *Belfast Telegraph*, 24 Jan. 1945.
99. Ibid., 25 Jan. 1945.
100. Ibid., 5 June 1945.
101. N.I. Cabinet papers 9D/1/11 contains copies of correspondence between Sir Shane Leslie of Glaslough, Co. Monaghan and the Prime Minister (N.I.) in late March and early April 1945, together with notes commenting on same written by Brownell of the Ministry of Education to Gransden, secretary to the N.I. cabinet. A letter dated 23 Mar. 1945 from Leslie to the cardinal confirming contact with Brooke is amongst the MacRory papers in the Diocesan Archive, Armagh.
102. Ibid. Brownell to Gransden.
103. Ibid.
104. Ibid., Leslie to Prime Minister, 15 Mar. 1945.
105. Ibid.
106. Ibid., 22 Mar. 1945.
107. *Irish Times*, 28 Mar. 1945.
108. Leslie to Prime Minister, 4 Apr. 1945.
109. *Irish Times*, 28 Mar. 1945.
110. Ibid.
111. Ibid.
112. Ibid.
113. Mageean papers, E11/45
114. Ibid.
115. Note on meeting held in the Law Courts, London, 11 Jan. 1945, N.I. Cabinet papers, 9D/1/12.

116. Home Office, London, to Gransden 16 Jan. 1945, N.I. Cabinet papers, 4/61.
117. Ministry of Education note on cabinet discussion of a possible enabling bill to amend Government of Ireland Act. N.I. Cabinet papers, 9D/1/12.
118. N.I. Cabinet papers, 4/621, 29 Mar. 1945.
119. Akenson, *Education and enmity*, p. 171.
120. N.I. Cabinet papers, 4/626/1, 25 May 1945.
121. Ibid.
122. Ibid.
123. *T.E.S.*, 30 July 1945.
124. *Irish Times*, 25 May 1945.
125. Akenson, *Education and enmity*, p. 171.
126. Ed 13/1/2130, 16 July 1945.
127. Ibid.
128. Ibid., 24 Sept., 1945.
129. Copy dated 14 Nov. 1945, N.I. Cabinet papers, 9D/1/14.
130. Copy dated 30 Nov. 1945, N.I. Cabinet papers, 9D/1/13.
131. Copy dated 29 Nov. 1945, N.I. Cabinet papers, 9D/1/13.
132. Copies in N.I. Cabinet papers, 9D/1/14.
133. *Irish News*, 8 Feb., 1946.
134. Ibid., 4 Mar. 1946.
135. 'Management of primary and secondary schools', Clauses 12–17 of Education Bill (N.I.), 1946.
136. Ibid.
137. Ibid.
138. N.I. H.C., v. 30, cols 2000–04 (15 Oct. 1946).
139. Ibid.
140. Ibid.
141. Letter to the Prime Minister, N.I. Cabinet papers, 9D/1/14.
142. Ibid., 15 Oct. 1946.
143. N.I. Cabinet papers, 9D/1/14.
144. *Belfast Telegraph*, 29 Oct. 1946.
145. Ibid., 30 Oct. 1946.
146. *Irish News* , 30 Oct. 1946.
147. *Belfast Telegraph*, 9 Nov. 1946.
148. Ibid., 26 Oct. 1946.
149. Ibid., 11 Nov. 1946.
150. Ibid.
151. Ibid., 16 Nov. 1946.
152. Quin, N.I. H.C., v. 30, cols 2250–70 (24 Oct. 1946).
153. Ibid., Milne-Barbour, col. 2317.
154. Ibid., Quin, col. 2270.
155. Ibid., col. 3405 (10 Dec. 1946).
156. Ibid., Beattie, col. 2074, (17 Oct. 1946).
157. Ibid., col. 2076.
158. Ibid., col. 2031.
159. Ibid., col. 2133.
160. Ibid., col. 3392 (10 Dec. 1946).
161. Ibid., col. 2165 (17 Oct. 1946).
162. Ibid., col. 3311 (5 Dec. 1946).
163. Ibid., col. 3314.
164. Ibid., col. 3473, (10 Dec. 1946).
165. *Belfast Telegraph*, 23 Oct. 1946.
166. 16 Oct. 1946.
167. Copy in N.I. Cabinet papers, 9D/1/14.
168. Ibid.
169. *Belfast Telegraph*, 14 Nov. 1946.
170. Ibid., 30 Oct. 1946.
171. Ibid., 15 Nov. 1946.
172. Ibid.

Chapter 8

1. School Attendance Act, 1942.
2. D.H. Akenson, *A mirror to Kathleen's face* (Montreal and London, McGill-Queen's University Press, 1975), p. 129.
3. Ibid.
4. O'Connell, *I.N.T.O.*, p. 391.
5. Ibid.
6. Dáil Éireann, v. 92, cols 2122–23 (18 Nov. 1942).
7. *Bunreacht na hÉireann*, article 42.
8. I.N.T.O., *Report of the committee of inquiry into the use of Irish as a teaching medium to children whose home language is English* (Dublin, I.N.T.O., 1941).
9. Ibid.
10. *T.E.S.*, May 1942.
11. Ibid.
12. O'Connell, *I.N.T.O.*, p. 390.
13. *Irish Times*, 8 Apr. 1942.
14. A.S.T.I., *Schools and colleges yearbook 1940–1941* (Dublin, A.S.T.I., 1941).
15. *Irish Times*, 8 Apr. 1942.
16. Ibid.
17. Irish state papers, S 7801A.
18. Ibid.
19. Ibid.
20. Ibid.
21. Dáil Éireann, v. 87, col. 719 (1 June 1942).
22. Ibid.
23. Coiste Gnó Conradh na Gaeilge, May 1942. Copy in Irish state papers, S 7801.
24. Dáil Éireann, v. 87, col. 711 (1 June 1942).
25. Ibid., col. 666.
26. Dáil Éireann, v. 94, col. 276 (13 June 1944).
27. Ibid., col. 277.
28. Dáil Éireann, v. 96, cols 2660–79 (27 Apr. 1945).
29. Ibid., v. 94, col. 396 (13 June 1944).
30. Editorial, *The Bell*, Oct. 1944.
31. Ibid., July 1945.
32. *Studies*, Mar. 1940, pp 1–14.
33. *Irish Times*, 18 May 1947.
34. Brown, *Ireland*, ch. 6.
35. Ibid.
36. Dáil Éireann, v. 106, col. 402–3 (20 May 1947).
37. Ibid.
38. *Irish Times*, 9 Apr. 1947.
39. Ibid., 10 Apr. 1947.
40. Department of Education, Dec. 1947. Irish state papers S7801.
41. In May 1945 Derrig claimed that 60 per cent of secondary pupils were either in Class A (all-Irish) or in Class B (bilingual) schools: Dáil Éireann, 25 Apr. 1945.
42. Dáil Éireann, v. 113, col. 1369–70 (14 Dec. 1948).
43. Ibid.
44. Department of Education, *Rules and regulations for national schools, 1950* (Dublin, Stationery Office, 1950).
45. Post-war education policy. Irish state papers, S12891.
46. Ibid.
47. Correspondence between Derrig and Bishop Staunton of Ferns who was secretary to the Catholic hierarchy, 31 May 1943. Irish state papers, S 12891.
48. Dáil Éireann, v. 94, col. 243 (13 June 1944).
49. Derrig to Staunton, 31 May 1943. Irish state papers, S 12891.
50. Ibid.
51. Ibid.
52. Staunton to Derrig, 26 Oct. 1943. Irish state papers, S 12891.
53. Ibid.

54. Dáil Éireann, v. 94, col. 253 (13 June 1944).
55. Derrig to Staunton, 10 Jan. 1945. Irish state papers, S 12891.
56. Ibid.
57. O'Connell, *I.N.T.O.*
58. Ibid.
59. Smith to Derrig, 31 July 1945. Irish state papers, S 12891.
60. Dáil Éireann, v. 94, col. 394 (13 June 1944).
61. Seanad Éireann, v. 33, col. 1927 (22 May 1947).
62. Dáil Éireann, v. 94, col. 399 (13 June 1944).
63. De Valera to Derrig, 16 Dec. 1944. Irish state papers, S 12891
64. *Irish Times*, 12 Dec. 1944
65. Ibid., 15 Dec. 1944.
66. Ibid., 4 Apr. 1945.
67. Derrig to de Valera, 24 Feb. 1945. Irish state papers, S 12891
68. *Report of the commission on technical and vocational education* (Dublin, Stationery Office, 1927).
69. Inter-departmental committee, 29 June 1935. Irish state papers, S 12891.
70. *Final report of the departmental committee*, 27 June 1947. Irish state papers, S 13638.
71. Ibid.
72. Ibid.
73. Ibid.
74. Ibid.
75. Ibid.
76. Ibid.
77. Edward Leen, CSSp., *What is education* (London, Burns, Oates and Washbourne, 1943).
78. I.N.T.O., *Plan for education* (Dublin, I.N.T.O., 1947).
79. Ibid.
80. Election manifestoes of all the major parties contained a reference to the need to extend access to secondary education.
81. F.S.L. Lyons, *Ireland since the famine* (London, Fontana Press, 1985) p. 561.
82. Private secretary, Department of Education to the Commission on Vocational Organisation, 5 Mar. 1942. Irish state papers, S 1753.
83. Ibid.
84. Coolahan, *A.S.T.I.*, p. 172.
85. O'Connell, *I.N.T.O.*, p. 450.
86. Seanad Éireann, v. 25, col. 13 (22 Jan. 1941).
87. Ibid.
88. Ibid.
89. Dáil Éireann, v. 95, col. 1744 (23 Mar. 1945).
90. Ibid.
91. Department of Education, 19 Feb. 1945. Irish state papers, S 12891.
92. Seanad Éireann, v. 33, col. 1925 (18 June 1947).
93. The motion was introduced by Senator Michael Ó hAodha. Seanad Éireann, v. 33, col. 1902 (18 June 1947).
94. Ibid., col. 1926.
95. Dáil Éireann, v. 110, col. 1093 (4 May 1948)
96. Ibid.
97. Ibid., 17 Feb. 1949. The motion was moved by Mr. Patrick Palmer T.D. requesting that 'A Council of Education be established as a permanent advisory body to the Minister for Education'.
98. *Council of Education* (Dublin, Stationery Office, 1950).
99. Ibid.

Chapter 9

1. In the immediate post-war period and throughout the 1950s the Northern Irish government engaged in a campaign to attract investment from abroad. The man-made fibre industry was a sector that was especially targeted and considerable success was achieved. Multinational companies like Courtaulds, British Enkalon, I.C.I., Monsanto and Dupont located large manufacturing units in Northern Ireland.

2. Buckland, *History of Northern Ireland*, p. 94.
3. Anti-partitionism gained a degree of popular appeal in the years 1947–51. De Valera, especially when in opposition after the 1948 elections, frequently spoke on this theme. Amongst the government parties, Clann na Poblachta which was led by the veteran I.R.A. commander, Sean McBride, supported the move for pressure to be applied internationally against Britain. The result was the launching of an all-party anti-partition campaign. This campaign evoked, not unexpectedly, a very hostile reaction in the north. Lyons, *Ireland since the famine*, p. 90.
4. The I.R.A. began to show signs of renewed activity in the early fifties with a series of raids on British army armouries. Then in 1956 a campaign of border raids, bombings and shootings was launched and lasted until 1962. See Buckland, *History of Northern Ireland*, pp 104–5.
5. A year marked by many demonstrations of devotion to Mary, the Mother of Jesus Christ.
6. Buckland, *History of Northern Ireland*, p. 104.
7. The civil rights campaign focused, in its initial stages, 1968–70, on such matters as reform of the local government franchise, housing allocation, fair employment opportunities, and policing.
8. The General Assembly of the Presbyterian Church, *The General Assembly and the new Education Act* (Belfast, Presbyterian Church in Ireland, 1947).
9. Ibid.
10. Ibid.
11. *Defence of Ulster*, a pamphlet published by a committee established in 1946 during the agitation against the Education Bill. Copy in P.R.O.N.I., Ministry of Education, Ed 13/1/.
12. Akenson, *Education and enmity*, pp 186–7.
13. Ibid.
14. N.I. H.C., v. 33, col. 1106 (14 June 1949).
15. Ibid., col. 1108 (14 June 1949).
16. The minister tendered his resignation on the 14 Dec. 1949 and in a speech to the house the following day made clear that the bill had been intended to meet needs in Protestant as well as Catholic schools. N.I. H.C., v. 33, cols 2283–4 (15 Dec. 1949).
17. Education (Miscellaneous Provisions) Act, 1949.
18. Akenson, *Education and enmity*, p. 186.
19. *Belfast Telegraph*, 14 Dec. 1949.
20. *Irish News*, 17 Jan. 1950.
21. N.I. Cabinet papers, 9D/78/1, 24 Oct. 1949 in which a memorandum refers to Derry County Education Committee's decision and the grounds offered for it.
22. Ibid.
23. Ibid.
24. Ibid.
25. Ibid. This file also contains details of protracted efforts to deal with similar cases in Armagh and Tyrone where the authorities wished to refuse travel payments to Catholic pupils on the grounds that they were living within walking distance of county secondary schools. The minister feared that denial of payments would be in breach of parents' right to choose schools for their children, but he also obviously wished to avoid antagonising local unionist feelings.
26. Memorandum to his cabinet colleagues from the Minister of Education, 2 Jan. 1952. N.I. Cabinet papers, 9D/78/1.
27. Ibid.
28. Ed 13/1/2463.
29. Ibid.
30. N.I. Cabinet papers, 4/964.
31. Ibid.
32. St Patrick's High School for boys and St Brigid's Secondary School for girls.
33. *Belfast Telegraph*, 16 Mar. 1952.
34. N.I. H.C., v. 39, col. 1921–34 (12 June 1956).
35. Ibid. col. 1934.
36. Ibid., v. 39. Debate on grants to voluntary schools (12 & 20 June 1956).
37. Cardinal D'Alton's circular was quoted by Minford in this debate. N.I. H.C., v. 39, cols 1923–4 (12 June 1956).
38. Ibid.
39. Midgley, N.I. H.C., v. 39, col. 1960 (12 June 1956).

40. N.I. H.C., v. 41 col. 584–5 (12 Mar. 1957).
41. Ibid., col. 585 (20 Mar. 1957).
42. In his House of Commons speech, 20 March 1957, Midgley quoted from a communication he had received from the Association of Education Committees making the same point as had Henderson.
43. Ibid.
44. Midgley's death occurred in April 1957. An *Irish News*, 30 April, comment following his death summed up the predominant Catholic attitudes towards him: 'his deep rooted bias against Catholic education made it impossible to discover what were his views as a Minister of Education generally'.
45. N.I. Cabinet papers, 9D/86/1.
46. Ibid.
47. *Annual report of the Ministry of Education (N.I.), 1955–56.*
48. Catholic dioceses were quite expeditious in preparing and submitting plans as papers in Ed 13/1/2463 reveal. Derry and Dromore, for example, had plans with the ministry by the end of October 1948.
49. Ibid.
50. Ibid.
51. Ibid.
52. N.I. H.C., v. 42, col. 1269 (5 June 1958).
53. 5 June 1958.
54. Ibid.
55. Education Act (England and Wales), 1959.
56. N.I. H.C., v. 46, col. 418 (24 Feb. 1960).
57. Ibid.
58. Ibid., Healy.
59. In the course of the educational estimates debate in 1957, for example, May's references to the work of voluntary schools was notably conciliatory. In particular he expressed considerable satisfaction at the rate of progress then being made in providing new voluntary intermediate schools. N.I. H.C., v., col. (30 May).
60. *Annual report of the Ministry of Education (N.I.), 1960–61.*
61. The motion was introduced by H. Diamond. N.I. H.C., v. 59, col. 1276 (2 Mar. 1965).
62. Ibid., cols 1276–90.
63. Ibid.
64. Ibid., cols 1308–10.
65. Education (Amendment) Act (Northern Ireland), 1968.
66. N.I. H.C., v. 37, col. 856 (16 Apr. 1953).
67. Ibid., v. 41, col. 1608 (12 June 1957).
68. Ibid., v. 44, col. 782 (19 Mar. 1959).
69. Ibid., v. 41, col. 1376 (13 Nov. 1956).
70. Ibid., Morgan, v. 42, col. 1266 (5 June 1958).
71. Official letter from the Minister of Education reproduced in the *Irish News*, 2 Mar. 1956.
72. N.I. H.C., v. 40, col. 394–98 (1 Mar. 1956).
73. Ibid.
74. Ibid.
75. Ibid.
76. Ministry of Education (N.I.) *Programme for primary schools* (Belfast, H.M.S.O., 1956).
77. *Annual report of the Ministry of Education 1955–56.*
78. Ibid.
79. Ministry of Education (N.I.) *Educational development in Northern Ireland* (Belfast, H.M.S.O., 1964).
80. Dáil Éireann, 22 May 1952.
81. *Report of the Department of Education, 1960–61.*
82. Ibid.
83. J.A. O'Brien (ed.), *The vanishing Irish* (London, W.H. Allen, 1954).
84. *Irish Independent*, 28 May 1952.
85. Lyons, *Ireland since the famine, part IV*, ch. 4.
86. Ibid.
87. The Marian celebrations held on almost a nation wide basis on 16 May 1954 were widely reported in the press, e.g. *Irish Times*, 17 May.

88. Brown, *Ireland*, p. 221.
89. Lyons, *Ireland since the famine*, pp 576–8.
90. Ibid., p. 577. The church seems to have been particularly concerned about the possibility of advice of which it might not approve being given in the area of family planning.
91. Whyte, *Church and state*, ch. 7 provides a very detailed account of the 'Mother and Child' controversy.
92. Ibid.
93. J. Whyte, *Church and state*, p. 271. Dr Lucy, Coadjutor Bishop of Cork is quoted as saying that 'This is the age of the State, the age of the eclipse of the individual by the government department and civil servant . . . In some countries this eclipse is complete . . .'
94. Dáil Éireann, v. 125, col. 784 (1951).
95. Cited in Lyons, *Ireland since the famine*, p. 578.
96. *Belfast Telegraph* , 14 Apr. 1951, just one of several editorials which this newspaper carried at the time. Others in the same month were published on the 21 and 28.
97. These regulations intended to provide guidelines as to the penitential exercises which Catholics should undertake during Lent. They also contained general instructions such as those warning against attendance at Trinity College. They first appeared in 1941 carrying the explicit prohibition on attendance at Trinity College and are extensively quoted and discussed in St John Ervine, *Craigavon*.
98. W. Philbin, 'A City on the Hill' in *Studies*, 46, Autumn, 1957, pp 259–70.
99. Ibid.
100. Lyons, *Ireland since the famine*, pp 567–8.
101. Ibid. p. 564.
102. Ibid.
103. In particular the funerals of two members of the I.R.A. from the south, F. O'Hanlon and Sean South, killed in a border raid were attended by very large numbers of people, including public representatives and the Catholic clergy. *Irish Times* 4 and 5 Jan. 1957.
104. Four Sinn Féin members were elected to the Dáil in 1957, but, in accordance with Sinn Féin policy, did not take their seats. Lyons, *Ireland since the famine*, p. 582.
105. Ibid., pp 581–2.
106. All three required negotiations between ministers and officials of both governments and in all three cases agreements were reached to their mutual satisfaction.
107. *Irish Times*, 15 Oct. 1957.
108. The most dramatic evidence of this was to be the visit made by Lemass to Belfast in 1965 for talks with Prime Minister O'Neill and the latter's return visit later that same year. See Lyons, *Ireland since the famine*, p. 587.
109. Lyons, *Ireland since the famine*, pp 589–98.
110. While a national television service was not available until 1961, British channels were being received along the east coast from the early 1950s.
111. Air travel developed quite rapidly with transatlantic services through Shannon and European services through Dublin.
112. Dáil Éireann, v. 126, col. 1725 (July 1951).
113. Ibid., 16 June 1954.
114. Ibid.
115. *Irish Press*, 6 Sept. 1952, address to the Fianna Fail Ard-Feis.
116. Dáil Éireann, v. 146, col. 233 (16 June 1954).
117. T.J. McElligott, *Education in Ireland*, p. 38.
118. Dáil Éireann, v. 132, col. 24 (28 May 1952).
119. Ibid., v. 146, col. 245 (16 June 1954).
120. O'Connell, *I.N.T.O.*, p. 437.
121. Ibid., p. 443.
122. Ibid., p. 440.
123. J. Lynch, Minister of Education, in his estimates speech in 1957 reported that 53 new schools had been built and that 23 schools had undergone major repairs or extensions in the previous year while 85 new schools were being built and 28 existing schools extended. Dáil Éireann, v. 165, cos 495–8 (1 May 1957).
124. Ibid., Noel Browne, col. 660 (2 May 1957).
125. O'Connell, *I.N.T.O.* , pp 444–9.
126. Ibid.
127. *Irish Times*, 2 Aug. 1953.

128. Council of Education, *Report of the Council of Education on the function and curriculum of the primary school* (Dublin, Stationery Office, 1954). (Hereafter cited as Council of Education, *Primary report*).
129. Ibid.
130. Áine Hyland, 'The multi-denominational experience in the national school system in Ireland' in *Irish Educational Studies*, vol. 8, 1, 1989, pp 89–114.
131. Akenson, *The Irish education experiment*, ch. 5
132. Ibid., ch. 7.
133. Lucy and Brennan, quoted in ch. 6. *Irish Ecclesiastical Record*, 52 (1938).
134. Given the pre-eminence accorded parental rights in the 1937 constitution the constitutionality of the recommendation was highly questionable.
135. Council of Educaton, *Primary report*, para. 129.
136. Ibid.
137. Ibid., para. 127
138. Ibid., para. 130.
139. Ibid., para. 132.
140. Ibid.
141. Ibid., para. 137.
142. Ibid., para. 196.
143. Ibid., para. 197.
144. Ibid.
145. Ibid., para. 205.
146. Ibid., para. 207.
147. Ibid., para. 244.
148. Ibid.
149. Ibid., para. 245.
150. Bilingualism and multilingualism in the classroom have received considerable attention in recent debates on the curriculum in England. See H. Sava, 'The rights of bilingual children' in R. Carter (ed.), *Knowledge about language* (London, Hodder and Stoughton, 1990), pp 248–68.
151. Council of Education, *Report 1954*, para. 216.
152. Ibid. Minority Report No. 1 by Canon W. Nesbitt Harvey, Dr Henry Kennedy and Dr Patrick Moran, pp 296–304.
153. Ibid.
154. Ibid.
155. Ibid.
156. Ibid.
157. Ibid., para. 15
158. Ibid.
159. *Irish Times*, 13 Aug. 1954.
160. Ibid., 11 Oct. 1954.
161. Ibid.
162. P. Birch, in *Irish Ecclesiastical Record*, 83 (1954) pp 1–11.
163. S. Ó Catháin 'The report of the Council of Education' in *Studies*, 43 Winter (1954), pp 361–74.
164. Dáil Éireann, v. 159, col. 1192 (18 July 1956).
165. Ibid.
166. Ibid. v. 182, cols 86–7 (24 May 1960)
167. Local Authorities (Scholarships) Act, 1961 increased the number of scholarships available to pupils transferring to secondary education. However, since the scholarships were still competitive their number was not sufficient to meet the demand for them.
168. Fianna Fail was returned to office in 1957. De Valera led the government for two years before retiring in 1959 when his deputy Sean Lemass became Taoiseach.
169. Dáil Éireann, 1 May 1957.
170. *Irish Times*, 25 Apr. 1957.
171. *Report of the commission on youth unemployment* (Dublin, Stationery Office, 1951) p. 17.
172. *Irish Times*, 5 Apr. 1956.
173. E. O'Doherty, 'Bilingual schools policy' in *Studies*, 47, Autumn (1958), pp 259–68.
174. R. Breathnach, 'Revival or survival' in *Studies*, 46, Summer (1956), pp 129–45.
175. Seán Ó Catháin, *Secondary education in Ireland* (Dublin, The Talbot Press, 1956). (Hereafter cited as Ó Catháin, *Secondary education*).

176. Ibid., p. 12.
177. Ibid., p. 15.
178. Ibid.
179. The commission was established in 1959 and was chaired by Fr. T. Ó Fiaich of St Patrick's College, Maynooth.
180. *Report of the commission on the restoration of the Irish Language* (Dublin, Stationery Office, 1965).
181. The terms of reference for the second investigation to be conducted by the Council of Education were focused on the curriculum of secondary education.
182. Ó Catháin, *Secondary education*, p. 46.
183. A. Wickham, 'International context of national systems: the Irish case' in *Comparative Education Review*, 24, 3, Oct. (1980), pp 323–37.
184. Professor Wheeler, University College, Dublin, *Irish Times*, 18 Apr. 1962.
185. Lynch, Dáil Éireann, v.165, cols 495–98 (1 May 1957).
186. 'Schools and teachers – north and south', *Irish Times*, 23 and 24 Apr. 1957.
187. *Irish Times*, 19 Apr. 1960.
188. Ibid.
189. J. O'Meara, *Reform in education* (Dublin, Mount Salus Press, 1957).
190. Ibid.
191. *Sunday Press*, 4 Oct. 1959, cited in E. Randles, *Post-primary education in Ireland 1957–1970* (Dublin, Veritas, 1975), p. 39. (Hereafter cited as Randles, *Post-primary education*).
192. Ibid.
193. *Report of the Department of Education, 1956–57*.
194. Dáil Éireann, v. 177, cols 188–200 (21 Oct. 1959).
195. Ibid.
196. Ibid.
197. Ibid., col. 200.
198. Ibid., col. 204.
199. Randles, *Post-primary education*, pp 41–2.
200. *Irish Times*, 2 Nov. 1959.
201. Ibid.
202. Dáil Éireann , 28 Oct. 1959.
203. Lyons, *Ireland since the famine*, p. 629.
204. Council of Education, *The secondary school curriculum* (Dublin, Stationery Office, 1962).
205. Ibid., paras 163–171 summarize the basic philosophy which underlay the council's approach to the curriculum, and its endorsement of an essentially liberal-humanistic-Christian basis to secondary education.
206. Ibid., para. 150.
207. Ibid., para. 152.
208. Ibid., para. 155.
209. Ibid., para. 189.
210. Ibid., paras 213–228.
211. Ibid., para. 220.
212. Ibid., para. 217.
213. Ibid., para. 309.
214. Ibid., para. 249.
215. Ibid.
216. Ibid., paras 428–31.
217. Ibid., para. 429.
218. Ibid., para. 428.
219. Ibid., para. 430.
220. *Irish Times*, 26 Apr. 1962; cited in Randles, *Post-primary education*, p. 98.
221. Ibid., chap. 2 & chap. 3. In these chapters Randles discusses several of the sources of international influence on educational policy in the south at this period.
222. *Irish Times*, 23 June 1962.
223. The full terms of reference are set out on page xxxix of the survey team's report *Investment in education* (Dublin, Stationery Office, 1965).

Bibliography

Government Papers
Public Record Office of Northern Ireland
Cabinet Papers (Cab 4, 9)
Ministry of Education (Ed 13,32)

National Archives, Dublin
State Papers
S 855,1 730,2 512,3 092,3 891,12 753 (A–B),4 650/9,4828, 12 891, 13 638, 7 801 (A–B), 15
  561, 1 973/A/B, 879, 4 522, 3 835, 1973 A, 6 554.

Private Papers
Armagh Archdiocesan Archive, Armagh
Michael Logue papers.
Joseph MacRory papers.
Patrick O'Donnell papers.

Down and Connor Diocesan Archives, Belfast
Miscellaneous documents relating to the diocese.

Parliamentary Debates
Northern Ireland: House of Commons and Senate Reports .
Irish Free State/Republic of Ireland: Dáil Éireann and Seanad Éireann Reports.
United Kingdom Parliament: House of Commons Reports.

Government Publications
Ireland pre-1921
Eighth report of the commission of inquiry into education in Ireland 1824–26 (509),
  vol. 13 (122).
Ninth report of the commission of inquiry into education in Ireland 1824–26 (510),
  vol. 13 (122).
Reports of the Commissioners of National Education, 1834–1920.
Reports of the Commissioners of Intermediate Education, 1879–1923.
Report of the royal commission of inquiry into primary education (Ireland) vol. 1, pt. 1
  and vol. iii & iv (minutes of evidence) (Powis Commission). H.C., 1870.
Report of the commission on manual and practical instruction in primary schools
  under the Board of National Education in Ireland. H.C., 1897.
Commission on intermediate education (Ireland), 1898.
Report of Mr. F. H. Dale, His Majesty's Inspector of Schools, Board of Education, on
  primary education in Ireland. H. C., 1904.
Report of Messrs. F. H. Dale and T.A. Stephens, His Majesty's Inspectors of Schools,
  Board of Education, on intermediate education in Ireland. H C., 1905.
A bill to provide for the establishment and functions of an administrative council in
  Ireland and for other purposes connected therewith. H.C., 1907.

A bill to provide for the heating of national schools in Ireland. H.C., 255. 1907.

Education (Belfast) Bill, 1919. H.C., 1919.

A bill to make further provision with respect to education in Ireland, and for other purposes therewith. H.C., 1919.

Report of the vice-regal committee of inquiry into primary education (Ireland), 1918. H.C., 1919.

Report of the vice-regal committee on intermediate education in Ireland, 1919. H.C., 1919.

Northern Ireland

Annual reports of the Ministry of Education 1922–67 (Belfast, H.M.S.O).

Correspondence between the Ministry of Education and the Armagh Regional Education

Committee on the subject of Bible instruction in transferred schools (Belfast, H.M.S.O., 1928).

Education Bill (Northern Ireland), 1923 (Belfast, H.M.S.O., 1923).

Education (Amendment) Bill (Northern Ireland), 1925 (Belfast, H.M.S.O., 1925).

Education (Amendment) Bill (Northern Ireland), 1930 (Belfast, H.M.S.O., 1930).

Education (Raising of the school leaving age) Bill (Northern Ireland), 1938 (Belfast, H.M.S.O., 1938).

Education Bill (Northern Ireland), 1946 (Belfast, H.M.S.O., 1946).

Education Bill (Northern Ireland), explanatory memorandum (Belfast, H.M.S.O., 1946).

Education (Amendment) Bill (Northern Ireland), 1968 (Belfast, H.M.S.O., 1946).

Educational development in Northern Ireland, 1964 (Belfast, H.M.S.O., 1964).

Educational reconstruction in Northern Ireland (Belfast, H.M.S.O., 1944).

Educational reconstruction in Northern Ireland: the first ten years (Belfast, H.M.S.O., 1959).

Final report of the departmental committee on the educational services in Northern Ireland (Belfast, H.M.S.O., 1923).

Interim report of the departmental committee on the educational services in Northern Ireland (Belfast, H.M.S.O., 1922).

List of books in history, citizenship and economics approved for use in public elementary schools for the school year 1934 (Belfast, H.M.S.O., 1934).

Programme of instruction for public elementary schools (Belfast, H.M.S.O., 1924).

Programme of instruction for public elementary schools (Belfast, H.M.S.O., 1946).

Programme of instruction for primary schools (Belfast, H.M.S.O., 1956).

Irish Free State/Republic of Ireland

Annual reports of the Department of Education 1923–64 (Dublin, Stationery Office).

Bunreacht na hÉireann (Dublin, Stationery Office, 1937).

Investment in education, report of the survey team appointed by the Minister for Education, 1962 (Dublin,Stationery Office, 1965).

National education statistics 1920–1925 (Dublin, Stationery Office, 1926).

Notes for teachers: history, 1933.

Report of the second National Programme Conference (Dublin, Stationery office, 1926).

Report of the commission on technical education (Dublin, Stationery Office, 1927).

Report of the commission on vocational organisation (Dublin, Stationery Office, 1944).

Report of the commission on youth unemployment (Dublin, Stationery Office, 1952).

Report of the Council of Education on the function of the primary school (Dublin, Stationery Office, 1954).

Report of the Council of Education on the curriculum of the secondary school (Dublin, Stationery Office, 1962).

Report of the commission on the restoration of the Irish language (Dublin, Stationery Office, 1963).
Rules and regulations for national schools published annually.
Rules and regulations for secondary schools published annually.
Tuarascail Comisiun na Gaeltachta (Dublin, Stationery Office, 1926).

Church of Ireland Training College, Dublin
Annual reports, 1920 –.

Unpublished Theses
Coolahan, J., 'Curricular policy for the primary and secondary schools of Ireland 1900–1935'. Ph.D. thesis, Trinity College, Dublin, 1973.
Holmes, E., 'Public opinion and educational reform in the North of Ireland 1900–1954'. M.A. thesis, Queen's University, Belfast, 1969.
Jacques,W., 'Factors determining developments in primary education in Ireland 1831–1947'. Ph.D. thesis, Queen's University, Belfast, 1952.
O'Connor, D., 'Curriculum development at second level in the Republic of Ireland'. Ph.D. thesis, St Patrick's College, Maynooth, 1976.
O'Leary, K., 'Post-primary education in Eire since 1922'. Ph.D. thesis, Queen's University, Belfast, 1962.
Spence, W.R., 'The growth and development of the secondary intermediate school in Northern Ireland since the Education Act of 1947'. M.A. thesis, Queen's University, Belfast, 1959.

Newspapers and Periodicals
Belfast Newsletter
Belfast Telegraph
The Bell
The Catholic Bulletin
Church of Ireland Gazette
Irish Catholic Directory
Irish Ecclesiastical Record
Irish Education Review
Irish Educational Studies
Irish Historical Studies
Irish Independent
Irish News
Irish Press
Irish School Weekly
Irish Times
An Muinteoir Naisiunta
Oideas
Schools and Colleges Yearbook
Studies
Times Educational Supplement
U.T.U. Bulletin

School texts referred to in Chapter 6
Browne and Nolan Publications:
The New Sterling Readers, 1929.
The Oriel Readers, 1929.
Inis Aoibhinn, 1930.
Irish World Readers, 1933.
New Model Readers, 1936.

Christian Brothers Publications
Senior Reader, 1934

Educational Company Publications
Educational Class Readers, 1931.
Léitheoirí Inse Fáil, 1931.

Books and Pamphlets
Akenson, D.H., *The Irish education experiment.* (London, Routledge and Kegan Paul, 1970).
—— *Education and enmity: the control of schooling in Northern Ireland 1920–1950.* (Newton Abbot, David and Charles, 1973).
—— *A mirror to Kathleen's face: education in independent Ireland 1922–1960* (Montreal and London, McGill-Queen's University Press,1975).
Andrews, L., *The decline of Irish as a school subject in the Republic of Ireland* (An Conradh Celiteach agus Craobh n dTeicneolaithe de Chronradh na Gaeilge a d'fhoilsigh, 1978).
A.S.T.I., *Schools and colleges yearbook* (Dublin, A.S.T.I., 1941).
Atkinson, N., *Irish education: a history of educational institutions* (Dublin, Allen Figgis, 1969).
Barritt, D. and Carter, C., *The Northern Ireland problem: a study in group relations* (London, Oxford University Press,1962).
Batterbury, R., *Oideachas in Eirinn, 1500–1946* (Dublin, Stationery Office, 1955).
Bardon, J., *A history of Ulster* (Belfast, Blackstaff, 1993).
Bell, B. *The secret army, a history of the I.R.A.* (Dublin, Academy Press, 1979).
Bell, R., Fowler, K. and Little, K., *Education in Great Britain and Ireland* (London, Routledge and Kegan Paul, 1973).
Birmingham,G., *An Irishman looks at his world* (London, Hodder and Stoughton, 1919).
Blake, J.W., *Northern Ireland in the second world war* (Belfast, H.M.S.O., 1956).
Brennan, N., *Dr Mannix* (London, Angus and Robertson, 1965).
Brown, T., *Ireland a social and cultural history 1922–1979* (London, Fontana Paperbacks, 1981).
Buckland, P., *Irish Unionism 1: the Anglo-Irish and the new Ireland 1885–1922* (Dublin, Gill and Macmillan, 1972).
—— *Irish Unionism 2: Ulster Unionism and the origins of Northern Ireland 1886–1922* (Dublin, Gill and Macmillan,1976).
—— *The factory of grievances* (Dublin, Gill and Macmillan, 1979).
—— *A history of Northern Ireland* (Dublin, Gill and Macmillan, 1981).
—— *Irish Unionism 1885–1922: a documentary history* (Belfast, H.M.S.O., 1986).
Burns, J.F., *Shop window on the world, Masonic Boys' School 1867–1967* (Dublin, Board of Governors Masonic School, 1967).
Butler, M., *Irish women and the home language* (Dublin, Gaelic League Pamphlets, n.d.)
Cahill, Edward, *The framework of a Christian state* (Dublin, Gill and Son, 1932).
Campbell, J.J., *Catholic schools* (Belfast, Fallons Educational Supply Company, n.d.).
Carter, R., *Knowledge about language* (London, Hodder and Stoughton, 1990).
Christian Brothers, *A century of Catholic education* (Dublin, Brown and Nolan, 1916).
Collins, M., *The path to freedom* (Cork, Mercier Press, 1968).
Coolahan, J., *Irish education history and structure* (Dublin, Institute of Public Administration, 1981).
—— *The A.S.T.I. and post-primary Education 1909–1984* (Dublin, A.S.T.I., 1985).
Corcoran, T., *State policy in Irish education* (Dublin, Fallon, 1916).
—— *Education systems in Ireland from the close of the middle ages* (Dublin, University College Dublin, 1928).

—— *The Catholic schools of Ireland* (Louvain, H. Bomans, 1931).

Corkery, D., *The philosophy of the Gaelic League* (Dublin, Conradh na Gaeilge, 1948).

—— *The fortunes of the Irish language* (Cork, Mercier Press, 1968).

Corkey, W., *The Church of Rome and Irish unrest: how hatred of Britain is taught in Irish schools* (Publication details unknown, copy available in the National Library of Ireland).

—— *Episode in the history of Protestant Ulster 1923–1947* (details unknown).

—— *Glad did I live* (Belfast, Newsletter, 1963).

Curtis, S.J., *History of education in Great Britain* (London, University Tutorial Press, 1948).

Dallat, M. (ed.), *Aspects of Catholic education* (Belfast, St Joseph's College of Education, 1971).

Darby, J., *Northern Ireland: the background to the conflict* (Belfast, Appletree Press, 1983).

Dineen, P., *Native history in national schools* (Dublin, Gill and Son, 1905).

Dowling, P.J., *A history of Irish education* (Cork, Mercier Press, 1968).

Duffy, P.J., *The lay teacher in Ireland* (Dublin, Fallon, 1967).

Duggan, G.C., *Northern Ireland – success or failure* (Dublin, Irish Times Publications, 1950).

Ellis, T.H., *Noisy mansions, reflections on a career in Ulster schools* (Lisnaskea, Whitethorn Press, 1983).

Ervine, St John, *Craigavon* (London, George Allen and Unwin, 1946).

Fenton, S., *It all happened* (Dublin, Gill and Son, 1949).

Finlay, P., *The church and secular education* (Dublin, Irish Messenger Office, 1922).

Fitzpatrick, J.D., *Edmund Rice founder and first Superior General of the Brothers of the Christian Schools of Ireland* (Dublin, Christian Brothers, 1945).

Forde, P., *The Irish language movement: its philosophy* (Dublin, Gaelic League Pamphlet 21, 1899).

General Assembly of the Presbyterian Church in Ireland, *The General Assembly and the new Education Act* (Belfast, Presbyterian Church in Ireland, 1947).

Geraghty, M., *Idols of modern society* (Dublin, Irish Messenger Press, 1931).

Good, H.G., *A history of western education* (New York, Macmillan Company, 1960).

Gordon, P. and Lawton, D., *Curriculum changes in the nineteenth and twentieth centuries* (London, Hodder and Stoughton, 1978).

Harris, M., *The Catholic Church and the foundation of the northern Irish state* (Cork, University of Cork Press, 1993).

Hopkinson, M., *Green against green: the Irish civil war* (Dublin, Gill and Macmillan, 1988).

Hurley, M. (ed.), *Irish Anglicanism* (Dublin, Allen Figgis, 1970).

Hyland, A. and Milne, K. (eds), *Irish educational documents volume 1* (Dublin, C.I.C.E., 1987).

—— *Irish educational documents volume 2* (Dublin, C.I.C.E., 1992).

—— *Irish educational documents volume 3* (Dublin, C.I.C.E., 1995).

I.N.T.O., *Report of the inquiry into the use of Irish as a teaching medium to children whose home language is English* (Dublin, I.N.T.O., 1941).

—— *Plan for education.* (Dublin, I.N.T.O., 1947).

Irish Labour Party and Trades Union Congress, *Policy on education* (Dublin, Irish Labour Party, 1926).

Kennedy, D., *The widening gulf: northern attitudes to an independent Irish state 1919–1949* (Belfast, Blackstaff Press, 1988).

Keogh, D., *The Vatican, the bishops and Irish politics 1919–1939* (London, C.U.P., 1986).

Kingsmill Moore, Dr H., *Reminiscences and reflections from some sixty years of life in Ireland* (London, Longmans, 1930).

Larkin, E., *The consolidation of the Roman Catholic Church in Ireland 1860–1870* (Dublin, Gill and Macmillan, 1987).

Lee, J. *Ireland 1912–1985, politics and society* (Cambridge, Cambridge University Press, 1989).

Leen, E., *What is education* (London, Burns Oates and Washbourne, 1943).

Lyons, F.S.L., *Ireland since the famine* (London, Fontana Press, 1971).

—— *Culture and anarchy in Ireland 1890–1939* (Oxford, Clarendon Press, 1979).

McElligott, T.J., *Education in Ireland* (Dublin, Institute of Public Administration, 1966).

—— *Secondary education in Ireland 1870–1921* (Dublin, Irish Academic Press, 1981).

McIvor, J., *Popular education in the Irish Presbyterian Church* (Dublin, Scepter Books, 1969).

MacManus, F., *The years of the great test 1926–39* (Cork, Mercier Press, 1967).

McNeilly, N., *Exactly 50 years: the Belfast Education Authority and its work (1923–1973)* (Belfast, Belfast Education and Library Board, 1973).

McQuaid, J.C., *Wellsprings of faith* (Dublin, Clonmore and Reynolds, 1956).

—— *Catholic education: its function and scope* (Dublin, C.T.S., 1942).

McSweeney, B., *Roman Catholicism: the search for relevance* (London, Blackwell, 1980).

MacSuibhne, P., *Paul Cullen and his contemporaries Volume I,* (Naas, Leinster Press, 1961).

—— *Paul Cullen and his contemporaries Volume II* (Naas, Leinster Press, 1961).

—— *Paul Cullen and his contemporaries Volume III* (Naas, Leinster Press, 1965).

Mandle, W.F., *The Gaelic Athletic Association and Irish nationalist politics 1884–1924* (London and Dublin, Croom Helm and Gill and Macmillan, 1987).

Mansergh, N., *The government of Northern Ireland: a study in devolution* (London, 1936).

Marnane, J., *A guide for Catholic teachers* (Dublin, Gill and Son, 1952).

Martyn, E., *Ireland's battle for her language* (Dublin, Gaelic League Pamphlets, n.d.).

Mescal, J., *Religion in the Irish system of education* (Dublin, Clonmore and Reynolds, 1957).

Miller, D., *Church, state and nation in Ireland* (Dublin, Gill and Macmillan, 1973).

Miller, J., *Clericalised education in Ireland* (Dublin, Maunsel, 1907).

Moran, D.P., *The philosophy of Irish Ireland* (Dublin, James Duffy, 1905).

Morrissey, T.J., *Towards a national university: William Delaney (1835–1924)* (Dublin, Wolfhound Press, 1983).

Mulcahy, D.G., *Curriculum and policy in Irish post-primary education* (Dublin, Institute of Public Administration, 1981).

Murphy, I., *A history of Irish Catholicism: the church since emancipation, volumes 5 and 6: primary education* (Dublin, Gill and Macmillan, 1971).

National Programme Conference, *National programme of primary instruction* (Dublin, The Educational Company, 1922).

National Programme Conference, *Report and Programme* (Dublin, Stationery Office, 1926).

Northern Ireland Labour Pary, *Education policy* (Belfast, N.I.L.P., 1944).

Nowlan, K.B. and Williams, T.D. (eds.), *Ireland in the war years and after, 1939–51* (Dublin, Gill and Macmillan,1969) pp 80–93.

O'Brien, J. A. (ed), *The vanishing Irish* (London, W.H. Allen, 1954).

Ó Buachalla, S., *A significant Irish educationalist* (Cork and Dublin, Mercier Press, 1980).

—— *Educational policy in twentieth century Ireland* (Dublin, Wolfhound Press, 1988).

Ó Catháin, S., *Secondary education in Ireland* (Dublin, Talbot Press, 1958).

Ó Conaire, B. (ed.), *Language, lore and lyrics, essays and lectures of Douglas Hyde* (Dublin, Academic Press, 1986).

O'Connell, T.J. (ed.), *Proceedings of the fifth biennial conference of the W.F.E.A.* (Dublin, I.N.T.O., 1933).

O'Connell, T.J., *History of the I.N.T.O.* (Dublin, I.N.T.O., 1969).

Ó Cuív, B. (ed.), *A view of the Irish language* (Dublin, Stationery Office, 1968).

O'Farrelly, A., *The reign of humbug* (Dublin, Gaelic League Pamphlets, n.d.).

O'Hickey, M., *The nationalisation of Irish education* (Dublin, Gaelic League Pamphlets, n.d.).
—— *The Irish language movement* (Dublin, Gaelic League Pamphlets, n.d.).
O'Leary, M., *The Catholic Church and education* (London, Burns Oates and Washbourne, 1943).
O'Meara, J., *Reform in education* (Dublin, Mount Salus Press, 1957).
Ó Muimhneacháin, A., *Dóchas agus duaineís* (Corcaigh, Mercier Press, 1974).
O'Rourke, T.A., *The future of the Irish language* (Dublin, Towards a New Ireland Pamphlet no. 16, n.d.).
Ó Snodaigh, S., *Hidden Ulster – the other Ireland* (Dublin, Clodhanna Teoranta, 1977).
Ó Suilleabháin, D., *Cath na Gaeilge sa chóras oideachais 1893–1911* (Ath Cliath, Conradh na Gaeilge, 1988).
Ó Suilleabháin, S., *A history of Irish Catholicism: the church since emancipation, Catholic Education, Volumes 5 and 6: secondary education* (Dublin, Gill and Macmillan, 1971).
Ó Tuama, S (ed.)., *The Gaelic League idea* (Dublin and Cork, Mercier Press, 1972).
Parkes, S., *Kildare Place: history of the Church of Ireland Training College* (Dublin, C.I.C.E., 1984).
Pearse, P.H., *Political writings and speeches* (Dublin, Talbot Press, 1962).
Phoenix, E. , *Northern nationalism, nationalist politics, partition and the Catholic minority in Northern Ireland 1890–1940* (Belfast, Ulster Historical Foundation, 1994).
Pope Pius XI, *The Christian education of youth* (London, Catholic Truth Society, 1970).
—— *Quadragesimo Anno (The Christian state)* (London, Catholic Truth Society, 1931).
Pritchard, R.M.O.P. (ed), *Motivating the majority – modern languages in Northern Ireland* (London, C.I.L.T., 1991).
Puirséal, P., *The G.A.A.and its times* (Dublin, Purcell, 1982).
Randles, Sr. E., *Post-primary education in Ireland 1957–1970* (Dublin, Veritas, 1975).
Rooney, W., *Prose writings* (Dublin and Waterford, Gill and Son, 1909).
Seaver, G., *John Allen Fitzgerald Gregg, Archbishop* (London, Faith Press, 1963).
Starkie, W., *Recent reforms in Irish education* (Dublin, 1902).
Stenhouse, L., *Culture and education* (London, Thomas Nelson and Sons, 1967).
Tierney, M., *Education in a free Ireland* (London, Martin Lester, 1926)
Titley, E. Brian *Church, state and the control of schooling in Ireland 1900–1944* (Dublin, Gill and Macmillan and Kingston and Montreal, McGill-Queen's University Press, 1983).
'Torna', *You may revive the Gaelic language* (Dublin, Gaelic League, 1936).
Ulster Unionist Council, *Education in Northern Ireland* (Belfast, Ulster Unionist Council, 1949).
Walker, G., *The politics of frustration* (Manchester, Manchester University Press, 1986).
Walsh, W., *Denominational education* (Dublin, Talbot Press, n.d.).
White, G.K., *History of St Columba's College* (Dublin, Old Columbian Society, 1980).
White, J., *Minority report, the Protestant community in the Irish Republic* (Dublin, Gill and Macmillan.1975).
Whyte, J., *Church and state in modern Ireland 1923–1970* (Dublin, Gill and Macmillan, 1971)
—— *Interpreting Northern Ireland* (Oxford, Clarendon Press, 1990).
Wilson, T., *Ulster under Home Rule* (London, Oxford University Press, 1955).
Windle, B., *The prospects of education in Ireland Today* (Cork, University College, 1917).

Articles

Akenson, D., 'National education and the realities of Irish life 1831–1900' in *Eire–Ireland*, 4, 4 (1969), pp 42–51.
Airmeas, P., 'The ideal of the state in Irish education'in *Irish Education Review,* 4 (1914), pp 256–61.

Andrews, L.S., 'The Irish language in the education system of Northern Ireland: some political and cultural perspectives' in R.M.O.P. Pritchard (ed.), *Motivating the Majority*. (London, C.I.L.T., 1991), pp. 1–17.

Bergin, O., 'Revival of Irish language' in *Studies*, 16 (1927), pp 17–20.

Birch, P., 'Report of the Council of Education' in *Irish Ecclesiastical Record*, 83 (1954), pp 1–11.

Breathnach, R., 'Revival or survival' in *Studies*, 45 (1956), pp 129–45.

Brennan, M., 'The Catholic school system of Ireland' in *Irish Ecclesiastical Record*, 52 (1938), pp 257–72.

——— 'The Netherlands solution to the education question' in *Irish Ecclesiastical Record*, 53 (1939), p. 261.

——— 'The vocational schools II' in *Irish Ecclesiastical Record*, 53 (1939), pp 406–18.

——— 'The restoration of Irish' in *Studies*, 53 (1964), pp 263–77.

Brown, P.,'Revival of the Irish language' in *Studies*, 16 (1927), pp 15–17.

Byrne, M.J., 'Education – wanted a definition' in *Irish Education Review*, 1 (1907–8), p. 373.

Byrne, P., 'Primary education in Ireland – a retrospect' in *Irish Ecclesiastical Record*, 5, 2 (1914), pp 225–40.

Cahill, E., 'Perversion of Irish education' in *Irish Ecclesiastical Record*, 53 (1939), pp 577–92.

——— 'The social question in Ireland' in *Ecclesiastical Record*, 34 (1929), p. 225.

Coolahan, J. 'The education bill of 1919 – problems of educational reform' in *Proceedings of the Educational Studies Association of Ireland Conference,1979* (Galway, Galway University Press, 1980), pp 11–31.

Corcoran, T., 'The new secondary programmes in Ireland: classical studies' in *Studies*, 11 (1922) p. 359.

——— 'The new secondary programmes in Ireland' in *Studies*, 12 (1923), p. 24 .

——— 'How the Irish language can be revived' in *Irish Monthly*, 47 (Jan., 1923), pp 26–30.

——— 'Education through Anglo-Irish literature' in *Irish Monthly*, 51 (May, 1923), p. 599.

——— 'The Irish language in Irish schools' in *Studies*, 14 (1925), pp 377–88.

——— 'The Catholic philosophy of education' in *Studies*, 19 (1930), p. 199.

——— 'Structural principles of Catholic education' in T.J. O'Connell (ed.), *Proceedings of the fifth biennial conference of the W.F.E.A.* (Dublin, I.N.T.O., 1933).

Cullen, P. 'The Irish hierarchy and Catholic education' in *Irish Ecclesiastical Record*, 10 (1873), pp 81–82.

Devane, R.S., 'Indecent literature' in *Irish Ecclesiastical Record* 25 (1925), pp 182–204.

Doherty, E. 'Bilingual schools policy' in *Studies*, 47 (1958), pp 259–68.

Farren, S. 'Culture and education in Ireland' in *Compass, Journal of the Irish Association for Curriculum Development*, 3, 2 (1976), pp 22–38.

——— 'Divergence and convergence in Irish education – a study of the educational systems in Ireland, north and south'. An unpublished paper delivered at a seminar in the School of Social Administration, New University of Ulster (1978).

——— 'Unionist–Protestant reaction to educational reform in Northern Ireland 1923–1930' in *History of Education*, 14, 3 (1985), pp 227–36.

——— 'Nationalist–Catholic reaction to educational reform in Northern Ireland, 1921–1930' in *History of Education*, 15, 1 (1986), pp 1921–1930.

——— 'Teacher education, the collapse of its all-Ireland dimensions in 1922' in *Irish Educational Studies*, 8, 1 (1988), pp 56–73.

——— 'Catholic–nationalist attitudes to Education in Northern Ireland 1921–1947' in *Irish Educational Studies*, 8, 1 (1989), pp 37–55.

——— 'A lost opportunity: education and community in Northern Ireland 1947–1960' in *History of Education*, 21, 1 (1992), pp 71–82.

—— 'A divided and divisive legacy: education in Ireland 1900–1920' in *History of Education*, 23, 2 (1994), pp 207–24.

—— 'Irish model schools: models of what?' in *History of Education*, 14, 1 (1995), pp 40–60.

Graham, E. 'Religion and education – the constitutional problem' in *Northern Ireland Legal Quarterly*, 33, 1 (1982), pp 20–51.

Hallinan, Mgr. D., 'State aggressiveness in education I' in *Irish Education Review*, 1 (1907–8), pp 226–29.

—— 'State aggressiveness in education II' in *Irish Education Review*, 1 (1907–8), pp 284–90.

—— 'State aggressiveness in education III' in *Irish Education Review*, 1 (1907–8) p. 409.

Harper, T., 'Authority and education' in *Irish Ecclesiastical Record*, 79 (1953), p. 115.

Hayes, C., 'The educational ideas of Paul Cullen' in *Proceedings of the Educational Studies Association of Ireland Conference, 1979* (Galway, Galway University Press), pp 1–10.

Hislop, H., 'The 1806–12 Board of Education and non-denominational education in Ireland' in *Oideas*, 40 (1993), pp 48–60.

Hyland, A., 'The treasury and Irish education 1850–1922: the myth and the reality' in *Irish Educational Studies*, 3, 2 (1983), pp 57–82.

—— 'The multi-denominational experiences in the national school system in Ireland' in *Irish Educational Studies*, 8,1 (1989), pp 89–114.

Kearns, C. 'The revival of Irish' in *Irish Ecclesiastical Record*, 81 (1954) p. 184.

Kelly, A. 'The Gaelic League and the introduction of compulsory Irish into the Free State education system' in *Oideas*, 41 (1994) pp 46–57.

Kennedy, David, 'Catholic Schools in Northern Ireland 1921–1970' in M. Dallat (ed.), *Aspects of Catholic Education* (Belfast, St Joseph's College of Education, 1971).

Kennedy, Denis, 'Northern responses to the Irish language movement.' A paper to the annual conference of the Irish Association, Queen's University, Belfast (September,1988).

Londonderry, Lord 'Public education in Northern Ireland – the new system' in *The Nineteenth Century*, (March 1924), pp 328–44.

Lucy, C. 'Making the school system of Ireland Catholic' in *Irish Ecclesiastical Record*, 52 (1938), pp 405–17.

—— 'A guild for education' in *Irish Ecclesiastical Record*, 51(1938), pp 582–92.

MacCartney, Donal, 'Education and language 1938–51' in K.B. Nowlan and T.D. Williams (eds.) *Ireland in the war years and after, 1939–51* (Dublin, Gill and Macmillan,1969), pp 80–93.

Mac Con Midhe, P. 'Staid na Gaeilge i scoileanna na sé gcontae I' in *An tUltach*, (Bealtaine,1971), pp 5–8.

—— 'Staid na Gaeilge i scoileanna na sé gcontae II' in *An tUltach*, (Meitheamh, 1971) 6–7.

McElligott, T.J. 'Some thoughts on our educational discontents' in *University Review*, 1, 5 (1955) pp 27–36.

—— 'Schools and teachers' in *Irish Times*, 23 and 24 Apr. 1957.

—— 'Secondary education: a privileged class' in *Irish Times*, 19 Apr. 1960.

McEvoy, J., 'Catholic hopes and Protestant fears', paper presented to the New Ireland Forum (1983).

MacGearailt, T., 'The great power-sharers' in *The Education Times* (29 May 1975).

McKenna, L., 'State rights in education' in *Studies*, 16 (1927), pp 215–30.

McKeown, M., 'The Irish educational scene: the past' in *Christus Rex Journal of Sociology*, 22, 2 (1968), p. 86.

MacMathúna, L., 'The potential for Irish-English dual medium instruction in the primary school' in *Oideas*, 32 (1988), pp 5–21.

MacNéill, Eoin, 'A view of the state in relation to education' in *The Irish Review*, 1, 1 (Oct. 1922) 3, 4; 1, 3 (Nov.,1922), 28, 29.

—— 'Irish education policy I' in *The Irish Statesman*, 4 (17 Oct. 1925).

—— 'Irish education policy II' in *The Irish Statesman*, 4 (24 Oct. 1925).

Mulcahy, R., 'The revival of the Irish language' in *Studies*, 16 (1927), pp 10–15.

Murphy, A.(A.M.), 'The teaching of history I' in *Irish Education Review*, 1 (1907–8), p. 111.

—— 'The teaching of history II' in *Irish Education Review*, 1 (1907–8), p. 182.

Murphy, G., 'Irish in our schools' in *Studies*, 37 (1948), p. 481.

Ó Buachalla, S. 'Education as an issue in the first and second Dáil' in *Administration*, 25, 1 (1980), pp 57–75.

—— 'Educational policy and the role of the Irish language from 1831–1981' in *European Journal of Education*, 19, 1 (1984), pp 75–91.

O'Callaghan, M., 'Language, nationality and cultural identity' in *Irish Historical Studies*, 24, 94 (1984), pp 226–45.

Ó Canainn, S., 'The educational inquiry of 1824–1826 in its social and political context' in *Irish Educational Studies*, 3, 2 (1983), pp 1–20.

Ó Catháin, S., 'The report of the Council of Education' in *Studies*, 43 (1954), pp 361–74.

O'Connor, J., 'The teaching of Irish, testament of a pioneer' in *Capuchin Annual* (1949), pp 205–20.

Ó Croinín, B., ' An Ghaeilge sa choras bunoideachais i dtus an cheid seo' in *Oideas*, 30 (1988), pp 19–27.

O'Doherty, E., 'Bilingual school policy' in *Studies*, 47 (1958), pp 259–68.

O'Dwyer, Bishop E. T., 'Marlborough House' in *Irish Education Review*, 2 (1909–10), pp 1–10.

Ó Faoláin, S., 'The priest in politics' in *The Bell* (Jan. 1947), pp 4–24.

Ó Móráin, D., 'Forbairt na hathbheochana' in *Feasta* (Nollaig 1956), pp 8–12.

O'Neill, J., 'Departments of Education: church and state' in *Studies*, 38 (1949), pp 418–29.

Ó Raifeartaigh, T., 'Changes and trends in our educational system since 1922' in *Journal of the Statistical and Social Inquiry Society of Ireland*, 20 (1957–8), pp 42–51.

Ó Suilleabháin, P., 'Teagasc trí Ghaeilge sna meanscoileanna' in *Feasta* (Samhain 1957), pp 5–8.

Panza, S., 'Survival without revival' in *Studies*, 46 (1957), pp 34–43.

Pearse, P.H., 'An ideal in education' in *Irish Review*, 14 (1914), pp 171–73.

—— 'Education and Home Rule' in *Irish Review*, 2 (1912–3), pp 617–20.

Philbin, W., 'A city on the hill' in *Studies*, 46 (1957), pp 259–70.

Púichín, An, 'Naisiúntacht agus oideachas 1' in *Irish Education Review*, 1 (1907–8), p. 30.

—— 'Naisiúntacht agus oideachas 2' in *Irish Education Review*, 1 (1907–8), p. 291.

Reynolds, L., 'Secondary education' in *Irish Times* (18 Aug. 1953).

Rigney, I. 'Educational ingredients' in *Irish Ecclesiastical Record*, 35 (1930), p. 492.

—— 'Irish education; how to improve it' in *Irish Ecclesiastical Record*, 36 (1930), p. 289.

Tierney, M., 'The revival of the Irish language'in *Studies*, 16 (1927), pp 1–10.

—— 'The problem of partition' in *Studies*, 27 (1938), pp 637–64.

—— 'Ireland and the Anglo-Irish heresy' in *Studies*, 29 (1940), pp 1–14.

—— 'The origin and growth of modern Irish nationality' in *Studies*, 30 (1941), pp 321.

—— 'Culture and education' in *Studies*, 30 (1941), pp 488.

—— 'Nationalism, a survey' in *Studies*, 34 (1945), pp 474–82.

Tynan, M., 'General review of education in Ireland' in *Lumen Vitae*, 4, 2 (1949), pp 377–407.

Wall, P.J., 'The bishops and education' in *Oideas*, 25 (1982), pp 5–13.

Ward, M.H. 'The Irish language movement' in *Irish Educational Review*, 1 (1907–8), p. 610.

Wickham, A., 'International context of national systems: the Irish case' in *Comparative Education Review*, 24, 3 (1980), pp 323–37.

Wilkinson, R., 'Educational Endowments Act (Ireland) 1885 as part of nineteenth century educational reform'in *Irish Educational Studies*, 3, 2 (1983), pp 98–121.

Index

98. Dáil Éireann, v. 8, col. 559 (7 July 1924).
99. *Appendix to the annual report of the Department of Education 1924–25.*
100. O'Connell, *I.N.T.O.*, p. 355.
101. Ibid.
102. National Programme Conference, *Report and programme* (Dublin, Stationery Office, 1926).
103. Kingsmill Moore, *Reminiscences.*
104. National Programme Conference, *Report and programme.*
105. Ibid.
106. Ibid.
107. Earnán de Blaghd (Ernest Blythe) was an enthusiastic member of the language movement who became a Sinn Féin activist and eventually served in Cumann na nGael governments in the 1920s. His three-part autobiography *Trasna na Bóinne, Slán le hUltaibh* and *Gaeil ar Mhúscailt* was published by Sairseal and Dill 1957,1970 and 1973. See also D. Greene 'The founding of the Gaelic League' in *The Gaelic League idea,* edited by Seán Ó Tuama, (Cork and Dublin, Mercier Press, 1972), pp 9–19.
108. Kingsmill Moore, *Reminiscences*, p. 287.
109. Ibid., p. 288.
110. *Annual report of the Church of Ireland Training College 1923–24.*
111. Ibid., 1925–26.
112. Ibid.
113. Whyte, *Church and state,* p. 37.
114. Ibid., p. 34–9.

Chapter 6

1. Miller, *Church, state and nation.*
2. Pope Pius XI, *The Christian education of youth* (London, Catholic Truth Society, 1970). (Hereafter cited as Pius XI, *Christian education.*)
3. Kennedy, *Widening gulf*, ch. 13.
4. Buckland, *History of Northern Ireland*, p. 35 and p. 32.
5. *Irish News*, 18 Dec. 1931.
6. Ibid.
7. Akenson, *Education and enmity*, p. 125.
8. Memorandum 'Stranmillis Training College: demand of the Committee of the Protestant Churches', 27 July 1931, N.I. Cabinet papers, 4/289/15.
9. Ibid.
10. Corkey to Craig, 19 Aug. 1931, N.I. Cabinet papers, 4/270/15.
11. Ibid.
12. Ibid.
13. Craig to Corkey, 21 Aug. 1931, N.I. Cabinet papers, 4/290/16.
14. Akenson, *Education and enmity*, p. 132.
15. A new primary programme was introduced in 1932, *Programme of instruction for public elementary schools* (Belfast, H.M.S.O., 1932).
16. Norman McNeilly, *Exactly 50 years: the Belfast education authority and its work* (Belfast, Belfast Education and Library Board, 1973), ch. 6. (Hereafter cited as McNeilly, *Exactly 50 years.*).
17. Ministry of Education (N.I.), *Annual report of the Ministry of Education (N.I.), 1932–33,* H.C. 294.
18. Ibid., 1937–38, H.C. 440.
19. Ibid., 1933–34, H.C. 315.
20. *Irish News*, 30 Oct. 1934.
21. Ibid., 13 Nov. 1934.
22. Ibid., 9 Nov. 1934.
23. Ibid., 14 Nov. 1934.
24. Ibid., 9 Nov. 1934.
25. Ibid., 15 Nov. 1934.
26. Ibid., 13 Nov. 1934.
27. Board of Education, *The education of the adolescent* (Hadow Report), (London, H.M.S.O., 1926).
28. Advisory Committee on Education, June 1926 (P.R.O.N.I.).

29. Ministry of Education (N.I.), *Annual report of the Ministry of Education (N.I.) 1932–33*, H.C. 294.
30. Ibid., 1936–37, H.C. 410.
31. N.I. H.C., v. 18, cols 1224–26 (30 Apr. 1936).
32. Ibid., v. 19, col. 1316 (6 May 1937).
33. Ibid., v. 21, cols 1472–80 (11 Oct. 1938).
34. The act was due to take effect in 1939, but was postponed and never came into effect.
35. T. Campbell, N.I. H.C., v. 21, col. 1529 (12 Oct. 1938).
36. N.I. H.C., v. 21, col. 1544 (12 Oct. 1938).
37. Ibid., v. 15, col. 1077 (25 Apr. 1933).
38. Ibid., v. 15, col. 919 (16 Mar. 1933).
39. Ministry of Education (N.I.), *Annual report of the Ministry of Education (N.I.), 1928–29*, H.C. 180.
40. Ibid., 1929–30, H.C. 211.
41. Ibid., 1930–31, H.C. 242.
42. T. Henderson, N.I. H.C., v. 15, col. 960 (21 Mar. 1933).
43. W. Grant, N.I. H.C., v. 15, col. 772 (9 Mar. 1933).
44. *Belfast Telegraph*, 26 Apr. 1933.
45. J. Beattie, N.I. H.C., v. 15, col. 1095 (25 Apr. 1933).
46. Cahill, *Christian state*, p. 611.
47. Ibid.
48. Ibid., p. 353.
49. Ibid., p. 376.
50. Ibid.
51. Address to World Federation of Education Associations Congress. *T.E.S.*, July–August 1933.
52. Bunreacht na hÉireann (Dublin, Stationery Office, 1937).
53. Pius XI, *Christian education*, p. 18.
54. C. Lucy, ' Making the school system of Ireland Catholic' in *Irish Ecclesiastical Record*, 52 (1938), pp 405–17.
55. Ibid.
56. Pope Pius XI , *Quadragesimo anno*, 1931.
57. *Irish Ecclesiastical Record*, 52 (1938), p. 116.
58. Ibid.
59. Ibid.
60. Whyte, *Church and state*.
61. M. Brennan, 'The Catholic school system of Ireland' in *Irish Ecclesiastical Record*, 52 (1938), pp 257– 72.
62. Michael Geraghty S.J., *Idols of modern society* (Dublin, Irish Messenger Press, 1931).
63. *Report of the Department of Education, 1931–32.*
64. Ibid.
65. Department of Education, 'Teaching through the medium of Irish', Circular 11/31.
66. Dáil Éireann, v. 43, col. 1090 (15 July 1932).
67. Ibid., v. 51, col. 1604 (11 Apr. 1934).
68. Dáil Éireann, v. 46, col. 2318 (5 Apr. 1933).
69. Ibid., v. 51, col. 1591 (11 Apr. 1934).
70. *T.E.S.*, 1 Apr. 1933.
71. O'Connell, *I.N.T.O.*, p. 363.
72. Ibid.
73. The withdrawal of the lower course was announced in the department's *Rules and regulations for national schools, 1934.*
74. *Rules and regulations for national schools, 1935.*
75. Derrig, Dáil Éireann, v. 55, col. 1850 (3 Apr. 1935).
76. Ibid., v. 55, col. 1919 (4 Apr.1934).
77. Ibid.
78. Ibid.
79. Ibid.
80. *Rules and regulations for secondary schools, 1934 .*
81. Irish language tests were gradually introduced and extended throughout the public service from 1922. Even positions requiring quite low general educational standards became subject to an Irish language test.